Peacebuilding in Crisis

The 1990s saw a constant increase in international peace missions, predominantly led by the United Nations, whose mandates were more and more extended to implement societal and political transformations in post-conflict societies. However, in many cases these missions did not meet the high expectations and did not acquire a sufficient legitimacy on the local level. Written by leading experts in the field, this edited volume brings together 'liberal' and 'post-liberal' approaches to peacebuilding. Besides challenging dominant peacebuilding paradigms, the book scrutinizes how far key concepts of post-liberal peacebuilding offer sound categories and new perspectives to reframe peacebuilding research. It thus moves beyond the 'liberal'/'post-liberal' divide and systematically integrates further perspectives, paving the way for a new era in peacebuilding research which is theory guided, but also substantiated in the empirical analysis of peacebuilding practice!

This book will be essential reading for postgraduate students and scholar-practitioners working in the field of peacebuilding. By embedding the subject area into different research perspectives, the book will also be relevant for scholars who come from related backgrounds, such as democracy promotion, transitional justice, statebuilding, conflict and development research and international relations in general.

Tobias Debiel is professor for international relations and development policy at the University of Duisburg-Essen, where he is the director of the Institute for Development and Peace as well as director of the Käte Hamburger Kolleg/Centre for Global Cooperation Research, Germany.

Thomas Held is the managing director of the German Foundation for Peace Research (DSF), which was founded in 2000 to strengthen peace research in Germany.

Ulrich Schneckener is professor of international relations and peace and conflict studies, University of Osnabrück, and director of the university's Center for Democracy and Peace Research as well as a member of the governing board of the German Foundation for Peace Research, Germany.

Routledge Global Cooperation Series

This series develops innovative approaches to understanding, explaining and answering one of the most pressing questions of our time – how can cooperation in a culturally diverse world of seven billion people succeed?

We are rapidly approaching our planet's limits, with trends such as advancing climate change and the destruction of biological diversity jeopardising our natural life support systems. Accelerated globalisation processes lead to an ever-growing interconnectedness of markets, states, societies and individuals. Many of today's problems cannot be solved by nation states alone. Intensified cooperation at the local, national, international and global levels is needed to tackle current and looming global crises.

Series editors

Tobias Debiel, Claus Leggewie and Dirk Messner are codirectors of the Käte Hamburger Kolleg/Centre for Global Cooperation Research, University of Duisburg-Essen, Germany. Their research areas are, among others, global governance, climate change, peacebuilding and cultural diversity of global citizenship. The three codirectors are, at the same time, based in their home institutions, which participate in the Centre, namely the German Development Institute/Deutsches Institut für Entwicklungspolitik (DIE, Messner) in Bonn, the Institute for Development and Peace (INEF, Debiel) in Duisburg and the Institute for Advanced Study in the Humanities (KWI, Leggewie) in Essen.

Titles

Global Cooperation and the Human Factor in International Relations
Edited by Dirk Messner and Silke Weinlich

Peacebuilding in Crisis
Rethinking paradigms and practices of transnational cooperation
Edited by Tobias Debiel, Thomas Held and Ulrich Schneckener

Humanitarianism and Challenges of Cooperation
Edited by Volker Heins, Kai Koddenbrock and Christine Unrau

Peacebuilding in Crisis

Rethinking paradigms and practices
of transnational cooperation

Edited by Tobias Debiel, Thomas Held and Ulrich Schneckener

LONDON AND NEW YORK

Centre for
**Global
Cooperation
Research**

SPONSORED BY THE

Federal Ministry
of Education
and Research

Zentrum für
Demokratie- und
Friedensforschung

DSF

Deutsche
Stiftung
Friedensforschung
german foundation for peace research

First published 2016
by Routledge

2 Park Square, Milton Park, Abingdon, Oxfordshire OX14 4RN
711 Third Avenue, New York, NY 10017

Routledge is an imprint of the Taylor & Francis Group, an informa business

First issued in paperback 2017

British Library Cataloguing-in-Publication Data
A catalogue record for this book is available from the British Library

Library of Congress Cataloging-in-Publication Data
Names: Debiel, Tobias, 1963– editor. | Held, Thomas (Managing director), editor. | Schneckener, Ulrich, 1968– editor.
Title: Peacebuilding in crisis : rethinking paradigms and practices of transnational cooperation / [edited by] Tobias Debiel, Thomas Held and Ulrich Schneckener.
Description: Abingdon, Oxon ; New York, NY : Routledge, [2016] | Includes bibliographical references and index.
Identifiers: LCCN 2015034079 | ISBN 9781138858596 (hbk) | ISBN 9781315717852 (ebk)
Subjects: LCSH: Peace-building—International cooperation.
Classification: LCC JZ5538 .P374294 2016 | DDC 327.1/72—dc23
LC record available at http://lccn.loc.gov/2015034079

ISBN: 978-1-138-85859-6 (hbk)
ISBN: 978-0-8153-6446-7 (pbk)

Typeset in Goudy
by Apex CoVantage, LLC

Contents

Tables

Contributors

Pol Bargués-Pedreny is a research fellow at the Centre for Global Cooperation Research, University of Duisburg-Essen, and was formerly visiting lecturer at the University of Westminster. He is interested in dilemmas of global governance, and explores questions of culture, resilience and self-determination.

Michael Barnett is university professor for political science and international affairs at George Washington University.

Morgan Brigg is senior lecturer in peace and conflict studies in the School of Political Science and International Studies at the University of Queensland. His research explores cultural difference, governance and selfhood in conflict resolution, peacebuilding and international development.

Susanne Buckley-Zistel is director of the Center for Conflict Studies and professor for peace and conflict studies, Philipps Universität Marburg as well as senior fellow, Käte Hamburger Kolleg/Centre for Global Cooperation Research in Duisburg.

David Chandler is professor of international relations and director of the Centre for the Study of Democracy, Department of Politics and International Relations, University of Westminster. He is the founding editor of the journal *Resilience: International Policies, Practices and Discourses*, and writes on a wide variety of themes connected to shifting paradigms of international policy-making.

Tobias Debiel is professor for international relations and development policy at the University of Duisburg-Essen, and director of the Institute for Development and Peace and of the Käte Hamburger Kolleg/Centre for Global Cooperation Research. He does research on state fragility and development cooperation, crisis prevention and peacebuilding, governance and corruption, the role of emerging powers in global cooperation (focus: India) and the responsibility to protect.

Martina Fischer is a political scientist and director of the Southeast Europe Programme at the Berghof Foundation in Berlin. She has done research on peacebuilding in postwar societies and the role of civil society in conflict transformation. Furthermore she investigated the interaction of different actors in transitional justice processes and reconciliation with a particular emphasis on the Balkan region.

Thomas Held is the managing director of the German Foundation for Peace Research (DSF), which was founded in 2000 to strengthen peace research in Germany.

Keith Krause is professor of international relations at the Graduate Institute of International and Development Studies in Geneva, Switzerland, as well as director of the Centre on Conflict, Development and Peacebuilding (CCDP). His research interests include concepts of security, the changing character of contemporary armed violence, multilateral security cooperation, arms control and disarmament, peacekeeping, peacebuilding and reconstruction policy.

Roger Mac Ginty is professor of peace and conflict studies at the Humanitarian and Conflict Response Institute and in the Department of Politics, School of Social Sciences, University of Manchester. His research has been on peace processes, political violence, and local responses to international peace-support interventions.

Andreas Mehler is director of the Arnold Bergstraesser Institute and professor of political science at University of Freiburg. Born in 1963, he is a political scientist and honorary professor at the Free University/Berlin. He also serves as vice president of the Association for African Studies in Germany (VAD) and as a board member of the Africa-Europe Group for Interdisciplinary Studies (AEGIS). He is co-editor of the *Africa Spectrum and Africa Yearbook* and member of the "Beirat Zivile Krisenprävention" of the Federal German government. His major fields of expertise include peace processes in Africa south of the Sahara (particularly power-sharing pacts); security, state and statehood; and French and German Africa policies.

Thania Paffenholz is project director and senior researcher at the Graduate Institute Geneva, Switzerland, Centre on Conflict, Peacebuilding and Development. Her main fields of research are conflict analysis and peacebuilding, the conflict-development nexus and the role of development actors in peacebuilding, critical analysis of the role of the aid system in peacebuilding/conflict, international peacemaking strategies, and the role of civil society in peacebuilding. She also works as a policy advisor in different peace processes for the UN, government and other organisations.

Michael Pugh is visiting professor, at the Institute of Management Research, Centre for Conflict Analysis and Management, Radboud University Nijmegen, and emeritus professor at the University of Bradford.

Patricia Rinck is a researcher and editorial assistant at the Käte Hamburger Kolleg/Centre for Global Cooperation Research. Her main research interests include post-conflict peacebuilding, power-sharing, and democratisation in post-conflict societies. She has a special interest in nonethnic power-sharing, peacebuilding and democratisation in Sierra Leone, and conducted respective field research in 2013.

Ulrich Schneckener is professor of international relations and peace and conflict studies at the University of Osnabrück and director of the University's Center for Democracy and Peace Research. He is a member of the Governing Board of the German Foundation for Peace Research. His main areas of research include international security policy, international conflict management, peace- and statebuilding processes and the role of armed nonstate actors.

Jonas Wolff is head of the research department "Governance and Societal Peace" at the Peace Research Institute Frankfurt (PRIF) and teaches at Goethe University Frankfurt and Kassel University. His research interests include Latin American politics, democratization and international democracy promotion as well as foreign and development policies.

Preface

"Crisis! What Crisis?" one might ask when considering the enormous scope and complexity of international peacebuilding operations that have emerged since the end of the Cold War. However, the high expectations placed on the efforts to achieve sustainable peace processes in areas of conflict have only partially been fulfilled. Especially the approaches to peacebuilding that were based on the idea of simply transferring standardised conceptions of democratisation, rule of law, and market economy largely failed to meet their targets. There were increasing indications that the idea to socially reengineer post-conflict societies by nation and institution building proved to be insufficient and illusionary and was not appropriately adjusted to the local conditions peace operations were confronted with. Reflecting on these experiences, refined conceptions like local ownership and inclusivity gained prominence in academia and policy circles and, among others, were taken up in the 'New Deal for Engagement in Fragile States', endorsed at the 4th High Level Forum on Aid Effectiveness in Busan, South Korea, in November 2011.

This volume, published in the newly established Routledge Global Cooperation Series, critically takes stock of most recent academic and policy-related debates that are characterised by critiques of the 'liberal peace' model and increasingly shaped by new understandings of the local, resilience and hybrid political orders. Moreover, the contributions aim at providing new perspectives for research on peacebuilding and at reframing the respective policy agendas.

This volume traces back to the international symposium 'Peacebuilding in Crisis – Experiences and New Perspectives' hosted by the German Foundation for Peace Research and the Centre for Democracy and Peace Research at the University of Osnabrück from 23–25 January 2014. The papers for this conference in Osnabrück, city of the Westphalian Peace, provided the basis for the chapters published in this volume and were complemented by further contributions. The publication is a collaboration project between the organisers of the conference and the Käte Hamburger Kolleg/Centre for Global Cooperation Research of the University of Duisburg-Essen, where related research and debates on peacebuilding have figured prominently.

Our special thanks go to the organisation teams of the hosting institutions for helping to make the symposium a great success. Furthermore, we would like to thank all those who supported the editing process, among them Helen Bell from Routledge, who accompanied this publication with great patience and helpful advice. We owe special gratitude to Patricia Rinck from the Centre for Global Cooperation Research for managing the editorial process with enthusiasm and efficiency.

Tobias Debiel, Thomas Held and Ulrich Schneckener

Duisburg and Osnabrück, July 2015

1 Peacebuilding in crisis?

Debating peacebuilding paradigms and practices

Ulrich Schneckener

Introduction: peacebuilding in crisis?

In International Relations textbooks, the Westphalian Peace of 1648 is often portrayed as the birthplace of the international system of states, labelled as the Westphalian system characterised by the notion of sovereign statehood. As all historians and most IR specialists know, this reference is merely a myth or a metaphor but hardly an adequate description of the historical record. Nonetheless, the Westphalian Peace treaties, negotiated and concluded in the cities of Münster and Osnabrück (from 1643 to 1648) in order to end the so-called Thirty Years' War in Central Europe, represent one of the early historical manifestations of a complex peacebuilding process. In particular, the Osnabrück treaty (*Instrumentum Pacis Osnabrugensis*), dealing with the postwar order in the Holy Roman Empire of the German Nation, included a number of provisions which can be regarded as faintly reminiscent of peacebuilding packages nowadays. In its famous article 2, the treaty called for everlasting oblivion and amnesty (*perpetua oblivio et amnestia*) regarding all atrocities and activities of the war and explicitly ruled out any attempts to legitimise future conflicts with past events and sufferings. This general postulation was however accompanied by detailed regulations on restitution and compensation among the warring feudal parties in order to restore a minimum of justice. Moreover, the treaty aimed at solving disputes over territories and religious as well as constitutional matters within the empire. Translated into modern terms, the peace accord established a new power-sharing arrangement and multilayered structure by reassessing rights and duties of German provinces, bishoprics, feudal states and the Kaiser. In essence, the result was a much stronger position of the Reichsstände (those individuals and political entities with a seat in the Reichstag) and a weakening of the German Kaiser. The result was a fragile bargain which was heavily influenced by outside powers, most notably by the Swedish and the French crown. To put it in a nutshell, the Westphalian Peace dealt with the questions of legitimate rule and of peaceful coexistence inter alia between the Protestant and the Catholic churches, the Kurfürsten and the Kaiser, and different European feudal states. In one way or another, the treaties addressed peace settlement and peacebuilding at the societal level, the state level and the international (European) level, and thereby linked intrastate peace with interstate (European) peace (*pax universalis*).

Today's international peacebuilding efforts take place under completely different circumstances in a globalised, post-colonial world shaped by the universalisation of independent statehood (the so-called Westphalian System) and by the spectacular increase of international organisations, regimes, fora and transnational nongovernmental organisations (NGOs) (post-Westphalia). And, of course, modern peacebuilding is rather different in shape, scope and content. Nevertheless, as in 1648, the rationale of building peace is still essentially about assuring nonviolent conflict resolution among various segments of a society on the one hand as well as organising beneficial state–society relations on the other hand. In this regard, peacebuilding remains an enduring task for each and every society. Peacebuilding, understood as a holistic approach to building peaceful relations among people, covering political, economic, social, cultural-symbolic, educational and psychological aspects, is not in crisis (see Lederach 1997). Fundamentally, peacebuilding is about achieving and sustaining "positive peace" (Galtung) and, thereby, is linked to the Kantian ideal of *si vis pacem, para pacem* (Senghaas 1995, 2004). Thus, when we talk about "peacebuilding in crisis" in this volume, we refer specifically to *the way how and by whom peacebuilding is conceptualised and conducted*. The concern is basically about the disputed role of international, mostly Western peacebuilders, about their concepts and approaches vis-à-vis post-conflict societies. The following observation may serve as a point of departure: on the one hand, throughout the 1990s and 2000s, efforts in internationally sponsored peacebuilding have drastically increased. This trend can be illustrated by the growing numbers of UN or regional organisations' peace operation missions of different sizes, by the seconded personnel and experts, and by resources assigned.[1] More and more external actors have become involved in war-torn regions, mostly in Africa, in order to support, to implement, to aid and assist, to monitor or, in extreme cases, to enforce peace. At the same time, key aspects of the peacebuilding concept have become standardised, "tool-boxed", mainstreamed and institutionalised, mainly at the level of international organisations and major donors who became the central nodes of what has been called the "international peacebuilding regime" (Suhrke 2014, 270). In 2005, the UN even set up a new body – the Peacebuilding Commission. Although this institution has a rather limited mandate, controls only a small budget and deals de facto with very few, less prominent cases, its establishment nonetheless highlighted the growing relevance of this field of international policy (Schneckener and Weinlich 2005). At least at the surface, a peacebuilding consensus has emerged among organisations such as the UN, the European Union (EU), the Organisation for Economic Co-operation and Development (OECD), the World Bank and regional development banks focusing on issues such as security, legitimate institutions, rule of law, free elections and socioeconomic development.[2]

On the other hand, the ever-increasing efforts of international peacebuilding in terms of numbers, activities and resources have coincided with vivid debates and critiques in academia about the normative and ethical foundations, the underlying premises and the sociopolitical practices of peacebuilding. In other words, the more peacebuilding became a standard operating procedure and an established field of international engagement in local affairs, the more it became controversial and contested in the academic world. During the past years, an essential part of the (Anglo-Saxon) peacebuilding literature was dominated by the critics and defenders of the so-called liberal peace paradigm (cf. the volumes of Newman et al. 2009 and Campbell et al. 2011) and its follow-up debates on "post-liberal peace" (Richmond 2011), "hybrid peace" (Mac Ginty 2010) or the "local turn" (Mac Ginty and Richmond 2013). Despite these important contributions, the debates on the raison d'être of peacebuilding seem to be much more diverse and driven by different epistemological interests. It makes a great difference whether critics see peacebuilding primarily as a *normative project* (either to be promoted, reframed or dismissed), as an *analytical tool or concept* (aiming at describing or explaining social processes or political outcomes) or as a *distinct set of social practices* involving different actors and levels (to be studied and evaluated). Sometimes the different perspectives are mixed together in order to deliver a radical and fundamental critique of peacebuilding. However, according to my understanding, these avenues for research should be distinguished analytically since they involve different research agendas and methods, study different objects and result in different kinds of critique.[3]

Therefore, the peacebuilding crisis refers to three different but interrelated debates (and their subdebates). The *first* contestation revolves around the normative and ethical foundations of peacebuilding. Here, peacebuilding is understood as a set of controversial universalised norms which is related to other contested norms of international politics (e.g. "responsibility to protect") and which is embedded in concepts of a Western-dominated international order. Ethical concerns are raised in particular about paternalistic attitudes of external peacebuilders and their attempts to impose or transfer norms. The *second* debate focuses on the conceptual-analytical level by questioning the rationale of the standard peacebuilding concept and its underlying theoretical assumptions, in particular the various assumed causal links between peace, good governance, statehood, democracy and market economy. The *third* debate relates to the critical assessment of the strategies and operational policies of international peacebuilders. Here, concerns are mainly raised about the apparently limited prospects of success of peacebuilding operations, methods and instruments. Typical problems and dilemmas are addressed such as conflicting strategies and goals, the sequencing and coordination of international approaches, the gap between supply and demand and different logics of action at headquarter and field levels.

At the centre of the three arenas, however, seems to be a fourth dimension – the ambivalent interaction and relation between "external" actors (i.e. states, international organisations and international NGOs) and "local" actors, ranging from political elites to civil society groups. This theme cuts across the other three debates by concentrating on both the categorisation and the relationship of various actors in peacebuilding, in particular by unpacking the binary categories of external/international and internal/local. This distinction, constantly reproduced by both peacebuilding analysts and policy-makers (for example by introducing the concept of "local ownership"), has triggered a number of reservations. Authors call inter alia for a blurring of these abstract categories, for the use of a more complex multiagency framework, and for a rethinking of the interaction of different actors (e.g. by using concepts such as "relational sensibility" or "hybridity").

The chapters in this volume relate to all arenas of debate; however, the topic of the externals/locals divide can be seen as the core aspect of the book since it is addressed and problematised in one way or another by almost all chapters. This introductory chapter provides an overview of these debates, before focusing on the cross-cutting issue in order to arrive at some desiderata and prospects for peacebuilding research. In concluding, the chapter argues that peacebuilding research should be more empirical and less occupied with promoting or critically deconstructing abstract categories, concepts or labels. My reading is that such debates not only run the risk of becoming self-referential, but also tend to underestimate the intriguing role of agency and its complexity when it comes to the rather messy politics of peacebuilding.

Debating normative and ethical foundations of peacebuilding

This arena covers a number of arguments which all challenge the normative and ethical foundations of peacebuilding. They certainly do not question the value of "peace" or of peaceful relations as such, but they oppose the view that peacebuilding is inherently a "good thing" associated with substantial and procedural norms such as nonviolence, nondiscrimination, emancipation, equality, liberty, justice, solidarity, inclusion or dialogue. There are at least four lines of arguments which are often used in combination but in fact follow from slightly different worldviews. The first and probably most fundamental critique rooted in neo-Marxist, post-colonial or Foucaultian thinking argues that peacebuilding, like any other international concept, simply reflects the unjust world order and the asymmetric power relations between a Western-dominated centre and a post-colonial periphery (see in particular Duffield 2007; Jabri 2007; Dillon and Reid 2009). Moreover, peacebuilding (together with its twin statebuilding) should be regarded as part and parcel of a greater project of transforming the notion of sovereignty and undermining the self-determination of peoples and states (cf. Chandler 2008). Peacebuilding – albeit a softer approach – therefore needs to be seen in the same light as other forms of intervention justified on humanitarian grounds or by the emerging norm of responsibility to protect (R2P) which may allow for (military) intervention in cases where governments are assumed to be unable or unwilling to end or prevent mass violence (Jabri 2013, 9). By initiating and imposing these norms, Western hegemony will be extended and reproduced. According to Jabri (2013, 6) peacebuilding therefore follows a "colonial rationality" since it views "the juridical-political boundaries of the postcolonial state as irrelevant in its calculations and formulations of schemes of government." Furthermore, by referring to Foucault's concept of *gouvernementalité*, Jabri (2013, 13–14) points to the "governmentalizing design imperative" of peacebuilding which is "already scripted elsewhere, in the structuration of peacebuilding as a norm constitutive of the normative ordering of the international." The second argument, articulated by both post-colonial and "liberal peace" critics, accuses peacebuilding of being inherently Eurocentric since all norms and values attributed to the concept have been developed throughout the European history and by (Western) European societies, in particular those regarding human rights and liberal democracy (for this debate, see Sabaratnam 2013, 261–263). Therefore, peacebuilding as a normative project has – be it intended or unintended – a strong bias towards universalising these norms and transferring them to non-European contexts. The imperative seems to be that others should learn from European experience and follow a similar path to consolidated peace. This ambition (or, better, hubris) is normatively questionable – not only because it offers a simplistic and teleological understanding of Europe's contradictory history, but also because it neglects and potentially marginalises non-European experiences, traditions and cultures and hence often meets with local resistance. Eurocentric peacebuilding violates non-discrimination, autonomy and (collective) self-determination instead of respecting these fundamental principles; it may even create instability and tensions in the first place rather than accommodate intrasociety conflicts. The third critique derived mainly from critical security studies is to a lesser extent occupied with the projection of Western power, order or ideas, but sees peacebuilding primarily as a management or control mechanism in order to secure industrial and democratic societies from violent conflicts, failing states, terrorism or mass migration to other parts of the world. In particular post-9/11, peacebuilding – like statebuilding – became an expression of the widespread securitisation of international politics and has to be regarded in the context of counter-terrorism, counter-insurgency or global policing policies (cf. Newman 2010; Tschirgi 2013).

While the aforementioned critiques portray peacebuilding not as an end itself but as instrumental either for upholding the international Western-dominated order, for the universalisation of European ideas or for Western security concerns, the fourth layer of critique is less concerned with the normative biases of the concept but rather with the ethics of peacebuilding itself. The main argument is that international peacebuilding is inevitably paternalistic since it always involves those actors who need to claim to know better what is good for someone else. In this case, external peacebuilders have to maintain that their recipes for stable peace are not only superior but will work if one is prepared to strictly follow the guidelines given. The paternalistic formula of "care and control," as Barnett in this volume puts it, seems to be an essential and almost inescapable feature of peacebuilding. Even if it comes with different faces and varying doses, paternalism is nevertheless regarded as highly problematic since it constantly reproduces the asymmetric relationship between "teachers" and "students" of peacebuilding with all its well-known adverse effects. The key ethical dilemma seems to be this: on the one hand, peacebuilding (like R2P), if taken seriously, implies that one has a moral obligation to assume responsibility for the fate of others (in particular if nonintervention means the loss of lives); on the other hand, peacebuilding at the same time does harm the political autonomy, pride and dignity of those who become recipients of particular policy interventions. As Brigg discusses in this volume, thinking in different forms of "relationality" between externals and locals may be one ethical perspective in order to soften these tensions, since they cannot be overcome.

These critiques, often articulated in fairly generalised and abstract forms, certainly have their merits. However, despite their differences, it is interesting to note that they all point in the same direction: they see peacebuilding basically as a normative project which mainly suits Western ideas, concepts and agendas. Even if this might be true, it seems to be only one side of the equation. Most notably, the "other" is ominously absent or simply reduced to a rather passive "object" of highly dubious neo-colonial, Eurocentric, securitised or paternalistic peacebuilding projects. Sabaratnam (2013, 263–264) speaks about the "methodological and analytic bypassing of subjects" and the "avatars of Eurocentrism" in critical thought. Therefore, to varying degrees, the various critiques tend to reproduce the positioning of externals and locals they want to criticise and overcome in the first place. By doing so, they largely overestimate both the intention and ability of (Western) peacebuilders to intervene, to control or to govern others, while at the same time underestimating the role of the recipients in resisting, shaping or adapting to external peacebuilding efforts. There may even be the danger of a "reverse paternalism" since by rightfully questioning the normative and ethical basis of Western-dominated peacebuilding some critics implicitly assume that they know what is good or bad for populations in war-torn societies. Or, to put it bluntly: is it not also a form of paternalism to tell others that Western paternalism, norms or liberal ideas are not good for them?

Debating conceptual and analytical dimensions of peacebuilding

The second arena critically addresses a number of analytical claims made implicitly or explicitly by the concept of peacebuilding and by international peacebuilders. Most of the literature about the pros and cons of the so-called liberal peace struggles with these questions (cf. inter alia Paris 2004, 2006, 2011; Richmond 2006, 2011; Mac Ginty and Richmond 2007; Chandler 2010; Zaum 2012; Selby 2013; Richmond and Mac Ginty 2015). There are essentially two main arguments which question the rationale of the concept: the first holds that the predominant peacebuilding paradigm, as coined by the 1990s, is informed by modernisation theory and by (neo)liberal concepts. In short, it aims at modernising a somewhat backward, violent society by various aspects of modern statehood and bureaucracy, of liberal democracy and of free market economy. By doing so, liberal peacebuilding hardly reflects the specific aspects of postwar societies but rather views them as a subtype of developing and transition countries. Peacebuilding has become an offspring of the wider field of development and transformation policy conducted by Western donors and international organisations. By aiming at a radical transformation of both state and society to sustain peace, peacebuilding is doomed to fall into the same traps of social engineering, top-down governance, one-size-fits-all approaches and mechanistic, linear thinking which are typical of international development policy even if concrete policies and priorities have shifted from time to time (e.g. from the neo-liberal

"Washington Consensus" of the 1980s and 1990s to the "post-Washington Consensus" with its poverty reduction agenda of the mid-2000s).

The second critique is closely related to the first, but questions in a more nuanced way the underlying analytical assumptions of the concept and in particular the assumed causal links between democracy/democratisation, good governance and socioeconomic development (as independent variables) and peace (as a dependent variable). Hereby, peacebuilding draws on different liberal sources: first, by focusing on the peace–democracy link, peacebuilding is part of the general debate on the neo-Kantian "Democratic Peace Theory" (Russett 1993; Geis et al. 2007; Geis et al. 2013) or the "triangular peace" (Oneal and Russett 2001) in international relations and peace studies. Second, peacebuilding is closely associated with economic interdependence, market and competition mechanisms which are seen as necessary to foster development, prosperity and social change (for "economic peace theory," cf. Coulomb 2004, 39–74; for a critical account of "cooperated peace," see Pugh in this volume). Third, the concept follows the liberal conviction that the promotion and protection of individual human rights, of civil liberties as well as of the rule of law is fundamental for achieving lasting peace (cf. Carothers 2006; Ife 2007; Bell 2013); this includes the legal and social equality of men and women, which is often a highly contested issue in many post-conflict societies (for a review of human rights and gender, see Buckley-Zistel in this volume). Fourth, peace rests on a strong and vibrant civil society; peacebuilding, therefore, needs to mobilise and empower civil society forces and encourage political participation of wider segments of the society (cf. Paffenholz 2010). And finally, peacebuilding has to be accompanied by a process of statebuilding and institution-building, since functioning state institutions and administrative structures are see as a prerequisite for public order and a peaceful society (cf. Fukuyama 2004; Paris 2004, 2006). No matter which route liberal peacebuilding takes, it tends to follow a "cause-and-effect model" (see Chandler in this volume) rooted in positivist thinking. Critics of liberal peace such as Richmond and others acknowledge different variations within the liberal paradigm, for instance, by distinguishing between "conservative" versions of peacebuilding (based on hegemony and domination), "orthodox" versions (based on state-centric peace) and "emancipatory" versions (based on bottom-up processes) (Richmond 2006). But they nonetheless reject the whole approach as insufficient to analyse the complexities of peace processes, as incapable of understanding local dynamics and as insensitive to the inherent contradictions of the concept and of its adverse effects regarding peace and stability. As summarised by Richmond:

> The liberal approach to peacebuilding often leads to empty states, a virtual peace, and a focus on institutions over the variations of everyday life. The neoliberal approach denies the post-conflict individual and community the resources needed to engage in the liberal social contract, and to express the locality of peace. The rationalist and institutional focus of liberal peacebuilding denies cultural agency.
>
> (Richmond 2011, 95)

The overall claim is not only that the underlying causal assumptions are ill-conceived and ignorant regarding important factors and (social-cultural) contexts but that liberal peace is neither liberal by its own standards nor peace in terms of "positive peace" since it prolongs societal cleavages or even establishes new ones.

This critique, however, has provoked replies from different angles.[4] On the one hand, there are those voices for which the critics of liberal peace are not critical enough because they still question liberal peace largely on liberal grounds, they do not include an analysis of power (Chandler 2010) and they do not escape from Eurocentric categories, including the divide between the West and the non-West or the "liberal" and the "non-liberal" (Sabaratnam 2013). On the other hand, for some authors the liberal peace critique is "hyper-critical" (Paris 2011) or simply constitutes a "straw man" (Zaum 2012; Selby 2013). In order to "save liberal peacebuilding", Paris (2011, 40–43) suggests that the critics not only "conflate post-conquest and post-settlement peacebuilding" by taking cases of US invasion such as Iraq or Afghanistan as representatives of liberal peacebuilding, but moreover define liberal peace far too broadly (for a similar position see Debiel/Rinck in this volume). Thereby, liberal peace became a catch-all phrase for international, Western policies in general and itself lacks the analytical rigour to distinguish between various strands of liberalism and other peacebuilding approaches. A complementary point made by Zaum (2013, 110) is that by framing the liberal peace paradigm the critics assume "a degree of coherence and consensus within liberal thought" and "that external peace-builders act for liberal reasons." Both claims, however, cannot be defended on empirical grounds.

Debating approaches and dilemmas of peacebuilding practices

The debate about the analytical shortcomings of (liberal) peacebuilding as well as of its critiques already builds a bridge from theorising peacebuilding to studying peacebuilding practices. To a large extent, the claims made by both camps are informed by empirical observations and the argument often boils down to the question which conclusions should be drawn from the findings. This strand of the peacebuilding literature is mainly characterised by applied and policy-oriented research based on quantitative analysis, comparative studies or field research. The debates are less characterised by major controversies than by a number of concerns and empirical insights regarding the operational approaches and the overall performance of international peacebuilders, not at least by discussing dilemmas (e.g. effects of short-term stabilisation versus prospects for long-term transformation) and unintended consequences (cf. Cousens and Kumar 2000; Stedman et al. 2002; Chesterman 2004; Newman et al. 2009; Paris and Sisk 2009; Dayton and Kriesberg 2009). In order not to get lost in issue-specific or case-specific details, this introduction will focus on a few central themes.

Most importantly, there is a debate about the effectiveness, the impact or the success of peacebuilding. This includes two main questions: how to measure these aspects and how to explain them (see Schröder 2013, 222–225). Both involve tricky methodological problems related to choosing useful yardsticks and indicators as well as verifying the significance of explanatory variables or contributing factors. For measuring effectiveness or success different benchmarks are used: a minimum standard would be the absence of violence or, more precisely, the nonrecurrence of organised violence over time (measuring "negative peace"); a medium standard would be the implementation of specific objectives based on the mandate of the peacebuilding operation (measuring goal attainment); and a high standard would be the achievement of sustainable peace (measuring degree of conflict transformation or "positive peace"). Surely, depending on the approach, the result and the policy recommendations will be very different (see Page Fortna 2004). On the whole, most studies conclude that international peacebuilding missions – most notably those with peacekeeping as a key component – are generally able to reduce violence and to ease tensions among conflict parties, but that they often meet neither their own narrowly defined objectives (apart from achieving technical benchmarks such as delivering particular services or training of personnel) nor higher expectations concerning sustainable peace. Notwithstanding this, there is still a widely shared belief that international assistance makes a great difference. Based on statistical analysis and case studies, Doyle and Sambanis (2006), for example claim that the prospects for success depend on the interplay of three key variables which constitute a "peacebuilding triangle": the degree of hostility of the factions, the extent of local capacities remaining after the war and the amount of international assistance. Their main argument goes as follows: "the deeper the hostility, the more the destruction of local capacities, the more one needs international assistance to succeed in establishing a stable peace" (Doyle and Sambanis 2006, 4). In other words, the more a violent conflict has been escalated, the more international efforts are needed in order to increase the probability of peacebuilding success. This winning formula, however, underestimates the fact that the greater the peacebuilding tasks, the more complex missions and activities are required and the more external actors have to be involved. Inevitably, the result is an increasing number of context-related or actor-related factors which makes it extremely difficult to identify those explaining variables and causal links responsible for success or failure of peacebuilding (see Schröder 2013, 228–230).

Closely linked to the question of effectiveness, scholars also disagree about the appropriate approach and the sequencing of various dimensions of peacebuilding (cf. Schneckener 2005, 2011; Barnett et al. 2007; Newman 2009, 30–38). On the one hand, authors discuss the merits of minimalist ("light-footprint") versus maximalist ("heavy-footprint") peacebuilding. The first concentrates international peacebuilding on a few key aspects such as the promotion of basic security and basic services while leaving the responsibility for the peace process to a large extent in the hands of local authorities and parties (so-called local ownership). As observed during the first years after 2001 in Afghanistan, this approach may lead to forms of warlord governance, to illegitimate institutions, to widespread corruption, to the recurrence of massive violence and, eventually, to mission creep. The second model, which can be illustrated by internationally run transitional administrations in Kosovo, Bosnia or East Timor, involves a comprehensive, transformative approach for state and society, covering a wide range of policy areas. External actors, in this case bodies led by the UN or EU, are in charge of virtually all political decisions and governance functions before transferring powers step-by-step back to local actors ("transfer of responsibility") (cf. Caplan 2005). This resource-intensive model runs not only the risk of severely overstretching international capacities, but it often lacks legitimacy, denies self-determination and sovereignty and provokes opposition from society and local elites. Most peacebuilding missions, however, in fact oscillate between the two models, depending not at least on the intensity of the violent conflict, on the degree of political attention paid by outside actors and on the amount of resources mobilised by international peacebuilders. On the other hand, the debate refers to various strategies and to the question of what comes first in peacebuilding. In an ideal-type manner, one may differentiate between *Liberalisation First*, *Institutionalisation First*, *Security First* and *Civil Society First* approaches (cf. Schneckener 2005, 22–27; 2011, 235–245). Each of them prioritises different issues and policies; they also differ considerably concerning their assumptions about the root causes of the conflict, the role of the state in peacebuilding, the time frame allotted to projects and programs and the required resources. Moreover, they result from different conceptions about the "right" political order, based on different worldviews. The first two are widely discussed within the liberal peace debate, not at least stimulated by the work of Paris (2004), who advocated "institutionalization before liberalization" and preferred the building of public institutions over the "liberal ideal" of early elections and market reforms (for parallels in democratisation and peacebuilding studies, see Wolff in this volume). In a similar vein, some emphasise especially the quest for the establishment of power-sharing institutions after civil wars in order to secure inclusive politics (for a critical assessment, see Mehler in this volume). The second two are derived from different positions: *Security First* can be associated with a realist paradigm by focusing on the promotion of a secure environment in particular by (re)establishing and strengthening of the state's monopoly on the use of force, by containing or demobilising nonstate armed groups and by reforming the security sector (cf. Marten 2004 and Etzioni 2007; for a critical account see Krause in this volume). While this approach is characterised by a top-down perspective, *Civil Society First* argues for the opposite by emphasising the need for bottom-up, grassroots-level processes (cf. Pouligny 2005; Van Tongeren et al. 2005; Verkoren and Van Leeuwen 2013). The premise here is that peace will only be sustainable when peacebuilding empowers and mobilises societal forces, improves opportunities for participation, secures access to rights and services and strengthens social cohesion. That often includes inter alia the outside support of peace alliances, of marginalised groups, of reconciliation and transitional justice processes and of gender aspects (cf. Fischer and Buckley-Zistel in this volume). The various approaches both complement each other and at the same time compete with each other. At least in theory, they could go hand in hand and reinforce each other. In practice, however, each strategy is advocated by certain peacebuilders who all compete for funding and political attention at the level of international organisations' and donors' headquarters. Consequently, the sequencing debate remains rather hypothetical since international peacebuilding practices are shaped by a mixture of approaches, often less orchestrated by comprehensive, strategic planning than by ad hoc decisions, political compromise, expected outcomes and internal bureaucratic interests at the level of peacebuilders' headquarters (cf. Barnett et al. 2007).

The same applies to constant complaints about the lack of coordination and coherence. Considering the multitude of actors, approaches and activities in peacebuilding, such problems both among and within organisations inevitably arise (Paris 2009). The results are duplicating, competing or even contradicting efforts. On the one hand, each external actor wants to ensure autonomy and control over its own policies, projects and budgets. On the other hand, the lack of coordination with others may severely harm one's own ambitions. Moreover, even if all major actors could agree on strategic peacebuilding objectives and follow largely the same agenda (as for example discussed within the framework of the OECD or the UN Peacebuilding Commission), there remains the intriguing problem of different logics of action for political decision-makers at the headquarters and for international personnel at the field level. What has been drafted in New York, Geneva or Brussels by no means translates into operational policies in post-conflict societies since the seconded personnel, directly confronted with the local situation, may set different priorities or simply have a different reading of the headquarters' decisions. Still, calls for improvement of coordination and coherence have become a permanent item in practitioners' discourses. The oft-repeated assumption is "we could do better, if we just coordinate better." This mantra has led to the establishment of new coordination mechanisms and bodies, reporting systems, evaluation schemes, best practices and lesson-learned studies. Frequently, the effect has been increasing bureaucratic procedures and technocratic checklists for peacebuilders. These undertakings, however, neglect the fact that incoherence is a "resource" often welcomed by political actors – not only by external peacebuilders themselves, but more so by powerful local actors who know perfectly well how to take advantage of incoherent policies (on the gap between the rhetoric and reality of coordination, see also Hensell 2015).

At the same time, external actors are confronted in various ways with the question of legitimacy. On the one hand, their activities abroad must be considered legitimate by their own societies back home; otherwise they will lose political and material support. For example, German politicians would have great difficulties in supporting measures which are not in line with international law, human rights or democratic values. On the other hand, peacebuilders have to respond to the expectations and needs of local societies in order to gain some legitimacy; often, however, this involves cooperating with those parties and elites who have been responsible for atrocities and violent conflict in the first place. In addition, at both levels, input and output legitimacy correspond with each other. If peacebuilders do not respect local aspirations and ensure participation, then even successful output may be seen as illegitimate and cause resistance. If, however, they aim at increasing input legitimacy by involving a number of local actors (in particular former warring parties), then this may hamper effective implementation of policies, resulting in suboptimal or unintended outcomes, which in turn causes opposition in the peacebuilder's own constituencies.

Reflecting on these debates on peacebuilding practices, one has to admit that most of the literature is written from the perspective of external actors. It is largely about the peacebuilders' successes and failures, performances and dilemmas. The relationship with local actors comes into the picture, but is merely conceptualised as an intervening variable or a contextual variable with which to explain or evaluate the outcome of peacebuilding practices. In this sense, most studies are unidirectional: they regard peacebuilding as a transfer of resources, capacities and know-how from externals to locals and ask the ultimate policy question of how this transfer can be improved and go more smoothly. From this perspective, "local ownership" – a concept invented by donors – is seen as an enabling factor to make the medicine go down. Strangely, local ownership is part and parcel of peacebuilding practices, which implies that ownership does not exist per se, but needs to be established and nurtured by external actors (see Bargués-Pedreny in this volume). This static view, however, does not systematically take into consideration the interactions between internationals and locals as such, their multiplicity, dynamics and feedback effects.

The cross-cutting issue: debating the international–local divide

Be it explicit or implicit, all three debates have their conceptualisation of externals and locals as well as assumptions about their relationship. As Mac Ginty in this volume points out, both categories are analytically co-constitutive; the one necessarily takes the other as point of reference. The local exists only in relation to the international and vice versa. As most authors admit, both terms remain overdetermined and undertheorised at the same time. They are overdetermined because by using these abstractions everything can be attributed to internationals or locals. In many debates there is, for example a tendency to assume that peacebuilders (read the "North" or the "West") act on a clear, coherent set of intentions and actually know what they want and what they are doing (at least in theory). In contrast, the local is largely portrayed in a reactive mode – either ignoring, resisting or adapting to external peacebuilding activities (see Mehler in this volume). Both categories are undertheorised because the binary vocabulary captures neither the multitude of actors nor the different constellations in which they typically interact. This refers to the simple fact that both concepts notably cover a wide range of different actors and types of actors (e.g. state and nonstate actors). In most empirical studies, therefore, the use of these terms does not make a great deal of sense since it is much more appropriate to talk about specific actors and call them what they are: international organisations, NGOs, development agencies, governments, state officials, national elites, clans, political parties, social movements, armed groups, religious authorities, elders, individuals and so on (see Mac Ginty, Debiel/Rinck and Paffenholz in this volume). Most notably, cross-cutting dimensions are often neglected as in particular feminist theorists show with regard to gender, to the relationship between men and woman (externals as well as locals) and how this affects the very understanding of justice and human rights (cf. Buckley-Zistel in this volume).

Moreover, the internationals–locals divide oversimplifies the multilevel architecture of peacebuilding and the dynamics of interaction not only between various international and local actors, but also among locals and among internationals. Analytically, different levels or arenas of interaction can be distinguished (cf. Schneckener 2011, 245–246): the interactions among locals (in particular those between former warring parties), the interactions between local elites and external peacebuilders, the interactions among internationals working in the same post-conflict theatre and, finally, the interactions among peacebuilders and donors at the level of distant capitals and headquarters. At each layer, interactions follow different logics and are shaped by different contexts. In plain words, the rules of the game at the UN or EU headquarters are rather different from those among local power-holders. Still, these arenas do not act independently from each other, but rather affect each other (see also Schlichte and Veit 2012). Political decisions and peacebuilding activities at one level have an impact on expectations, behaviour and (re)actions of actors at other layers and, thereby, influence their way of interacting with others. Most importantly, between the various layers one has to acknowledge feedback effects which make peacebuilding a rather complex, multidirectional undertaking where different actors perform at different levels and address different audiences (e.g. communal, national and international).

From a sociological perspective, the interactions and feedback loops in the process of peacebuilding blur the external–local divide. On the one hand, the involvement of peacebuilders means the "internationalisation of local conflicts" and, thereby, linking local actors of different kinds to international politics. On the other hand, over time peacebuilding also leads to the localisation of the internationals. External actors become part of the local political landscape and are drawn into power politics of local elites, often shaped by neo-patrimonial rule, forms of patronage and clientelism, informal power-sharing and the mobilisation of traditional structures such as clan, ethnic or kinship networks. For them, the internationals may offer new opportunities and strengthen their role as gatekeepers or intermediaries between the local population and the outside world. Moreover, in many ways, local elites are able to instrumentalise resources or to manipulate policies introduced by peacebuilders for their own purposes (for some illustrations, see Krause in this volume). In other words, while external actors certainly have an impact on the behaviour of the recipients, nonetheless their activities are also shaped by the skilful manoeuvring of local political forces. Based on the tripartite interactions of international peacebuilders, national and subnational elites, the result is, as Barnett and Zürcher (2009) put it, "cooperative", "compromised", "captured" or "conflictive" peacebuilding. In reality, however, these modes can change quickly or simply coexist depending on the issue or the constellation of actors involved.

Another aspect neglected by the binary coding is the emergence of the "transnational" and the long-term effects of "transnationalisation." Peacebuilding by its multilevel architecture produces new transnational social spaces and, thereby, transnationalises actors who are able to act on various levels at the same time; these may include, for example societal actors, business actors, churches, NGOs, diasporas and cross-border networks. As Mac Ginty and Richmond (2013, 773) conclude: "local actors, whether elites, societal groups or individuals, are regionally and globally aware and connected."

Furthermore, peacebuilding – like any other policy interventions – can be regarded as part of the historical process of transnationalisation and globalisation which obviously not only extends to post-colonial or post-Soviet societies but also affects the democratic societies of the industrial North.

The effects of these and other mechanisms on peace processes are largely discussed under different concepts. Once again, the recent "local turn" in peacebuilding studies highlights the neglected role of local agency. Mac Ginty and Richmond (2013), for example call for the "decolonisation of knowledge about peace making and peace building" by analysing "localized modi vivendi". For them the local turn is closely linked to the "post-liberal peace", which is about "notions of particularism and local variations that confront universalist ideas and practices" and about a "communitarian ethos" which challenges the "liberal-international peace architecture" (Mac Ginty and Richmond 2013, 772). Others might be less enthusiastic regarding the prospects for "bottom-up processes", "local peace" or "everyday peace", not least because they see the role of local actors – in particular of elites – more sceptically (cf. Barnett and Zürcher 2009; see also Krause and Paffenholz in this volume). Nonetheless, most observers agree that the notion of local remains inherently problematic. Not just because of the variety of actors, but the (re)discovery of the local in international peacebuilding discourses runs the risk of reproducing the asymmetry by constructing the local – be it as an actor-related or spatial concept – according to the needs of external peacebuilders. In other words, the local is what liberal or post-liberal peacebuilders make of it (see Mac Ginty and Debiel/Rinck in this volume).

At the same time, a number of scholars have put forward new concepts in order to capture the encounter of the international and local (however defined) and its effects for peacebuilding. By pointing to mixed international–local institutions or bodies in cases such as Afghanistan, Bosnia, East Timor or Kosovo, be it for joint decision-making, for consultation or coordination purposes, some speak about "new modes of governance" or forms of "transnational governance" emerging in post-conflict societies (Schneckener 2011, 250–254). Transitional justice processes, conducted by courts or commissions, are also a case in point since they are often shaped by hybrid institutional settings (see Fischer in this volume). More broadly, others refer to the "hybridity" or "hybridisation" of peacebuilding: they coin concepts such as "hybrid peace" (Mac Ginty 2010), "hybrid peace governance" (Belloni 2012) or "hybrid political orders" (Boege et al. 2009). Notwithstanding their differences in detail, the various frameworks aim at uncovering the coexistence, the overlap, the competition and the interplay of different notions of peace, institutions and order, composed of internationally supported (liberal peace), state-centric, traditional, "indigenous" or customary, formal or informal approaches. Mac Ginty describes four elements of the process of hybridisation: the compliance powers of the liberal peace; the incentive powers of the liberal peace; the ability of local actors to resist, ignore or subvert the liberal peace; and the ability of local actors to formulate and maintain alternatives to liberal peace. (Mac Ginty 2010, 398–404)

In his model, nevertheless, the liberal peace paradigm still remains the fixed star for all actors while others try to analyse more closely governance or power structures based on interactions of different actors (see Debiel/Rinck in this volume). However, it is not always clear whether these concepts are seen as analytical tools in order to describe better what *is* actually happening or as normative claims what *should* happen in peacebuilding. Is, for instance, hybrid peace a matter of fact or an ideal? Moreover, the notion of hybridity has its downsides since it is analytically not very precise. In fact, it covers a range of rather different constellations and options in peacebuilding which can all be regarded as hybrid in one way or the other. Additionally, hybridity needs to be based on ideal types from which it derives. Thus, the concept cannot transcend the international–local divide, but builds upon it. A hybrid peace or hybrid order is still a peace or an order which has identifiable international and local components.

This discussion reveals that it is indeed very difficult to move beyond the binary conceptualisation which is not only constitutive of peacebuilding practices, but also of most (Western) peacebuilding research. On the one hand, as described, almost all authors agree that the categories need to be abandoned, either on sociological or on normative grounds. On the other hand, in order to pinpoint different roles, patterns of behaviour, capacities and responsibilities, mind maps and power structures, the international–local divide still has some analytical relevance – at least as a starting point for research and as a shorthand description. Also, for ambitious ethical concepts such as "relational peacebuilding" (cf. Brigg in this volume) blurring or denying the lines would not be helpful, since both sides have distinct roles which define their relationship and their positioning in the first place. The interesting point, however, is what happens when the peacebuilding process is under way and when roles, relations and responsibilities become less clear.

Concluding remarks

This stock-taking exercise unveils that not only practitioners but also academics seem to struggle with peacebuilding. Over the years, an impressive and rich body of literature has been produced and has stimulated various disputes and critiques. In many respects, the peacebuilding debates mirror the more general contestation about the justification, the practices and the consequences of any kind of intervention from outside into a distinct polity. One might even argue, as proposed by Chandler in this volume, that peacebuilding became "indistinguishable from other policy spheres" and, therefore, meaningless. If this is case, should not the term be dismissed – at least by peace and conflict researchers? According to my reading, there are two main reasons why this radical option is not convincing. First, in contrast to other policy interventions, peacebuilding as a concept and practice still raises the question about the foundations of peace. Surely, the meaning of peace itself is contested territory and the notion of peace is oftentimes used to justify very different policies (including fighting wars). Nonetheless, most would probably agree with a sociological understanding of peace which refers to constructive, nonviolent responses to social conflicts within and between societies (or communities). In other words, recognising and acknowledging social conflicts has to be a precondition for building peace. Consequently, peace is not a state of affairs (as in negative peace), but a process which requires the tireless efforts of many actors at all levels of society and which can never be taken for granted. For realist or neo-Marxist thinkers, this may sound hopelessly naïve since peace is, like all politics, a field of struggle, largely shaped by power and interests. A world, however, in which different actors can pursue their agendas by peaceful coexistence, by peaceful means and within a regulated setting, seems to be a much better place – notwithstanding remaining power asymmetries. And peacebuilding seems to be the only concept which gives sustainable peace a chance, even if many peacebuilders in their operational policies have lost sight of it (which, in turn, we only know if we have a concept like peacebuilding). Second, abandoning the term would not make it easier to study the phenomenon as such. It will certainly not abandon or alter those practices and policies which the protagonists or we as observers used to call peacebuilding and now call X or Y. Do we really believe that new terms and frameworks will better inform us about the normative, analytical and practical problems discussed under the umbrella of the (rightfully disputed) peacebuilding perspective? What would be a candidate to replace the concept – simply "intervention," "involvement" or another member of the "building" family?

As this example shows, there is a diminishing utility in the academic ritual of constructing, deconstructing or replacing paradigms and concepts. Such debates certainly fill academic journals, but to some extent they tend to go around in circles with limited impact on politics, as Richmond and Mac Ginty (2015, 173) admit in a self-critical manner regarding the intense debate on liberal peace over the past 10 years. This should by no means imply that a critical assessment and deconstruction of concepts such as peacebuilding from different perspectives is not needed at all – quite the contrary. Indeed, through the debates presented earlier, peacebuilding paradigms and practices have been placed in the wider context of international relations, social science theories and political philosophy. This exercise is and will still be necessary, also in order to open up the rather narrow field of peace and conflict research. Nonetheless, the question remains: where do all these debates lead us to – in particular regarding further research? My reading is that the various debates – at least partly – can be regarded as contributions to an emerging *political sociology of peacebuilding* which aims at integrating inter alia the body of social science theories on power, rule and domination, on political legitimacy, on political economy, on policy-making and decision-making, on political bargaining and negotiating, on social processes and dynamics, on discourses and narratives and so forth. Such a perspective applies in particular to the cross-cutting issue of the complex web of relations and interactions by various actors involved in peacebuilding practices. This would imply being less occupied with the concept and the approaches of peacebuilding and its discontents, instead focusing more on the role of agency, that is on interactions and its effects, on patterns of behaviour, on sometimes erratic political actions and on social practices conducted by different actors, most prominently by the triads of peacebuilders, national elites and local subelites (as well as their opponents or rivals). There still seems to be a field open to both conceptual and theoretical innovation as well as empirical studies, be they comparative case studies or in-depth ethnographical studies. Furthermore, peacebuilding research could profit from a broader time horizon and from a comparative historical perspective which addresses not only earlier cases of peacebuilding (which may have not been called that way) but also long-term processes taking place over generations. In particular, the history of European states and societies can be seen as a laboratory of failed and successful peacebuilding undertakings. Thereby, today's peacebuilders could reflect more about their own experiences as locals, about their controversial ways of responding to conflict and violence and about the pitfalls of peacebuilding in their own history – even if one does not want to go back as far as 1648.

Notes

1 For 2013, SIPRI counted 57 peace operations (2012: 53, 2011: 52, 2010: 52, 2009: 54, 2008: 60, 2007: 60) of different kinds involving more than 200,000 people (SIPRI Yearbook 2014). In October 2014, the German Centre for International Peace Operations (ZIF) published a list of 70 ongoing peace operations, including 26 UN and 17 EU missions and 16 by the Organization for Security and Co-operation in Europe (OSCE) (www.zif-berlin.org).

2 See, for example, UN Peacebuilding: An Orientation, New York: UN Peacebuilding Support Office, 2010, http://www.un.org/en/peacebuilding/pbso/pdf/peacebuilding_orientation.pdf. One recent attempt has been the formulation of five Peace- and Statebuilding Goals (PSG), formally concluded at the 4th High Level Forum on Aid Effectiveness in Busan/Korea (December 2011) within the framework of the OECD/DAC (Development Assistance Committee). The PSGs consist of "legitimate and inclusive politics" (including conflict resolution), "security" (including strengthening people's security), "justice" (including access to justice), "economic foundations" (including employment and improving livelihoods) and "revenues and services" (including capacity-building).

3 According to my reading, therefore, the distinction between "critical" and "problem-solving" paradigms in peacebuilding (see Pugh 2013), based on Robert Cox, is misleading since it not only represents a widespread misunderstanding of the *Frankfurt Critical School*, which was in fact very productive in empirical, applied research and in policy advice, but also insinuates a division of research in either critical or affirmative ways of thinking.

4 In a recent article Richmond and Mac Ginty (2015) listed 17 different critiques of the critique of the liberal peace and responded to them.

References

Barnett, M., Kim, H., O'Donnell, M., and Sitea, L. (2007). Peacebuilding: What is in a name? *Global Governance*, 13(1), 35–58.

Barnett, M., and Zürcher, C. (2009). The peacebuilder's contract. In R. Paris and T. Sisk (Eds.), *The Dilemmas of Statebuilding: Confronting the Contradictions of Postwar Peace Operations*. Taylor & Francis, London, 23–52.

Bell, C. (2013). Peacebuilding, law and human rights. In R. Mac Ginty (Ed.), *Routledge Handbook of Peacebuilding*. Routledge, Abingdon, 249–260.

Belloni, R. (2012). Hybrid peace governance: Its emergence and significance. *Global Governance*, 18(1), 21–38.

Boege, V., Brown, A., and Nolan, A. (2009). Building peace and political community in hybrid political orders. *International Peacekeeping*, 16(5), 599–615.

Campbell, S., Chandler, D., and Sabaratnam, M. (Eds.). (2011). *A Liberal Peace? The Problems and Practices of Peacebuilding*. Zed Books, London.

Caplan, R. (2005). *International Governance of War-Torn Territories*. Oxford University Press, Oxford.

Carothers, T. (Ed.) (2006). *Promoting the Rule of Law Abroad: In Search of Knowledge*. Carnegie Endowment for International Peace, Washington, DC.

Chandler, D. (2008). Post-conflict statebuilding: Governance without government. In M. Pugh, N. Cooper, and M. Turner (Eds.), *Whose Peace? Critical Perspectives on the Political Economy of Peacebuilding*. Palgrave, London, 337–355.

Chandler, D. (2010). The uncritical critique of "liberal peace". *Review of International Studies*, 36(1), 137–155.

Chesterman, S. (2004). *You, the People. The United Nations, Transitional Administration and State-Building*. Oxford University Press, Oxford.

Coulomb, F. (2004). *Economic Theories of Peace and War*. Routledge, London.

Cousens, E. M., and Kumar, C. (Eds.). (2000). *Peacebuilding as Politics. Cultivating Peace in Fragile Societies*. Lynne Rienner, Boulder, CO.

Dayton, B., and Kriesberg, L. (Eds.). (2009). *Conflict Transformation and Peacebuilding*. Routledge, London.

Dillon, M., and Reid, J. (2009). *The Liberal Way of War: Killing to Make Life Live*. Routledge, London.

Doyle, M. W., and Sambanis, N. (2006). *Making War & Building Peace*. Princeton University Press, Princeton, NJ.

Duffield, M. (2007). *Development, Security and Unending War: Governing the World of Peoples*. Polity Press, Cambridge.

Etzioni, A. (2007). *Security First. For a Muscular, Moral Foreign Policy*. Yale University Press, New Haven, CT.

Fukuyama, F. (2004). *State-Building: Governance and World Order in the 21st Century*. Cornell University Press, Ithaca, NY.

Geis, A., Müller, H., and Schörnig, N. (2013). *The Militant Face of Democracy. Liberal Forces for Good*. Cambridge University Press, Cambridge.

Geis, A., Müller, H., and Wagner, W. (Eds.). (2007). *Schattenseiten des Demokratischen Friedens. Zur Kritik einer Theorie liberaler Außen- und Sicherheitspolitik*. Campus Verlag, Frankfurt.

Hensell, S. (2015). Coordinating intervention: International actors and local "partners" between ritual and decoupling. *Journal of Intervention and Statebuilding*, 9(1), 89–111.

Ife, J. (2007). Human rights and peace. In C. Webel and J. Galtung (Eds.), *Handbook of Peace and Conflict Studies*. Routledge, Abingdon, 160–172.

Jabri, V. (2007). *War and the Transformation of Global Politics*. Palgrave Macmillan, Basingstoke.

Jabri, V. (2013). Peacebuilding, the local and the international: A colonial or a postcolonial rationality? *Peacebuilding*, 1(1), 3–16.

Lederach, J.-P. (1997). *Building Peace. Sustainable Reconciliation in Divided Societies*. United States Institute for Peace, Washington, DC.

Mac Ginty, R. (2010). Hybrid peace: The interaction between top-down and bottom-up peace. *Security Dialogue*, 41(4), 391–412.

Mac Ginty, R., and Richmond, O. (2007). Myth or reality: Opposing views on the liberal peace and the post-war reconstruction. *Global Society*, 21(4), 491–497.

Mac Ginty, R., and Richmond, O. (2013). The local turn in peace building: A critical agenda for peace. *Third World Quarterly*, 34(5), 763–783.

Marten, K. Z. (2004). *Enforcing the Peace: Learning from the Imperial Past*. Columbia University Press, New York.

Newman, E. (2009). "Liberal" peacebuilding debates. In E. Newman, R. Paris, and O. Richmond (Eds.), *New Perspectives on Liberal Peacebuilding*. United Nations University Press, Tokyo, 26–53.

Newman, E. (2010). Peacebuilding as security in failing and conflict-prone states. *Journal of Intervention and Statebuilding*, 4(3), 305–322.

Newman, E., Paris, R., and Richmond, O. (Eds.). (2009). *New Perspectives on Liberal Peacebuilding*. United Nations University Press, Tokyo.

Oneal, J., and Russett, B. (2001). *Triangulating Peace. Democracy, Interdependence and International Organizations*. W. W. Norton, New York.

Paffenholz, T. (Ed.) (2010). *Civil Society and Peacebuilding: A Critical Assessment*. Lynne Rienner, Boulder, CO.

Page Fortna, V. (2004). Does peacekeeping keep peace? International intervention and the duration of peace after civil war. *International Studies Quarterly*, 48(2), 269–292.

Paris, R. (2004). *At War's End: Building Peace after Civil Conflict*. Cambridge University Press, Cambridge.

Paris, R. (2006). Bringing the Leviathan back in: Classical versus contemporary studies of the liberal peace. *International Studies Review*, 8(3), 425–440.

Paris, R. (2009). Understanding the "coordination problem" in postwar statebuilding. In R. Paris and T. Sisk (Eds.), *The Dilemmas of Statebuilding: Confronting the Contradictions of Postwar Peace Operations*. Taylor & Francis, London, 53–78.

Paris, R. (2011). Critiques of liberal peace. In S. Campbell, D. Chandler, and M. Sabaratnam (Eds.), *A Liberal Peace? The Problems and Practices of Peacebuilding*. Zed Books, London, 31–54.

Paris, R., and Sisk, T. (Eds.). (2009). *The Dilemmas of Statebuilding: Confronting the Contradictions of Postwar Peace Operations*. Taylor & Francis, London.

Pouligny, B. (2005). Civil society and post-conflict peacebuilding: Ambiguities of international programmes aimed at building "new" societies. *Security Dialogue*, 36(4), 495–510.

Pugh, M. (2013). The problem-solving and critical paradigms. In R. Mac Ginty (Ed.), *Routledge Handbook on Peacebuilding*. Routledge, Abingdon, 11–24.

Richmond, O. (2006). The problem of peace: Understanding the "liberal peace". *Conflict, Security and Development*, 6(3), 291–314.

Richmond, O. (2011). *A Post-liberal Peace*. Routledge, Abingdon.

Richmond, O., and Mac Ginty, R. (2015). Where now for the critique of liberal peace? *Cooperation and Conflict*, 50(2), 171–189.

Russett, B. (1993). *Grasping the Democratic Peace: Principles for Post–Cold War World*. Princeton University Press, Princeton, NJ.

Sabaratnam, M. (2013). Avatars of Eurocentrism in the critique of the liberal peace. *Security Dialogue*, 44(3), 259–278.

Schlichte, K., and Veit, A. (2012). Three arenas: The conflictive logic of external state-building. In B. Bliesemann de Guevara (Ed.), *Statebuilding and State-Formation. The Political Sociology of Intervention*. Routledge, Abingdon, 167–181.

Schneckener, U. (2005). Frieden Machen: Peacebuilding und peacebuilder. Die Friedens-Warte. *Journal of International Peace and Organization*, 80(1–2), 17–39.

Schneckener, U. (2011). State building or new modes of governance? In T. Risse (Ed.), *Governance without a State? Policies and Politics in Areas of Limited Statehood*. Columbia University Press, New York, 232–261.

Schneckener, U., and Weinlich, S. (2005). The United Nations Peacebuilding Commission. Tasks, Mandate, and Design for a New Institution, *SWP-Comments*, C 38, September 2005, Stiftung Wissenschaft und Politik, Berlin.

Schröder, U. (2013). Gauging the effectiveness of post-conflict peace- and state-building. In H. Hegemann, R. Heller, and M. Kahl (Eds.), *Studying "Effectiveness" in International Relations*. Barbara Budrich, Opladen, 217–235.

Selby, J. (2013). The myth of liberal peacebuilding. *Conflict, Security and Development*, 13(1), 57–86.

Senghaas, D. (Ed.) (1995). *Den Frieden Denken. Ci vis pacem, para pacem*. Suhrkamp, Frankfurt.

Senghaas, D. (2004). *Zum iridischen Frieden*. Suhrkamp, Frankfurt.

Stedman, S. J., Rothchild, D., and Cousens, E. M. (Eds.). (2002). *Ending Civil Wars. The Implementation of Peace Agreements*. Lynne Rienner, Boulder, CO.

Suhrke, A. (2014). Post-war states: Differentiating patterns of peace. In C. Stahn, J. Easterday, and J. Iverson (Eds.), *Jus post bellum: Mapping the Normative Foundations*. Oxford University Press, Oxford, 269–284.

Tschirgi, N. (2013). Securitization and peacebuilding. In R. Mac Ginty (Ed.), *Routledge Handbook of Peacebuilding*. Routledge, Abingdon, 197–210.

Van Tongeren, P., Brenk, M., Hellema, M., and Verhoeven, J. (Eds.). (2005). *People Building Peace II: Successful Stories of Civil Society*. Lynne Rienner, Boulder, CO.

Verkoren, W., and Van Leeuwen, M. (2013). Civil society in peacebuilding: Global discourse, local reality. *International Peacekeeping*, 20(2), 159–172.

Zaum, D. (2012). Beyond the liberal peace. *Global Governance*, 18(1), 121–132.

Zaum, D. (2013). International relations theory and peacebuilding. In R. Mac Ginty (Ed.), *Routledge Handbook of Peacebuilding*. Routledge, Abingdon, 105–116.

Part I

Reflecting peacebuilding paradigms

2 Peacebuilding and paternalism

Michael Barnett

Peacebuilding is accused of many things. It is criticized for having a predetermined idea about what a proper state should look like: liberal, democratic, and market-oriented. Peacebuilding, in this way, is operating in the long, modernist tradition, supported by reformers and radical of all political ideologies, attempting to "bring" progress, through heavy-handed means if necessary. As peacebuilders seek the "liberal peace," they do so in a very illiberal manner. They know, even before they arrive, what they need to do; thanks to their "to-do list," they do not even need to consult with the local population to ascertain its needs. Although they preach partnership, they treat the local population as afterthoughts at worst and as service providers at best, reserving for themselves the major decisions and avoiding any accountability to those directly affected by their decisions. Peacebuilding is done for the local population, not with them. Their position of superiority turns otherwise well-meaning, down-to-earth individuals into arrogant know-it-alls. For these and many other reasons, critics of peacebuilding accuse it of possessing a colonial mentality.

What do peacebuilders say in their defense? Some plead innocent of the charges. Others will argue that the characterization is true of other organizations, a comment often heard when a nongovernmental organization (NGO) worker talks about the United Nations. Another response is to insist that the colonial charge is patently unfair because colonialism was exploitative, whereas peacebuilding attempts to help states and societies in need; in short, they have radically different purposes. Another, more interesting response is to provide reasons for their illiberal character. In other words, they plead guilty to some of the accusations but point to extenuating circumstances that justify their otherwise transgressive actions. Populations emerging from war and disaster often are too devastated to know how to pick up the pieces. If peacebuilders are going to "build back better," then they have to be willing to take action without necessarily waiting for all the voices to be heard. Do local populations really know the best way to build peace? And, who is the "local"? Often men with guns who were largely responsible for producing the devastation. To do what the locals want, in short, would merely reproduce the status quo and the causes of the conflict. And, most of the places hosting peacebuilding operations have high rates of illiteracy, little education, and few experts who actually know how to get things

done. In many respects, the peacebuilders are there to perform governance functions that cannot be performed by the state or local municipalities, not only
because there is not enough money, but also because there is a shortage of know-
how. Let the experts do their job. The argument, in short, is that peacebuilders,
under the right conditions, can justifiably use power over the population for
their betterment.

There is a concept that captures this mixture of care and control: paternalism. Paternalism has many different meanings, as I will soon discuss, but
the gist is that one actor is substituting his judgment for another's in order to
further the target's welfare and well-being. Similar to many concepts, paternalism is both a concept of analysis and a concept of evaluation. As a concept of
analysis, defining the meaning and boundaries of the concept helps us identify
when it exists and what distinguishes it from, for instance, an act of pure compassion or pure domination. And, similar to most concepts of analysis, there is
an active debate over how to define it and which are its essential properties.
As a concept of evaluation, paternalism is almost always considered to be a sin
for various reasons: it is disrespectful, infantilizing, violates someone's autonomy and dignity, and on and on. Yet scholars have identified conditions under
which it might be justified. It might be all the things that its critics say it is, but
if a little paternalism improves the well-being of an individual or a population,
hurt feelings seem like a small price to pay. Indeed, the justification for the use
of power by peacebuilders overlaps with some standard, and widely accepted,
defenses of paternalism.

This chapter explores the paternalism in peacebuilding, with two objectives in
mind. The main goal, and the bulk of the chapter, explores how elements associated with various definitions of paternalism illuminate distinctive criticisms of
peacebuilding. Specifically, peacebuilding has the following maladies associated
with paternalism: ineffectiveness, heavy-handedness, the imposition of reasoning, the creation of relations of superiority and inferiority, a lack of consent, a
lack of legitimacy, and a lack of democracy. Although a sensitivity analysis would
reveal the different shades and degrees of paternalism across different kinds of
peacebuilding actors, this chapter is interested in identifying the elements of
paternalism that underlie much of peacebuilding. These various paternalist-
informed criticisms of peacebuilding have a common element: the failure to
incorporate the local. Exactly how and why peacebuilding silences the local,
though, varies from critique to critique.[1] And, like all indictments, some charges
are seen as more fundamental than others, and might even be justifiable given
the reasons. This feeds into my second point, which I address briefly in the conclusion: paternalism in peacebuilding might be justified but nevertheless be difficult to legitimate. There might be times when outsiders feel as if they cannot
or should not incorporate the views of local populations, precisely because doing
so would harm their well-being and welfare. "Do no harm," in this view, might
require intentionally disregarding the preferences of local populations who, if
they had their way, might lead to self-harm.

How is peacebuilding paternalistic?

There is an endless supply of definitions of paternalism.[2] Merriam-Webster defines it as "the attitude or actions of a person, organization, etc., that protects people and gives them what they need but does not give them any responsibility or freedom of choice" ("Paternalism," n.d.a.). According to the Oxford English Dictionary, paternalism is "the policy or practice on the part of people in positions of authority of restricting the freedom and responsibilities of those subordinate to them in the subordinates' supposed best interest" ("Paternalism," n.d.b.). Other definitions highlight not the attempt by one person to improve the circumstances of another, but instead the intent to "prevent him from harming himself, either when he would harm himself voluntarily or when he would do so involuntarily" (Claassen 2014, 61). According to another, frequently cited definition by Gerald Dworkin, it is "the interference with a person's liberty of action justified by reasons referring exclusively to the welfare, good, happiness, needs, interests or values of the person being coerced" (Dworkin 1972, 70–76). In a recent review of the contending definitions, Dworkin marches through seven candidates, including Seana Shiffrin's influential version, which emphasizes not the interference with another actor's interests but rather the interference in another actor's proper sphere of autonomy and judgment (Dworkin 2013; Shiffrin 2000). More recently, Cass Sunstein and Robert Thaler observe that paternalism exists when an action is intended to affect the choices available to the person whose welfare is a source of concern (Thaler and Sunstein 2003, 2008; Sunstein 2006).

Scholars of paternalism have generated a long list of alternative definitions. There are some definitions that appear to avoid taking a position on whether, normatively speaking, it is good or bad; indeed, preventing someone from harming himself sounds like a good deed, not a sin. There are other definitions that vary in terms of what sort of action is required to be a paternalist; some set the bar at the use of coercion and the active suspension of liberty, others at the act of trying to help someone without incorporating their views, and still others include almost any action that restricts choice in order to improve the well-being of the target actor. Also, there are differences over which first-order values have been violated: liberty, autonomy, and dignity are not the same things. Given these definitions, it is difficult to imagine that peacebuilding, or any professionalized ethics of care, could escape the charge of paternalism; indeed, it might not be able to do its job without it. In any event, different definitions of paternalism illuminate different lines of critique of peacebuilding. In what follows I use the literature on paternalism to identify seven different criticisms of peacebuilding.

Ineffective

Although this might seem to be a trivial place to start, in fact it is central. Paternalism rests on an ethic of consequentialism: suspending someone's liberty, restricting their choices, or encroaching on their autonomy is justified because doing so is in the best interest of the target. The presumption, of course, is that the paternalizer knows what he is doing and that good intentions translate into good results. Yet one of the constant criticisms of peacebuilding is that peacebuilders, in fact, do not know what they are doing. The reasons for their ignorance are many. They do not know the local language and lack a basic familiarity with the country's history. They think that they know best. They rely on bureaucratic and expert logics that are used in a cookie-cutter formulation without any nuance or attention to local conditions. Their models, logframes, formulas, and checklists are, in fact, gobbledygook – pseudo-science that better resembles alchemy than it does geometry. It is because of their ignorance that good intentions almost always go awry. One obvious antidote to paternalism is to incorporate local voices into all aspects and stages of the peacebuilding process. However, resting the case against paternalism on effectiveness offers a backdoor defense of the paternalism in peacebuilding. Peacebuilding is based not only on an ethics of consequences but also on counterfactual scenarios. The implied counterfactual in the recommendation to incorporate the local is that doing so would improve the results. However, this is an empirical question and the jury is still out. Said otherwise, if it can be shown, empirically, that peacebuilding outcomes are either outcome neutral or better with limited local participation, then peacebuilders are justified being paternalistic. The case for paternalism is premised on the result; the case against only partly so.

Coercion

For many, the problem with paternalism is that it is, quite literally, heavy-handed. For instance, in Dworkin's classic definition, paternalism is not just interference, but interference that includes some degree of coercion. In this respect, the grievance is the application of power in its most traditional sense – one actor compelling another to do something that he would otherwise not do. Consequently, paternalism does not exist simply when someone tells us what he thinks we should be doing for our own good, but rather when someone actually redirects our behavior. Said otherwise, while being told by another what to do is never pleasant, the transgression is not someone speaking their mind but rather using force. The tools of coercion can vary from the direct application of physical force to the indirect introduction of incentives that significantly raise the cost of resistance through some combination of carrots and sticks. A central problem with paternalism concerns the means that are used.

If peacebuilding's paternalism rested solely on the use of force, then it would probably be fairly difficult to find instances when peacebuilders are, in fact, paternalistic. Indeed, one of the criticisms of peacebuilding is not the excessive use of force but rather its scarcity – especially when it comes to civilian protection. In any event, peacebuilders do not have the standard tools of coercion. However, they do have other means of influence which can be equally attention-grabbing and incentive-shaping. Most importantly, peacebuilders come with resources to areas and populations that have next to nothing. In these situations of gross asymmetries of power, where peacebuilders have an exit option or can tie their aid to the acceptance of conditions, words can sound like commands backed by unspoken threats. Yet many studies of peacebuilding highlight that peacebuilders cannot impose their preferences but rather must bargain with, and ultimately persuade, the local populations to follow their recommended path – and the local populations are not without their means of resistance, ability to capture the resources provided by peacebuilders, and even capacity to shape the preferences of the peacebuilders (Barnett et al. 2014). Peacebuilders do have tools of coercion available to them, but it is not clear how effective they are, or even how often they are deployed. Consequently, peacebuilders are reputed to rely on tools of persuasion, but even such tools, coupled with the ability to distribute and withhold assistance, can have a coercive dimension (Tsai 2014).

Imposition of reasoning

Force is bad, but according to others, the original sin is the imposition of reasoning. Coercion, in other words, only adds injury to insult. In many definitions of paternalism, the central feature is the substitution of one person's judgment for another in order to further the latter's betterment. Sometimes this action owes to a self-conscious decision to forgo soliciting the views of the actor because his interests are obvious. If someone is starving or dehydrated, why waste time asking them if they would like something to eat or drink? If someone's house was destroyed by a natural disaster, it seems fairly obvious that they will need shelter. Solidarity, rather than paternalism, might be the more accurate description of these acts because the benefactor is responding to the apparent interests of the beneficiary.

Yet it is common for those who profess to be acting in solidarity with others to be accused of sliding into paternalism, because they have failed to properly listen to the views of those they want to help and unilaterally substituted their judgment for theirs. Those in the West spend a lot of time attempting to save those in the third world, but it is not always clear that those in the third world feel as if they need to be saved, at least not in the way perceived by Westerners. Those living under oppressive conditions are quite likely to want to better their human rights but might have a very different idea about what those rights are and which rights should be prioritized.

Moreover, at other times, and especially in non-life-threatening circumstances, the needs and interests are not so obvious, yet the paternalist proceeds to decide for himself what they are. The substitution of one person's judgment for another, in many of these instances, owes to an unconscious or self-conscious decision that the person is unable to judge what their interests are. It is irrelevant whether or not the target would have made the same choice if asked. The point is that he was not asked and should have been. It is equally irrelevant whether or not the decision improved the welfare of the target. It has nothing to do with the results.

If it turns out for the best, it might make the offender feel vindicated and the offended a little less willing to hold a grudge, but results can only mitigate, not erase, the wrongdoing. It is the act itself – the usurpation of someone else's right to decide for himself – that is the offense.

Many charges of paternalism against peacebuilders fall into this category. A fairly standard accusation of peacebuilding operations concerns their failure to canvas the local population about their perceived needs and how to achieve them. In the attempt to remedy this dogmatism, the humanitarian sector intro-duced the idea of needs assessment, which was supposed to allow local popula-tions to decide and communicate their needs. All good in theory, but it is not clear that it has had any practical effects (Garfield et al. 2011). Moreover, the human rights community does not wait for individuals to "discover" their rights and then ask for outside assistance; instead it often operates on the assumption that it must spread and enforce "natural rights." These rights exist, in other words, whether or not local populations recognize them and ask for help from outsiders (Hopgood 2013).

The substitution of one actor's judgment for another connects to a common criticism of peacebuilding in general and liberal peacebuilding in particular – it arrives with a predetermined idea of what societies need and what they should look like. In this respect, peacebuilding is reminiscent of colonialism and its civi-lizing missions. The liberal John Stuart Mill defended British imperialism in India on the grounds that it would help the Indians develop the mental capacities and social institutions to become free-thinking, reasoning peoples who were capa-ble of self-governance (which would benefit the British) (Hopgood 2013, 175; Habibi 1999). His sentiments were hardly radical, for many colonizing peoples genuinely believed that colonialism could and should benefit the colonized popu-lation. Indeed, accusations that colonial administrators and commercial elites were exploiting the colonial peoples could unleash a torrent of outrage by the British public on the grounds that Britain was failing in its role of trustee (Dirks 2006). A similar logic and dynamic also exists in contemporary peacebuilding operations. Peacebuilding operations might not use force, unlike the civilizing missions of yesteryear, but they attempt to impose their own visions of what other societies need for progress.

Relations and attitudes of superiority and inferiority

Frequently when the paternalism charge is slapped on peacebuilding, the insinu-ation is that peacebuilders believe themselves to be superior to the local popula-tion. This critique has a mixture of layers. The first is the assumption that one person's judgment is superior to another's. He is smarter, more knowledgeable, better educated, more rational, or wiser. Why such confidence? It can be a matter of faith. Faith-based paternalism exists when confidence derives from preternatu-ral commitments that leave little room for doubt, most obvious when claims to know better cannot be challenged by empirical evidence. These nearly founda-tional claims help orient the self in relationship to humankind and the cosmos.

Religious theology has this characteristic. "Theological propositions are unverifiable because the existence they posit – God, immortal souls, and so forth – do not, even if they exist, intrude on human experience in such a way as to provide compelling evidence for their verification" (Westbrook 2003, 194). Some secular thought has these very qualities as well. For instance, many statements on human rights are founded on natural law and nonverifiable commitments; they cannot be proven or disproven but rather are a matter of faith. In terms of its effects, then, belief in God is not that different from a belief in humanity (Hopgood 2009; Feldman and Ticktin 2011). Although it is not very fashionable for peacebuilders to refer to faith, claims to operate in the name of the values of international community or transcendental and universal values have faith-like qualities.

Alternatively, confidence can be founded on claims to superior knowledge. Evidence-based paternalism exists when confidence derives from potentially verifiable claims that can be supported or challenged by empirical evidence. In other words, it rests on science in its broadest possible meaning: the systematic effort to organize, develop, and accumulate knowledge in the form of verifiable and testable explanations and predictions, most often based on the idea of establishing causal links between different social phenomena. Importantly, scientific inquiry and rationalization processes have produced a new kind of actor that is central to contemporary evidence-based paternalism: the expert. The sociological category of expert is a modern creation, emerging in the late nineteenth century with the expansion of capitalism, the growth of a more specialized division of labor, the heightened importance of services in the modern economy and, ultimately, the emphasis of modernity on knowledge gained by formal training and education. Although not all recognized knowledge is general (sometimes referred to as local) or obtained through education (sometimes referred to as experiential or practical), the presumption is that in modern society credentialed knowledge trumps local and practical knowledge.[3] This is a standard criticism of peacebuilders and the aid world more generally (Easterly 2007, 2013).[4]

The second layer is the belief that the other actor is not only not as smart as the superior actor, but also not smart enough, mature enough, rational enough, or competent enough to make decisions for himself. If they had crossed some threshold of competence, rationality, maturity, or wisdom, then they would be allowed to make their own decisions, even if the decisions were not equal to those that would have been made by the superior actor. The civilizing missions of the nineteenth century presupposed that the colonial peoples had not reached a sufficient level of judgment to enjoy self-rule, and the civilizing powers had a responsibility to help them to the point where they had such judgment, not that such judgment would be equal to the civilized country. So, too, for peacebuilders.

These discourses and binaries of civilized/uncivilized and advanced/traditional generate relations of superiority and inferiority. To return to the category of expert, expertise generates hierarchies of superiority and inferiority. Experts claim to know more and expect to be treated with deference. Global governance institutions are increasingly staffed by experts who, by virtue of their superior knowledge, feel as if they know best and that others should listen and do as they say. Such mentalities, according to many in the humanitarian sector, are particularly prevalent when those with advanced knowledge are asked to help "victims" who, almost by definition, are victims because they were and, and continue to be, unable to act in their own best interests. Lastly, the belief that some people just know more and better, and are willing to use their insights to help others, creates the space to interfere without consent.

Another layer, which is a residue of the first two, is the assault on someone's dignity. Our dignity is insulted whenever someone assumes that we are unfit to understand, speak, or act in our own best interest. Paternalism offends not only because of the act, but also because of the attitude. The typical synonyms for paternalism include high-mindedness, condescension, arrogance, conceit, and haughtiness. Indeed, according to the various listening projects and surveys of recipients, these are common criticisms of peacebuilders (Abu-Sada 2012; Anderson 2012).

Lack of consent

According to some definitions, paternalism exists whenever an actor interferes in the affairs of another without his or her consent. There might be times when consent is not given but can be reasonably inferred from the circumstances. Emergency room doctors must frequently act first and get patient consent later. Humanitarian intervention, at least from the perspective of the victims, is probably applauded by the recipients; the standard question is, "what took so long?" Indeed, delaying action until consent can be acquired might very well mean waiting until it is too late. During humanitarian emergencies and mass refugee flight, aid workers must frequently make decisions without being able to canvass the views of the affected population, but nevertheless have a pretty good idea that they have some basic needs, such as water, food, medicine, and shelter that must be met. In these situations, then, international actors might justifiably act with implied consent.

However, reasonable in some circumstances, implied consent is a slippery slope, especially once the absence of a registered dissent becomes taken as an indicator of consent. Consider, for instance, when the UN High Commissioner for Refugees (UNHCR) must decide whether or not to repatriate refugees to their homeland. Because international refugee law prohibits the repatriation of refugees to their home countries if they believe that they cannot return without exposing themselves to harm, UNHCR is expected to survey the refugees to ascertain their preferences. Such assessments are incredibly difficult to carry out, the validity of the responses is highly debatable, and it is often quite difficult to interpret the wishes of the refugees. Given this uncertainty, UNHCR often relies on its own judgment, issues a decision, and then assumes that if there is no major outcry from refugees then their decision is probably consistent with preferences of the refugee population. But there are lots of reasons why refugees might not vocally protest a decision that they believe puts them at risk, including the concern that they have no choice or the fear that UNHCR might engage in punitive action, such as cutting rations, if they do not comply. It is because implied consent is such a slippery slope that many ethicists prefer to err on the side of caution, insisting that consent must either be explicit or "obvious" from what "most" people would want under the circumstances (Hartogh 2011).

Although the obvious remedy to implied consent is explicit consent, this is easier assumed than corroborated. There is, of course, the previously mentioned problem of how to ascertain consent from large populations, especially in contexts where substantial portions have lived their lives in authoritarian countries and have never been asked for their consent or opinion about anything. And, in many local settings where peacebuilders operate, there are preexisting social structures that are constituted by patrimonialism and neo-patrimonialism, which have elements of paternalism. Consequently, their "consent" might represent someone else's choice. Relatedly, while no choice is made outside of constraints, constraints can quickly become so severe that consent can be seen as coerced in some form. What does consent mean in conditions of gross power asymmetries? Also, consent is granted in relationship to an assessment of objectives. However, do individuals always know their objective interests and how to achieve them? What if they articulate preferences that really seem to be in the interests of others? One of the most potent effects of power occurs when an actor adopts the interests of the more privileged. Can individuals make informed decisions if they are, for instance, locked down by a culture that has taught them to blindly accept an outward and inward orientation that stifles their human development? One way out is to lean heavily on informed consent and try to persuade them, but this has its own limitations (O'Neill 2003; Tsai 2014).

There might also be occasions when actors transfer rights to give or deny consent to a third party – that is, voluntarily delegating to another the authority to act in ways that the authority believes is in the best interest of the actor in the subordinate position. Why would anyone do such a thing? Presumably because she believes that it is in her best interest to enter into an arrangement where another actor has the authority to restrict or guide her choices in the future. We might do so when we experience collective action problems, possess the self-awareness that we are sacrificing long-term gains for immediate gratification, or want to improve our welfare by seeking out another's assistance (Talbott 2010, 277). To perform this welfare-enhancing role, the agent must be relatively autonomous from the (most powerful) members. Institutionalist and principal-agent approaches capture this logic and have been used to understand why states might voluntarily surrender some part of their sovereignty to a third party (Lake 2011; Cooley 2008). This logic also informs Thaler and Sunstein's notion of "libertarian paternalism" (Thaler and Sunstein 2003), wherein an authorized third party is given the authority to limit the choices available to the principals in order to further their well-being. Drawing from psychology and behavioral economics, they begin with the finding that individuals do not make choices as suggested by rational choice models; humans process information in ways that depart substantially from rationality. Consequently, individuals often make suboptimal decisions. If so, then this opens up the space for a third party to arrange the options available in such a manner that steers the actor toward the most welfare-enhancing outcome. They call this a "nudge." Their defense of nudges by the government also applies to peacebuilding, and the broad insights from decision-making judgment have become quite influential in development assistance (World Bank 2014).

Lack of legitimacy

Sometimes the charge of paternalism is about the lack of legitimacy of the authority who is claiming the right to interfere.[5] Briefly, legitimacy has two dimensions (Suchman 1995). There is procedural legitimacy, in which decisions made by the authority are seen by the audience as having followed the correct path. There is also substantive legitimacy, in which the authority's decisions are seen as being consistent with the audience's values. To the extent that the authority gets high marks for both procedural and substantive legitimacy, then the audience is more likely to see the authority's decisions as reflecting their interests and more likely to comply with its decisions; to the extent that the authority gets low marks, the audience is more likely to feel removed from, threatened by, and resistant to the authority's decisions.

Interference is most easily legitimated, and paternalism most easily excused, when it is undertaken by those authorities that have procedural and substantive legitimacy. As paternalism scales up from the intimate and continuous interaction to the itinerant and the imaginary, the sense of legitimacy appears to decline. Parents are seen as having authority over their children and as most likely to have their best interests at heart; they are paternalists, expected to be so, and if they fail to enact their role, they might lose their parental rights. The government enforces various regulations that are intended to limit the liberty of its citizens, for example, motorcycle helmet laws in many states. In response to the accusation that these laws are paternalistic, defenders of such laws typically resort to one of two answers: (1) they are paternalistic but justifiable because those who do not wear helmets are not simply risking harm to themselves but are also increasing the welfare costs to society; or (2) they are not paternalistic because the laws were passed through a democratic process (laws imposed by fiat are another matter).

The conditions that make paternalism potentially legitimate in the family and the state are largely absent in the international context. The sovereign state is the highest authority in international affairs. It enjoys the principle of noninterference. Its consent is required for those who want permission to enter its territory or to act within its realm. And, it justifies its sovereignty on legal and moral grounds: according to international law, it has various kinds of prerogatives, and the state is supposed to represent the nation and community within its borders (Anghie 2007). The legitimacy of an act of international interference is based on prior consent by the recipient government, that is, the interference is lawful and not illegal. The same is true for peacebuilding operations: before the peacebuilders are issued a visa or deployed, they must first get the legal permission of the host government.

Yet sovereignty is not a given or natural right, but rather depends on recognition; and what the society of states can grant, the society of states also can withdraw. After all, why assume that the state truly represents the wishes of the population within its borders? And what about those instances when the state is not a source of protection but rather a major threat to the lives of the population? John Stuart Mill and John Rawls argued, in different ways, that the principle of noninterference does not extend to barbarians or states that are not well ordered, respectively (Rawls 1999).[6]

If the state does not adequately represent or protect its population, then who does and who should? Perhaps outsiders such as the international community.[7] During the colonial period, well-meaning and not so well-meaning imperialists, missionaries, and liberal humanitarians frequently operated with the belief that they were an upgrade over the backward despots who exploited their own people. Although this might be seen as nothing more than swapping one absolutist rule for another, at least they were committed to the welfare of the population. "Such power-backed paternalism, while admittedly despotic, was at the same time progressive and thus was superior to the indigenous forms of self-rule found in less developing societies, which, while no less despotic, were evidently less progressive" (McCarthy 2009, 171). A similar logic informs the Responsibility to Protect doctrine and many peacekeeping and peacebuilding operations.

What is the legal and moral basis for the international community or its representatives to substitute their judgment for that of the state? Peacebuilding operations cite UN Security Council authorizations, which themselves are based on a negotiation between the United Nations and the host country. Yet often peacebuilders cite not formalities but rather discourses of natural law and universalism. In contrast to positive law, which presumes that law exists when there is an agreement between two or more states that have the legal authority to enter into binding agreements, natural law presumes that we have certain kinds of rights, protections, privileges, and responsibilities that owe from the simple fact of our humanity. Universalism and the idea that there are (however thin) ethics that envelop all individuals make territorial borders less fortified and encourage us to see each other as bound by a common morality. The authority and legitimacy to intervene, consequently, is tied to broader, metaphysical discourses that transcend the explicit preferences of those who are living in the material world.

Undemocratic

The lack of consent and legitimacy are often combined in the critique that peacebuilding is not democratic. Peacebuilders do not pretend to be operating under the influence of democracy; they claim to be representing the true interests of the local people, not that they are agents that take their marching orders from local actors who are the principals. Sometimes the accusations rest less on the specific lack of democratic controls and more on the general absence of accountability. This is not the place to review the debate on the multiple meanings of accountability; for my purposes, what matters most is whether the affected populations have the ability to hold accountable those who claim to be their trustees.[8]

Contemporary peacebuilding operations have a well-deserved reputation for being accountability challenged. Following trends in global governance, contemporary peacebuilding operations have now established various kinds of local accountability mechanisms (Sriram et al. 2009; Chesterman 2004). Yet there is widespread acceptance that accountability is preached more than it is practiced. This gap between ideology and reality is particularly evident in the rise of "participation" and discourse of partnership. Similar to accountability, participation has an elusive set of meanings, though most definitions imply that local populations are meaningfully involved in the entire life cycle of a program, from design to implementation to evaluation (Darcy et al. 2013, 31). There are many reasons why peacebuilders, like so many of those who arrive pledging to work in solidarity with the local populations, are unable to hold up their side of the spirit of participation and partnership. There is the simple fact that those who have power do not like to give it up. They plead that if they are going to do their job, then they cannot be too attentive or beholden to local populations. In other words, their lack of accountability is in the best interests of those they want to help, especially if the most powerful locals are also the most opposed to progressive reforms. This sort of reason is typical of most experts; in the competition between the rule of technocracy and the rule of the people, sometimes the former must trump the latter. Also, if peacebuilders defer to the entrenched elites, then they are likely to reproduce existing inequalities and fail to promote political and economic liberalization (Mitchell and Doane 1999). And, lastly, there are those who claim that peacebuilding, if it is going to be more effective, has to centralize and bureaucratize; it cannot keep allowing the different pieces to act on their own or reinvent the wheel. Centralization and bureaucratization, however, do not generally mix well with participation and partnership. In short, peacebuilders find themselves pulled in different directions, but they almost always lean away from the local.

Peacebuilding stands accused of various offenses which frequently dovetail with some offenses associated with paternalism. Yet not all offenses are equal; some are more offensive than others. The failure to consult might be more insulting than the deliberate disregard of someone's explicit preferences. In fact, some offenses can seem trivial, or even as if they are condemning peacebuilders for doing what they were hired for. There might be no good reason to have a series of conversations regarding how to distribute latrines around a refugee camp; if the leader of the refugees is insulted because he wishes he was consulted, and consultation would not have changed the action, then how offensive is the act of paternalism? Whether we think that an offensive is minor or major often depends on whether we believe that the peacebuilder is interfering in someone else's proper sphere of autonomy, whether more consultative mechanisms might have changed the outcome or made the beneficiaries feel less insulted without too much added cost or energy. What these criticisms have in common, though, is that they fault peacebuilders for failing to adequately incorporate, and be more responsive to, local voices. And the failure to incorporate local populations into the decision process can lead to feelings of infantilization, inferior outcomes, and even a culture of dependency. Consequently, peacebuilders are constantly being told to be more participatory and accountable to local populations. Yet it also is not clear that the remedies are always desirable; they might, in fact, make it more difficult for peacebuilding to succeed.

Paternalism in peacebuilding: occasionally justified, chronically illegitimate

Regardless of how we try to modify peacebuilding, whether we call it liberal, post-liberal, republican, hybrid, social welfare, subaltern, postmodern, or localized, it is quite likely to contain elements of paternalism. Part of the reason for paternalism's apparently constant presence is because it can be defined so loosely that almost any act of care will have its residue. Another reason is that intervention, no matter how well intended or how deeply motivated by compassion, can easily take on qualities of paternalism. It also might be that interference is an occupational hazard: peacebuilders would not be doing their job if they were not attempting to improve the lives of others. Yet there is a fourth reason: on occasion, it might be justified.

Although anti-paternalist sentiments circulated prior to the ascendance of liberal political theory in the nineteenth century, liberals can be credited with making paternalism something of a sin. Paternalism violates nearly every cherished principle of liberalism. John Stuart Mill, the patron saint of the anti-paternalism camp, famously wrote:

> The sole end for which mankind are warranted, individually or collectively, in interfering with the liberty of action of any of their number, is self-protection. That the only purpose for which power can be rightfully exercised over any member of a civilised community, against his will, is to prevent harm to others. His own good, either physical or moral, is not a sufficient warrant.
>
> (Mill 1975, 10–11)

And the list of objections goes on and on. Autonomy and liberty are central to human dignity. No one can know better than us what we want, and we can never know what is best for another. Even if individuals act in ways that appear to be irrational or to demonstrate poor judgment, to stop them from acting on their perceived interests violates their dignity. It also denies them an opportunity to learn from their mistakes. Nor can paternalism be defended on the grounds that the interference improves the welfare of the individual – ends do not justify the means. Paternalism presumes that an individual is incompetent or inferior. Worryingly, an actor might give reasons of care, but the powerful typically delude themselves into believing that they know what is best for everyone. We should be worried whenever actors become convinced of their benevolence. Henry David Thoreau spoke for many when he exclaimed, "if I knew for certainty that a man was coming to my house with the conscious design of doing me good, I should run for my life."

Yet liberal political theorists, among others, have attempted to identify the conditions under which paternalism might be warranted – that is, when it might be proper to substitute one person's judgment for another's on the grounds that it is in the latter's interests. This is not the place to review this highly contested terrain, but I want to flag three cautionary questions that intentional and accidental paternalists must address. First, are there grounds for concluding that some individuals or groups are unable to make reasoned decisions? What are they? Are they owing to mental or cognitive deficiencies? Extraordinary circumstances? Is it because of a crisis? Critically, judgments about the competence of another should be based not on an assessment of an individual's rationality but rather on the institutional circumstances that might inhibit choice and the ability to make informed decisions. In this spirit, Sigal Ben-Porath (2010, 19) argues that institutions will foster meaningful choice if they help individuals develop an awareness of their options and the capacity to exercise them, enable rights, and foster what T.H. Marshall called social rights. To what extent, in short, have peacebuilders helped to expand the choices – and the ability to make choices – for local populations?

Second, is the interference in an area that is central to their well-being? Intervention should not be in a trivial or tertiary domain of life, but should only happen in domains arguably fundamental to being able to live a full life. But, often the most trivial areas of life can be tied to human flourishing, opening the door to intrusive and potentially wide-ranging interventions. To what extent, in short, have peacebuilders begun to encroach into areas that are not critical to fundamental well-being, dignity, and welfare?

The third and perhaps most difficult question is, how will the global paternalist be held accountable? Part of the defense of paternalism in liberal societies is the claim that those who are given the authority to impose their views can be held accountable to those who are affected by their decisions. As already discussed, a central problem for humanitarian and global governance is the nearly complete lack of accountability mechanisms. Ideally, the state would help perform this function. But in the absence of effective state institutions, which is almost always the normal state of affairs where humanitarian governance operates, there must be other kinds of mechanisms in place. Until today, and perhaps for the foreseeable future, those who are quite prepared to engage in a global ethics of care are also quite resistant to being held responsible for their actions and to the objects of their concern. Accountability without responsibility. And accountability is probably what separates responsible from irresponsible paternalizers.

Peacebuilding and paternalism share two final features. First, they are premised on an ethic of consequentialism. A necessary justification for peacebuilding is that it improves the lives of the local population relative to the no-peacebuilding alternative. But the ethic of consequentialism does not stop there, because it also demands that the intervener attempt to minimize the costs of such an interference. What are the costs? As students of policy analysis know, cost calculation is treacherous and unscientific. That said, the cost calculation must include not only material but also affective costs. There are welfare costs. And there are the costs to the autonomy and dignity of the objects of the interference. Neither peacebuilding nor paternalism assumes that interference will be cost-free in this respect. All they assume is that the overall net benefits are greater than any short-term hurt feelings.

Peacebuilding and paternalism also share a second feature: they can be justified but difficult to legitimate. To recall, I noted that legitimacy has two dimensions, procedural and substantive. An action has legitimacy if it is consistent with the broader community standards. But which community? The international? The domestic? And then which international and which domestic? And is not the point of peacebuilding, quite frequently, to overturn local community standards because they are the root causes of suffering and destruction? Sometimes peacebuilders hook their legitimacy to the implied consent that accompanies the permission granted by the state and local officials. But, no one would ever mistake peacebuilding for a democracy, either direct or republican. Indeed, it cannot meet the basic metrics of accountability. Peacebuilding, so it seems, might frequently be paternalistic and lack legitimacy, but is nevertheless justified.

Notes

1 Perhaps the most important and recent statement on these issues is Séverine Autesserre's *Peaceland* (2014). Also see Freire and Lopes (2013); Hellmuller (2013); Millar, Van der Lijn, and Verkoren (2013); Cubitt (2013); Curtis (2012); Richmond (2012a); Mac Ginty (2013); Wallis (2012); Doneis (2009); Richmond (2012b); and Richmond (2012c).
2 For a sampling of the definitional debate, see Thompson (1990); Archard (1990); Garren (2006); Garren (2007); Dworkin (1972); Sartorius (1983); Gert and Culver (1976); Vandeveer (1986); Mead (1997); Husak (2003); Young (2008); Dworkin (2000); Kelman (1981); Grill (2007); Shafer-Landau (2005); Hanson (2008); and Talbott (2010).
3 For various statements on these issues, see Sunstein (1997) and Brint (1994).
4 See Easterly (2007, 2013).
5 This is neither the time nor the place to devolve into a discussion regarding the concept of political community. For three contrasting views see Kymlick (1991), Sandel (2005), and Kukathas (2003). My reading of this literature, moreover, suggests that much of the battle is fought over the domestic terrain, and the dominant view is that any deep sense of community does not exist in cross-boundary relations.
6 For a discussion of this Rawlsian-centered analysis and the general question of interference in postwar situations, see Recchia (2009).
7 This is why many scholars of international relations oppose any weakening of sovereignty. See Jackson (2000) and Bain (2003a, 2003b, 2006). However, see Søbjerg (2007).
8 For broader discussions regarding the globalization of accountability, see Ebrahim and Weisband (2007).

References

Abu-Sada, C. (2012). *Dilemmas, Challenges and Ethics of Humanitarian Action: Reflections on Médicens Sans Frontières Perception Project*. McGill Queens University Press, Montreal.

Anderson, M. (2012). *Time to Listen: Hearing People on the Review End of International Aid*. CDA Learning Collaborative Project, Boston.

Anghie, A. (2007). *Imperialism, Sovereignty and the Making of International Law*. Cambridge University Press, New York.

Archard, D. (1990). Paternalism defined. *Analysis*, 50(1), 36–42.

Autesserre, S. (2014). *Peaceland*. Cambridge University Press, New York.

Bain, W. (2003a). *Between Anarchy and Society: Trusteeship and the Obligations of Power*. Oxford University Press, Oxford, 26, 173.

Bain, W. (2003b). The political theory of trusteeship and the twilight of international equality. *International Relations*, 17(1), 59–77.

Bain, W. (2006). In praise of folly: International administration and the corruption of humanity. *International Affairs*, 82(3), 525–538.

Barnett, M., Fang, S., and Zurcher, C. (2014). Compromised peacebuilding. *International Studies Quarterly*, 58(3), 608–620. doi:10.1111/isqu.12137

Ben-Porath, S. (2010). *Tough Choices: Structured Paternalism and the Landscape of Choice*. Princeton University Press, Princeton, NJ.

Brint, S. (1994). *In an Age of Experts: The Changing Role of Professionals in Politics and Public Life*. Princeton University Press, Princeton, NJ.

Chesterman, S. (2004). *You, the People: The United Nations, Transitional Administration, and State-Building*. Oxford University Press, New York.

Claassen, R. (2014). Capability paternalism. *Economics and Philosophy*, 30(1), 57–73.

Cooley, A. (2008). *The Logics of Hierarchy: The Organization of Empires, States, and Military Occupations*. Cornell University Press, Ithaca, NY.

Cubitt, C. (2013). Responsible reconstruction after war. *Review of International Studies*, 39(1), 91–112.

Curtis, D. (2012). The international peacebuilding paradox: Power sharing and post-conflict governance in Burundi. *African Affairs*, 112(446), 72–91.

Darcy, J., Alexander, J., and Kiani, M. (2013). *2013 Humanitarian Accountability Report*. Humanitarian Accountability Partnership International, Geneva.

Dirks, N. (2006). *The Scandal of Empire: India and the Creation of Imperial Britain*. Harvard University Press, Cambridge, MA.

Doneis, T. (2009). Empowerment or imposition? Dilemmas of local ownership in post-conflict peacebuilding processes. *Peace and Change*, 34(1), 3–26.

Dworkin, G. (1972). Paternalism. *Monist*, 56(1), 64–84.

Dworkin, G. (2013). Defining paternalism. In C. Coons and M. Weber (Eds.), *Paternalism: Theory and Practice*. Cambridge University Press, New York, 25–38.

Dworkin, R. (2000). *Sovereign Virtue: The Theory and Practice of Equality*. Harvard University Press, Cambridge, MA.

Easterly, W. (2007). *The White Man's Burden: Why the West's Efforts to Aid the Rest Have Done So Much Ill and So Little Good*. Penguin Books, New York.

Easterly, W. (2013). *The Tyranny of Experts: Economists, Dictators, and the Forgotten Rights of the Poor*. Basic Books, New York.

Ebrahim, A., and Weisband, E. (Eds.). (2007). *Global Accountabilities: Participation, Pluralism, and Public Ethics*. Cambridge University Press, New York.

Feldman, I., and Ticktin, M. (2011). Introduction: Government and humanity. In I. Feldman and M. Ticktin (Eds.), *In the Name of Humanity: The Government of Threat and Care*. Duke University Press, Durham, NC, 1–26.

Freire, M., and Lopes, P. (2013). Peacebuilding in Timor-Leste: Finding a way between external intervention and local dynamics. *International Peacekeeping*, 20(2), 204–218.

Garfield, R. (2011). *Common Needs Assessments and Humanitarian Action*. Overseas Development Initiative: Humanitarian Practice Network, London. (http://www.odihpn.org/documents/networkpaper069.pdf) Accessed: 9 September 2014.

Garren, D. (2006). Paternalism, Part I. *Philosophical Books*, 47(4), 334–341.

Garren, D. (2007). Paternalism, Part II. *Philosophical Books*, 48(1), 50–59.

Gert, B., and Culver, C. (1976). Paternalistic behavior. *Philosophy & Public Affairs*, 6(1), 45–58.

Grill, K. (2007). The normative core of paternalism. *Res Publica*, 13(4), 441–458.

Habibi, D. (1999). The moral dimensions of J. S. Mill's colonialism. *Journal of Social Philosophy*, 30(1), 125–146.

Hanson, R. (2008). Making sense of medical paternalism. *Medical Hypotheses*, 70(5), 910–913.

Hartogh, G. (2011). Can consent be presumed? *Journal of Applied Philosophy*, 28(3), 294–307.

Hellmuller, S. (2013). The power of perceptions: Localizing international peacebuilding approaches. *International Peacekeeping*, 20(2), 219–232.

Hopgood, S. (2009). Moral authority, modernity and the politics of the sacred. *European Journal of International Relations*, 15(2), 229–255.

Hopgood, S. (2013). *The Endtimes of Human Rights*. Cornell University Press, Ithaca, NY.

Husak, D. (2003). Legal paternalism. In H. Lafollette (Ed.), *The Oxford Handbook of Practical Ethics*. Oxford University Press, New York, 387–412.

Jackson, R. (2000). *The Global Covenant: Human Conduct in a World of States*. Oxford University Press, New York, 412.

Kelman, S. (1981). Regulation and paternalism. *Public Policy*, 29(2), 219–254.

Kukathas, C. (2003). *The Liberal Archipelago: A Theory of Diversity and Freedom*. Oxford University Press, Oxford.

Kymlick, W. (1991). *Liberalism, Community, and Culture*. Oxford University Press, New York.

Lake, D. (2011). *Hierarchy in International Relations*. Cornell University Press, Ithaca, NY.

Mac Ginty, R. (2013). Hybrid governance: The case of Georgia. *Global Governance*, 19(3), 443–461.

McCarthy, T. (2009). *Race, Empire, and the Idea of Human Development*. Cambridge University Press, New York.

Mead, L. (1997). The rise of paternalism. In L. Mead (Ed.), *The New Paternalism: Supervisory Approaches to Poverty*. Brookings Institution Press, Washington, DC, 1–38.

Mill, J. (1975). *On Liberty*. W. W. Norton, New York.

Millar, G., Van der Lijn, G., and Verkoren, W. (2013). Peacebuilding plans and local reconfigurations: Frictions between imported processes and indigenous practices. *International Peacekeeping*, 20(2), 137–143.

Mitchell, J., and Doane, D. (1999). An ombudsman for humanitarian assistance? *Disasters*, 23(2), 115–124.

O'Neill, O. (2003). Some limits of informed consent. *Journal of Medical Ethics*, 29(1), 4–7.

Paternalism. (n.d.a.). In *Merriam-Webster's online dictionary*. (http://www.merriam-webster.com/dictionary/paternalism) Accessed: 8 September 2014.

Paternalism. (n.d.b.). In *Oxford online dictionary*. (http://www.oxforddictionaries.com/us/definition/american_english/paternalism) Accessed: 8 September 2014.

Rawls, J. (1999). *The Law of Peoples: With "The Idea of Public Reason Revisited."* Harvard University Press, Cambridge, MA.

Recchia, S. (2009). Just and unjust postwar reconstruction: How much external interference can be justified? *Ethics and International Affairs*, 23(2), 165–187.

Richmond, O. (2012a). Beyond local ownership in the architecture of international peacebuilding. *Ethnopolitics*, 11(4), 354–375.

Richmond, O. (2012b). A pedagogy of peacebuilding: Infrapolitics, resistance, and liberation. *International Political Sociology*, 6(2), 115–131.

Richmond, O. (2012c). *A Post-liberal Peace*. Routledge, New York.

Sandel, M. (2005). *Public Philosophy: Essays on Morality in Politics*. Harvard University Press, Cambridge, MA.

Sartorius, R. (Ed.). (1983). *Paternalism*. University of Minnesota Press, Minneapolis.

Shafer-Landau, R. (2005). Liberalism and paternalism. *Legal Theory*, 11(3), 169–191.

Shiffrin, S. (2000). Paternalism, unconscionability doctrine, and accommodation. *Philosophy and Public Affairs*, 29(3), 205–250.

Søbjerg, L. (2007). Trusteeship and the Concept of Freedom. *Review of International Studies*, 33(3), 475–488.

Sriram, C., Martin-Ortega, O., and Herman, J. (2009, February). *Strategies of peacebuilding and accountability: An assessment of contemporary trends in practice*. In Annual Meeting of the International Studies Association, New York. (http://citation.allacademic.com/meta/p_mla_apa_research_citation/3/1/2/3/1/pages312311/p312311–1.php) Accessed: 8 September 2014.

Suchman, M. (1995). Managing legitimacy: Strategic and institutional approaches. *Academy of Management Review*, 20(3), 571–610.

Sunstein, C. (1997). *Free Markets and Social Justice*. Oxford University Press, New York.

Sunstein, C. (2006). Preferences, paternalism, and liberty. *Royal Institute of Philosophy Supplement*, 59, 233–264.

Talbott, W. (2010). *Human Rights and Human Well-Being*. Oxford University Press, Oxford.

Thaler, R., and Sunstein, C. (2003). Libertarian paternalism. *American Economic Review*, 93(2), 175–179.

Thaler, R., and Sunstein, C. (2008). *Nudge: Improving Decisions about Health, Wealth, and Happiness*. Yale University Press, New Haven, CT.

Thompson, D. (1990). *Political Ethics and Public Office*. Harvard University Press, Cambridge, 148–177.

Tsai, G. (2014). Rational persuasion as paternalism. *Philosophy & Public Affairs*, 42(1), 78–112.

Van der Lijn, G., and Verkoren, W. (2013). Peacebuilding plans and local reconfigurations: Frictions between imported processes and indigenous practices. *International Peacekeeping*, 20(2), 137–142.

Vandeveer, D. (1986). *Paternalistic Intervention: The Moral Bounds of Benevolence*. Princeton University Press, Princeton, NJ.

Wallis, J. (2012). A liberal-local hybrid peace project in action? The increasing engagement between the local and liberal in Timor-Leste. *Review of International Studies*, 38(4), 735–761.

Westbrook, R. (2003). An uncommon faith: Pragmatism and religious experience. In S. Rosenbaum (Ed.), *Pragmatism and Religion: Classical Sources and Original Essays*. University of Illinois Press, Urbana, 190–205.

World Bank. (2014). *World Bank Development Report 2015: Mind, Society, Behavior*. World Bank, Washington, DC.

Young, R. (2008). John Stuart Mill, Ronald Dworkin, and paternalism. In C. L. Ten (Ed.), *Mill's "On Liberty": A Critical Guide*. Cambridge University Press, New York, 209–227.

3 The future of peacebuilding

David Chandler

Introduction

This chapter considers whether peacebuilding as a strategic policy framework can survive growing policy-maker and academic concern with the problems of unintended consequences, understood to stem from the underestimation of relational interconnections, alterity and complexity. It will be argued that the last 10 years have seen a major shift in how peacebuilding under complexity is understood. Roland Paris's (2004) monograph, *At War's End*, could be seen as the last gasp of liberal peacebuilding, arguing that its goals – of peace, elections and markets – needed to be implemented by external actors rather than be assumed to exist without guidance. This was a top-down approach to peacebuilding. Since then we have seen the rise of alterity and complexity – in the view that liberal peacebuilding interventions are inadequate, producing hybrid and problematic outcomes, and that bottom-up approaches are necessary: building civil society, engaging and empowering local agency. In the space of a few years, even bottom-up peacebuilding initiatives have been problematised, also for their lack of attention to alterity and complexity. It has been argued that every intervention policy practice necessarily produces unintended outcomes, dilemmas and contradictions and that 'dilemma analysis training' and 'muddling through' are the only answer (Paris and Sisk 2009). More recently, Charles Call at the US State Department suggested in a high-level policy/academic seminar at George Washington University that external policy actors should reject acting on the basis of instrumental goals, merely 'finding the organic processes and plussing them up', effectively reducing peacebuilding to generic capacity-building and posing the question of the future of peacebuilding itself as a policy area (cited in Chandler 2015, 43).

In the 1990s, international peacebuilding intervention was often conceived of as an exception to the norm of international politics, which was still based on a sovereign order. Intervention was posed as necessary in the case of crises that threatened the peace and security of international society, and the UN Security Council incrementally relaxed its restrictions, making intervention increasingly permissible (Chesterman 2002). This assumption of external problem-solving capabilities is central to liberal conceptions of peacebuilding: first, the undermining of sovereign rights was legitimised by the assumption of the superior knowledge and resources of the policy-interveners; and, second, because intervention necessarily assumed that knowledge and power operated in linear and reductive ways. This chapter heuristically focuses on the cause-and-effect ontology of peacebuilding to explain how interventions have been reconceptualised – from an emphasis on the asymmetrical and potentially oppressive discourse of the 'right' or need for intervention (based on the superior knowledge and resources of the policy-intervener) to an increasing emphasis on the problem of the linear and reductive understandings of peacekeeping intervention itself (and the unintended consequences of such mechanistic approaches in the international sphere).

Debates over international peacebuilding intervention have seen a shift from critical concerns over infringements of rights to autonomy and self-government to increasingly pragmatic concerns of stability and effectiveness. It seems that the difficulties associated with peacebuilding intervention, designed to address the causes of conflict and to create a sustainable peace, have become a greater concern for international interveners than the problems ostensibly to be addressed. This can be illustrated through contrasting the difference between the confidence – today, critics would say 'hubris' (Mayall and Soares de Oliveira 2011) – of late-1990s understandings of the transformative nature of peacebuilding intervention with current, much more pessimistic, approaches. In the late 1990s, leading advocates understood international peacebuilding intervention as able to address the 'causes' of problems in a global and interconnected world (for example, Blair 1999). Following the apparent successes of ethical and humanitarian interventions in the 1990s, the response to the shock of the terrorist attacks of 9/11 appeared to intensify the trend towards international peacebuilding. The 2002 US National Security Strategy (NSS) expanded and securitised the interventionist remit, arguing that 'America is now threatened less by conquering states than we are by failing ones' (US Department of State 2002, 1). The recognition that we lived in a globalised and interconnected world seemed to bind the needs of national security with those of human rights, democracy and development, creating a powerful interventionist consensus around the peacebuilding discourse (see Mazarr 2014).

Today, analysts are much more likely to highlight the fact that complex interactions and processes cannot be subordinated to linear cause-and-effect models, aspiring to address problems at the level of causal relations (for example, Ramalingam et al. 2008; Ramalingam 2013). The pessimistic approach to the limits of liberal peacebuilding as a transformative framework of intervention can therefore be seen as a retreat from the commitments of earlier interventionist approaches of the 1990s and early 2000s, in terms of both resources and policy goals. However, it is the shifting conceptualisation of peacebuilding itself which is the concern of this chapter and whether peacebuilding is, in fact, still a discrete sphere of policy activity. Peacebuilding interventions are increasingly conceptualised in ways which relocate the subject position of the intervener both in relation to the problem of peacebuilding – which is seen as much less amenable to external policy solutions – and the society or community being intervened upon – which is no longer constructed as lacking knowledge or resources, but as being the key agency of transformation. Transformation comes not through external cause-and-effect policy-interventions but through the facilitation or empowerment of local agential capacities. This shift has major consequences for the understanding of peacebuilding interventions and their limits.

The liberal model of peacebuilding

The cause-and-effect model, the archetypal model of peacebuilding intervention, was developed in the policy debates of the late-1990s and 2000s, particularly during the post-conflict reconstructions following humanitarian intervention and regime change under the auspices of the War on Terror. In this framing, the policy-response tended to be one of centralised direction, under UN or US and EU control, based upon military power or bureaucratic organisation, which often assumed that peacebuilding operated in a vacuum, where social and political norms had broken down, and little attention needed to be given to the particular policy-context. The cause-and-effect models of liberal peacebuilding approaches share three key aspects: they are universalist, mechanistic, and reductionist.

Universalist

First, this framework is universalist. Intervening states and international institutions were understood to have the power, resources and objective scientific knowledge necessary to solve the problems of conflict and human rights abuses. Debates in the 1990s assumed that Western states had the knowledge and power to act and therefore focused on the question of the political will of Western states (see, for example, Held 1995; Wheeler 2000). Of particular concern was the fear that the United States might pursue national interests rather than fully support comprehensive peacebuilding efforts (Kaldor 2007, 150). In this framework, problems were seen in terms of a universalist and linear understanding. It was believed that peacebuilding interventions could be successful on the basis that a specific set of policy solutions could solve a specific set of policy problems. This framework of intervention reached its apogee in international peacebuilding in the Balkans, with long-term protectorates established over Bosnia and Kosovo, and was reflected in the RAND Corporation's reduction of such interventions to simple cost and policy formulas that could be universally applied (Dobbins et al. 2007). This set up a universalist understanding of good policy-making – the idea that certain solutions were timeless and could be exported or imposed – like the rule of law, democracy and markets.

   The universalist model legitimising peacebuilding intervention thereby established a hierarchical and paternalist framework of understanding. Western liberal democratic states were understood to have the knowledge and power necessary to solve the problems that other 'failed' and 'failing' states were alleged to lack. It was therefore little surprise that these interventions challenged the sovereign rights to self-government, which had long been upheld after decolonisation in the

1950s and 1960s. Many commentators have raised problems with the idealisation of liberal Western societies and the holding up of abstract and unrealistic goals which tended to exaggerate the incapacity or lack of legitimacy of non-Western regimes (see, for example, Heathershaw and Lambach 2008; Lemay-Hébert 2009). Beneath the universalist peacebuilding claims of promoting the interest of human rights, human security or human development, critical theorists suggested new forms of international domination were emerging, institutionalising market inequalities or restoring traditional hierarchies of power reminiscent of the colonial era (see, for example, Chandler 2006; Douzinas 2007; Duffield 2007; Pugh et al. 2008; Dillon and Reid 2009).

Mechanistic

This policy framework was also mechanistic. The peacebuilding problems of non-Western states were understood in simple terms of the need to restore the equilibrium of the status quo – which was understood as being disrupted by new forces or events. This was illustrated, for example, in the popular 'New Wars' thesis, which argued that sustainable peace was disrupted by exploitative elites seeking to destabilise society in order to cling to resources and power (Kaldor 1999) or that the lack of human rights could be resolved through constitutional reforms (Brandt et al. 2011). The assumption was that society was fundamentally healthy and that the problematic individuals or groups could be removed or replaced through external policy-intervention which would enable equilibrium to be restored. This was a mechanistic view of how societies operated – as if they were machines and a single part had broken down and needed to be fixed. There was no holistic engagement with society as a collective set of processes, interactions and interrelations. The assumption was that external peacebuilders could come up with a 'quick fix' – perhaps sending troops to quell conflict or legal experts to write constitutions – followed by an exit strategy. The problems of policy based upon these mechanistic assumptions led to an extension of the cause-and-effect paradigm of peacebuilding into extended statebuilding attempts to understand the endogenous causal processes at play and the search for the societal preconditions necessary for the establishment of liberal regimes of markets, democracy and the rule of law (Paris 2004; Chandler 2010).

Reductionist

Further, this framework was reductionist. This approach left out the interactive relationship between the state and society and multiple possible responses to the appearance of certain problems or governance failings (see Scott 1998). First, certain societies may be more prone to some problems rather than others. Rather than viewing these problems as discrete threats to otherwise healthy systems, vulnerability to conflict should therefore be seen as a product of the social, economic and political systems in place, and addressed at that level (see, for example, Commission for Africa 2005). Second, conflict, corruption, poverty or other problems of peacebuilding manifest themselves differently in different societies and have different consequences and impacts, making any external measure or comparison impossible (with regard to development and poverty, see Sen 1999). Some societies may be better able to cope with the stresses and strains of poverty or inequality than others, for example, or conflict, corruption or other problems might be understood as reflecting processes of change and development and therefore be seen as coping mechanisms or as positive, depending on the context of the society concerned (see, for example, Cramer 2006). Clearly, even the idea that peacebuilding was somehow a discrete policy area or that the barriers to sustainable peace could somehow enable a discrete set of policy-interventions, somehow separate from economic, social and political processes, was deeply reductionist and problematic.

The universalist, mechanistic and reductionist approach to international peacebuilding assumed that international intervention was the prerogative of leading Western states and that the subjects of intervention were non-Western states, and that Western international specialists had the knowledge, technology and agency necessary to fix the problems. Traditionally, in the discipline of international relations, critical commentators have understood this as a paternalistic framework, reproducing relations of inequality and reinforcing or constituting more open hierarchies of power, through the challenge to post-colonial sovereignty claims to political equality and self-government (see, for example, Chandler 1999; Bain 2003; Bickerton et al. 2007; Hehir and Robinson 2007; Barnett 2010).

However, as will be considered further later, a second way of critically conceptualising peacebuilding has developed rapidly since the early 1990s, which engages with the knowledge assumptions at play in the legitimisation of intervention on the basis of universalist, mechanistic and reductionist understandings of the nature of social and political processes. These critics suggest that the claims of Western knowledge and power are false and hubristic and that Western modernist understandings of knowledge as context free and universally valid are problematic (see further Law 2004; Shilliam 2011). Peacebuilding interventions assuming discrete and linear cause-and-effect relations are therefore criticised increasingly on practical and functionalist grounds rather than on ethical and political ones. Critics working within the second critical paradigm tend to reframe problems as emergent outcomes of complex processes rather than as discrete problems amenable to linear and reductionist policy-interventions. This process is well articulated by Michael Dillon's (2007) conception of 'the emergency of emergence', in terms of a shift in policy concerns from sovereign power over territory to biopolitical concerns over the circulatory and contingent processes of life.

Problems of sustainable peace are thus less likely to be construed as amenable to sovereign forms of top-down power and cause-and-effect interventions but rather seen as a result of complex interconnected processes with no clear lines of causation (see also Dillon and Lobo-Guerrero 2008). Rearticulating problems in terms of emergent or complex outcomes necessarily prevents peacebuilding from being understood as a technique of external crisis solving. The alternative to addressing causes is governance at the level of coping with and managing in the absence of a liberal peace. Peacebuilding without the goal of liberal peace no longer necessitates claims of sovereign power and direction and thereby no longer poses the problem of political autonomy and state sovereignty. In this framing, conflict, poverty and humanitarian disasters become normalised, leading to coping strategies rather than crisis-driven discourses of political exception. The governance of nonliberal peace relies on a systems- or process-based ontology, suggesting that policy-interventions need to work with rather than against organic local practices and understandings and that there is a need for more homeopathic forms of policy-intervention designed to enhance autonomous processes rather than undermine them (see, for example, Drabek and McEntire 2003; Kaufmann 2013). These forms of intervention cannot be grasped within the liberal modernist paradigm of peacebuilding.

Peacebuilding and the law of unintended consequences

The shift from peacebuilding intervention addressing the causes of conflict to much more light-touch and content-less interventions has been predominantly discussed in relation to the need to take into account the 'law of unintended consequences'. The problem of unintended consequences has become a policy trope regularly used as a shorthand expression for the profound shift in the understanding of intervention, addressed in this chapter, and can be understood as a generalised extension of Ulrich Beck's view of 'risk society' with the determinate causal role of 'side effects' or of Bruno Latour's similar analysis of today's world as modernity 'plus all its externalities' (see further, Beck 1992; Latour 2003). It seems that there is no way to consider peacebuilding in terms of intended outcomes without considering the possibility that the unintended outcomes will outweigh these.

The shift to the focus on unintended effects rather than the original causes of conflict acknowledges the limits of policy intentionality based on cause-and-effect assumptions and explicitly challenges the rationalist and reductionist assumptions prevalent in disciplinary understandings of peacebuilding intervention. By 2012, a decade after the US extension of peacebuilding as a way of addressing state failure, the US Defense Strategic Guidance (DSG) policy was operating on a different set of assumptions: that US forces would pursue their objectives through 'innovative, low-cost, and small-footprint approaches' rather than the conduct of 'large-scale, prolonged stability operations' (DSG 2012, 3, 6).

As Michael Mazarr argued in the State Department's in-house journal, *Foreign Affairs*, in 2014 securing US goals of peace, democracy and development in failing and conflict-ridden states could not, in fact, be done by instrumental cause-and-effect external policy-interventions: 'It is an organic, grass-roots process that must respect the unique social, cultural, economic, political, and religious contexts of each country . . . and cannot be imposed' (Mazarr 2014). For Mazarr, policy would now follow a more 'resilient mindset, one that treats perturbations as inevitable rather than calamitous and resists the urge to overreact', understanding that policy-intervention must work with rather than against local institutions and 'proceed more organically and authentically' (Mazarr 2014). This is also reflected by high-level policy experts in the US State Department; according to Charles T. Call, senior adviser at the Bureau of Conflict and Stabilization Operations, current US approaches seek not to impose unrealistic external goals but instead to facilitate local transformative agency through engaging with local 'organic processes and plussing them up' (cited in Chandler 2015, 43).

In the discipline of international relations today, it has become increasingly commonplace for radical critics, drawing on a wide range of critical social theory, such as new materialism, complexity approaches, actor network theory and philosophical realism, to suggest that the 'lessons learned' from the limited successes and outright failures of international intervention since 1990 concur with those drawn by pragmatic US policy-advisors. This is a far cry from the understandings of peacebuilding in the 1990s and early 2000s, when intervention was supported not on the basis of technical or pragmatic considerations but as part and parcel of the moral standing and meaning of international institutions and the leading states which composed and directed them. It was precisely the grand narratives of liberal internationalist promise and social and political transformation, under the guidance of leading Western democracies, which inspired support for the extension of cause-and-effect policy understandings and the extension of claims of external interventionist authority. Liberal states were understood to have the right and the authority to undertake peacebuilding interventions on the basis of ideological grounds, altruism and international security concerns.

Peacebuilding today is increasingly understood to be problematic if it is based upon the grand narratives of liberal internationalism, which informed and drove the debate on international intervention in the 1990s, when issues of intervention and nonintervention in Africa and the Balkans were at the centre of international political contestation. International policy-intervention is not opposed per se or on principle, but on the basis of the universalist and hierarchical knowledge assumptions which informed policy-interventions and produced the hubristic and reductionist promises of transformative outcomes (see, for example, Mayall and Soares de Oliveira 2011; Owen 2012; Stewart and Knaus 2012; Mazarr 2014). According to the critical consensus, international policy-makers need to liberate themselves from the constraints of their outmoded mechanistic models, inherited from the Enlightenment in the seventeenth century and associated with Descartes's strict mechanical division between the mind and the body and Isaac Newton's view of the universe as a mechanical clockwork model of timeless universal laws.

Today, the organic processes of endogenous development tend to be prioritised over universalising, mechanistic or reductionist approaches to peacebuilding which seek to introduce policy-solutions from the outside. For example, while markets, development, democracy, security and the rule of law might be good when they develop organically, it is often argued that when they are extracted from their context and applied in a 'pure' form they can be dangerous, as they lack the other ingredients connected to institutions and culture. This perspective was first argued in relation to intervention in the Balkans in the mid- and late-1990s, when interventionist policy-making began to shift attention to the endogenous or internal capacities and capabilities of the local society rather than seeking externally managed 'military solutions, quick fixes [and] easy, early exits' associated with simple cause-and-effect understandings (Bildt 2003). However, the critique of cause-and-effect assumptions, which focused on the knowledge and expertise of external policy-interveners, rapidly extended beyond the critique of coercive interventions to cover a broad range of peacebuilding interventions associated with liberal internationalist goals of promoting markets, democracy and the rule of law.

Peacebuilding without content

Classical peacebuilding programmes tended to exclude the specific internal and external historical, social, political and economic environment and also any understanding of what was necessary to encourage the state or society's own capacities and capabilities to manage effects. The shift to a focus on alterity, complexity and unintended outcomes inverts this and tends to thereby reject ready-made international policy solutions that can simply be applied or implemented, and therefore implies little possibility of learning generic lessons from intervention that could be applied to all other cases of conflict on the basis that if the symptoms appeared similar, the cause must be the same. Crucially, this framing takes peacebuilding intervention out of the context of policy-making and policy-understanding and out of the political sphere of democratic debate and decision-making. The focus therefore shifts away from international policies (supply-driven policy-making) and towards engaging with the internal capacities and capabilities that are already held to exist. In other words, there is a shift from the agency, knowledge and practices of policy-interveners to that of the society, which is the object of policy concerns. This shift opens to question whether peacebuilding still exists as a discrete set of policy practices. As the 2013 updated UK Department for International Development (DfID) Operational Plan states: 'We will produce less "supply-driven" development of product, guidelines and policy papers, and foster peer-to-peer, horizontal learning and knowledge exchange, exploiting new technologies such as wiki/huddles to promote the widest interaction between stakeholders' (DfID 2013, 8).

Supply-driven policies – the stuff of politics and of democratic decision-making – are understood to operate in an artificial or nonorganic way and to lack an authentic connection to the effects which need to be addressed. The imposition of (accountable) external institutional and policy-frameworks has become increasingly seen as artificial and thereby as having counterproductive or unintended outcomes. Content-less approaches thereby seek to move away from the 'liberal peace' policy interventions – seeking to export constitutional frameworks, to train and equip military and police forces, to impose external conditionalities on the running of state budgets, to export managerial frameworks for civil servants and political representatives or to impose regulations to ensure administrative transparency and codes of conduct – which were at the heart of international peacebuilding prescriptions in the 1990s and early 2000s (Action-Aid 2006; Eurodad 2006; World Bank 2007).

It is argued that the supply-driven approach of external experts exporting or developing liberal institutions does not grasp the complex processes generative of instability or insecurity. Instead, the cause-and-effect model of intervention is seen to create problematic 'hybrid' political systems and fragile states with little connection to their societies (Roberts 2008; Mac Ginty 2010; Richmond and Mitchell 2012; Millar 2014). The imposition of institutional frameworks, which have little connection to society, is understood as failing, not only in not address-ing causal processes but, as making matters worse, through undermining local capacities to manage the effects of problems, shifting problems elsewhere and leaving states and societies even more fragile or vulnerable. This approach is alleged to fail to hear the message of problematic manifestations or to enable societies' own organic and homeostatic processes to generate corrective mecha-nisms. Triggering external interventions is said to shortcut the ability of societies to reflect upon and take responsibility for their own affairs and is increasingly seen as a counterproductive overreaction by external powers (see further Desch 2008; Maor 2012). There is an increasingly prevalent view that, contrary to ear-lier assumptions, peacebuilding solutions can only be developed through practice by actors on the ground. This can be seen through an examination of the policy shifts in the key areas of peacebuilding concern: security and the rule of law, democracy and rights.

Policy-interventions are increasingly shifting in relation to the understanding of conflict. There is much less talk of conflict prevention or conflict resolution and more of conflict management. As the UK government argues, in a 2011 combined DfID, Foreign and Commonwealth Office and Ministry of Defence document, conflict per se is not the problem: 'Conflict is a normal part of human interaction, the natural result when individuals and groups have incompatible needs, interests or beliefs' (UK Government 2011, 5). The problem which needs to be tackled is the state or society's ability to manage conflict: 'In stable, resil-ient societies conflict is managed through numerous formal and informal insti-tutions' (ibid.). Conflict management, as the UK government policy indicates, is increasingly understood as an organic set of societal processes and practices, which international policy-intervention can influence but cannot import solu-tions from outside or impose them. As leading peace theorist, Jean Paul Leder-ach, has long argued, 'the greatest resource for sustaining peace in the long term is always rooted in the local people and their culture' (1997, 94). For Lederach, managing conflict means moving away from cause-and-effect forms of instrumen-tal external intervention which see people as recipients of policy, and instead see-ing people as resources, integral to peace processes. Therefore it is essential that

> we in the international community adopt a new mind-set – that we move beyond a simple prescription of answers and modalities for dealing with

conflict that come from outside the setting and focus at least as much attention on discovering and empowering the resources, modalities, and mechanisms for building peace that exist within the context.

(Lederach 1997, 95)

One of the central shifts in understanding conflict as something that needs
to be coped with and managed rather than something that can be solved or prevented is the view that state-level interventions are of limited use. Peace treaties
can be signed by state parties, but unless peace is seen as an ongoing and transformative inclusive societal process these agreements will be merely superficial and
nonsustainable (Lederach 1997, 135).

Just as peace and security are no longer understood to be able to be secured
through cause-and-effect forms of intervention, reliant on policy-interveners
imposing solutions in mechanical and reductive ways, there has also been a
shift in understanding the counterproductive effects of attempts to export the
rule of law (Cesarini and Hite 2004; Zimmermann 2007; Chandler 2015). The
peacebuilding approach is increasingly driven by a realisation of the gap between
the formal sphere of law and constitutionalism and the social reality of informal
power relations and informal rules. The social reality of countries undergoing
post-conflict transition could not be understood merely by an analysis of laws
and statutes. These points are highlighted, for example, in Bruno Latour's critical
engagement with modernist modes of understanding – arguing that Western societies have forgotten the lengthy processes which enabled them to build liberal
institutions dependent on the lengthy process of the establishment of a political
culture, which has to be steadily maintained, renewed and extended and cannot
be exported or imposed (Latour 2013, 343).

This shift away from formal universalist understandings is increasingly evidenced in the shifting understanding of peacebuilding approaches to empowerment. Understanding empowerment in instrumental cause-and-effect terms
based upon the external provision of legal and political mechanisms for claims
is increasingly seen to be ineffective. Peacebuilding nongovernmental organizations (NGOs) now seek not to empower people to access formal institutional
mechanisms but to enable them to empower themselves. This approach places
the emphasis on the agency and self-empowerment of local actors, not on the
introduction of formal frameworks of law, supported by international human
rights norms (Moe and Simojoki 2013, 404). The approach of enhancing local
or organic processes is not limited to government policy-interventions but has
been increasingly taken up as a generic approach to overcome the limits of cause-
and-effect understandings. A study of Finnish NGOs highlights that rather than
instrumentally selecting groups or civil society elites, new forms of intervention appear as anti-intervention, denying any external role in this process and
stressing that there is no process of external management or selection, as policy-
interveners work with whatever groups or associations already exist and 'have
just come together . . . it is not our NGO that brought them together but we just
found them that way' (Kontinen 2014).

A similar study, in southeastern Senegal, notes that policy-interveners are concerned to avoid both the 'moral imperialism' of imposing Western peacebuilding norms, but also to avoid a moral relativism which merely accepts local traditional practices (Gillespie and Melching 2010, 481). The solution forwarded is that of being nonprescriptive and avoiding and 'unlearning' views of Western teachers as authorities and students as passive recipients (ibid.). Peacebuilding intervention is articulated as the facilitation of local people's attempts to uncover traditional practices and in awakening and engaging their already existing capacities: 'By detecting their own inherent skills, they can more easily transfer them to personal and community problem solving' (ibid., 490). These processes can perhaps be encouraged or assisted by external policy-interveners but they cannot be transplanted from one society to another, and even less can they be imposed by policy-actors. Tackling the effects of these problems as if they were the product of direct causal relations thereby misunderstands peacebuilding needs through being trapped in the reductionist mind-sets of liberal governance understandings.

In these examples, it is clear that problems are no longer conceived as amenable to political solutions in terms of instrumental peacebuilding interventions on the basis of cause-and-effect understandings. Peacebuilding, thus reduced to generic forms of empowerment and capacity-building, seemingly can no longer be distinguished from similar shifts in approach in the fields of development and disaster risk reduction and seems unlikely to continue to demarcate itself as a distinct or separate policy field (DfID 2011; Aradau 2014; Nicholson 2014).

Conclusion

The shift in understanding peacebuilding from addressing the causes of conflict to focusing on the problem society's own capacities and needs and internal and organic processes has been paralleled by a growing scepticism of attempts to export or impose Western models. In depoliticising discourses of peacebuilding as empowerment there is no assumption that the peacebuilding intervener is any way limiting the freedom or the autonomy of the state or society intervened upon, and the discourse does not establish the intervening authority as possessing any greater power or knowledge or establish a paternalist relationship of external responsibility. Peacebuilding intervention, in this framing, is articulated as one that respects the autonomy of the other and even enables the development of autonomous capacities and 'spaces'. Interventions of this sort require no specialist knowledge and, in fact, tend to problematise such knowledge claims, and instead could be understood to require more therapeutic capacities and sensitivities, more attuned to open and unscripted forms of engagement, mutual processes of learning and unpredictable and spontaneous forms of knowledge exchange (see, for example, Duffield 2007, 233–234; Jabri 2007, 177; Brigg and Muller 2009, 130).

While cause-and-effect problem-solving peacebuilding interventions, with crude levers of external power, might be out of fashion, peacebuilding nominally still appears to be alive and well, thriving on the noninterventionist move towards approaches oriented towards developing existing local capacities and capabilities.

The depoliticisation of peacebuilding and the removal of its former content – the goals of liberal peace – may, of course, be understood as positive. It enables peace-builders to evade the criticisms made of classical 1990s and 2000s peacebuilding approaches. However, the question remains whether, in evading the problems of political accountability and external responsibility for peacebuilding outcomes, peacebuilding has, in fact, lost its meaningfulness and become indistinguishable from other policy spheres. If the goal is no longer peace and if there is no structure of goals and development from which success and failure can be judged, then peacebuilding certainly does not seem a particularly fitting description for the forms of international intervention still discussed and pursued under this rubric.

References

ActionAid (2006). *What progress? A shadow review of World Bank conditionality.* Action-Aid, Johannesburg. (http://www.actionaid.org.uk/sites/default/files/what_progress.pdf) Accessed: 19 May 2015.

Aradau, C. (2014). The promise of security: Resilience, surprise and epistemic politics. *Resilience: International Practices, Policies and Discourses,* 2(2), 73–87.

Bain, W. (2003). *Between Anarchy and Society: Trusteeship and the Obligations of Power.* Oxford University Press, Oxford.

Barnett, M. N. (2010). *The International Humanitarian Order.* Routledge, Abingdon.

Beck, U. (1992). *Risk Society: Towards a New Modernity.* Sage, London.

Bickerton, C. J., Cunliffe, P., and Gourevitch, A. (Eds.). (2007). *Politics without Sovereignty: A Critique of Contemporary International Relations.* University College London Press, Abingdon.

Bildt, C. (2003, 3 April). Europe's future in the mirror of the Balkans. *openDemocracy.* (http://www.opendemocracy.net/democracy-open_politics/article_1123.jsp) Accessed: 19 May 2015.

Blair, T. (1999). *Doctrine of the international community.* (http://webarchive.national archives.gov.uk/+/www.number10.gov.uk/Page1297) Accessed: 20 May 2015.

Brandt, M., Cottrell, J., Ghai, Y., and Regan, A. (2011). *Constitution-Making and Reform: Options for the Process.* Interpeace, Geneva. (http://www.constitutionmakingforpeace.org/sites/default/files/Constitution-Making-Handbook.pdf) Accessed: 19 May 2015.

Brigg, M., and Muller, K. (2009). Conceptualising culture in conflict resolution. *Journal of Intercultural Studies,* 3(2), 121–140.

Cesarini, P., and Hite, K. (2004). Introducing the concept of authoritarian legacies. In K. Hite and P. Cesarini (Eds.), *Authoritarian Legacies and Democracy in Latin America and Southern Europe.* University of Notre Dame Press, Notre Dame, IN, 1–24.

Chandler, D. (1999). *Bosnia: Faking Democracy after Dayton.* Pluto, London.

Chandler, D. (2006). *Empire in Denial: The Politics of State-Building.* Pluto, London.

Chandler, D. (2010). *International Statebuilding: The Rise of Post-Liberal Governance.* Routledge, London.

Chandler, D. (2015). Resilience and the "everyday": Beyond the paradox of "liberal peace". *Review of International Studies,* 41, 27–48.

Chesterman, S. (2002). *Just War or Just Peace?: Humanitarian Intervention and International Law.* Oxford University Press, Oxford.

Commission for Africa. (2005). *Our Common Interest: Report of the Commission for Africa.* (http://www.commissionforafrica.info/wp-content/uploads/2005-report/11–03–05_cr_report.pdf) Accessed: 19 May 2015.

Cramer, C. (2006). *Civil War Is Not a Stupid Thing: Accounting for Violence in Developing Countries*. Hurst, London.

Desch, M. C. (2008). America's liberal illiberalism: The ideological origins of overreaction in US foreign policy. *International Security*, 32(3), 7–43.

DfID. (2011). *Saving Lives, Preventing Suffering and Building Resilience: The UK Government's Humanitarian Policy*. DfID, London. (https://www.gov.uk/government/uploads/system/uploads/attachment_data/file/67468/The_20UK_20Government_s_20Humanitarian_20Policy_20-_20September_202011_20-_20Final.pdf) Accessed: 19 May 2015.

DfID. (2013). *Operational Plan 2011–2015 DFID Growth and Resilience Department*. DfID, London.

Dillon, M. (2007). Governing terror: The state of emergency of biopolitical emergence. *International Political Sociology*, 1(1), 7–28.

Dillon, M., and Lobo-Guerrero, L. (2008). Biopolitics of security in the 21st century: An introduction. *Review of International Studies*, 34(2), 265–292.

Dillon, M., and Reid, J. (2009). *The Liberal Way of War: Killing to Make Life Live*. Routledge, London.

Dobbins, J., Jones, S. G., Crane, K., DeGrasse, and Cole, B. (2007). *The Beginner's Guide to Nation-Building*. RAND, Santa Monica, CA.

Douzinas, C. (2007). *Human Rights and Empire: The Political Philosophy of Cosmopolitanism*. Routledge-Cavendish, Abingdon.

Drabek, T. E., and McEntire, D. A. (2003). Emergent phenomena and the sociology of disaster: Lessons, trends and opportunities from the research literature. *Disaster, Prevention and Management*, 12(2), 97–112.

DSG. (2012). *Sustaining US Global Leadership: Priorities for 21st Century Defense*. White House, Washington, DC.

Duffield, M. (2007). *Development, Security and Unending War: Governing the World of Peoples*. Polity, Cambridge.

Eurodad. (2006). *World Bank and IMF Conditionality: A Development Injustice*. European Network on Debt and Development, Brussels. (http://www.eurodad.org/uploadedfiles/whats_new/reports/eurodad_world_bank_and_imf_conditionality_report.pdf) Accessed: 19 May 2015.

Gillespie, D., and Melching, M. (2010).The transformative power of democracy and human rights in nonformal education: The case of Tostan. *Adult Education Quarterly*, 60(5), 477–498.

Heathershaw, J., and Lambach, D. (2008). Introduction: Post-conflict spaces and approaches to statebuilding. *Journal of Intervention and Statebuilding*, 2(3), 269–289.

Hehir, A., and Robinson, N. (Eds.). (2007). *State-Building: Theory and Practice*. Routledge, Abingdon.

Held, D. (1995). *Democracy and the Global Order: From the Modern State to Cosmopolitan Governance*. Polity, Cambridge.

Jabri, V. (2007). *War and the Transformation of Global Politics*. Palgrave, Basingstoke.

Kaldor, M. (1999). *New and Old Wars: Organized Violence in a Global Era*. Polity, Cambridge.

Kaldor, M. (2007). *Human Security: Reflections on Globalization and Intervention*. Polity, Cambridge.

Kaufmann, M. (2013). Emergent self-organisation in emergencies: Resilience rationales in interconnected societies. *Resilience: International Policies, Practices and Discourses*, 1(1), 53–68.

Kontinen, T. (2014, 13–14 March). *Rights-based approach in practice? Dilemmas of empowerment in a development NGO*. Unpublished paper, presented for After Human Rights workshop, University of Helsinki.

Latour, B. (2003). Is re-modernization occurring – And if so, how to prove it? A commentary on Ulrich Beck. *Theory, Culture & Society*, 20(2), 35–48.

Latour, B. (2013). *An Inquiry into Modes of Existence: An Anthropology of the Moderns*. Harvard University Press, Cambridge, MA.

Law, J. (2004). *After Method: Mess in Social Science*. Routledge, Abingdon.

Lederach, J. P. (1997). *Building Peace: Sustainable Reconciliation in Divided Societies*. United States Institute of Peace, Washington, DC.

Lemay-Hébert, N. (2009). Statebuilding without nation-building? Legitimacy, state failure and the limits of the institutionalist approach. *Journal of Intervention and Statebuilding*, 3(1), 21–45.

Mac Ginty, R. (2010). Hybrid peace: The interaction between top-down and bottom-up peace. *Security Dialogue*, 41(4), 391–412.

Maor, M. (2012). *Policy overreaction*. Working paper, Hebrew University of Jerusalem. (http://portal.idc.ac.il/he/schools/government/research/documents/maor.pdf) Accessed: 19 May 2015.

Mayall, J., and Soares de Oliveira, R. (Eds.). (2011). *The New Protectorates: International Tutelage and the Making of Liberal States*. Hurst, London.

Mazarr, M. J. (2014, January–February). The rise and fall of the failed-state paradigm: Requiem for a decade of distraction. *Foreign Affairs*. (http://www.foreignaffairs.com/articles/140347/michael-j-mazarr/the-rise-and-fall-of-the-failed-state-paradigm) Accessed: 20 May 2015.

Millar, G. (2014). Disaggregating hybridity: Why hybrid institutions do not produce predictable experiences of peace. *Journal of Peace Research*, 51(4), 501–514.

Moe, L. W., and Simojoki, M. V. (2013). Custom, contestation and cooperation: Peace and justice in Somaliland. *Conflict, Security & Development*, 13(4), 393–416.

Nicholson, G. (2014, 22 July). *Inequality and its impact on the resilience of societies*. Association of Caribbean States. (http://www.eturbonews.com/48253/inequality-and-its-impact-resilience-societies) Accessed: 20 May 2015.

Owen, D. (2012). *The Hubris Syndrome: Bush, Blair and the Intoxication of Power* (Rev. ed.). Methuen, York.

Paris, R. (2004). *At War's End: Building Peace after Civil Conflict*. Cambridge University Press, Cambridge.

Paris, R., and Sisk, T. D. (2009). *The Dilemmas of Statebuilding: Confronting the Contradictions of Postwar Peace Operations*. Routledge, Abingdon.

Pugh, M., Cooper, N., and Turner, M. (Eds.). (2008). *Whose Peace? Critical Perspectives on the Political Economy of Peacebuilding*. Palgrave Macmillan, London.

Ramalingam, B. (2013). *Aid on the Edge of Chaos: Rethinking International Cooperation in a Complex World*. Oxford University Press, Oxford.

Ramalingam, B., Jones, H., Reba, T., and Young, J. (2008). *Exploring the science of complexity: Ideas and implications for development and humanitarian efforts*. ODI Working Paper, 285. Overseas Development Institute, London.

Richmond, O. P., and Mitchell, A. (Eds.). (2012). *Hybrid Forms of Peace: From Everyday Agency to Post-Liberalism*. Palgrave, Basingstoke.

Roberts, D. (2008). Hybrid polities and indigenous pluralities: Advanced lessons in statebuilding from Cambodia. *Journal of Intervention and Statebuilding*, 2(1), 63–86.

Scott, J. C. (1998). *Seeing Like a State: How Certain Schemes to Improve the Human Condition Have Failed*. Yale University Press, New Haven, CT.

Sen, A. (1999). *Development as Freedom*. Oxford University Press, Oxford.

Shilliam, R. (2011). The perilous but unavoidable terrain of the non-west. In R. Shilliam (Ed.), *International Relations and Non-western Thought: Imperialism, Colonialism and Investigations of Global Modernity*. Routledge, Abingdon, 12–26.

Stewart, R., and Knaus, G. (2012). *Can Intervention Work?* W. W. Norton, London.

UK Government. (2011). *Building stability overseas strategy*. Department for International Development, Foreign and Commonwealth Office, Ministry of Defence, London. (https://www.gov.uk/government/uploads/system/uploads/attachment_data/file/67475/Building-stability-overseas-strategy.pdf) Accessed: 20 May 2015.

US Department of State. (2002). *The National Security Strategy of the United States of America*. White House, Washington, DC. (http://www.state.gov/documents/organization/63562.pdf) Accessed: 20 May 2015.

Wheeler, N. J. (2000). *Saving Strangers: Humanitarian Intervention in International Society*. Oxford University Press, Oxford.

World Bank. (2007). *Conditionality in Development Policy Lending*. World Bank, Washington, DC. (http://siteresources.worldbank.org/PROJECTS/Resources/40940–1114615847489/Conditionalityfinalreport120407.pdf) Accessed: 20 May 2015.

Zimmermann, A. (2007). The rule of law as a culture of legality: Legal and extra-legal elements for the realisation of the rule of law in society. *E-Law – Murdoch University Electronic Journal of Law*, 14(1), 10–31. (https://elaw.murdoch.edu.au/archives/issues/2007/1/eLaw_rule_law_culture_legality.pdf) Accessed: 3 November 2015.

4 Relational peacebuilding
Promise beyond crisis

Morgan Brigg

Introduction

The enthusiasm for peacebuilding that blossomed after the Cold War has recently met with practical and ethical limits. The task of implementing ambitious societal and political transformations in conflictual settings, frequently across strong cultural and religious differences, has often not achieved expectations. Shortcomings have been accompanied by critiques of liberal hubris and questions about the relevance of liberal frameworks for pursuing peace. The challenges of gaining traction in local contexts alongside the dawning recognition of local capacity has given rise, against liberal peace approaches to peacebuilding and statebuilding, to discussion of hybrid political orders (e.g. Roberts 2008; Boege et al. 2009), hybrid peace governance (e.g. Belloni 2012) and diverse processes of peace formation (Richmond 2013). Liberal frameworks continue to hold sway in policy-making capitals from New York to Brussels to Tokyo – and yet here, too, there is recognition of need for change. There are both increasing attention to the pursuit of greater local engagement and more critical self-reflexivity on the part of interveners. These dynamics may be read as a decolonial moment within contemporary peacebuilding: the approaches of the former colonisers are brought to recognise and engage with local constituencies – not the elites that inhabit and direct the institutional architecture of states and participate in the states-system, but the people themselves.

While the current state of play in peacebuilding presents possibilities for reworking relationships between liberal international peacebuilders and local peoples as well as peacebuilding practice, it also risks confusion. The liberal peace is under question, but there also appears to be no clear alternative ideology or theoretical framework (Chandler 2013, 20). The world of peacebuilding, as with much globalised politics, is so complexly entangled that it is difficult for peacebuilding researchers and practitioners to identify key phenomena – the 'international' and 'local', for instance – let alone begin to theorise relations between them. Similar complexities plague the notion of hybrid political orders, regardless of the utility of this notion. In these circumstances the language of hybrid peacebuilding and peace formation is diverse. There is talk of various forms of local engagement and ownership, complex networks, flexibility and continuous learning. In parallel there are efforts to acknowledge and embrace innovative practice alongside non-linear understandings and emergent effects of policy and practice.

One prominent scholar, David Chandler, argues that the logical conclusion of these developments is 'that problems are no longer conceived as amenable to political solutions in terms of instrumental governing interventions on the basis of cause-and-effect understandings' (2015, 84). He goes so far as to suggest that the result is the disappearance of politics (ibid.). It seems likely that Chandler overstates the implications of recent developments, but his analysis is also helpful. On the one hand, Chandler highlights the risks of vagueness and indeterminacy associated with the current self-reflexive trajectory; on the other, he gives expression to nostalgia for a less complex and complicated world – a desire no doubt widely shared. The appeal of solutions and cause–effect understandings is clear, and yet the critique of liberal peacebuilding has shown that it is the easy appeal to precisely these types of conventional understandings that masks state-centric and Eurocentric approaches (Richmond and Mac Ginty 2015). This closes down the search for alternatives borne of people themselves. The challenge, then, is to find ways forward that manage complexity and confusion without closing down possibilities, or politics.

This chapter argues that the language of relationality is a useful vehicle for navigating the complexities of contemporary peacebuilding and for articulating the best impulses and possibilities of recent developments while retaining a focus on meaningful change and on politics. Attention to relations in peacebuilding emerges as the language of relationality is burgeoning in many other fields across the natural and social sciences and humanities. In the social sciences alone the contributions range from sociology (Emirbayer 1997) to politics (Stacy 2003; Nexon 2010), law (Nedelsky 2011), geography (Nash 2005) and anthropology (Strathern 1995; Thelen et al. 2014). Relationalists also come in all shades, including postmodern (Steiner and Helminski 1998), realist (Somers 1998) and feminist (Keller 1997). As is usually the case with such phenomena, relationality is not wholly new. Relationality has antecedents and analogues in minor traditions of dominant scholarship, and in non-Western traditions and a variety of religions.

In peacebuilding, relationality captures the ways in which practitioners and scholars are increasingly focused, in the wake of failures and critiques of liberal peacebuilding, on partnership, relationship and exchange, particularly with local counterparts and populations. It arises out of practical and ethical challenges as many interveners try to move beyond binaries such as 'liberal versus local' and 'Western versus non-Western' to seek out more balanced and reciprocally empowering exchanges, including for mutual learning that enables effective solutions developed through hybrid political orders. Interveners increasingly facilitate or advise rather than directing or doing, and host societies are encouraged to realise their own capacities and abilities while interveners take less prominent, assertive and knowledgeable stances in their interactions with local people. These shifts are increasingly considered necessary to enable the realisation of peacebuilding objectives and goals.

The possibilities of relational peacebuilding, though, do not arise automatically with the emergence of relationality as an idiom. This signals the need to engage more thoroughly with relationality, including by drawing upon relevant scholarship to clarify the concept and by considering the risks and possibilities associated with it. To do so, this chapter first disaggregates and explains relationality in ontological terms before considering the risks and promise associated with different forms of relationality. I argue that while relationality certainly comes with risks, it also contains substantial promise for navigating and advancing contemporary peacebuilding.

Thin, thicker and thick relationality

Neologisms are routinely associated with definitional confusion and contestation. Consider, for example debates around the meaning of 'sustainable development' and even peacebuilding itself. Because such matters are rarely settled decisively it is both unnecessary and unhelpful to attempt to trace the multiple and sometimes competing provenance of contemporary interest in relationality. Instead, this section distinguishes between different ontological forms of relationality by using the terms 'thin', 'thicker' and 'thick' to identify the differing weight that the idea of relation can be given in conceptualising and engaging the social and political world of peacebuilding. Thin relationality refers to relationships among entities (for example individuals, organisations or states) without questioning how entities come into being. This might also be termed minimal or shallow relationality. Thicker relationality identifies the ways entities are mutually conditioned and changed through interaction. This ontologically stronger form of relationality asserts, for instance, that no individual, organisation or state can exist unaffected by others. Thick relationality, finally, gives conceptual priority to relations over entities and thus embraces a more fluid and fundamentally dynamic understanding of the social and political world of peacebuilding.

By referring to relationships among entities or structures, thin relationality draws attention to neglected or underappreciated relationships in peacebuilding, whether between or among individuals, peoples, institutions, systems, or other entities or structures. Thin relationality suggests the importance, for instance, of paying attention to the interpersonal dimensions of lives affected by conflict and of the exchanges that occur in processes of bringing peace and rebuilding political order, including through reparations, reconciliation and processes of state formation. To this extent, relationality reflects long-standing commitments in the field of peace and conflict studies. Relational ethics, for instance, is arguably central to the forgiveness and reconciliation that is necessary among individuals who have harmed or been harmed by each other in order that they can be able to live together with each other in the wake of violent conflict (Ducommun-Nagy 2009). Micro-level interpersonal relational exchanges have also long been recognised as important in mediation and other conflict resolution processes, and some now argue that this needs to be taken further (e.g. Leary 2004; Noll 2011).

Thin relationality can equally be drawn upon to analyse relationships in the more technical realms of peacebuilding governance. Visoka and Doyle (2014), for instance, invoke the idiom of relationality to analyse international responsibility and accountability in the relationship between the UN Interim Administration Mission in Kosovo and local authorities. These and similar relationships are crucial to analysing and advancing the governance and effectiveness of peacebuilding interventions. Relationships are also at the centre of recent discussion of hybrid political orders and hybrid peace governance. This is explicitly recognised in the important concept of peace formation recently introduced by Oliver Richmond (2013). As a wide range of local organisations 'have become involved in everyday matters of peace and its infrastructures, in security, political, economic and social realms' (2013, 380), they have entered into relationships with the modern state and international actors, asserting the value of local agency, organisation and mobilisation.

The relational engagements that lead to hybrid political orders and constitute peace formations exemplify thin relationality to the extent that they refer to relations between or among preexisting individuals, peoples, institutions, systems and structures. But, as Richmond notes, part of what is most interesting and important about peace formation is the way processes reshape governance and the mechanisms for pursuing peace and order, leading to the emergence of post-liberal forms of peace associated with emerging post-colonial forms of civil society (2013, 397). In these 'thicker' relational engagements, 'indigenous or local agents of peacebuilding, conflict resolution or development . . . find ways of establishing peace processes and dynamic local forms of peace, which are also constitutive of their state' through exchange with 'external praxes of intervention' (ibid., 383). Such engagements do not accept or assume the existing institutional, social or political order. Rather than accepting indigenous customary law or the modern state as fixed, for instance, each is transformed through interaction with the other.

Thicker relationality thus involves the ways in which entities or structures or systems – whether individuals, customary law or states, for instance – are engaged in processes that are mutually conditioning or transformative. Relationship is not conceived as involving simple negotiation and exchange between, for instance, an INGO (international nongovernmental organisation) and a local counterpart, that takes the form of shuffling between self-subsistent entities. Instead, interactions condition the entities, with each changing through time through relationship. In thicker forms of relationality, entities and structures are changed through interaction. Where thin relationality conceives of (apparently) preexisting entities and structures, allowing these phenomena to stand, thicker relationality evokes interactive and dynamic processes through which entities or structures come into being and are transformed through relations.

Thicker understandings of relationality, then, deeply challenge efforts to understand the world primarily in terms of entities. Building upon Greek heritage, mainstream social science places entities such as individuals and states at the centre of analysis, with such 'things' conceived as internally consistent and having the character of 'substance' which sets them apart from other things (Aristotle 1941, 740). But if an entity arises in relation to another entity, gaining its characteristics through exchange, then its substance may be less important than the relations it shares with other entities. In this perspective, the state, for instance, a core operational entity in much peacebuilding, arises through myriad social and political relations, including with other states (for a classical discussion of some these matters, see Abrams 1988). Thicker relationality thus contends that 'what distinguishes subject from subject, subject from object, or object from object is mutual relation rather than substance' (Schaab 2013, 1975).

This thicker relational approach to social and political life has distinct advantages for dealing with the complexities of peacebuilding because it enables a conceptual nimbleness suited to understanding forms of relating that are apparently contradictory in the terms of mainstream science. Consider, for example, that individuals frequently hold overlapping roles within a given social or political order such that one may simultaneously be the same as and different from others. A local interlocutor in a peacebuilding intervention may simultaneously be a member of a particular cultural community, a traditional chief and a government administrator. What makes the individual different (e.g. the administrator role) does not make him or her separate from the cultural community, but rather differently the same (see Albrecht and Moe 2014). Thicker relationality enables a focus on the workings of mutual and overlapping relations among community, chief and government.

What, though, of thick relationality, and of the notion of 'hybridity' that has been used to evoke relational interactions in recent peacebuilding debates? The point of distinction between thicker and thick relationality arises when 'the relations between entities are ontologically more fundamental than the entities themselves' (Wildman 2010, 55; Durie 2002). Hybridity points to both these types of relations and to underlying entities or categories – the local or international, or customary and state conflict management, for instance. It thereby exemplifies thicker relationality, but *thick* relationality requires that relations do not derive from, or be beholden to, preexisting entities or structures. Instead, thick relationality involves giving 'logical consistency to the in-between' and thus 'realigning with a logic of relation' (Massumi 2002, 70).

While hybridity has certainly advanced peacebuilding debates, it is not an instance of thick relationality because the hybrid is always necessarily a derivative effect of already constituted entities. Hybridity requires that underlying phenomena (e.g. the local or international) are assumed, but such assumptions cannot stand scrutiny because detailed historical and social analysis typically reveals hybrids 'all the way down'. What is local or international, or customary or state law, for instance, is almost always a relational effect of long historical dynamics, including relations brought about through trade and colonialism. Hybridity conceals and contravenes the logic of relationality because without the underlying entities or categories to which it refers, the hybrid 'vaporize[s] into logical indeterminacy' (Massumi 2002, 69).

Thick relationality, then, reverses the prevailing priority of entity over relation in mainstream social science to focus attention on how entities continually arise or emerge through relations and processes. Ontological privilege shifts to the relations for it is relations that constitute the field from which entities arise (Massumi 2002, 8). As a result, thick relationality is fundamentally dynamic. An entity conceived in the terms of thick relationality, whether individual, organisation or state, exists in an 'unfolding relation to its own nonpresent potential to vary' (ibid., 4). Entities, structures and the connections between and among them continually re-form in dynamic relation, even as these relations regularly affirm and reproduce existing entities and structures.

The dynamism evoked by relationality tends to confound conventional social science because existing analytic tools usually 'avoid emphasis on dynamic processes and focus on equilibrium states' (Miller and Page 2007, 83). Nonetheless, scholars focusing on dynamic systems have in recent decades been struck by the importance of phenomena that are dynamically self-organising through local interaction (e.g. neurons in brains, birds in flocks, people in cultures). These phenomena, which are beginning to be analysed as examples of chaos, emergence and complex adaptive systems – including in peace and conflict studies (Körppen et al. 2011) – operate in nonlinear and semi-ordered ways. Organisation arises through mutual contagion, susceptibility or transmission of information among interacting parts, leading to dynamic changes on the whole that operate beyond conventional understandings of cause and effect that rely upon proportional and linear understandings of interactions among entities. A proportionally small event, for instance, may trigger an outbreak of conflict or, conversely, a breakthrough in a peace process (e.g. Coleman et al. 2011, 41).

By approaching the limits of conventional ways of knowing, thick relationality opens onto other ways of thinking and of ordering social and political life. These possibilities may already exist, in the underappreciated forms of kinship-based or otherwise laterally networked political community practised by some indigenous or local peoples in their everyday lives. Or they may be prospective, able to be developed as organic networks resulting from myriad complex exchanges that occur in efforts to build peace in the processes of peace formation described by Richmond (2013). The case of Somaliland likely represents some combination of both possibilities (Menkhaus 2007). To open to other possibilities in these ways speaks directly to decolonial possibilities in contemporary peacebuilding by reopening the possibility for people to participate in the governing of their lives somewhat outside the framework of dominant institutions. By foregrounding fluid and dynamic relations, thick relationality provides a way of thinking beyond existing entities or structures, including beyond dominant understandings of state, democracy, rule of law, rights or markets.

Where thin relationality assumes and draws attention to underappreciated relationships between existing social and political entities or structures, thicker relationality points to the interactive and mutually conditioning ways in which entities come into existence. Thick relationality goes a step further by giving priority to relations over entities to break with conventional approaches and embrace a fundamentally dynamic understanding of the social and political world. Peacebuilding practitioners may have limited use for debates about the nature of social and political reality, but disaggregating relationality and thinking carefully about forms of relationality – although in a schematic way – provides a way of engaging burgeoning relational commitments and applying the idiom of relationality to maximise its potential in peacebuilding.

Risk and promise

Relations are both necessary and commonsensical in peacebuilding, so to draw attention to them is in many respects intrinsically worthwhile. However, the burgeoning interest in relationality also comes with ethical, political and practice risks. This section maps a selection of these risks before arguing that a disaggregated understanding of relationality helps to largely – though not wholly – mitigate risks. The risks associated with thin forms of relationality, for instance, can be partially managed by drawing upon thicker forms. This leads to the argument that relationality does indeed hold promise for advancing peacebuilding. Even so, emancipatory political outcomes are not guaranteed, and it is consequently necessary to pay attention to the differing forms of relationality and the political and practice possibilities that are thereby stifled or enabled.

The contemporary pursuit of relationality in peacebuilding is often associated with everyday ideas of relationship and accompanied by the language of participation and empowerment. In this idiom, interveners are open to local insights and ownership, and listening for local input is often accompanied by self-deprecation about what can be achieved by outsiders. These ways of relating appear to directly counter the liberal hubris that has been critiqued in recent scholarship, and to acknowledge and respond to the limitations of many externally driven peacebuilding efforts. Such ways of relating also reflect core procedural goods of human relationships: listening carefully, respectful exchange and so on. These ideas and exchanges, then, seem to reflect an appropriate level of modesty that begins to redress long-standing iniquitous power relationships, in part by enabling those targeted in peacebuilding interventions to develop and realise their own capacity and agency.

However, an everyday approach to relationships can be profoundly unsatisfactory for understanding the politics of peacebuilding and for advancing peacebuilding practice. The notion that interveners and local people can enter into a mutually appreciative relationship belies the asymmetrical power relationships that characterise most peacebuilding settings. Even more concerning than asymmetry itself is the fact that the language of partnership and exchange can prevail even as the interveners maintain firm control of key political, policy, bureaucratic, administrative and resourcing levers. This is not to suggest that local people exercise absolutely no power in relationships with interveners, but rather that the language and practice of everyday relationships can mask power relations. These dynamics may be quite obvious (taking the form of control of key resourcing, for instance), but can also involve people as participants in their own governance. As governmentality scholarship following Michel Foucault (1991) shows, the most effective form of power in liberalism involves people governing themselves in accordance with dominant policy programs as they pursue their peace, freedom and well-being.

No doubt a focus of everyday relationships and appropriate levels of humility are important in peacebuilding practice, but downplaying international peace-builder capacity to effect change alongside emphasis on local participation and ownership through the language of relationality carries substantial risks. These risks include:

1   diminishing responsibility for outcomes, thereby downplaying, reproducing or exacerbating recent peacebuilding failures;
2   obscuring peacebuilders' complicity with the governing mechanisms and effects of liberal peacebuilding;
3   leaving unchallenged a range of structural forces – at national, regional and global levels – that generate conflict and put people at risk;
4   shifting responsibility for remedying problems back to micro-level local communities and populations, thereby obscuring possibilities for collective political action and advances in intervener peacebuilding practice.

As interveners turn to progressive liberal humanitarian sensibilities to guide rela-tionships with local people, they risk pursuing relationships predominantly on liberal terms while assuaging guilt about the likelihood of peacebuilding failures and the iniquities of contemporary global politics.

The everyday approach to relationships in peacebuilding is an example of thin relationality because it pays little or no attention to the relations through which individuals or institutions come into existence. Listening to people, openness to exchange and input, and the facilitation of participation or empowerment *can* be much more, but frequently risk a tendency to overlook the structuring of the world through power and political relationships, and this is likely to reproduce or exacerbate existing ethical, political and practice problems in peacebuilding. It is important to state that neither thin relationality nor a focus on the everyday relationships in peacebuilding necessarily leads to ethical, political or practice problems, and attention to relations of both everyday interpersonal and other forms (such as between external and local peacebuilding organisations) is cru-cial for advancing effective peacebuilding efforts. Thin relationality also does not preclude self-reflexivity, but if self-reflexivity simply returns to the individual self it risks reproducing the current patterning of entities, structures and problems of peacebuilding. Thin relationality, then, comes with the risk of conceptualising the world 'as it stands' by leaving entities and structures intact and not attending to the political and practice risks associated with an everyday approach to rela-tionships in peacebuilding.

Thicker forms of relationality, though, provide ways of mitigating the forego-ing risks precisely by calling attention to the interactive and dynamic processes through which entities or structures come into being in relation to each other. To examine how individuals and institutions in peacebuilding are mutually conditioning, for instance, and to attend to this task carefully and seriously, is to engage with a wide array of forces and effects that constitute and position individuals, institutions and the practices and resource flows that constitute and shape contemporary peacebuilding efforts. Where thin relationality may mask these important dynamics, thicker relationality provides the conceptual means for critically engaging and hence combatting the risks of thin relationality. In turn, thicker relationality can lay foundations for mutually transforming relationships between, for instance, external and local peacebuilding organisations, and these have prospects for both improving outcomes and addressing structural inequalities and power imbalances in peacebuilding.

Thicker relationality also suggests more thoroughgoing forms of self-reflexivity. Where thin relationality takes in reflexivity about one's self, thicker relationality requires reflexivity about the mode of self-reflexive positioning. Thin modes of self-reflexivity, for instance, are associated with advanced liberal societies and accompanying forms of subjectivity, including those heavily relied upon and promoted by the self-help industry. Thicker relationality suggests that peacebuilders resist simply on implementing such forms of self-reflexivity, and instead critically inquire about the constitution of such modes of being and their relationship with other ways of being encountered in peacebuilding practice. Pursuing thicker relationality does not guarantee the risks that can arise with thin relationality will or can be adequately addressed, but does provide a mechanism for revealing and engaging them.

While thin and thicker forms of relationality do reflect differing conceptual orientations to the world, they are not mutually exclusive in practice, and to this extent advocacy for thicker relationality does not militate against everyday relationships, and it certainly cannot do away with the need for them. Indeed, relationships are a core site for the development of deeply ethical modes of relating, as evidenced, for instance, in the work of philosophers including Emmanuel Levinas (1991a; 1991b) and Martin Buber (1947/1961; 1937/2004). It is precisely relationships among people that prompt actions that lead to changes to institutions, structures and practices in hybrid political orders and through processes of peace formation, for instance. Thicker relationality, in short, both draws attention to the ways in which the world is structured and provides a vehicle for addressing the risks associated with enacting thin forms of relationality.

Meanwhile, deploying a combination of thin and thicker relationality is central to pursuing opportunities for innovative shared learning and partnering that can draw upon a blend of both local and introduced approaches and capacities for addressing difficult conflict challenges and building peace. Programs and practices developed in this mode are more flexible and able to tap into local forms of legitimacy, and are hence likely to have more traction on the ground. These developments begin to grapple with some of the key shortfalls of peacebuilding interventions of recent decades, including by addressing long-standing unequal power relationships through support for and development of local people's agency.

What, though, of the thickest form of relationality discussed in the previous section: thick relationality, which reverses the prevailing priority of entities over relations in order to embrace a logic of relation? This ontological shift deeply challenges conventional approaches, including cause–effect understandings. Thick relationality emerges in contemporary peacebuilding in the form of increasing interest in complex and nonlinear systems and a willingness to explore – and in some cases to embrace – the possibilities of unintended consequences and emergent change. A risk here is the surrender of peacebuilder agency and responsibility, including for self-reflexivity: doing away with entities and structures through thick relationality risks the notion that peacebuilders have very limited or no ability to generate effects in the world. This can, much like the risks that can be associated with thin relationality, mask power relations and politics. What, then, for instance, are the prospects for driving toward equity, justice and peace? As the perceived ability to effect an intended consequence declines, so too might responsibilities, leading to the risk of accepting 'whatever happens' as 'what needed to happen'. This creates space for interpreting what would be failures on conventional modernist measures as new opportunities, or even successes. A world evacuated of cause and effect where process, interaction and exchange reign runs the risk of removing responsibility for effects, whether positive or negative.

The desire for a clear compass to guide the pursuit of justice and peace is understandable, particularly when such a compass is not readily available, and yet thick relationality is not the cause of uncertainty. The problem is, rather, that in recent decades the 'crucial collective stories in modernity' that provided ready guidance 'have been disturbed or undermined' (Brown 2001, 3). The critique and undermining of the liberal peace is part of this larger pattern in which previously trustworthy touchstones – freedom, progress, democracy, development, equality and the like – have become less certain and reliable. Thick relationality does not provide a comforting path back to previous liberal modernist certainties. Quite the opposite. As a corollary, though, it can provide a way of opening onto other ways of thinking and of ordering social and political life – such as kinship-based or otherwise laterally networked political community practised by some indigenous or local peoples – precisely because it exceeds conventional modernist ways of knowing and ordering. In this way it may become possible to pursue peace in new ways that are not beholden to linear processes or anchored to ideas of sovereignty, state, liberal freedom, and rule of law or the market economy.

To the extent that peacebuilders surrender agency as agents of liberal peace, in other words, thick relationality may help to guide experimentation with new forms of peace through dynamic processes of peace formation. This is likely to bring uncertainty and unpredictable diversity, but deserves to be embraced rather than viewed as an unacceptable risk. Thick relationality may challenge conventional understandings of modernist agency, but this opens possibilities for reworking political orders introduced through colonialism and ramified through nationalism, developmentalism, and liberal peacebuilding and statebuilding. In this way, thick relationality reflects a democratising impulse and suggests possibilities for new forms of order that are simultaneously innovative, practical and emancipatory because they emerge beyond preexisting entities and structures as the creations of peacebuilders and local populations.

Responsibility, though, seems a rather different matter, for it appears harder to accept the proposition that peacebuilders should be able to avoid their social and political responsibilities by deferring them to relational or emergent system-effects. However, as with the risks associated with thin relationality, the broader phenomenon of relationality suggests ways of mitigating risks associated with its particular forms. Despite the more radical ontological stance suggested by thick relationality, embracing the logic of relation does not exclude relationship. Rather, to embrace thick relationality is to deeply commit to relationship, including through the recognition that human beings invariably come into being together such that all being is co-being (Nancy 2000). With co-being comes responsibility for the others that one is involved with, and for outcomes. This thicker form of relationality in which entities (in this case individuals) are mutually conditioned and changed through interaction provides an ethical foundation – theorised by Levinas and Buber, among others – for engaging with the politics of peacebuilding practice and effects. Deep relational commitments thus contribute greatly to mitigating the risk, per Chandler (2015, 84), that politics disappears.

Conclusion

The language of relationality is burgeoning in peacebuilding as in many other fields across the sciences and humanities. Relationality alone cannot pilot peacebuilding beyond crisis or resolve the complexities of contemporary peacebuilding practice. Nonetheless, this chapter has suggested that disaggregating and clarifying the meaning of relationality increases its potential for navigating and advancing peacebuilding. A threefold schema is offered. Thin relationality draws attention to underappreciated relations among entities or structures. Thicker relationality directs attention to the mutual constitution of entities or structures through relations. Thick relationality breaks with conventional thinking by prioritising relations over entities. Thin relationality reaffirms the centrality of relationships of all types to peacebuilding and provides a useful idiom for clarifying lines of responsibility. Thicker relationality offers a way of focusing upon how entities emerge in relation to each other and the politics and power relations at stake in these processes. Thick relationality draws attention to the deeply ethical responsibilities of relating and helps to open onto nondominant ways of ordering the world and pursuing peace – and hence to democratising and decolonising. Overall, relationality provides an idiom for advancing participatory, inclusive, pluralist, innovative, ethically responsible, grounded and legitimate approaches to processing conflict and building peace.

Relationality also certainly comes with ethical, political and practice-related risks, and these are cause for caution. However, many of the risks that accompany particular forms of relationality can also be managed through relationality itself.

Thin relationality can mask asymmetric power relations and structural iniquities, thereby depoliticising peacebuilding practice, but thicker relationality provides a way of focusing upon and critically engaging with exactly these relations. Thick relationality can compromise cause–effect understandings, diminish the capacity to plan for and deliver linear change, and hence compromise peacebuilders' agency and responsibility, but it also suggests deeply ethical responsibilities for others that take the form of thicker relationality by committing peacebuilders to responsibility for both the effects of peacebuilding practice and to respecting peoples' ways of organising political community and pursuing peace. Thicker relationality, by focusing upon how entities are mutually conditioned and changed through interaction, is in many respects a middle path for grappling with the risks associated with relationality and the challenges of contemporary peacebuilding. It avoids the risks accompanying a straightforward focus on relationships associated with thin relationality and moderates the very conceptually challenging and at times open-ended approach associated with thick relationality. Nonetheless, thicker relationality requires straightforward relationships, and some of the most exciting possibilities of relationality are associated with its thick forms.

Relationality cannot guarantee improved peacebuilding practice or that the power and political relations that circulate through the networks, entities and structures of peacebuilding will be addressed or resolved satisfactorily. It is also the case that relationality cannot address the risks of contingency and uncertainty in contemporary peacebuilding. For some a relational ontology undermines politics, including the possibility of driving toward equity, peace and justice, because it gives ground to emergent effects of interactions rather than subscribing to pre-programmed objectives. Yet, this chapter has suggested that politics is changing its form rather than disappearing. We are living through a time in which the touchstones of liberal modernist political narrative – including equity, peace and justice – are fractured and yet have not been replaced (Brown 2001, 3). In these circumstances the risks of uncertainty and diversity need to be embraced in order to advance peacebuilding. Politics arises in relations among people, and accessing the possibilities of other ways of ordering the world, and of participatory, pluralist, grounded, democratising and decolonising peacebuilding requires embracing and working with and among these relations rather than pushing them aside.

References

Abrams, P. (1988). Notes on the difficulty of studying the state (1977). *Journal of Historical Sociology*, 1, 58–89.

Albrecht, P., and Moe, L. W. (2014). The simultaneity of authority in hybrid orders. *Peacebuilding*, 3, 1–16.

Aristotle. (1941). *The Basic Works of Aristotle* (Ed. R. McKeon). Random House, New York.

Belloni, R. (2012). Hybrid peace governance: Its emergence and significance. *Governance: A Review of Multilateralism and International Organizations*, 18, 21–38.

Boege, V., Brown, A. et al. (2009). On hybrid political orders and emerging states: What is failing – States in the Global South or research and politics in the West? *Berghof*

Handbook Dialogue No. 8, Building Peace in the Absence of States: Challenging the Discourse on State Failure. Berghof Research Center for Constructive Conflict Management, Berlin.

Brown, W. (2001). *Politics Out of History.* Princeton University Press, Princeton, NJ.

Buber, M. (2004). *I and Thou.* Continuum, London. (Original work published 1937)

Buber, M. (1961). *Between Man and Man.* Collins, London. (Original work published 1947)

Chandler, D. (2013). Relational sensibilities: The end of the road for "liberal peace". In W. Chadwick, T. Debiel, and F. Gadinger (Eds.), *Relational Sensibility and the "Turn to the Local": Prospects for the Future of Peacebuilding (Global Dialogues 2).* Käte Hamburger Kolleg/Centre for Global Cooperation Research (KHK/GCR21), Duisburg, 19–26.

Chandler, D. (2015). Reconceptualizing international intervention: Statebuilding, "organic processes" and the limits of causal knowledge. *Journal of Intervention and Statebuilding, 9,* 70–88.

Coleman, P., Vallacher, R., Bartoli, A., Nowak, A., and Bui-Wrzosinska, L. (2011). Navigating the landscape of conflict: Applications of dynamical systems theory to addressing protracted conflict. In D. Körppen, N. Ropers, and H. Gießmann (Eds.), *The Non-linearity of Peace Processes – Theory and Practice of Systemic Conflict Transformation.* Barbara Budrich Verlag, Opladen, 39–56.

Ducommun-Nagy, C. (2009). Forgiveness and relational ethics: The perspective of the contextual therapist. In A. Kalayjian and R. F. Paloutzian (Eds.), *Forgiveness and Reconciliation: Psychological Pathways to Conflict Transformation and Peace Building.* Springer, Dordrecht, 33–54.

Durie, R. (2002). Immanence and difference: Toward a relational ontology. *Southern Journal of Philosophy, 40,* 161–189.

Emirbayer, M. (1997). Manifesto for a relational sociology. *American Journal of Sociology, 103,* 281–317.

Foucault, M. (1991). Governmentality. In G. Burchell, C. Gordon, and P. Miller (Eds.), *The Foucault Effect: Studies in Governmentality.* Harvester Wheatsheaf, London, 87–104.

Keller, J. (1997). Autonomy, relationality, and feminist ethics. *Hypatia, 12,* 152–164.

Körppen, D., Ropers, N., and Giessmann, H. (Eds.). (2011). *The Non-linearity of Peace Processes – Theory and Practice of Systemic Conflict Transformation.* Barbara Budrich Verlag, Opladen.

Leary, K. (2004). Critical moments as relational moments: The Centre for Humanitarian Dialogue and the conflict in Aceh, Indonesia. *Negotiation Journal, 20,* 311–338.

Levinas, E. (1991a). *Otherwise than Being or Beyond Essence.* Kluwer Academic, Dordrecht.

Levinas, E. (1991b). *Totality and Infinity.* Kluwer Academic, Dordrecht.

Massumi, B. (2002). *Parables for the Virtual: Movement, Affect, Sensation.* Duke University Press, Durham, NC.

Menkhaus, K. (2007). Governance without government in Somalia: Spoilers, state building, and the politics of coping. *International Security, 31,* 74–106.

Miller, J., and Page, S. (2007). *Complex Adaptive Systems.* Princeton University Press, Princeton, NJ.

Nancy, J. (2000). *Being Singular Plural.* Stanford University Press, Stanford.

Nash, C. (2005). Geographies of relatedness. *Transactions of the Institute of British Geographers, 30,* 449–462.

Nedelsky, J. (2011). *Law's Relations: A Relational Theory of Self, Autonomy, and Law.* Oxford University Press, New York.

Nexon, D. (2010). Relationalism and new systems theory. In M. Albert, L. Cederman, and A. Wendt (Eds.), *New Systems Theories of World Politics*. Palgrave, New York, 99–126.

Noll, D. (2011). *Elusive Peace: How Modern Diplomatic Systems Could Better Resolve World Conflicts*. Prometheus, New York.

Richmond, O. (2013). Failed statebuilding versus peace formation. *Cooperation and Conflict*, 48, 378–400.

Richmond, O., and Mac Ginty, R. (2015). Where now for the critique of the liberal peace? *Cooperation and Conflict*, 50, 171–189.

Roberts, D. (2008). Hybrid polities and indigenous pluralities: Advanced lessons in statebuilding from Cambodia. *Journal of Intervention and Statebuilding*, 2, 63–86.

Schaab, G. (2013). Relational ontology. In A. Runehov and L. Oviedo (Eds.), *Encyclopedia of Sciences and Religions*. Springer, Netherlands, 1974–1975.

Somers, M. (1998). "We're no angels": Realism, rational choice, and relationality in social science. *American Journal of Sociology*, 104(3), 722–784.

Stacy, H. (2003). Relational sovereignty. *Stanford Law Review*, 55, 2029–2059.

Steiner, D., and Helminski, K. (1998). The politics of relationality: From the postmodern to post-ontology. *Philosophy & Social Criticism*, 24, 1–21.

Strathern, M. (1995). *The Relation: Issues in Complexity and Scale*. Prickly Pear Press, Cambridge.

Thelen, T., Vetters, V., and von Benda-Beckmann, K. (2014). Introduction to stategraphy: Toward a relational anthropology of the state. *Social Analysis*, 58, 1–19.

Visoka, G., and Doyle, J. (2014). Peacebuilding and international responsibility. *International Peacekeeping*, 21, 673–692.

Wildman, W. (2010). An introduction to relational ontology. In J. Polkinghorne and J. Zizioulas (Eds.), *The Trinity and an Entangled World: Relationality in Physical Science and Theology*. Eerdmans, Grand Rapids, 55–73.

Part II

Revisiting peacebuilding practices

5 Peacebuilding and democracy promotion

What current challenges to the latter might tell us for rethinking the former

Jonas Wolff

Introduction[1]

In some way or another, peacebuilding is in crisis. This observation is the point of departure of this volume. More specifically, there is a crisis – or rather multiple crises – of liberal peacebuilding. At times, however, there is the notion that the current challenges to liberal peacebuilding are due to rather specific, and in a way superficial, problems: poor and incoherent implementation; the specific challenges that come with the promotion of liberal democracy in post-conflict settings; and/or the idiosyncratic effects produced by Bush's Freedom Agenda and the so-called regime change wars in Afghanistan and Iraq (cf. Paris 2010). In this chapter, I will argue that such a reading tends to lose sight of the much more fundamental problems with which liberal peacebuilding is confronted.

I will make this argument by looking at the related subfield of democracy promotion. The promotion of norms and institutions associated with liberal democracy constitutes a core element of mainstream peacebuilding strategies as practiced since 1990. However, international activities that aim at promoting democracy in the Global South go beyond the specific field of peacebuilding. Since 1990, they have become standard elements in the foreign and development policies of established (North-Western) democracies and international organizations. In discussing experiences with this kind of "normal" international democracy promotion, I suggest that current challenges concern the very normative premises and conceptual underpinnings of the overall liberal template that guides both peacebuilding and democracy promotion. We are confronted, in this sense, with a crisis of the liberal project of creating "a world after its own image," to use the famous phrase from Marx and Engel's *Communist Manifesto*. The crisis at hand, that is, involves a serious questioning of both the feasibility and the legitimacy of the external promotion of a particular (liberal-democratic) set of norms and institutions.

This chapter starts with a brief exercise in defining, relating and delimiting peacebuilding and democracy promotion. Then, current challenges to democracy promotion are summarized before I discuss in more detail some fundamental problems that are, in my view, crucial for understanding the contemporary crisis of democracy promotion. The chapter ends with concluding thoughts on the implications that recent scholarship on democracy promotion has for the debate about peacebuilding.

Democracy promotion in and outside of peacebuilding

According to a broadly accepted definition, democracy promotion refers to all measures of external actors that aim explicitly and directly at establishing, strengthening, improving or defending democracy in a given country (Azpuru et al. 2008, 151; cf. Burnell 2000a, 3–33). Such measures range from development aid projects and diplomatic appeals to democratic conditionality (incentives and sanctions) to the use of military force. External actors can be states and international and nongovernmental organizations (NGOs).[2] Democracy assistance refers to the subset of activities that are nonviolent and concern the delivery of economic resources and technical know-how through foreign/development aid; it includes the support of political institutions (parliament, judiciary or oversight bodies), political processes (e.g., elections) and sociopolitical actors (civil-society groups, political parties). This definition implies that democracy promotion is whatever measure a given external actor declares as being aimed towards promoting democracy. The kind of democracy that is supported in any individual case is thus dependent on the particular conception of democracy upheld by the particular democracy promoter. With a view to the actual practice of democracy promotion, which is dominated by North-Western governments including the European Union, this implies that democracy promotion usually means liberal democracy promotion (Kurki 2010, 363).

As mentioned in the introduction, international peacebuilding as practiced since 1990 usually includes the introduction and/or strengthening of liberal-democratic norms and institutions (cf. Jarstad and Sisk 2008; Newman et al. 2009; Paris 2004). Still, in the context of peacebuilding, democracy promotion is "only" a means to another end (peace) and, therefore, only one component of a larger package of reform measures. At the same time, both liberal peacebuilding and democracy promotion pursue their liberal and/or democratic objectives by using illiberal and/or nondemocratic means. This is very clear in cases of peacebuilding and democracy promotion programs that are implemented by external authorities with coercive powers such as in the cases of Afghanistan, Bosnia-Herzegovina or Kosovo (cf. Chesterman 2004; Grimm 2010; Tadjbakhsh 2011), but it is also true in the more benign cases. Given the international power asymmetries on which both peacebuilding and democracy promotion are based, any external activity that aims at exerting a significant influence upon the political regime in a given country (i.e., that aims at "making a difference") clashes with liberal and democratic core values such as autonomy and self-determination (Poppe and Wolff 2013). To the extent that both autonomy and self-determination also have a collective dimension that includes the right of a given political community to decide on its own path and shape of political development, external support for a particular model of (liberal) democracy is generally problematic, even if only nonviolent means are used.[3] Bolivia is a case in point in which this inherent tension in the external promotion of democracy has recently come to the fore. Under the current government led by President Evo Morales (since 2006), Bolivia has seen a transformation of democracy that includes a partial deviance from the conception of liberal democracy promoted by external actors such as the US or Germany (cf. Wolff 2012).

While democracy promotion is a core element of peacebuilding programs, a lot of democracy promotion activities take place outside the specific field of peacebuilding, that is, in countries that are not (supposed to be) in a process of transitioning from war to peace. Usual targets or recipients of democracy promotion include "young" democracies that are considered in need of external support in order to deepen, consolidate and/or protect their democratic regime; countries in which authoritarian rule is breaking down and which are thus considered to be undergoing a process of transition to democracy; and authoritarian regimes in which external actors may try to promote gradual liberalization or outright regime change. These different contexts can be illustrated with a view to Latin America – a region that has played an important role in the emergence of the set of international practices that today constitutes the field of democracy promotion (cf. Carothers 1991; Robinson 1996; Smith 1994). Here, US and European democracy promoters, for instance, supported the transitions from military dictatorships to elected civilian governments in the 1980s and engaged in electoral observation, political party-building and the strengthening of democratic institutions in the 1980s and 1990s.[4] The same kinds of activities can today be observed across the globe. The example of Latin America also confirms that democracy promotion is far from a neutral or altruistic practice: the kind of transition and the type of democracy actually promoted by external actors such as the US is clearly related to particular interests and ideologies (cf. Robinson 1996).

The crisis of democracy promotion

In recent contributions on the topic, it is widely acknowledged that the 1990s boom in the international promotion of democracy has been followed by a period of growing challenges (cf. Burnell and Youngs 2010; Diamond 2008, 56–87; Grimm et al. 2012; McFaul 2010, 1–24; Poppe and Wolff 2013; Wolff et al. 2014). Since the turn of the twenty-first century, frustrated expectations, public delegitimation, a shrinking power base and increasing resistance have converged. Breaking with the notion that the end of the Cold War would lead to a progressive enlargement of the zone of democracies, scholars have declared "the end of the Transition Paradigm" (Carothers 2002) and identified a phase of "democratic recession" (Diamond 2008, chap. 3). At the global level, the Freedom Agenda put forth by US President George W. Bush as well as the 2003 invasion of Iraq widely discredited the entire idea of democracy promotion. This exacerbated the general credibility problem of democracy promotion that is caused by the double standards which more generally characterize the foreign policies of the North-Western democracies.[5] At the same time, the rising power of non-Western states with non- or semi-democratic regimes such as China and Russia is weakening the global dominance of the North-West, thereby decreasing the vulnerability of developing countries to North-Western pressure and the leverage of would-be democracy promoters (Levitsky and Way 2005, 21–22).[6] Finally, and related to these trends, scholars and practitioners have noted an outright "backlash against democracy promotion," that is, open resistance by recipient governments to external support for democratic reforms and civil-society groups (Carothers 2010; National Endowment for Democracy [NED] 2006). Recent developments such as the Arab uprisings, which initially led to a certain revival of the liberal optimism from the 1990s, quickly reconfirmed the notion of growing challenges to democracy promotion.

From the perspective of those that are engaged in democracy promotion, the perception of a crisis – or at least of serious challenges – basically results from a loss of trust in the feasibility of democracy promotion. On the one hand, disappointment with the results of democracy promotion, and of democratization processes in general, have raised questions concerning the capability of external actors to effectively promote liberal democracy. On the other hand, the distrust of, or even active resistance to, democracy promotion activities calls into question the expectation that recipients will, in general, be happy to adopt liberal democracy and accept corresponding external support. As a recent Carnegie report has summarized, in recent years "dozens of governments in Asia, Africa, Latin America, the Middle East, and the former Soviet Union have taken steps to limit the space for external support for democracy and human rights within their borders" (Carothers and Brechenmacher 2014, 5), in particular by imposing restrictions on the external support of civil-society organizations. "Especially disconcerting," for the authors and democracy promoters alike, is the fact that this trend also includes "some relative democratic governments that for decades encouraged or at least tolerated international democracy and rights support" such as "Bangladesh, Bolivia, Ecuador, Honduras, India, Indonesia, Kenya, Nicaragua, and Peru" (ibid., 7). A notable example is the so-called Arab Spring: in post-revolutionary Egypt, almost directly following the fall of President Hosni Mubarak, foreign-based democracy promotion organizations from the US and Germany had to face raids, trials and convictions. At that time, Egypt was certainly not a democracy, but the decision still plausibly reflected the popular mood: according to opinion polls from December 2011, a wide majority of Egyptians opposed the delivery of US economic aid to Egyptian civil-society groups (Sharp 2012, 14). Very clearly, recent developments in Egypt and Tunisia, in Ukraine and Russia – or for that matter, in Spain and Greece – show that a lot of people do continue to call for democracy and/or freedom, often in combination with demands for dignity and social justice. But this is obviously not to say that there is a global consensus on what these demands actually consist of, how they may be fulfilled and who is it that should actually be in charge of defining and fulfilling them.

In the following, I will argue that these challenges to democracy promotion result inter alia from a multiple crisis of legitimacy, and that this crisis of legitimacy can be traced to fundamental normative problems with which the overall idea of promoting democracy from the outside is confronted. For the sake of systematizing the multiple crisis of legitimacy, I will make creative use of an established typology that distinguishes between three dimensions of the legitimacy of political order (output, input and throughput)[7] and discuss three sources of legitimacy as related to democracy promotion that, in recent years, have become increasingly problematic (see Table 5.1): the *instrumental legitimacy* that is based on the empirical expectation that, by being the subject of external democracy promotion, countries will also benefit in terms of intrastate peace or socioeconomic development; the *intrinsic legitimacy* that is based on the normative assumption that, by promoting democracy, external actors help the people in recipient countries to realize their human rights; and the *procedural legitimacy* that is based on the combined assessment that democracy promotion is basically demand-driven, thereby respecting local "ownership," and an established international practice.

Instrumental legitimacy: problematizing the instrumental value of liberal democracy

In democratic theory, output legitimacy is the kind of legitimacy that results from the capacity of a given political regime "to solve problems requiring collective solutions" (Scharpf 1999, 11). More generally speaking, it is outcomes that make those subject to a given authority or policy believe that this particular authority or policy is legitimate. With a view to democracy promotion, democratization is usually associated with a series of beneficial consequences, based on the notion of an instrumental value of liberal democracy (Sen 1999). The promotion of democracy is thus often seen as contributing to intrastate and interstate peace, to economic development, social justice and poverty reduction.[8]

In contrast to this optimistic expectation that shaped the rise of the democracy promotion paradigm in the 1990s, recent scholarship has rather emphasized that conflicting objectives pervade the strategy and practice of democracy promotion (cf. Grimm et al. 2012; Wolff et al. 2014). These conflicting objectives, on the one hand, take the well-known shape of *extrinsic* conflicts of objectives: the outcomes of democracy promotion and of democratization processes, in general, frequently go against the interests of those engaged in promoting democracy.

Table 5.1 The crisis of democracy promotion: a multiple crisis of legitimacy

Output legitimacy	Questioning of the *instrumental value* of democracy promotion (concerns strategy to promote peace, socioeconomic development, etc., through democratization)
Input legitimacy	Questioning of the *substantive justice* of democracy promotion (concerns notion of liberal democracy as the universal template of a just political order)
Throughput legitimacy	Questioning of the *procedural justice* of democracy promotion (concerns ways in which external actors intervene in the shaping of the political order in other countries)

Broadening political participation can, for instance, bring political forces to power that challenge the economic and/or security interests of democracy-promoting states. The 2006 election of Hamas in Palestine and the 2005 election of the indigenous and left-wing coca grower Evo Morales as president of Bolivia are (very different) cases in point. On the other hand, however, these conflicting objectives often also have an *intrinsic* dimension in the sense that the very aim to promote democracy is challenged. To the extent that processes of democratization provoke political destabilization, lead to escalating conflict or threaten the governability of a given political regime, the prospects of democracy itself are thwarted. In this sense, the aforementioned electoral victory of Hamas also sparked the fear that a Hamas-led Palestinian government might, once in power, undermine democracy. In the case of Bolivia, the political changes initiated by the Morales government did in fact provoke open resistance in the country – driven mainly by the former elites – and temporarily brought the country to the brink of civil war.

These examples already show that recipient countries face the same problem of conflicting objectives. Democratization may either be seen as threatening the interests in political power and/or economic resources of particular ruling individuals, political factions or social forces, or "collateral damages" of democratization may be regarded as undermining the very process of democratic development. Recent global developments have also more generally led to a questioning of the notion that democratization necessarily constitutes the best path towards peace and well-being. Prominent occurrences include the escalation of (violent) conflict that has accompanied recent transitions away from authoritarian rule (from Afghanistan and Iraq to Egypt and Libya) as well as the success of authoritarian developmental states (most notably of China) in terms of economic development and poverty reduction. In general, comparative research suggests that democratization does in fact increase the risk of civil war (cf. Cederman et al. 2010), while "there is little evidence that democracies are better at promoting economic growth than non-democratic systems" (Beetham 2012, 384).[9]

For peacebuilding, the expectation that democratization along the lines of liberal democracy is good or even necessary for the establishment of a lasting civil peace is obviously crucial. This is, in the end, what the paradigm of liberal peace is largely about. Now, this paradigm has been heavily criticized by peacebuilding scholars. In general, it is broadly acknowledged that the actual ways in which liberal democracy is promoted in contemporary peacebuilding frequently does not meet this expectation.[10] Still, even those critical scholars that go beyond the claim that the problem lies either with a poor/incoherent implementation of the liberal peace paradigm or with the fact that it is being combined with (neo) liberal economic reforms tend to stick to fairly idealistic premises. These scholars convincingly argue that peacebuilding – and, thus, the promotion of democracy as a part of it – has to incorporate local voices and, as a consequence, should be open to somehow hybrid, and thus less liberal-democratic, solutions (cf. Jarstad and Belloni 2012; Leeuwen et al. 2013; Lidén 2009; Mac Ginty 2011; Millar et al. 2013; Richmond 2011). Yet, it is at times not sufficiently recognized that also a domestically driven search for locally appropriate (hybrid) ways of organizing political rule is prone to spark serious political conflict in the countries at hand. This can be exemplified, once again, by referring to the case of Bolivia. The fierce domestic resistance against the changes initiated by the Morales government was not merely an attempt of formerly privileged sectors to prevent a redistribution of political power and economic resources; it was also directly related to an attempt to profoundly transform the existing democratic regime in post-liberal ways so as to correspond better to the interests and values of the country's indigenous majority population (cf. Wolff 2013). For so-called post-conflict societies, the probability will be even higher that locals will hold divergent, if not mutually exclusive, conceptions about how to construct a just political order.

Another issue related to the problem of conflicting objectives is that, in parts of the (critical) scholarship on peacebuilding, there is a certain tendency to focus on the contestation of ideas and paradigms: liberal or Western versus local or alternative (cf. Chandler 2013, 32). At times, it seems that the official aim of peacebuilding – namely, to build peace – is not seen as problematic, but only the potentially divergent notions and conceptions of peace. In contrast, the research on conflicting objectives in democracy promotion suggests that it is crucial to also include the much more mundane interests – in terms of economic resources, political power or security – that coalesce with identities and values in the politics of international democracy promotion. In this sense, it is important to consider that the normative aim to promote democracy (and, for that matter, peace) is also regarded as a strategic interest, and that the ways in which normative goals such as democracy and peace are conceptualized are also shaped by particular interests and power relations – just as the definition of "material" interests is not objectively given but, in its own terms, is shaped by ideational and normative predispositions. Examples for this coalescing of interests and norms in democracy promotion include the US, with its explicit focus on promoting liberal (market) democracy and pro-Western segments of civil society, or Germany, with its Civilian Power–like preference for change through rapprochement, which is very much in line with the interests of Germany's export sector (cf. Wolff et al. 2014).

Intrinsic legitimacy: contesting the substantive justice of liberal democracy promotion

In democratic theory, output legitimacy is distinguished from (and then combined with) input legitimacy – the kind of legitimacy that is not based on results and effects but on what goes into the political process. In this sense, it is basically the participation of the people that is seen as endowing democratic regimes with legitimacy (cf. Scharpf 1999, 7–10). In a way, this is the intrinsic legitimacy of democracy: the legitimacy democratic regimes create by functioning democratically. In creatively appropriating this concept for the analysis of democracy promotion, one can now argue that the crucial input on which the intrinsic legitimacy of democracy promotion rests is, precisely, the intrinsic "goodness" of democracy. In normative terms, the legitimacy of democracy promotion is based on the assumption that there is a universal value of and, in fact, a commitment to democracy (Schraeder 2003, 25–26; Sen 1999). To the extent that all human beings have an entitlement – a moral, if not even a legal right – to democracy, bringing democracy to people living under nondemocratic or not sufficiently democratic conditions is legitimized in the name of global (political) justice.[11] From a critical perspective, the observation that "democracy is a universal aspiration and the claim to promote it has mass appeal" rather points to the "ideological dimension" of democracy promotion (Robinson 1996, 16). But for our discussion, the result remains the same: a crucial ingredient of the belief in the legitimacy of democracy promotion is the assumption that democracy – and, more precisely, liberal democracy – is the one universal embodiment of a just political order.[12]

Again, the debate and practice of democracy promotion in the 1990s was very much shaped by such a belief in liberal democracy as the virtually uncontested, universal template of political order (cf. Burnell 2000b, 39). In recent years, however, this ideological taken-for-grantedness of liberal democracy has been increasingly questioned, both in academic circles and in the political world. Recent scholarship in the area of democracy promotion has, for instance, demonstrated how a process of ideological decontestation has led practitioners and scholars of democracy promotion to forget about the essential contestability of democracy (Kurki 2010, 2013). Taking the contested nature of any concept of democracy into account implies that the aim of democracy promotion can no longer be regarded as intrinsically just and thus per se legitimate – but as the contingent (hegemonic) result of "conceptual politics" that necessarily involves power struggles (cf. Hobson and Kurki 2012). The *theoretically* contested nature of democracy as a concept is far from a new phenomenon. But, in contrast to the 1990s, it has today become *empirically* manifest in a revival of political contestation of, and actual divergence from, liberal democracy. In most different shapes and ways, many countries[13] outside the established democracies of the North-West claim their right to pursue their own path of political development, which frequently deviates more or less significantly from the mainstream concept of liberal democracy: examples include China and Putin's Russia, Turkey under the government of the Justice and Development Party (AKP) and post-revolutionary Egypt, Bolivia or Venezuela in Latin America, as well as African countries such as Ethiopia or Rwanda (cf. Burnell and Youngs 2010; Morozov 2013; Wolff 2013; Wolff et al. 2014).

As a result, the liberal universalist premises that either implicitly or explicitly underlie the whole endeavor to globally spread democracy are theoretically and empirically questioned. The set of norms and institutions associated with the mainstream model of liberal, representative democracy-cum-market economy[14] can no longer – in fact, could never – be assumed to necessarily represent the kind of political order that will be perceived as appropriate and just by the supposed beneficiaries. The need to recognize local conceptions of democracy (or of just political order, more broadly defined), however, raises difficult normative questions (Poppe and Wolff 2013): to what extent can or should democracy promoters revisit and adapt their own norms and values in light of specific local conditions and demands? What are democracy promoters to do if they find locally prevailing conceptions of political rule problematic or even unacceptable on normative grounds? And, given that there are competing conceptions of just political order within the target countries, to what extent should external actors take sides in favor of their own normative predispositions? In their day-to-day activities, democracy promoters are frequently confronted with these kinds of questions, for example when they have to decide whether (and under what conditions) they should support indigenous justice systems alongside ordinary state law – justice systems that often count on high local legitimacy but, at least in part, clash with core liberal rights. As far as I can see, such issues are usually dealt with in an ad hoc manner rather than being based on some kind of general normative reasoning that would require, for instance, identifying some core or basic rights that a given democracy promoter may regard as nonnegotiable.

In the debate about peacebuilding, this *problematique* is generally acknowledged, at least by a series of critical scholars that have increasingly pointed to the need to think about and study the emergence of hybrid or post-liberal forms of peace that may emerge from the interaction between externals and locals in peacebuilding (cf. Jarstad and Belloni 2012; Mac Ginty 2011; Mac Ginty and Richmond 2013; Millar et al. 2013; Richmond 2011). Still, most scholars tend to hold fast to some specific normative model, which is still regarded as universally just (democratic, emancipatory), even if more or less different from mainstream (neo)liberal conceptions (Leeuwen et al. 2013; Sabaratnam 2013; cf. Chandler 2013, 32). A case in point is the approach of "social peacebuilding" that emphasizes social and economic rights as sources of peace (Lidén 2009, 621).[15] In other cases, the recognition of hybridity does not at all affect the explicitly liberal normative stance of the scholars. For Jarstad and Belloni, for example, hybridity emerges from the interaction and coexistence of "liberal and illiberal norms, institutions, and actors"; the only peaceful alternative to "liberal peace governance" is then a "victor's peace" in which war has ended simply "because the opposition has been defeated decisively" (Jarstad and Belloni 2012, 1–2).

In general, there is little discussion about what to do when local values point in directions that are regarded as decidedly anti-emancipatory – as judged from the perspective of the given scholar. The scholarship on peacebuilding is certainly more advanced than democracy promotion research in terms of empirically assessing "local conceptions of peace and justice" (Lidén 2009, 622) as well as investigating the processes of interaction between externals and locals.[16] But there seems to be just as much need for normative considerations about how to deal, both academically and politically, with the unescapable tension between one's own substantive normative standards and the just as normative recognition that others have the right to also fundamentally disagree (cf. Leeuwen et al. 2013; Lidén 2009). At least as long as we are talking about democracy promotion (within or outside peacebuilding), external actors cannot but work towards a specific political regime (democracy) which may be defined more or less narrowly but, in any case, imposes normative limits to local adaptation.[17]

Procedural legitimacy: challenging the procedural justice of liberal democracy promotion

In research about the legitimacy of the European Union (EU), the dimension of throughput legitimacy has been added to the typology of input and output legitimacy in order to grasp "the space between the political input and the policy output." The focus here is "on the quality of the governance processes": "Throughput is process-oriented, and based on the interactions – institutional and constructive – of all actors engaged in EU governance" (Schmidt 2013, 5). With a view to democracy promotion, the notion of throughput legitimacy points to the question of how external actors intervene in the shaping of political order in other countries. This procedural dimension is arguably crucial for the acceptance or rejection of the very practice of democracy promotion. Even if, in a given target country, democratization along liberal-democratic lines is generally seen as both strategically promising (instrumental legitimacy) and substantively just (intrinsic legitimacy), local actors may still dispute the legitimacy of the ways in which external democracy promoters support such a process.

In general terms, there is basic agreement among scholars of democracy promotion that the more coercive the instruments employed by external actors, the higher the probability that it will be perceived as an unjust intervention in the internal affairs of another country (cf. Burnell 2008, 421; Pangle 2009, 33; Schraeder 2003, 26–27). In this sense, the use of military force or economic sanctions have rarely been seen as a legitimate way of promoting democracy.[18] Still, the backlash against democracy promotion has forced practitioners and scholars to also recognize the contested (procedural) legitimacy of even peaceful democracy promotion via democracy assistance: As Thomas Carothers has noted, the recent backlash has

> drawn attention to the question of norms concerning democracy assistance. When and in what ways is it legitimate for governments to regulate, and if they wish, to also prohibit externally sponsored democracy aid activities on their territory? Or looked at from the other side, what right do democracy aid providers have to carry out their work in other countries?
>
> (Carothers 2010, 67)

Remarkably, up to now democracy promoters have largely avoided addressing these kinds of questions – as can be seen in the case of the aforementioned debate about restrictions on the foreign funding of NGOs.

As was briefly summarized earlier, the so-called phenomenon of a closing space (Carothers and Brechenmacher 2014) for civil-society support reflects a worldwide trend that is neither limited to a certain region nor to certain types of political regimes. In terms of procedural legitimacy, the underlying problem that is brought up here concerns the lack of established, "formalized norms" that would internationally regulate (enable and constrain) democracy assistance, "despite decades of active democracy aid efforts in more than 100 countries" (Carothers

2010, 68). As Carothers recounts, the range of activities associated with democracy assistance – including civil-society support – largely emerged, in the 1980s and 1990s, as a de facto practice, which was focused on target governments that were moving towards democracy and generally welcomed the support.[19] Today, democracy promoters argue that what they do has already become a customary practice and is therefore legitimized. But, in the end, their core justification rests on the notion that "governments which fall short on democracy are entitled to less political sovereignty than democratic governments" (ibid., 70). Recipient governments, in contrast, frequently highlight problems associated with the issue of procedural legitimacy: they question the very nature of the process by which external actors select and then support domestic civil-society groups, often without any control, at times not even with knowledge of the government that is supposed to exercise the authority over the given country. While the legitimacy (democratic and otherwise) of those recipient governments may be questionable, there is no doubt that external actors, in and of themselves, have no democratic legitimacy whatsoever when it comes to participating in internal political struggles. Correspondingly, democracy promoters emphasize the nonpartisan nature of their involvement and the need for local ownership. Yet in terms of procedural legitimacy, the question remains largely unresolved of how "countries" can effectively "own" external democracy assistance programs if it is not through the control exercised by those state institutions that are to politically represent the society at hand.

While states have been the core actors in the area of democracy promotion, the field of peacebuilding has been very much shaped by the UN, namely by the Security Council, the Secretary-General and a series of specialized UN agencies. As a consequence, the establishment of international norms of peacebuilding is certainly more advanced. Security Council mandates have even included the legal use of coercive means by external actors to further goals related to democratization. The *legality* of such activities and missions, however, does not necessarily translate into procedural legitimacy in the eyes of those that are supposed to benefit from them. The problem at hand is that the same norms and decisions that officially empower external authorities thereby denounce the principle of ownership (Chesterman 2004, 237–242). As local ownership, however, is crucial for establishing procedural legitimacy, the ownership problem looms large in the debate about peacebuilding (cf. Chesterman 2004; Jarstad and Sisk 2008; Mac Ginty and Richmond 2013).

Discussion

In an ideal world for democracy promoters, the three sources of legitimacy mutually reinforce each other: the positive side effects of democratization confirm the notion that (liberal) democracy is the universal model of a good or just political order, just as universal support of democracy strengthens its capacity to contribute to peace and development. This (re)produces broad local approval of the measures taken by external democracy promoters, which by increasing the effectiveness of democracy promotion further strengthens legitimacy across all three dimensions. In the same way, however, doubts about or open challenges to the legitimacy of democracy promotion in the three dimensions can reinforce each other: if democracy does not perform as expected, this also tends to undermine the belief in its intrinsic quality. Doubts about the functional utility and the universal goodness of democracy mean that external actors that claim to promote it will also face greater scrutiny, just as mistrust of external democracy promoters may cause a general mistrust of the very concept of (liberal) democracy that is associated with a given external actor.

As shown, there are increasing signs that democracy promotion – certainly not everywhere, but in a rising number of countries – is confronted with the latter dynamic. As Carothers and Brechenmacher conclude, the current context of serious challenges to democracy promotion "is not a temporary aberration from the earlier trend of growing acceptance of democracy and rights support around the world," but "should be understood as the 'new normal'" (2014, 31). Dealing with this multiple crisis of legitimacy is, however, far from easy. Very generally, the previous discussion points to three basic dilemmas with which democracy promotion – and with it liberal peacebuilding – are confronted. The first dilemma concerns the need to democratize the way in which democracy promotion is conducted. This is, in fact, a dilemma because it can only be resolved if and when the recipient country is fully democratized (whatever that means) and the external actor is entirely deprived of any authority – but then there is no external democracy promotion left, and none needed. The second dilemma concerns the tension between intrinsic and procedural legitimacy. On the one hand, democracy promotion is justified by the supposedly universal nature of the thing it promotes. On the other hand, however, if the very process of promoting democracy is to be democratized, the very aim of democracy promotion has to become part of the political debate. The third dilemma concerns the issue of power. To the extent that external actors try to promote democracy in another country, they aim at empowering the respective society ("to govern itself"); however, in shaping political dynamics and structures in this country, democracy promoters necessarily exercise power over this society and, thus, contribute to a status of (relative) disempowerment. This problem is, again, fundamentally unresolvable because, on the one hand, any kind of democratization implies a redistribution of power and, therefore, meets with resistance on the part of those whose vital interests are threatened by this redistributive process. Democracy promotion, if it is to take its declared aim seriously, has to work against such powers. On the other hand, however, democracy promoters are themselves part and parcel of global structures of domination that pose systematic limits on collective self-determination – and that are reproduced, if not strengthened, by the very kind of practices that are supposed to promote democracy.

Concluding remarks

The crisis of peacebuilding is closely related to a set of serious challenges to the international practice of democracy promotion. Elsewhere (Wolff 2014b,

280–284), I have argued that these challenges should lead democracy promoters to stop promoting democracy as an aim and instead rethink their role in terms of being external actors that accompany complex and contradictory internal search processes that neither have a predefined end nor follow a known path. Rather than working towards a specific end point of political development, democracy promoters would then try to support a peaceful and inclusive process of constructing a political order appropriate for the specific country. This, strictly speaking, implies stopping democracy promotion as defined at the outset of this chapter.

The good news for peacebuilding is that there is not a correspondingly fundamental questioning of the very aim that constitutes this international practice, namely peace (important discussions about competing notions of peace notwithstanding). As democracy promotion *within peacebuilding* is but an instrument or strategy, this should enable scholars and practitioners of peacebuilding to much more openly ask the question whether external actors should at all actively promote a specific way of organizing/institutionalizing political rule.[20] As far as I can see, there is not yet much knowledge of what international peacebuilding that explicitly refrains from democracy promotion could look like. Very generally speaking, an alternative could be to rather support spaces and settings – "infrastructures for peace" (Kumar and De la Haye 2012), if you will – in which (competing) local actors figure out local solutions to local conflicts. In doing so, it might be promising to draw on some of the norms and institutions that are part of the broad and contested norm set we usually call democracy – but this would be a problem- and context-specific decision, not a dogmatic one. The primary normative guideline would then be the well-known "do no harm," modified in terms of the principle "to reduce harm" rather than the however genuine aim to "do good." In case of doubt, external actors would focus on the aim to minimize the use of physical violence and systematic political repression (reduce harm), and abandon objectives related, for instance, to competitive elections or liberal constitutionalist principles (do good). This would not only facilitate broad agreement about shared basic principles (of nonviolent conduct of conflict), both among and between external and local actors, but would also better respond to the uncertainties and risks that are inherent to processes of democratization.

Whether the aim is to promote democracy or to build peace, political experience and academic research tells us that what external actors can achieve is rather limited, while the potential for collateral damage is considerable. Beyond the need to critically review, rethink and redesign actual practices of democracy promotion and peacebuilding, there is, therefore, also good reason to refocus our attention – both as practitioners and as scholars – on the indirect contributions external actors make and can make to indirectly *enable* rather than directly *promote* democracy and peace: For instance, activities to reduce asymmetric interdependencies in the area of international economic relations, changes to the international trade and investment regime that increase the discretionary power of developing countries, and efforts to reregulate the global financial markets could all be crucial measures to create more policy space, reduce distributive tensions within countries and, generally, improve the international and/or socioeconomic conditions for democratic self-determination (cf. Teivainen 2009, 277). It might well turn out that such indirect contributions will prove more helpful to inclusive and peaceful processes of political change in other countries than the kind of direct interventions on which the debate is all too often focused.

Notes

1   This chapter is based on the presentation "Democratization, Legitimacy and Peace: Inspiration and Irritation for Peacebuilding from Democracy Promotion Research and Practice" held at the international symposium "Peacebuilding in Crisis?" January 23–25, 2014, Osnabrück. The author thanks the participants of this symposium and, in particular, the editors of this volume for comments.

2   These categories are far from neatly separated as the range of actors includes, for instance, para-state and consulting organizations that implement official development projects or the partially supranational/government-like (Commission of the) European Union.

3   This *problematique* only dissolves if we assume that (1) the collective right to autonomy/self-determination is, in the end, only the expression of an individual right held by all human beings and that (2) there is only one model of (liberal) democracy that satisfies this individual right to autonomy/self-determination. In this case, the right to collective self-determination becomes an individual right to liberal-democratic self-governance. I have discussed the relationship between self-determination and democracy (promotion) elsewhere (Wolff 2014a).

4   The Central American countries that experienced civil war have, of course, also been targets of international (liberal) peacebuilding (cf. Kurtenbach 2010; Pearce 1999).

5   In fact, US President George W. Bush likewise exacerbated the latter credibility problem as he also intensified the cooperation with and actual support of autocratic partners in the context of the so-called War on Terror (cf. Carothers 2007).

6   These changes have even led to a debate on "autocracy promotion" as a counterweight to democracy promotion (Burnell 2011, chap. 11) – a debate, however, that tends to lose sight of the fact that de facto support of authoritarian regimes is also common practice among North-Western democracies, both historically speaking and today.

7   The distinction between input and output legitimacy has been coined by Fritz Scharpf (1999, chap. 1). On the additional dimension of throughput legitimacy, see, for instance, Schmidt (2013). The extent to which my usage of this typology departs creatively from this typology is explained later with a view to each individual dimension.

8   This argument is summarized and critically assessed in Spanger and Wolff (2007).

9   As Beetham (2012, 384) summarizes, "there is evidence that they [democracies, JW] perform better in promoting human development, as defined by the United Nations Development Programme in a wide range of indicators, including life expectancy, literacy and educational achievement." However, this relation is at best "one of contingent probability" (ibid., 385), as exemplified by cases such as Cuba and Singapore (in terms of absolute levels of human development) or China and Vietnam (in terms of relative improvements in the recent past).

10   For only a small selection of prominent contributions from different theoretical perspectives, see Jarstad and Sisk (2008); Millar et al. (2013); Newman et al. (2009); Paris (2004); Tadjbakhsh (2011); and Zürcher et al. (2013).

11   Whether internationally established norms or even international law can be seen as containing something that resembles an entitlement or right to democracy, is, of course, very much contested (cf. Fox and Roth 2000). Still, in some way or another, the belief that democracy is based on universal values and/or universal human rights is a central source of legitimacy in democracy promotion.

12 This and the following discussion of the (in)justice of democracy promotion draws on Poppe and Wolff (2013).
13 Most notably, this concerns incumbent governments, but usually their claims find significant resonance within their respective societies.
14 Within this overarching mainstream model of liberal democracy there is, on closer examination, of course a great deal of variation between different democracy promoters and over time (cf. Kurki 2013).
15 To be sure, Oliver Richmond – the main representative of this approach as discussed by Lidén – is, at the same time, one of the scholars most aware of this problem (cf. Richmond 2011).
16 For an overview of this scholarship, see Mac Ginty and Richmond (2013).
17 Such limits may refer to free and fair elections (as in the minimalist definition of electoral democracy) or to a set of core political and civil rights (however specifically selected and defined).
18 A different (albeit related) question concerns the effectiveness of coercive instruments of democracy promotion. The mainstream view, here, is that coercing other countries to be free is not impossible but rarely successful (cf. Downes and Monten 2013; Grimm 2010).
19 Of course, democracy promoters at that time also directed "some work to authoritarian countries, such as Burma and Cuba. In those cases the question of norms was simply a standoff – the governments in question denied external actors any access, or greatly limited the access on the grounds of national sovereignty, and democracy promoters did what they could" (Carothers 2010, 68–69).
20 This suggestion is also supported by the empirical finding that peacebuilding missions "can bring peace to war-torn countries, but they seldom bring democracy" (Zürcher et al. 2013, 1).

References

Azpuru, D., Finkel, S. E., Pérez-Liñán, A., and Seligson, M. A. (2008). Trends in democracy assistance: What has the United States been doing? *Journal of Democracy*, 19(2), 150–159.
Beetham, D. (2012). Democratization and human rights. Convergence and divergence. In J. Haynes (Ed.), *Routledge Handbook of Democratization*. Routledge, London, 381–394.
Burnell, P. (2000a). Democracy assistance: The state of the discourse. In P. Burnell (Ed.), *Democracy Assistance. International Co-operation for Democratization*. Frank Cass, London, 3–33.
Burnell, P. (2000b). Democracy assistance: Origins and organizations. In P. Burnell (Ed.), *Democracy Assistance. International Co-operation for Democratization*. Frank Cass, London, 34–64.
Burnell, P. (2008). From evaluating democracy assistance to appraising democracy promotion. *Political Studies*, 56(2), 414–434.
Burnell, P. (2011). *Promoting Democracy Abroad. Policy and Performance*. Transaction, New Brunswick, NJ.
Burnell, P., and Youngs, R. (Eds.). (2010). *New Challenges to Democratization*. Routledge, London.
Carothers, T. (1991). *In the Name of Democracy. U.S. Policy Toward Latin America in the Reagan Years*. University of California Press, Berkeley.
Carothers, T. (2002). The end of the transition paradigm. *Journal of Democracy*, 13(1), 5–21.
Carothers, T. (2007). The democracy crusade myth. *National Interest*, 90, 8–12.

Carothers, T. (2010). The continuing backlash against democracy promotion. In P. Burnell and R. Youngs (Eds.), *New Challenges to Democratization*. Routledge, London, 59–72.

Carothers, T. and Brechenmacher, S. (2014). *Closing Space. Democracy and Human Rights Support Under Fire*. Carnegie Endowment for International Peace, Washington, DC.

Cederman, L.-E., Hug, S., and Krebs, L. F. (2010). Democratization and civil war: Empirical evidence. *Journal of Peace Research*, 47(4), 377–394.

Chandler, D. (2013). Peacebuilding and the politics of non-linearity: rethinking "hidden" agency and "resistance". *Peacebuilding*, 1(1), 17–32.

Chesterman, S. (2004). *You, the People: The United Nations, Transitional Administration, and State-Building*. Oxford University Press, Oxford.

Diamond, L. (2008). *The Spirit of Democracy. The Struggle to Build Free Societies Throughout the World*. Times Books, New York.

Downes, A. B., and Monten, J. (2013). Forced to be free? Why foreign-imposed regime change rarely leads to democratization. *International Security*, 37(4), 90–131.

Fox, G. H., and Roth, B. R. (Eds.). (2000). *Democratic Governance and International Law*. Cambridge University Press, Cambridge.

Grimm, S. (2010). *Erzwungene Demokratie. Politische Neuordnung nach militärischer Intervention unter externer Aufsicht*. Nomos, Baden Baden.

Grimm, S., Leininger, J., and Freyburg, T. (Eds.). (2012). Do all good things go together? Conflicting objectives in democracy promotion [Special issue]. *Democratization*, 19(3), 391–414.

Hobson, C., and Kurki, M. (Eds.). (2012). *The Conceptual Politics of Democracy Promotion*. Routledge, London.

Jarstad, A. K., and Belloni, R. (2012). Introducing hybrid peace governance: Impact and prospects of liberal peacebuilding. *Global Governance*, 18(1), 1–6.

Jarstad, A. K., and Sisk, T. D. (Eds.). (2008). *From War to Democracy: Dilemmas of Peacebuilding*. Cambridge University Press, Cambridge.

Kumar, C., and De la Haye, J. (2012). Hybrid peacemaking: Building national "infrastructures for peace". *Global Governance*, 18(1), 13–20.

Kurki, M. (2010). Democracy and conceptual contestability: Reconsidering conceptions of democracy in democracy promotion. *International Studies Review*, 12(3), 362–386.

Kurki, M. (2013). *Democratic Futures: Re-visioning Democracy Promotion*. Routledge, Abingdon.

Kurtenbach, S. (2010). Why is liberal peace-building so difficult? Some lessons from Central America. *European Review of Latin American and Caribbean Studies*, 88, 95–110.

Leeuwen, M., Verkoren, W., and Boedeltje, F. (2013). Thinking beyond the liberal peace: From utopia to heterotopias. *Acta Politica*, 47(3), 292–316.

Levitsky, S., and Way, L. A. (2005). International linkage and democratization. *Journal of Democracy*, 16(3), 20–34.

Lidén, K. (2009). Building peace between global and local politics: The cosmopolitical ethics of liberal peacebuilding. *International Peacekeeping*, 16(5), 616–634.

Mac Ginty, R. (2011). *International Peacebuilding and Local Resistance: Hybrid Forms of Peace*. Palgrave Macmillan, Basingstoke.

Mac Ginty, R., and Richmond, O. P. (2013). The local turn in peace building: A critical agenda for peace. *Third World Quarterly*, 34(5), 763–783.

McFaul, M. (2010). *Advancing Democracy Abroad. Why We Should and How We Can*. Rowman & Littlefield, Lanham, MD.

Millar, G., Van der Lijn, J., and Verkoren, W. (Eds.). (2013). Frictions in peacebuilding interventions: The unpredictability of local-global interaction [Special issue]. *International Peacekeeping*, 20(2).

Morozov, V. (Ed.). (2013). *Decentering the West. The Idea of Democracy and the Struggle for Hegemony*. Farnham, Ashgate.

NED (2006). *The Backlash against Democracy Assistance. A Report Prepared by the National Endowment for Democracy for Senator Richard G. Lugar, Chairman, Committee on Foreign Relations United States Senate*. National Endowment for Democracy, Washington, DC.

Newman, E., Paris, R., and Richmond, O. P. (Eds.). (2009). *New Perspectives on Liberal Peacebuilding*. United Nations University Press, Tokyo.

Pangle, T. L. (2009). The morality of exporting democracy. A historical-philosophical perspective. In Z. Barany and R. G. Moser (Eds.), *Is Democracy Exportable?* Cambridge University Press, Cambridge, 15–34.

Paris, R. (2004). *At War's End. Building Peace after Civil Conflict*. Cambridge University Press, Cambridge.

Paris, R. (2010). Saving liberal peacebuilding. *Review of International Studies*, 36(2), 337–365.

Pearce, J. (1999). Peace-building in the periphery: Lessons from Central America. *Third World Quarterly*, 20(1), 51–68.

Poppe, A. E., and Wolff, J. (2013). The normative challenge of interaction: Justice conflicts in democracy promotion. *Global Constitutionalism*, 2(3), 373–406.

Richmond, O. P. (2011). *A Post-liberal Peace*. Routledge, London.

Robinson, W. I. (1996). *Promoting Polyarchy. Globalization, United States Intervention and Hegemony*. Cambridge University Press, Cambridge.

Sabaratnam, M. (2013). Avatars of Eurocentrism in the critique of the liberal peace. *Security Dialogue*, 44(3), 259–278.

Scharpf, F. W. (1999). *Governing in Europe: Effective and Democratic?* Oxford University Press, Oxford.

Schmidt, V. A. (2013). Democracy and legitimacy in the European Union revisited: Input, output and "throughput". *Political Studies*, 61(1), 2–22.

Schraeder, P. J. (2003). The state of the art in international democracy promotion: Results of a joint European-North American research network. *Democratization*, 20(2), 21–44.

Sen, A. (1999). Democracy as a universal value. *Journal of Democracy*, 10(3), 3–17.

Sharp, J. M. (2012). *Egypt: Transition under military rule*. Congressional Research Service. (http://fpc.state.gov/documents/organization/194799.pdf) Accessed: 1 March 2015.

Smith, T. (1994). *America's Mission. The United States and the Worldwide Struggle for Democracy in the Twentieth Century*. Princeton University Press, Princeton, NJ.

Spanger, H.-J., and Wolff, J. (2007). Why promote democratisation? Reflections on the instrumental value of democracy. In M. van Doorn and R. von Meijenfeldt (Eds.), *Democracy: Europe's Core Value? On the European Profile in World-Wide Democracy Assistance*. Eburon, Delft, 33–49.

Tadjbakhsh, S. (Ed.). (2011). *Rethinking the Liberal Peace. External Models and Local Alternatives*. Routledge, London.

Teivainen, T. (2009). The pedagogy of global development: The promotion of electoral democracy and the Latin Americanisation of Europe. *Third World Quarterly*, 30(1), 163–179.

Wolff, J. (2012). Democracy promotion, empowerment, and self-determination: conflicting objectives in US and German policies towards Bolivia. *Democratization*, 19(3), 415–437.

Wolff, J. (2013). Towards post-liberal democracy in Latin America? A conceptual framework applied to Bolivia. *Journal of Latin American Studies*, 45(1), 31–59.

Wolff, J. (2014a). *The question of self-determination in international democracy promotion.* PRIF Working Paper 19. (http://www.hsfk.de/fileadmin/downloads/PRIF_WP_19.pdf) Accessed: 1 March 2015.

Wolff, J. (2014b). Democracy promotion as international politics: Comparative analysis, theoretical and practical implications. In J. Wolff, H.-J. Spanger, and H.-J. Puhle (Eds.), *The Comparative International Politics of Democracy Promotion.* Routledge, London, 253–288.

Wolff, J., Spanger, H.-J., and Puhle, H.-J. (Eds.). (2014). *The Comparative International Politics of Democracy Promotion.* Routledge, London.

Zürcher, C., Manning, C., Evenson, K. D., Hayman, R., Riese, S., and Roehner, N. (2013). *Costly Democracy. Peacebuilding and Democratization after War.* Stanford University Press, Stanford, CA.

6 Adapted instead of imported

Peacebuilding by power-sharing[1]

Andreas Mehler

Introduction

Institutions proposed in a peacebuilding strategy or concomitant norms diffused
are not necessarily what is taking hold on the ground. Exporting something is one
act; importing is a different one. For instance, resistance and adaptation are typical strategies undertaken by elites of divided societies to avoid unwanted effects
of external brokerage. Agency has to be taken into account on what appears to
be the passive receiving end. Criticizing the foreign architects of peace orders as
overly self-confident, arrogant or naïve is probably allowed and justifiable, but
one would also be strongly naïve by chanting the song of 'the local'. Political,
juridical and administrative institutions have to be adapted to a context in order
to function, but there could be as well cases of overadaptation, that is a readiness of Western institution-builders to accommodate specific interests of politicians in the target society. Thereby, the question arises: who is defining what
the local contexts, culture, interests and concerns really are? There is in fact no
reason to believe that self-declared local actors know better or are well inten-
tioned. The 'local turn' is far from being able to provide a guarantee for better
outcomes in peacebuilding practice. More neutrality is indicated in analyzing the
international–local interplay at work in peacebuilding practices. In this chapter
I describe potential sources of resistance to the homogenous global discourse on
peacebuilding including its institutional devices, in particular regarding political power-sharing arrangements, as well as consequences of forms of adaptation
that could be fairly remote from initial intentions. Peacebuilding, if this ever
was the right word, is a political process that involves interests beyond that of
preserving peace, but which is also defined to a significant degree by legacies and
capacities[2] – both locally and internationally – that are not always favourable
for achieving the elusive goal of peace. Those motivations may revolve around
access to natural resources, preservation of geostrategic balances or ideological
preferences.

The line of argument of this chapter is as follows:

- Exporting political and administrative institutions without a look at the process of reception/import is only half of the story.

- The concept of power-sharing is one of the standards – and frequently translated into a set of various institutions – diffused to postwar settings.
- Local stakeholders always exhibit a behaviour towards power-sharing institutions – oscillating between adoption, adaptation and resistance. This behaviour may differ in different phases of peacebuilding, that is from the agreement to employ power-sharing in a post-conflict setting to the implementation process of power-sharing arrangements.
- Reasons for adaptation and resistance can be manifold and are path dependent. They may depend on culture including political culture, religion and ideologies, and (local or national) actor constellations, or also on the course or outcome of a war (and hence are not universal).
- Adaptation takes place in the blind spot of international engagement, in the lapse between political engagement and technical implementation of institutional reform meant to foster principles of power-sharing.
- Power-sharing could be at the same time a local standard and a recipe advocated by external institutional engineers. In this case, it may be chosen without much resistance.

The literature on norm diffusion is certainly at home in the political science's subdiscipline of international relations (e.g. Risse et al. 1999; Acharya 2004). It focuses on the way(s) in which international interdependence is shaping domestic decision-making. The focus is on ideas, norms and policies promoted by governments and international organizations. The reverse side of norm diffusion is norm reception and there is still little systematic research on the receiving end – with a problematic tendency to frame reactions on the ground in terms of 'compliance'. This chapter focuses on power-sharing as a concept containing norms (the principle that power should be shared between the main components of a polity/society) and related institutions. I do this more particularly with political power-sharing. I will first deal briefly with the issue of whether it qualifies as such a 'diffused norm', that is whether we can observe the diffusion of a standardized power-sharing norm, before turning to the receiving end. I will argue that studying processes of coercion, learning or emulation (see Gilardi 2012) is not about putting those in focus to whom the norm should be transferred. Instead, those at the receiving end have the options to resist, to ignore or to adapt a policy coming from outside. The perspective on norm reception allows for a deeper understanding of the nature of the relationship between norm-diffusing agencies and the multifaceted 'local' agency structure. The latter may have distinctive interests and sociocultural dispositions to deal with norm diffusion.

Power-sharing as a standard recipe for peacebuilding and war-ending?

Over the last two decades there has been a tendency to end violent intrastate conflicts with a worldwide standard recipe ("a dominant conflict-solving approach"; Binningsbø 2013, 89) that one may describe as power-sharing. Power-sharing contains norms, institutional arrangements and distinct policies. The established debate between 'consociationalists' (associated strongly with the name of Arend Lijphart) and 'centripetalists' (associated with the names of Donald Horowitz and Tim Sisk, for example) is mostly about the issue of making democracy work in divided societies. The more recent peacebuilding debate is rather dominated by the literature on post-conflict power-sharing; it is not aiming to reach a final verdict as to what mechanism (consociational or centripetal) is working better. Most influential in the contemporary debate on power-sharing in peace agreements is the distinction between political, economic, military and territorial power-sharing, vocally advocated by Hartzell and Hoddie (2003; 2007), for example. Political power-sharing mostly relates to the distribution of key positions in government among former belligerents, but potentially also constitutionally fixed quotas for their supposed (ethno-regional or religious) backers in that regard. Economic power-sharing varies between arrangements aiming at an equitable control of important state companies or wealth-sharing dispositions (e.g. with regard to income from the export of mineral resources). Military power-sharing deals with the filling of top military positions, could also include recruitment quota, or may regulate the incorporation of rebel army units in the national army. Territorial power-sharing is mostly about the introduction or modification of a federal system, decentralization or the attribution of territorial autonomy to one province. Though variations certainly matter, one could say that most recent peace agreements and processes contain one or more forms of power-sharing; this is particularly true in Africa (Mehler 2009).

The regional distribution of subforms of power-sharing displayed in Table 6.1 already suggests some significant variation. Take only two elements that could

Table 6.1 Peace agreements and power-sharing 1989–2006[1]

World region	Number of peace agreements	with Political power-sharing	. . . Military power-sharing	. . . Territorial power-sharing
Europe	9	2	1	7
Asia	17	4	3	6
Africa	48	20	32	15
Americas	5	0	1	1

(Note that the number of ongoing armed conflicts in Asia and Africa were more or less similar over this time span, but significantly lower in the Americas and in Europe, according to Uppsala Conflict Data Program (UCDP) figures; see Themnér and Wallensteen 2014.)

[1]Data from the Power-Sharing Event Dataset (PSED) at GIGA (www.giga-hamburg.de/en/project/PSED). Economic power-sharing, the fourth category of power-sharing according to Hoddie and Hartzell (2005), is rare and left out in this table. The PSED defines the present subforms of power-sharing in this way:

- Political power-sharing encompasses all instances when senior and/or nonsenior cabinet positions are shared between government and rebels. It also includes instances when rebel representatives are given guaranteed seats in the national parliament.
- Military power-sharing encompasses the military integration of rebel fighters into the national army, police or paramilitary forces and/or the establishment of shared command structures.
- Territorial power-sharing encompasses all instances of devolution and/or autonomy.

inspire some avenues of future reflection: power-sharing was not a standard solution to end violent conflict in Latin America. This may be related to the nature of violent conflicts that are perceived as occurring less between ethnic or religious groups (although the 'indigena' problematic has gained prominence over the last decade), and more between social classes (indigenas being more or less confined to the lower strata of the population) – but it could also be a function of the absence of indigena elites ready to be co-opted.[3] Europe shows a good deal of territorial power-sharing and this represents the opposite picture in an extreme way – violent conflicts were mostly about territorial autonomy (Bosnia, Kosovo, Georgia, Moldova and Macedonia).

I have argued elsewhere that the presence of strong norm-diffusing agents in peace processes translates systematically into efforts to enshrine consociational elements like grand coalition, mutual veto, proportionality as the standard for political representation and group autonomy in postwar constitutions (Mehler 2013). Evidence from Burundi, Comoros, the Democratic Republic of the Congo, Nepal and Sudan over the period 2001–2010 (where those conditions were present) was juxtaposed to cases where constitutional change in postwar situations did not include tangible efforts to manage the divisions within society by constitutional design. I found that external norm-diffusing agents – particularly UN agencies, the African Union and the European Union – were strong in the former and weak in the latter cases. Political power-sharing in the name of inclusivity was obviously the norm most strongly advocated.

But variation may be much more accentuated on the receiving end. One should not exclude different understandings of political power in different world regions or in different types of polities. For example, one preponderant interpretation of African power politics is to stress its patrimonial side. More frequently than not (but with notable exceptions and to varying degrees), African politics is about securing allegiance in exchange for sinecures – extended to upcoming young officials in one's own party, some opponents or 'independent' politicians credibly claiming to represent a certain ethno-regional constituency. To share power while remaining ultimately in a position to redistribute those power positions is a well-established behaviour for the heads of patrimonial regimes. The classical examples for such behaviour are probably DR Congo or Kenya. The patrimonial logic did not change with the occurrence and proposed solution of violent conflict.

In contrast, in some non-African civil wars we have witnessed a much more uncompromising behaviour from both rebels and governments. A case in point is Sri Lanka, suggesting that the disposition to sign power-sharing agreements is unevenly distributed around the globe. This disposition may be contingent on culture, religion, political ideologies (e.g. role of ethno-nationalism) and actor constellations, the outcome of a war as well as external military interventions – and while not completely area-bound, some combinations of factors, however, may then be contingent on world regions.

International peacebuilders and mediators favour negotiated solutions to civil wars that contain some form of power-sharing (*and* consociationalism). Reasons for this preponderant strategy may be either associated with political convictions or experiences of international mediators (e.g. solutions advocated by South African mediators may resemble the history of an elite pact solution to the country's own transition process in the early 1990s) or may look less costly than other forms of war termination necessitating more international commitment (Walter 1997). But certainly, what mediators and peacebuilders want and what they get is not identical: the growing convergence at the global stage in what is proposed to 'solve' a conflict is by no means identical with what is the outcome on the ground, as imported blueprint solutions face a mixture of resistance, ignorance or adaptation by local actors.[4]

Explaining varying responses to norm diffusion

This chapter seeks to sketch out a series of thinkable variants with alterations to the blueprint approach (as diffused by international norm-setting actors) and give illustrations of local rationales for reacting in specific ways from case evidence across two world regions. 'Compliance' versus 'noncompliance' is certainly an oversimplified dualism of reactions that can be observed.[5]

Generally, one may want to distinguish four different types of reactions to norm diffusion:

- Ignorance: local actors do not listen to or react to proposed norms from international norm diffusion agents.
- Resistance: local actors actively oppose the transfer or translation of norms and concomitant institutions.
- Adaptation: local actors change gradually, and to varying degrees, the name or content of norms plus their related institutions.
- Adoption: local actors accept norm diffusion and concomitant institutions as proposed from the outside.

Both adoption and ignorance will not be dealt with in this chapter, as agency on the receiving end appears to be absent. Adaptation and resistance, by contrast, involves action and potentially also strategic behaviour, while they could be based on quite different context conditions – this is what I want to investigate.

For the illustrative purpose of this chapter this will not be done in a *systematic* comparison between cases. I will concentrate on political power-sharing and select cases from Africa and Asia, as those are the two continents that have experienced similarly high numbers of armed conflicts and settlements over the period selected. The political culture, that is an established pattern of behaviour based on norms and attitudes of many African states (or their elites), is still strongly influenced by a patrimonial understanding of politics. One may want to argue that the adoption, or at least an adaptation, of political power-sharing devices is in conformity with important elements of the preponderant political culture here. It is less evident that a common heritage is at work all over Asia. But it appears as if the political culture of many Asian states is strongly uncompromising – potentially due to ideological divides, the relative weight of religion or bipolarity between contending groups. A winner-takes-it-all disposition is prevalent on both sides of many conflicts, government and rebels alike (see Sri Lanka). One may want to argue that resistance to political power-sharing is in conformity with such attitudes in this region. The schematic argument developing from this observation is that a patrimonial culture is more open to co-optation and coalition-building, while in a winner-takes-it-all culture it would be counterintuitive to accommodate winners and losers in a power-sharing mode. Although it is an exaggeration to speak of uniform African or Asian cultures in this regard – given some variations within each area – there is every reason to believe that such norms are not distributed equally over the globe.

The following paragraphs will shed some light on the supposed link between political culture and attitudes towards power-sharing with (1) an analysis of resistance to power-sharing at two stages (mediation and implementation) and (2) an analysis of adaptation processes.

Resistance to peacebuilding by power-sharing

The literature on peacebuilding is in general quick in using the term spoiler to characterize singular parties in the peace process when, from the perspective of peace negotiators, they fail to behave as expected (Stedman 1997). This terminology conceals more than it reveals: conflict parties have interests, sometimes very legitimate ones, and some of those may be harmed by the substance of a peace deal. Some rebel movements have won a war, but lost the peace, arguably this was the case for the Liberians United for Reconciliation and Democracy (LURD) rebels in Liberia after the 2003 peace agreement, manifesting itself in 2005.[6] A peace order is not necessarily favourable to everybody. As a consequence, resistance to peace negotiations and agreement implementation should not be described overtly in pejorative, but rather in analytical terms.

Robert D. Benjamin, dealing with problems of mediation in everyday conflicts, analyzes (US-specific) cultural (religious and moral) resistances to negotiation and mediation on the level of individuals (Benjamin 1999); there is no reason to believe that resistances by groups and/or their spokespersons should be less accentuated in intrastate conflict mediation. Resistance to imported blueprint solutions ending violent intrastate conflict can come in different ways. One may want to distinguish between the resisting actors (as they typically have different resources to resist) and also between moments of resistance. Obviously, there can be resistance both by government and rebel movements to engage in the initial mediation of power-sharing, as well as later in the process of implementation.[7]

Let me start with the timing aspect. One influential explanation of war termination, and particularly its timing, is the paradigm of "ripeness for resolution" put forward by I. William Zartman. He posits that enduring conflicts often lead to a situation of fatigue on both sides of a war or a "mutually hurting stalemate":

> Parties resolve their conflict only when they are ready to do so – when alternative, usually unilateral means of achieving a satisfactory result are blocked

and the parties feel that they are in an uncomfortable and costly predica-
ment. At that ripe moment, they grab on to proposals that usually have been
in the air for a long time and that only now appear attractive.

(Zartman 2001, 8)

It is obviously a rational choice assumption that war cannot be stopped at
any time, but only when its cost is perceived as unbearable, when it has become
a negative-sum game for both sides. War fatigue is then the explanation for
giving into a mediated end of hostilities. Zartman himself is more cautious in
further developing his argument. He admits that ripeness is a necessary condition but not a sufficient explanation of war termination. There must be more
to end a war. Ripeness theory is therefore not fully predictive, but could at least
identify necessary elements for productive inauguration of negotiations. And in
hindsight, Zartman admits that some refinements to his original thoughts were
necessary – mostly pertaining to the "pluralised politics on both the perceptions
and uses of ripeness." Perceptions arguably depend strongly on prior experiences.
One additional thought seems of particular interest for this study. Resistance may
develop from a particular hardliner strategy of quickly justifying renewed struggle
by focusing on *pain* (not synonymous with costs). 'Just' struggles call for greater
sacrifices, and it may be difficult for hardliners to admit that a stalemate will not
be overcome. This thought brings patterns of justification to the fore, and here
the relevant cultural registers may differ from one case to the next. One obvious
category of justifications for necessary sacrifices is of a religious nature. Conflict
parties with a faith-based mobilization strategy can, on the one hand, call on
their followers to resist pressure quite easily; on the other hand, they might find
it harder to compromise on problem-solving formulas that only partly meet the
group's original target goals (i.e. power-sharing). To illustrate, one may think of
the divide between moderate and radical Taliban in Afghanistan or the contrasting positions in Mali's civil wars between Tuareg (repeatedly open towards negotiating a power-sharing solution) and radical Islamists (though outside mediators
would also not have favoured their inclusion).

War fatigue is in fact a phenomenon frequently encountered, but it does not
necessarily translate into the end of war. Actor behaviour linked to specific political cultures may have to be taken into account. While most recent armed conflicts in sub-Saharan Africa ended with power-sharing agreements, this was not
the case in the Casamance conflict in Senegal. In fact, since about two decades
ago one can read reports from the Casamance province where a low-intensity
conflict is ongoing and where ordinary people from the Diola ethnic group (associated with the rebellion) would qualify as being *fatigué de la guerre*. But this
fatigue has not helped in completely ending the war. Why is this so? Organizational, material and more 'cultural' arguments can be found in the literature. The
segmentation of the rebel movement and the ensuing inability to make binding
decisions for all factions is an organizational argument. Additionally, one won-
ders whether the fatigue of the population needs to be complemented by a fatigue
of the combatants who live well from an ongoing war economy (export of cashew,
cannabis, timber; see Evans 2005); this is the material argument. Interestingly,

other, much more culturally specific arguments, have been put forward by country specialists with regard to the behaviour of combatants, including the better chances for young male combatants to get married in the context of a difficult 'wedding market' and the wish to stop migration of Diola women to the capital Dakar (Foucher 2005, 450) – a culture-bound argument not to give in to compromise solutions.

Power-sharing could be persuasive at least for those who are set to gain from it, and mostly on the rebel side, (a) when inner-core positions of a given polity are redistributed, it could solve the security dilemma of rebels (e.g. when defence and security portfolios are attributed to them), and (b) when important material sinecures are given out to a broader range of rebel leaders. One major result of a recent quantitative analysis is that inclusiveness of power-sharing is indeed a success factor, but just as suggested by option (b) – when this includes a broader range of rebel leaders in secondary positions (instead of distributing some critical top positions to only few rebel figures) (Mehler et al., forthcoming).

Resisting mediation towards power-sharing solutions

Obviously, not showing up at negotiations or not signing the final documents are forms of resistance at the disposal of all parties. For example, in Sudan's Darfur conflict, on numerous occasions only some rebel movements joined the negotiations.[8] Resisting mediation could be a tactical or a principled position, as will be shown in the following – potentially fitting Stedman's distinction between 'total' or 'greedy spoilers' – though, again, this perspective may contain a strong evaluative element and is likely to only look at the rebel side. Hard-line resistance to mediation can be found mostly when a conflict party views power as nonnegotiable absolute power.

On the rebel side, we frequently face one phenomenon in sub-Saharan Africa: rebel movements split when parts of the movement's leadership sign a ceasefire or peace agreement. This can frequently be explained tactically: only the signing leader reaps benefits from an agreement. Those left behind work for the next round of concessions (Tull and Mehler 2005). Alternatively, raising the stakes by stepping out of the peace process may result in a better deal in terms of demobilization arrangements or co-optation of more leading figures of a rebellion. But there might also be other factors at play for not accepting mediated solutions, including the valorization of organizational cohesion, path-dependency/ experience with prior peace negotiations/distrust setting in when commitments were not held and so forth. Those experiences include (respected/disrespected) power-sharing deals. Again, one could assume that a firmly entrenched patrimonial culture – where the sharing of spoils is 'normal' – strengthens the belief that promises are kept. However, just one failure to do so can harm trust between belligerents for a long period.

In DR Congo's multiple episodes of war in the Kivu provinces we have witnessed a recurrent pattern of splits/creation of new armed movements standing for mainly Tutsi interests and renewed attacks whenever a localized quasi-monopoly of power (i.e. per region) was given up in the course of the peace process. This can be observed from the first splits of the Rassemblement Congolais pour la Démocratie (RCD), over the rise and fall of Laurent Nkunda's Congrès national pour la défense du peuple (CNDP) to the more recent creation of the M23. Obviously, it is essential to understand the origin and early phases of the Congo war[9] to correctly interpret current behaviour of nominally different movements today (Simons et al. 2013). The readiness to negotiate by all belligerents was still comparatively strong, despite many instances of disrespect for a negotiated settlement (from both government and rebel side). A completely tactical use of resistance to mediation could be observed in the Liberian case where Movement for Democracy in Liberia (MODEL) and LURD delegates at the peace talks in Accra (Ghana) in 2003 were reported to have maintained contact with combatants on the ground by cell phone.

> On at least one or two occasions [. . .] a faction representative who was insistent on winning certain ministries in the government, but found himself blocked, used the shelling for leverage. He made a call on his cell phone to the front lines, ordering more shelling into Monrovia. All watched live on television as mortar rounds landed in Monrovia. The opposing parties at the talks then granted that faction what it wanted, witnesses say.[10]

Note that this was not resistance to power-sharing but to a proposed concrete formula of power-sharing.

The main impression when dealing with African cases is that it was fairly easy to convince conflict parties to agree, in general terms, to a power-sharing arrangement – be it Liberia, Côte d'Ivoire, Mali, Guinea-Bissau, Comoros, Sierra Leone, Chad, DR Congo or Burundi. But, as descriptive statistics from the PSED database show, nonsenior cabinet portfolios, not belonging to the 'inner core' positions within a regime, were frequently granted to African rebel groups (Ottmann and Vüllers 2014). Giving out positions of limited responsibility may not translate into the sharing of political power in a strict sense. However, in a patrimonial context, it could be highly valued – particularly as a material basis to organize a following and to strengthen patron–client relations.[11]

Cases in Asia look different: Cambodia's peace process in an early phase in 1988–1989 was characterized by the involvement of many outsiders (18 states, but also the UN). The peace conference in Paris 1991, cochaired by France and Indonesia, was failing inter alia in promoting a consensual power-sharing formula for a transitional period before elections, but some compromise solutions were signed (including on early elections and some principles of a new constitution). The Khmer Rouge resumed fighting in 1992, issued a boycott call for the upcoming legislative elections and tried to prevent citizens from voting (and consequently rejected election results). Instead of joining a unity government, the Khmer Rouge founded a schismatic Provisional Government of National Union and National Salvation of Cambodia. Only military setbacks and the defection of thousands of troops in 1996 created a new situation, and the organization dissolved in 1999. Resistance was therefore already recorded during a negotiation phase and continued during implementation on the battlefield.

The Philippines represent an interesting case where we have three instances of agreements without political power-sharing (1995 and 1996, both in the context of coup plots, and the 2001 Mindanao autonomy movement). In the first two events, a series of reform commitments in different sectors were given, but never did the association of rebels to public affairs stand at the centre. How can this be interpreted? One explanation could be the rather early occurrence of the two first events when the norm of power-sharing was eventually weaker than after 2001. Given the type of conflict we witness in the Philippines, it is remarkable that a form of political power-sharing was apparently never on the bargaining table. The main item was how much power would be vested in a new territorial unit on Mindanao. The government showed a strong reluctance to share the essential element of power with a clearly religiously motivated rebel movement.

It appears as if compromises on the sharing of political power in core decision-making positions were rather difficult to find for mediators in at least those Asian cases inspected in this chapter.

Resisting the implementation of power-sharing

Promises of power-sharing and actual implementation can be at strong variance; they can also have diverging effects (Ottmann and Vüllers 2014). While some ingredients of power-sharing can be rather quickly implemented (and under international scrutiny), like the formation of a unity government, this is more time-consuming for elements of power-sharing that need long technical prep-aration, for example, decentralization or the introduction of a federal system. Wealth-sharing formulas may also need a long technical preparation. However, governments of national unity as core elements of political power-sharing are sometimes formed only by name but not in substance. The belief not to have obtained a fair share in a peace deal or having accepted a deal at a time of weak-ness could push conflict parties to leave governments of national unity.[12]

After an initial failure, the conflict parties of Cambodia in 1991 finally signed a UN-sponsored peace agreement that included political power-sharing within the legislature. A balanced Supreme National Council was formed (six mem-bers of the Cambodian government, two members of Khmer People's National Liberation Front [KPNLF], one member of Front Uni National pour un Cam-bodge Indépendant, Neutre, Pacifique, et Coopératif [FUNCINPEC] and two members of the Khmer Rouge). However, at least one conflict party, the Khmer Rouge, resisted implementation and remained active until its last political lead-ers surrendered in late 1998. Considerable difficulties evolved also with regard to the establishment of transitional justice mechanisms. Whether this is simply the expression of a case-unspecific inability of societies to deal with widespread and brutal terror involving victims and perpetrators of the same society or whether it could rather be linked to a "theravada-buddhist and animist tradition of a Cam-bodian resistance to remember" (Oettler 2006, quoting Weggel 2006) may need further discussion. Cambodia is an example for upright resistance to the diffusion of power-sharing even in the long run.

Nepal is a case where a formal peace agreement between Maoist rebels and civilian parties in November 2006 went hand in hand with the elaboration of an interim constitution (2007), with strong elements of political power-sharing including a consensus government out of all 'seven parties' under the aegis of a prime minister selected by political consensus and participation of education-ally, socially or economically backward groups 'in state structures on the basis of principles of proportional inclusion'. It is noteworthy that the 'universal norms' behind all this were difficult to grasp in the period preceding the agreement, with the main active foreign power in Nepal's crisis, namely India, displaying considerable ambiguity with regard to the maintenance of the unpopular and manipulative monarchy under King Gyanendra (Destradi 2012). The complex text with many more consociational elements was not implemented and could only serve as a model for a permanent constitution to be elaborated by a Con-stituent Assembly (CA; elected in April 2008) whose mandate was prolonged time and again, without succeeding in elaborating a permanent constitution. However, the CA abolished the monarchy in a first spectacular move. Between the agreement and the end of 2011, the cabinet composition changed 10 times, mostly with Maoists moving in or out of the government. After a negative vote for its candidate for the job of prime minister in the CA, the CPN (M) (Communist Party of Nepal [Maoist]) still had a relative majority and refused to form a government. This move threatened to plunge the country into a new crisis and to undermine the peace agreement. After 10 days of negotiations, the Maoists' conditions for the formation of a government still failed to produce agreement. But finally, a compromise was found to elect the prime minister by a simple vote, and the CPN (M) leader Prachanda then won the premiership by a large margin; Prachanda stepped down in 2009 when he failed to get sup-port to sack the army chief, again producing a political crisis. In sum, there was strong resistance against the spirit of the mediated solution from the commu-nist party – the result of the mediation was not in conformity with its maximal-ist positions of aspiring to absolute power and there were many attempts to opt out of an agreement.

In the Central African Republic (CAR), a political dialogue with about 350 members was held in September 2003 in the presence of two African presidents (Omar Bongo and Denis Sassou Nguesso), but coup leader and President Fran-çois Bozizé did not feel forced to translate the detailed recommendations into practice, let alone constitutional change. The substance of power was not shared with his contestants. A second 'inclusive' political dialogue process was strongly suggested by the mediator Bongo (Gabon). From 8–20 December 2008, it culmi-nated in an important gathering of about 200 elite members in Bangui under the chairmanship of former Burundian President Pierre Buyoya. The formation of a government of National Unity was one of the main conclusions of the gather-ing. In its aftermath, Bozizé simply formed a somewhat extended government, but did not start palpable institutional reforms and also refrained from giving out inner-core power positions (Mehler 2011). One may speculate about the moral authority of a two-time coup leader (Buyoya) to sell the international norm of associating opponents in the exercise of power – as well as about the CAR experience in doing so: André Kolingba, in a post-electoral crisis phase in 1992 and under strong international pressure, associated his main challengers in the exercise of power during a transitional year before new elections were held (and lost by Kolingba). Ange-Félix Patassé, the winner of those elections faced three army mutinies in 1996–1997 and accepted the formation of a somewhat extended government – including rebel ministers – without curtailing his preeminent power position. It is the deep knowledge about precedents that may help in interpreting specific actor behaviour.

In short, resistance to the implementation of a power-sharing arrangement can be found in different cultural settings, but it may take different forms. While resistance to mediation is rather rare in most African cases, one would find more instances of resistance to implementation on the continent. However, the CAR example shows that it was not the principle of power-sharing as such that was contested; the Bozizé government rather subverted the norm of inclusivity in the blind angle of international engagement. It must be stated that Bozizé also lost internal acceptance due to this behaviour, provoking new rounds of violence and finally his downfall. The Khmer Rouge's outright rejection of the power-sharing formula is at the opposite end of the spectrum of potential reactions. Those features appear generalizable:

- Conflict parties' behaviour oscillates between adoption, adaptation and resistance to what is proposed in peace negotiations by outsiders.
- Tactical resistance – frequently found in the negotiation phase – can be overcome.
- Principled resistance – manifesting itself during the negotiation phase – is difficult to overcome.
- Legacies and path dependency can explain trust/distrust in proposed negotiated solutions or rather specific institutions. But the general political culture, religion and ideologies seem to explain much more the propensity to accept political power-sharing in the first place.
- Resistance to implementation may give way to strategies of adaptation that seek to alter the balance of power negotiated during a mediation phase.

Adaptation

In a two-case comparison between the settlement of post-electoral violence in Kenya and Zimbabwe, Cheeseman and Tendi (2010) have coined the Kenyan way out of the crisis as "politics of collusion." In Zimbabwe, by contrast, the political power-sharing deal had to be imposed upon the players and most prominently on President Robert Mugabe. Veto-players worked against the implementation of a power-sharing spirit resulting in "politics of continuity," that is holding the now associated opposition movements in junior positions (in our categorization this could be interpreted as "resistance to implementation"). Although those two cases are not cases of civil war termination but settlement of episodes of electoral violence, they underline one argument of this chapter: the disposition to accept power-sharing is variable and hinges probably on a specific preestablished 'culture' of inter-elite relations. Kenya would clearly qualify as a case of nonresistance. It may also be a case of adaptation. Agenda 3 of the peace accord (resolving the political crisis by power-sharing) translated into the formation of a grand coalition. But characteristic for Kenya's power-sharing agreement was the postponement of several aspects to be dealt with by a number of commissions. The so-called Agenda 4 (legal, constitutional and institutional reform; poverty and inequality; unemployment; land reforms; national cohesion and unity, as well as accountability and impunity) was left to Kenyan stakeholders and was effectively addressed only after negotiators had left the country.[13] This permitted opinion leaders and legislators to inquire and discuss at some length relevant reforms. Adaptation in this case could be equated with giving/taking an opportunity to find appropriate solutions to complicated questions – including power relationship between the office of the prime minister, the office of the vice president and the office of the head of civil service and secretary to the cabinet. In the end, the president's camp was seen as still retaining disproportionate power, at variance with the spirit of the mediated agreement.[14]

Resistance to power-sharing was limited in most African cases, as we have seen, although one finds many examples of delaying strategies and subtle subversions during the implementation of power-sharing agreements. Those are the precursors of adaptation strategies in the medium term, that is long after international mediators and peacebuilders have left the scene. Such adaptations have the potential to change the rationale of an original agreement. In Liberia, the members of the postwar power-sharing government formed in 2003 were excluded from the 2005 elections ending a transitional phase. Not excluded from elections were a number of strongly tainted, former political actors who were not part of this government. This resulted in the election of some warlords (e.g. Prince Johnson and Adolphus Dolo) into the country's senate – maybe not the most powerful position, but certainly also not an intended result of the international mediators.

Burundi's peace process has seen extraordinary efforts by outside mediators to move the conflict parties to accept a model strongly influenced by the consociational ideal. This paradoxically depoliticized to a fair degree the major Hutu–Tutsi split (as intended), but it was certainly not the intention of negotiators that a new dominant party with authoritarian habits would install itself within this framework. Precisely this happened, although one can still claim that the consociational constitution precluded the ruling Conseil National pour la Défense de la Démocratie–Forces pour la Défense de la Démocratie (CNDD-FDD) from more openly changing the rules of the game (Vandeginste 2011).

DR Congo's transitional government established in 2003 associated four vice presidents from three armed and one unarmed opposition movements with President Joseph Kabila. Cabinet positions included representatives of further armed movements and civil society.[15] The ensuing constitution, adopted by a popular referendum at the end of 2005, was already less inclusive with its semi-presidential content providing for both a president and a prime minister. However, it allowed for the president to retain a strong position, including, amongst others, the prerogative to appoint the prime minister, to dissolve the parliament and to rule by decree (Art. 69–89). Importantly, no regulations to continue a grand coalition government (for the period following the transition phase) were maintained. At the same time, devices for group autonomy were contained within the text. However, the situation in North and South Kivu during the transition was in contradiction to provisions of the national power-sharing accord: both provinces were under the control of a 'monopolist', with the RCD in charge of the former and the Kabila faction of the latter (Simons et al. 2013). One could safely say that this was not the intention of the mediators – again a case of adaptation.

Resistance may give way to adaptation, as adaptation can serve the interests of local stakeholders without generating much international concern: in Côte d'Ivoire the power-sharing formula mediated by France in 2003 attributed the defence and the interior portfolios to the rebels – ministries that would give them preponderance on all security issues. The presidential camp distanced itself immediately from the agreement upon the delegation's return, declaring the text a simple draft needing refinement. But the formation of a government of national unity remained on the agenda. At a new summit in Accra under the aegis of the Economic Community of West African States (ECOWAS) on 7 March 2003, the rebels of the Forces Nouvelles got two senior ministries (territorial administration and communication). The consensual Prime Minister Diarra was able to build a grand coalition including 10 ministries for the Front Populaire Ivoirien (FPI) and seven each for Rassemblement des Républicains (RDR) and Parti Démocratique de Côte d'Ivoire (PDCI), while nine went to the rebel union Forces Nouvelles plus six to smaller parties. A compromise was found regarding the interior and defence ministries, which went to technocrats. The façade of power-sharing was maintained, but the powers of the incumbent president were not strongly affected. The independent prime minister, together with the handful of technocrats in government, was still not able to influence government policy in key respects. The formation of this government was only about the sharing of spoils and the not sharing of power. The Ivorian example shows that a long drawn-out diplomatic process may also end up in adaptation to existing power relations.

In sum, while outright resistance to power-sharing is rare in most contemporary African cases, there are far more experiences with adaptation (i.e. efforts to twist elements of a peace deal in order to limit its intended effects perceived as dangerous in the eyes of strong local players). Simple adoption of a persuasive institutional package may be witnessed as a result of mediation, but the long drawn-out process of implementation of power-sharing institutions will result almost naturally in some form of adaptation, if not resistance leading to new crisis (and eventually new rounds of negotiation).

Conclusion

One could certainly find more examples where a clearly spelled-out intention by mediators met resistance or adaptation resulting in a much different outcome, suggesting that norm diffusion is not more than half of the story within norm transfer processes.

Two important lessons for peacebuilding practices can be drawn from this analysis:

- Different phases of peacebuilding may see different attitudes towards power-sharing. While negotiators representing belligerents may be less resistant to adopt power-sharing institutions during negotiations, the most powerful actors may try at least to adapt the proposed set of institutions to their preferences in the implementation phase – once international attention has waned. *For practitioners it is important to look into the effects of any modifications and delays during implementation of key institutions as they could reverse the logic of peacebuilding.*
- Political power-sharing, that is the distribution of core positions in the government and the state apparatus among the main conflict parties, may be in line with a dominant political culture among elites – or not. Experiences with certain types of institutions may preclude their use or help reinstating them. Peacebuilding agents can expect strongly varying degrees of acceptance, based on a dominant view of what the essence of politics is or should be. *This means that those involved in proposing institutional solutions need a strong knowledge of a country's history in order to select realistic options.*

Based on this sort of evidence, one could cautiously claim that the general tendency of less resistance and more adaptation in Africa, and more resistance without adaptation in Asia, is confirmed, although there are exceptions in both geographical zones where path dependency and the actual power relations determine strongly whether resistance is at all an option. We have seen that the variations in resisting, ignoring or adapting blueprint solutions are so important that it is perfectly advisable to look deeper into cases with particular actor constellations, cultural repertoires, ideologies and professed justifications, but also precursor events to refine more general assumptions. An in-depth case knowledge helps to explain not only why blueprint solutions are eventually rejected, but also to highlight the manner in which they are sometimes only half-heartedly or parsimoniously implemented or so strongly adapted to local contexts over time – after the political momentum of international mediation has waned – that they function quite differently from what the standard solution was proposing. This is in itself not a bad thing, adaptation may meet the often-raised call for tailor-made solutions, but it could also well be that adaptation translates into the continuation of a specific form of hybrid governance that was not innocent in creating the causes of violent conflict or civil war in the first place.[16] Path dependency looks important.

The vast majority of power-sharing occurs in Africa, and this disproportionately so, even when taking into account the number of terminated civil wars. Distinct event patterns across world regions suggest that power-sharing means different things in different contexts. This should invite generalists to be more cautious in proposing universal iron-clad rules. Scholars in the peacebuilding field may have to seek merely contingent generalizations.

In parallel, we have seen that some elements of resistance are well distributed over cases and areas, particularly moving in and out of governments of national unity in order to get a favourable adjustment of a peace deal or as a sign of protest against the watering down of the original spirit of power-sharing. This should invite case specialists to be less assertive about the particularity of their area of expertise.

Notes

1 The chapter builds on insights from two ongoing research projects funded by the German Research Foundation (DFG): 'Power-Sharing in Post-conflict Situations. On the Institutional Prerequisites for Lasting Peace' and 'The Local Arena of Power-Sharing. Patterns of Adaptation or Continued Disorder'. The latter is a four-country (eight-arena) qualitative comparison; the former works with a combination of methods including the building of a large-N dataset. I am indebted to Franzisca Zanker, Martin Ottmann and Johannes Vüllers who added important refinements to my argument. All imperfections are to be attributed to the author. An earlier version of this chapter was presented at the ISA convention in San Francisco in 2013.

2 Donald Horowitz in an oral input to the fourth Institutions for Sustainable Peace conference, held in Hamburg on 9–10 April 2015, made this point very vocally; antecedents would strongly determine institutional preference in target societies.

3 Indigena movements largely focus on material grievances and justice issues. Access to land, fighting corruption and so forth are on their agenda – much less so elite co-optation. For an overview of major issues see Flesken (2014).

4 The difference between promises and practice was first strongly made by Jarstad and Nilsson (2008).

5 Zimmermann (2015) looks into processes of resistance, compliance and localization of norm diffusion when it comes to human rights. Her discussion of a three-step translation process, including translation into domestic discourse, law and implementation could potentially also be relevant for power-sharing.

6 Or at least for the ethnic Mandingo constituency behind them, remaining in a very vulnerable position 10 years after the peace agreement of Accra in 2003 (one may interpret Liberia as a case of elite power-sharing without ensuing consociationalism).

7 Implementation may also meet societal resistance, but this will as a rule be motivated by majority resistance against minority quota/veto/rights (to be) enshrined in consociational constitutions (Horowitz 2008). I will therefore not deal with this perspective.

8 For example, on 5 May 2006 the government of Sudan signed an accord brokered by the African Union and the US in Abuja with one faction of the Sudan Liberation Army (SLA; the faction led by Minni Minnawi), but the agreement was rejected by the Justice and Equality Movement and a rival faction of the SLA. Libya-sponsored peace talks in October 2007 attracted only about half of the relevant movements.

9 And its link to the civil wars in both Rwanda and Burundi, where ethnocracies in power made it also very difficult to negotiate power-sharing agreements. The Burundian case deserves particular attention, the strongly institutionalized mode of conflict settlement after numerous failures in the end permitted an end to decades of violence, see Vandeginste (2009).

10 See Hayner (2007, 14). Note however, that there was obviously no clear blueprint for a postwar order in Liberia spelled out by the main negotiators. A US-inspired draft agreement keeping faction representatives out of the government was not accepted and resulted again in heavy shelling of Monrovia. The outcome is well known: all military factions were 'rewarded' with substantive positions in the interim government (see ibid., 20, criticized by Sawyer 2004).

11 Obtaining a position in public corporations in this sense could also be of benefit, even though not much power per se is attributed. In the case of Liberia, Hoffman (2004, 221) cites a LURD spokesman claiming that positions in the parastatal sector are to be preferred as the latter are too closely scrutinized by international donors; in the ports or telecommunications sectors "one was free to 'accumulate resources' without oversight."

12 The PSED database (Ottmann and Vüllers 2014) collects data on power-sharing events in 111 post-conflict periods from 1989 to 2011, including on conflict parties entering and leaving government.

13 Nigerian Foreign Minister Oluyemi Adeniji stayed on after Kofi Annan's departure, his mediation led to the signing of Agenda 4 on 4 March 2008, but not its implementation.

14 See the Kenya National Dialogue and Reconciliation Monitoring Project (2009), Agenda Item 3: Resolving the Political Crisis (Power Sharing), *Report on Status of Implementation*, January 2009. http://www.dialoguekenya.org/ (Accessed: 20 March 2013).

15 Tull and Mehler (2005) have argued, based on several cases, but most strongly concerning the DR Congo, that power-sharing of this sort creates incentives for rebels to engage in armed conflict in the first place.

16 In this sense I am much less optimistic with regards to the immediate outcomes of elite bargains rightly presented as important factors in statebuilding by Salmon and Anderson (2013).

References

Acharya, A. (2004). How ideas spread: Whose norms matter? Norm localization and institutional change in Asian regionalism. *International Organization*, 58(2), 239–275.

Benjamin, R. D. (1999). *Guerilla mediation: The use of warfare strategies in the management of conflict*. (http://www.mediate.com//articles/guerilla.cfm) Accessed: 24 March 2013.

Binningsbø, H. M. (2013). Power sharing, peace and democracy: Any obvious relationships? *International Area Studies Review*, 16(1), 89–112.

Cheeseman, N., and Tendi, M. (2010). Power-sharing in comparative perspective: The dynamics of "unity government" in Kenya and Zimbabwe. *Journal of Modern African Studies*, 48(2), 203–229.

Destradi, S. (2012). India as a democracy promoter? New Delhi's involvement in Nepal's return to democracy. *Democratization*, 19(2), 286–311.

Evans, M. (2005). Insecurity or isolation? Natural resources and livelihoods in the Casamance. *Canadian Journal of African Studies*, 39(2), 282–312.

Flesken, A. (2014, May). Indigene Mobilisierung in Lateinamerika: ein wenig genutztes Potenzial. *GIGA Focus Lateinamerika*. GIGA, Hamburg.

Foucher, V. (2005). Les relations hommes–femmes et la formation de l'identité casamançaise. *Cahiers d'études africaines*, 44(2), 431–455.

Gilardi, F. (2012). Transnational diffusion: Norms, ideas, and policies. In W. Carlsnaes, T. Risse, and B. A. Simmons (Eds.), *Handbook of International Relations*. SAGE, London, 453–477.

Hartzell, C., and Hoddie, M. (2003). Institutionalizing peace: Power sharing and post-civil war conflict management. *American Journal of Political Science*, 47(2), 318–332.

Hartzell, C., and Hoddie, M. (2007). *Crafting Peace: Power-Sharing Institutions and the Negotiated Settlement of Civil Wars*. Pennsylvania State University Press, University Park.

Hayner, P. (2007). *Negotiating peace in Liberia: Preserving the possibility for justice*. Center for Humanitarian Dialogue and the International Center for Transitional Justice. (https://www.ictj.org/publication/negotiating-peace-liberia-preserving-possibility-justice) Accessed: 22 May 2015.

Hoddie, M., and Hartzell, C. (2005). Power sharing in peace settlements: Initiating the transition from civil war. In P. G. Roeder and D. Rothchild (Eds.), *Sustainable Peace: Power and Democracy after Civil War*. Cornell University Press, New York, 83–106.

Hoffman, D. (2004). The civilian target in Sierra Leone and Liberia: Political power, military strategy, and humanitarian intervention. *African Affairs*, 103(411), 211–226.

Horowitz, D. (2008). Conciliatory institutions and constitutional processes in post-conflict states. *William and Mary Law Review*, 49(4), 1213–1248.

Jarstad, A., and Nilsson, D. (2008). From words to deeds: The implementation of power-sharing pacts in peace accords. *Conflict Management and Peace Science*, 25(3), 206–223.

Mehler, A. (2009). Peace and power sharing in Africa: A not so obvious relationship. *African Affairs*, 108(432), 453–473.

Mehler, A. (2011). Rebels and parties: The impact of armed insurgency on representation in the Central African Republic. *Journal of Modern African Studies*, 49(1), 115–139.

Mehler, A. (2013). Consociationalism for weaklings, autocracy for muscle men? Determinants of constitutional reform in divided societies [Special issue]. *Civil Wars*, 1(15), 21–43.

Mehler, A., Ottmann, M., and Vuellers, J. (forthcoming). *Slicing Up the Pie. A Disaggregated Analysis of Power-Sharing in Post-conflict Situations*. Unpublished manuscript.

Oettler, A. (2006). Vergangenheitspolitik zwischen globalen Normen und lokalen Verhältnissen. *GIGA Focus Global*, 6, 1–8.

Ottmann, M., and Vüllers, J. (2014). The power-sharing event dataset (PSED): A new dataset on the promises and practices of power-sharing in post-conflict countries. *Conflict Management and Peace Science*, 1–24.

Risse, T., Ropp, S. C., and Sikkink, K. (1999). *The Power of Human Rights: International Norms and Domestic Change*. Cambridge University Press, Cambridge.

Salmon, J., and Anderson, C. (2013). Elites and state-building. In D. Chandler and T. D. Sisk (Eds.), *Routledge Handbook of International Statebuilding*. Routledge, London, 42–51.

Sawyer, A. (2004). Violent conflicts and governance challenges in West Africa: The case of the Mano River basin area. *Journal of Modern African Studies*, 42(3), 437–473.

Simons, C., Zanker, F., Mehler, A., and Tull, D. (2013). Power-sharing in Africa's war zones: Translating peace to the local level? *Journal of Modern African Studies*, 51(4), 681–706.

Stedman, S. J. (1997). Spoiler problems in peace processes. *International Security*, 22(2), 5–53.

Themnér, L., and Wallensteen, P. (2014). Armed conflict, 1946–2013. *Journal of Peace Research*, 51(4), 541–554.

Tull, D., and Mehler, A. (2005). The hidden costs of power sharing: Reproducing insurgent violence in Africa. *African Affairs*, 104(416), 375–398.

Vandeginste, S. (2009). Power-sharing, conflict and transition in Burundi: Twenty years of trial and error. *Africa Spectrum*, 44(3), 63–86.

Vandeginste, S. (2011). Power-sharing as a fragile safety valve in times of electoral turmoil: The costs and benefits of Burundi's 2010 elections. *Journal of Modern African Studies*, 49(2), 315–335.

Walter, B. (1997). The critical barrier to civil war. *International Organization*, 51(3), 335–364.

Zartman, I. W. (2001). The timing of peace initiatives: Hurting stalemates and ripe moments. *Global Review of Ethnopolitics*, 1(1), 8–18.

Zimmermann, L. (2015). Same same or different? Norm diffusion between resistance, compliance, and localization in post-conflict states. *International Studies Review*, 1–19.

7 Transitional justice after violent conflict

The need for accountability, restorative justice and gender-sensitive approaches

Martina Fischer

Introduction

Transitional justice has come to play an important role in debates on peacebuilding – both in research and practice. The international human rights movement introduced the concept, referring to the judicial prosecution of human rights violations committed by repressive regimes in the course of democratic transition. Later on, the term also came to be used for addressing war crimes and massive human rights violations committed in violent conflicts (Kritz 1995; Minow 1998, 2002; Teitel 2000, 2014). The concept has since been adopted also by peacebuilders and its meaning has been extended. Today, it covers a variety of mechanisms, including the establishment of tribunals, truth commissions, lustration of state administrations, reparations, fact-finding initiatives, efforts for reconciliation and cultures of remembrance.[1]

The transitional justice paradigm is based on the idea that coming to terms with the past is a precondition for establishing sustainable peace between nations and social groups that have been at war with each other. From the perspective of peace and conflict research, it is necessary to assess both the chances and the risks that accompany initiatives aimed at facing the past: How can transitional justice processes be shaped in a way that enables the recognition of suffering, as opposed to fostering the burden for victims of war-related crimes? How can new conflicts be prevented from emerging from struggles over different interpretations of history? How should painful memories be addressed in a way that enables trust restoration and relationship-building in divided societies? And how can international actors support such processes?

This chapter presents an overview of the debate on transitional justice and discusses the potential of different approaches against the background of peacebuilding and conflict transformation. The chapter draws on previous publications and research. It makes reference to a more extended survey on the theory and practice of transitional justice published in the *Berghof Handbook for Conflict Transformation* (see Fischer 2011). Furthermore, it draws on results from empirical research – in particular findings from the research project *Dealing with the Past and Peacebuilding in the Western Balkans* that was conducted at the Berghof Foundation in 2010–2012 (see Fischer and Petrovic-Ziemer 2013).[2] The project focused on the interaction of international and local initiatives for transitional justice and reconciliation in Bosnia-Herzegovina, Croatia and Serbia. The field research encompassed a total of 160 interviews conducted in 28 municipalities. The comparative focus on Bosnia-Herzegovina, Croatia and Serbia was chosen because all three countries have a common history of violent ethnopolitical conflict that developed in the course of the dissolution of the former Yugoslavia. All three countries were involved in war operations that devastated Bosnia-Herzegovina in 1992–1995. The Dayton Peace Agreement obliged them to reach a peaceful settlement of conflicts, cooperation in the field of transitional justice, and unconditional support of the work of the International Criminal Tribunal for the Former Yugoslavia (ICTY).

Scholars and practitioners agree that the question of how and when a society decides to come to terms with the past is very much context-specific. Thoms et al. (2008), after having reviewed a great number of case studies and having undertaken a comprehensive literature review in the field of transitional justice, have warned that templatisation should be avoided, as what is helpful in one context may be irrelevant or even harmful in another. They have argued that practice-orientated research on the potential and limits of transitional justice approaches is needed and that policy recommendations are welcome, but that these must not aim to design blueprints in order to satisfy "policymakers' search for a 'winning formula' for broad application" (Thoms et al. 2008, 17). There are no general recipes for processes of facing the past. Experiences cannot simply be transferred from one historical or regional situation to another, but the appropriate forms for individuals and societies in coming to terms with a history of violence must develop out of specific contexts, taking account of the cultural background and societal dynamics. This chapter therefore does not seek to provide general recommendations or recipes for global application. However, some of the insights and experiences that have been made during the past two decades in the Western Balkans may be useful for enhancing the general debate.

The first section highlights the strengths and limits of international criminal justice. It argues that although legal approaches are necessary to end impunity for war crimes and gross human rights violations, their reconciliatory effects are limited, as the work of the ICTY shows; its achievements and limits have been analysed extensively both in scholarly discussions and practitioners' debates (see also our empirical findings later). Although both international and local transitional justice experts show a strong preference for legal prosecution of war crimes and crimes against humanity, they are convinced that restorative approaches are needed in addition to punitive mechanisms. Truth commissions have been applied in different contexts globally with ambivalent results. While these approaches have been framed as either-or options in scholarly debates and discussed as such by international human rights activists, activists from the Balkans hold that such mechanisms can only complement but never replace the work of the courts.

The second section outlines the need to overcome dichotomies in the debate in order to develop a more *holistic understanding of transitional justice*. It outlines the need for building institutions, establishing the rule of law and advancing human rights as a crucial element and precondition for dealing with the past in war-torn societies. Furthermore, it explains why transitional justice strategies need to be developed in a gender-sensitive way in postwar settings and illustrates how feminist discourses have so far contributed to the transitional justice debate and practice. This section finally points to blind spots, such as accountability gaps and protection gaps in international peacebuilding missions, arguing that such deficits draw into question the legitimacy of international organisations and damage the credibility of their transitional justice policies.

The third section identifies challenges for future research and practice. The chapter argues that the concepts of transitional justice and reconciliation should be seen as complementary in order to open spaces for reconciliation and conflict transformation in postwar societies. However, more conceptual clarity is still required, both in research and practice.

The potential and limits of criminal tribunals

For several decades, the literature on transitional justice has largely focused on retributive forms of justice, such as war crimes prosecution and the legal procedures of international, hybrid or domestic courts. In particular, the international tribunals established to prosecute war crimes committed in the former Yugoslavia, Rwanda, Sierra Leone and Lebanon have gained much attention. As the ICTY represented the first court implemented under the auspices of the UN, considerable research has been devoted towards evaluating its relevance for international law.[3] Together with the International Tribunal for Rwanda (ICTR), the ICTY can be considered as an important step towards the establishment of the International Criminal Court (ICC). Furthermore, the ICTY became a role model for the creation of ad hoc tribunals in Cambodia, Sierra Leone and East Timor. Hereby, the ICTY can be considered as an important example of international intervention for establishing accountability. It was explicitly mentioned in the Dayton Accords that were facilitated by international brokers between Bosnia-Herzegovina, Croatia and the Federal Republic of Yugoslavia[4] in 1995. Furthermore, international actors have insisted that the willingness of governments to cooperate with the Hague Tribunal will be a precondition for advancing EU integration. This conditionality became a crucial element of the EU Accession Policy. The literature that is available on the ICTY provides an excellent example of the potentials and limits of international criminal justice.

The Hague Tribunal as a role model of an international intervention for accountability

The ICTY, established by the UN in The Hague in 1993, has taken the lead in investigating and prosecuting war crimes and crimes against humanity committed during the 1990s in the Western Balkans. It has indicted 161 persons for serious violations of international humanitarian law[5] in a period when local institutions were unwilling or unable to investigate such crimes to an adequate extent. With regard to the relationship between external and internal actors, we find an ambivalent picture: although by signing the Dayton Peace Agreement in 1995, the governments of Bosnia-Herzegovina, Croatia and the Federal Republic of Yugoslavia had committed themselves to a peaceful settlement of conflicts; to address the consequences of war; and to cooperate in transitional justice, it took more than a decade until all of these states fully collaborated with the Hague Tribunal, and it took almost two decades until all suspects of war crimes were delivered to The Hague. Several prominent fugitives indicted by the ICTY remained at large unpunished during this period. As NATO forces had not managed to detain some of the most high-profile accused, it was argued that the ICTY lacked credibility (Kerr 2005, 325). In some areas these figures were even celebrated as heroes by nationalist politicians.[6]

The legitimacy of the tribunal has always been seen as controversial in the region itself (Banjeglav 2016; Subotic 2009, 2011). Although it had been created to command responsibility for individual guilt and war-related crimes, the ICTY was not able to communicate this message; instead, many verdicts were perceived as sentences aimed at establishing collective guilt and holding nations or countries at large responsible. In particular, many citizens in Serbia and the Republika Srpska (Bosnia-Herzegovina), regarded the ICTY from its outset as being biased – a kind of "justice of the victors" (although there is no empiric evidence to support this view, as Meernik [2005] concludes), or at least as a distant mechanism imposed from the outside (Arzt 2006; McMahon and Forsythe 2008; Spoerri and Freyberg-Inan 2008). Similar reactions were reported from Croatia (Banjeglav 2016). The limited acceptance of its jurisdiction was revealed by opinion polls, which, in turn, prompted the ICTY to set up regional offices in Sarajevo, Belgrade and Zagreb, and to initiate a public relations campaign ("outreach strategy") to maintain closer contact to the media and civil society. There are controversial assessments of the reasons for the ICTY's lack of acceptance and legitimacy. Distorted media reporting was an important factor for this dynamic (Allcock 2009; Sajkas 2007). However, the problems were also related to the tribunal's own procedures, a lack of clarity regarding its purposes and communication problems, particularly in communication between the ICTY and its local publics (Hodzic 2007a, 2007b; Mertus 2007). Trials and public declarations were published exclusively in English during the first years of the ICTY's existence.

The Hague Tribunal was criticised by human rights groups and women's organisations for focusing too strongly or exclusively on the perpetrators – assuring the protection of their rights, in part to the neglect of victims' needs. The lack of formal procedural law for victims and victims' associations was met with heavy criticism, as was the fact that victims could only be heard as witnesses. The main problem highlighted was the use of Anglo-American legal traditions, such as the practice of cross-examination, which proved to be extremely burdening for those who had been affected by crimes and who were now testifying (Franke 2006, 818). The practice of plea-bargaining, which led to extremely low sentences for several war criminals, was also seen as problematic and contributed towards damaging the tribunal's reputation. The ICTY's shortcomings have been acknowledged and explicitly named even by several insiders (Hodzic 2007a, 2007b; Hoffmann 2016).

While the ICTY's contribution to accountability has been widely acknowledged in the academic literature, the question of whether its work has contributed to the "restoration of peace and reconciliation" – as was stated in UN Resolution 1534 and promoted by high-ranking representatives of the tribunal[7] – is still a subject of controversy (Mertus 2004). On the one hand, it has been argued that the ICTY has countered the trend towards silencing or denying atrocities (Orentlicher 2008, 2010) and enhanced public discussions. On the other hand, scholars have pointed to the fact that the tribunal's sentences have also fuelled nationalist discourses (Allcock 2009, 367). There are clear indicators that some of these have fuelled hostilities in local communities, particularly in Bosnia-Herzegovina. Meernik (2005) has analysed the dynamics of conflict and cooperation among the principal ethnic groups in Bosnia-Herzegovina using statistical data from 1996–2003 and found little evidence to support the notion that the ICTY was having a positive impact on societal peace in Bosnia: "In fact, in more instances the effect was the opposite of that intended [. . .]. More often than not, ethnic groups responded with increased hostility towards one another after an arrest or judgement" (ibid., 287).

Several scholars therefore claim that it is unrealistic that the ICTY will be able to contribute towards reconciliation between former warring groups, and that expanding expectations beyond its legal mandate might "undermine the important contributions that international trials can make to post-conflict societies" (Fletcher and Weinstein 2004, 30). This example illustrates both the variety of opinions on the potentials and limits of prosecution by international criminal courts and the difficulty of assessing the impact of tribunals on war-torn societies. The legitimacy of the Hague Tribunal has always been contested and continues to be seen as controversial in the region also at present.

Although there has been and continues to be much open criticism by human rights activists regarding some of its legal practices, the ICTY has for a long period served as the only comprehensive cross-border mechanism for fact-finding and prosecution of war crimes, and it has thereby become an important point of reference for human rights and victims' groups. Even the most critical scholars and practitioners would agree that the ICTY has made an important contribution towards establishing a database of undeniable facts about massacres and atrocities, and that it has allowed for the identification of mass graves and the finding of missing persons. It is widely acknowledged that the ICTY has helped to set up important archives that will be helpful in establishing truth and accountability in the future. Local and international practitioners unanimously consider these archives as indispensable for informing future generations about the war events and crimes of the 1990s. Most of those practitioners who raised criticisms against the ICTY have also made it clear that there was no other alternative, as domestic courts were not capable of fostering accountability during the 1990s. The predominant opinion is, thus, that without this international mechanism the human rights movement in the Western Balkans would have been worse off.

The ICTY also became an important point of reference for the domestic judiciary (Petrovic-Ziemer 2013a, 2013b) because it contributed to the establishment of institutions for war crimes prosecution and training of judiciaries in the region.[8] These will continue to take on a central role and responsibility with regard to fact-finding and accountability in the future, particularly as the mandate of the ICTY is coming to an end[9] and several thousand war crime cases need to be concluded in the years to come (Hoffmann 2016).[10]

A strong preference for prosecution – results from field research

Among the protagonists of transitional justice, all actors that were interviewed in the project *Dealing with the Past and Peacebuilding in the Western Balkans* (including representatives of legal and fact-finding institutions, local civil society organisations [CSOs] and international actors) regarded war crime prosecution as indispensable. All of them explicitly acknowledged that the ICTY would contribute towards ending impunity (see Fischer 2013c, 133–135). The Commissions for Missing Persons pointed particularly to the ICTY's achievements in disclosing information on sites where atrocities had been committed. Domestic legal institutions emphasised the tribunal's role in setting norms and reforming judicial proceedings. At the same time, they considered some of its practices – in particular elements of common law, and the practice of plea bargaining – as highly problematic (see Petrovic-Ziemer 2013b). Among CSOs, divergent opinions were expressed. Most of them acknowledged that the ICTY has established evidence and created important archives, despite the serious criticisms that were voiced regarding its legal practices, effectiveness, and information policy. In contrast, representatives of war veterans' and victims' associations expressed more negative assessments, suspecting that the tribunal operated with an ethnic bias and treated criminals from the "other side" more leniently than those of "their own" constituency.

Furthermore, our study revealed that effective legal prosecution was very much dependent on a proactive cooperation with local CSOs, groups and individuals engaged in war crimes reporting and trial monitoring, those who provide psychological and legal support for victims and witnesses, or those who advance the documentation and finding of missing persons. Local human rights organisations have not only actively supported the establishment of the ICTY but also actively collaborated with the tribunal in fact-finding and in the exchange of documentation on human rights violations. In several cases, they have also provided evidence on war crimes; for instance, the videos uncovered by the Humanitarian Law Center that proved an active involvement of the Scorpions (special units from Serbia) in the murders committed after the fall of Srebrenica. CSOs have also collaborated in the accompaniment of victims and witnesses. Active support by local CSOs and legal experts, as well as the work of investigative journalists, is indispensable for implementing effective transitional justice initiatives. Such cooperation across levels is necessary in order to provide continuous war crimes monitoring and reporting and to secure psychosocial support for victims and witnesses. Experts from media and civil society served as important brokers translating the complex work of the ICTY within the broader reaches of society. Furthermore, the experience in the Balkans has shown that CSOs and investigative journalists are needed in order to pressure state institutions to open cases and create effective transitional justice mechanisms.

Our field research revealed that CSOs, transitional justice institutions and international actors have a common commitment towards legal accountability. Representatives of the judiciary, the Commissions for Missing Persons, local peace practitioners, human rights activists, representatives of victims' associations, and international organisations clearly shared the understanding that impunity cannot be tolerated, in view of the gross human rights violations committed in the territory of the former Yugoslavia during the 1990s. However, all of these transitional justice protagonists also clearly recognised the limits of legal prosecution and thus proposed additional (restorative) approaches that should complement the work of the courts.

The limits of retributive justice and the need for restorative approaches

The experience with the ICTY demonstrates the very limited scope of legal instruments in dealing with past violence. First, the international tribunal has only focused on large-scale crimes while several thousand minor cases are still pending and need to be investigated by the courts in the region. It is very unlikely, however, that all of these can be dealt with during the lifetimes of the accused and witnesses. Second, the work of the international and domestic war crimes chambers has not included compensation for the victims. This deficit was mentioned by the former president of the ICTY, Patrick Robinson, in a speech at the UN Security Council in December 2009. He in turn proposed that a "claims commission" be set up through which victims would be able to lodge compensation claims.[11] In November 2011, again, he called upon UN Member States to support the establishment of a trust fund, arguing:

> The Tribunal cannot, through the rendering of its Judgements alone, bring peace and reconciliation to the region. Other remedies must complement the criminal trials if lasting peace is to be achieved, and one such remedy should be adequate assistance to the victims for their suffering.[12]

For both of these reasons, transitional justice protagonists in the Western Balkans are convinced that, in addition to criminal justice, restorative forms of justice and truth-finding need to be advanced, giving a voice to the victims and address their wish for acknowledgement, material and symbolic compensations. The campaign for a Regional Commission for Truth-seeking and Truth-telling about War Crimes in the Former Yugoslavia (REKOM)[13] evolved around this idea.

The REKOM campaign was successful in engaging a variety of different actors, including peace practitioners, human rights activists, women's and youth groups, journalists, intellectuals, and also several veterans' and victims' groups (although only a small number of the latter are involved). Those who promoted the initiative all agreed on one common denominator: that a regional commission should mainly focus on *fact-finding*. Transitional justice protagonists in all three countries saw a need to establish a set of undeniable facts about past war events, as a point of reference for a "shared truth" and as a means of counteracting tendencies of silencing or the denial of war-related crimes. International promoters of the REKOM campaign also shared this expectation and hoped that a regional commission could help in establishing a climate that, in future, will enable people to accept the prevalence of different and opposing views, a space to create empathy, and a forum for debating history (Fischer 2013b). Peace practitioners and human rights activists also expressed hope that a regional commission would enhance societal debate and dialogue on the past and help to establish inclusive cultures of remembrance. Furthermore, a number of human rights activists and victims' representatives were convinced that REKOM should also provide space and give a *voice to the victims* of war-related crimes. Despite these positive sentiments, the hearings that have been held during the campaign have also aroused considerable controversy (Petrovic-Ziemer 2013b). In particular, the question of how to provide psychological support and protection for those who tell their stories in public settings remains unresolved. The same applies to the question of how the victim's testimonies can be verified and whether they can be transformed into "facts" so as to receive official acknowledgment.

Meanwhile, around 1,900 individuals and groups from different ex-Yugoslav countries support the initiative.[14] They have received support from several high-ranking politicians, as for instance former President Josipovic of the Republic of Croatia. But it remains to be seen whether the idea will gain the necessary support from a critical mass of political institutions and societal actors in the region. The idea of establishing a cross-border truth commission that addresses the regional dimension of the conflicts is historically unprecedented. It is important to mention that the consensus that has been found among those who promote the idea of a regional truth commission somehow reflects "lessons learned" from previous experiences with truth commissions: the protagonists have always discussed REKOM as a complementary tool, and not as an alternative instrument that should replace legal prosecution of war crimes and crimes against humanity. They have thereby followed a more holistic – and not a dichotomic – understanding of transitional justice.

Towards a holistic understanding of transitional justice

Overcoming dichotomies

Assessing the scholarly debates on transitional justice during the past two decades, one can summarise that to a considerable degree, these have centred on dichotomies.[15] In the debate on *peace versus justice*, one important strand of the earlier discussion has centred on amnesties, arguing that bargains rather than prosecution would be the best way to achieve agreements and to contain "spoilers" in peace processes. Later on, the idea of impunity was rejected more and more and seen as an imposition on the victims (Bell 2000; Hayner 2009; Minow 1998). During the 1990s, the *truth versus justice* debate balanced the merits of trials against other accountability mechanisms. Truth commissions have since been promoted as an alternative option to legal prosecutions. It has been argued that public and official exposure of truth provides redress for victims and may contribute towards individual and social healing and reconciliation (Hayner 1994). Kritz (2009) has emphasised that divided societies in particular need truth-seeking and truth-telling mechanisms, to counteract cultures of denial as well as nationalist myth-making and to prevent the distortion and instrumentalisation of facts and history. Especially after violent conflicts between ethnic and religious groups that have lived next to each other, and where extremists have been eager to tie responsibility for past crimes to their adversaries, a truth commission can counteract such tendencies by engaging the whole society in a national dialogue. Kritz (ibid., 18) has outlined that civil society is crucial for this. He is convinced that truth and reconciliation commissions should be established

> only where [. . .] a robust civil society remains intact. Where such conditions do not exist, the commission's mandate should be narrowly focused on documenting the truth along the lines of some earlier commissions rather than on the broader reconciliation goals established more recently.
>
> (Kritz 2009, 18)

However, research on truth commissions has also revealed that – apart from a strong civil society – there is a need for reliable allies in parliaments, governments and state administrations who are willing to engage in institutional reforms and in helping to reestablish the rule of law. Only state institutions themselves can initiate investigations on human rights violations and wrongdoings that have been committed by state employees (from police units, secret service, etc.) and reforms that help to prevent such behaviour in the future; furthermore they have to initiate the necessary reforms of structures and support mechanisms that guarantee democratic forms of control and the monitoring of state bodies.

Following a period in the 1990s that was marked by huge expectations regarding the potential of truth commissions, the human rights community has meanwhile come to view these instruments much more sceptically (Brouneus 2008; International Center for Transitional Justice 2014). An important aspect of this disillusionment was the enormous chasm between the commissions' mandates to develop detailed recommendations on societal reforms and the nonimplementation of these proposals by the governments that were addressed. It has therefore been recommended that international donors should reconsider strategies of tying aid to the implementation of truth commission recommendations (Kritz 2009; Laplante 2008). Kritz (2009, 17) has expressed concern that many countries in transition have decided to establish truth commissions without any clear understanding of what such endeavours are about and under which conditions they may function or not. The disillusionment has also contributed to broadening the discourse. Many more authors agree today that a holistic understanding of transitional justice is needed to support societies in recovering from oppression or violent conflict. As a consequence, *retributive* and *restorative* approaches are viewed as complementary and not mutually exclusive – an integrated approach thereby creating favourable conditions for conflict transformation and peacebuilding (see Johnstone and Van Ness 2006; Sullivan and Tifft 2006; Zehr 2002).

According to Alexander Boraine (former member of the South African Truth and Reconciliation Commission and founder of the International Center for Transitional Justice), a holistic interpretation of transitional justice encompasses five key elements, including accountability, truth recovery, reparations, reconciliation and institutional reform (Boraine 2006, 19–25). *Accountability* is indispensable as there are atrocities and crimes that a civilisation cannot tolerate ignoring, and societies emerging from violent conflict or dictatorship need to strictly adhere to the rule of law. Yet as in many cases of large-scale human rights violations, it is impossible to prosecute all incidences of human right violations. Additional efforts are needed and different forms of *truth* need to be established: forensic truth (evidence and facts about human rights violations and missing persons); narrative truth (storytelling by victims and perpetrators and communicating personal truths to a wider public); dialogical truth (by interaction, discussion and debate); and healing/restorative truth (documentation of facts to give dignity to the victims and survivors). In addition, *reparations* are crucial to acknowledge the suffering of victims – and, as such, are tied to the documentation of crimes. *Reconciliation* is seen as a long-term process that encompasses acknowledgement of the past, the acceptance of responsibility and steps towards (re)building trust. According to Boraine (ibid., 22), deeply divided societies need to achieve "at least a measure of reconciliation" by creating

> [a] common memory that can be acknowledged by those who created and implemented an unjust system, those who fought against it, and the many more who were in the middle and claimed not to know what was happening in their country.
>
> (Boraine 2006, 22)

Furthermore, Boraine states that *institutional reforms* form a prerequisite for truth and reconciliation, and therefore truth commissions should not necessarily take the form of individual hearings but focus instead on institutional settings that call to account the institutions that are responsible for the breakdown of a state, or the human rights violations committed.

The need for institutional reforms and establishing the rule of law

In order to establish functioning mechanisms of transitional justice, strong and reliable state institutions are necessary. Apart from independent legal institutions, such as courts and prosecutor's offices, reliable police institutions are needed that are able and willing to initiate and conduct investigations, get hold of war crimes suspects, and guarantee protection of the witnesses before, during and after the trials. In settings such as the Western Balkans, where fugitives often left their countries and where governments have decided not to extradite the suspects, there is also a great need for cooperation between police institutions, prosecutors and courts across borders on a regional level.

In the interviews conducted for the research project *Dealing with the Past and Peacebuilding in the Western Balkans*, many experts from international organisations have come to the conclusion that the performance of the war crimes chambers and prosecutors in Bosnia-Herzegovina, Serbia and Croatia has improved in the past decade. They mentioned that in a series of high-profile cases progress has been made in sentencing. International actors were convinced that the courts were less biased and more professional now in comparison to the postwar period. In particular, they pointed to the revision of in absentia trials; the increasing number of indictments and sentences in cases where crimes were committed by members of their "own" constituency. It was also positively emphasised that there is now more advanced cooperation between courts from different countries in the region. At the same time, problems and shortcomings were mentioned that have had an impact on the level of legitimacy and acceptance of these institutions. Slowness of proceedings and a lack of effective mechanisms for witness protection are the deficiencies that are most frequently mentioned. However, while representatives from international organisations were convinced that the legal institutions have changed and advanced their performance towards greater fairness and acquired more professional standards, in contrast, representatives from civil society organisations in all countries assumed an ongoing ethnopolitical bias and continued to advance a strong politicisation of the domestic judiciary.

In Bosnia-Herzegovina, international experts were convinced that the domestic courts have the capacity to deal successfully with pending war crimes cases ("they have qualified prosecutors and judges" [I-11], a department for witness protection, and a mechanism for impartiality" [I-21]).[16] It was reported that most of the war crimes, and in particular highly sensitive cases, have to be dealt with at the Court of Bosnia and Herzegovina (BiH), at state level. But by decision of the state court and prosecutors, several cases have been transferred back to lower level courts in municipalities where the crimes took place. Cantonal and district courts in various cities are also dealing with war crimes. It is reported that the courts in the urban centres Tuzla, Sarajevo and Banja Luka are handling the majority of cases "quite well" (I-14). But it is also mentioned that they are not as well-equipped as the Court of BiH, and that witness protection is nonexistent in many places (I-14). Furthermore, international experts in Bosnia-Herzegovina expressed strong concern that the legitimacy of the Court of BiH is questioned by the government of Republika Srpska (RS) – the administrative entity inhabited predominantly by Bosnian Serbs – as it had repeatedly been framed as internationally imposed by the RS prime minister Milroad Dodik (partly also due to the court's mandate to fight corruption and investigate RS leaders' performance). With regard to war crimes prosecution, it was reported that relevant parts of the

RS population see it as being biased, assuming "that it is only Serbs who are being tried at this court and Serb victims are not heard and their cases have not been prosecuted" (I-14). One expert reported that due to a high degree of distrust, Bosnian Serb victims still largely preferred to take proceedings to Belgrade instead of approaching the domestic courts in Bosnia (I-4).

In Serbia, meanwhile, most international representatives were convinced that the national prosecution office is well functioning, despite initial shortcomings (Fischer 2013b). They mentioned that the Serbian institutions' cooperation with prosecutor's offices in Croatia had substantially improved (I-11). However, the *legitimacy* of the judiciary was still considered to be low, due to various mistakes that had been made in earlier periods, in particular when the courts decided "to try a lot of people in absentia, because fugitives had escaped to other countries" (I-10). The international experts were convinced that in terms of outreach, the domestic legal institutions still suffer from many deficits and therefore organisations and agencies which promote war crimes prosecutions also need to be supported in the future. Finally, several interviewees insisted that the justice sector as a whole needs to be reformed and a lustration law is urgently needed (I-7).

In Croatia, international representatives gave predominantly positive assessments of the work of the chief prosecutor's office and the war crimes chambers.[17] They reported that the courts' performance was not satisfactory in the 1990s but had improved in the subsequent decade. The courts were considered to function more effectively and be less biased[18] than several years ago (I-1, I-15, I-8). Four specialised courts in Zagreb, Osijek, Rijeka and Split have been set up with staff and judges who are familiar with war crimes issues, and several new war crimes cases had been transferred to these courts, which will be in charge of war crimes prosecution in the future. This is seen as "a major move" that international organisations were pushing for (I-15). A war crimes prosecution action plan, initiated by the chief state prosecutor and adopted in 2008, was very much appreciated as a tool to improve witness protection (I-8). It was also acknowledged that the prosecutors' office has meanwhile revised several of the earlier in absentia trials and that it has established reliable procedures for the exchange of evidence with prosecutors in Serbia and Bosnia-Herzegovina. This guarantees that fugitive suspects can be put on trial in the respective countries, which is considered an important step forward (I-1).

Despite the positive assessments, several interviewees emphasised that a lot still needs to be done in Croatia in terms of accountability – especially with regard to the events during and after Operation Storm, the military activities that were undertaken in 1995 by the Croatian army aimed at ending the occupation of the Krajina region by Serbian military and that led to the flight and exodus of more than 200,000 Serbs from Croatia.[19] International experts complained:

> There has not been a single conviction of members of the Croatian army for war crimes during and after Operation Storm [. . .] There are 33 trials pending for the murder of civilians, but the state attorney has not addressed these as war crimes so far.
>
> (I-15)

It was argued that the willingness of the domestic courts to consider these cases of murder and convert them into war crime trials, and to investigate the fate of 677 civilians killed in the aftermath of the military operation, is the ultimate test for Croatia's commitment to deal with its past: "this is of particular importance because the ICTY will not pursue any other case in the context of Operation Storm" (I-15). International actors largely insisted that progress with regard to the investigation of these crimes will very much depend on the pressure from civil society (I-15, I-1, I-8). International actors in Croatia have explicitly emphasised that CSOs contributed substantially to fact-finding and improving the preparedness of the courts in this country and that they wished that the CSOs should continue to monitor courts' activities. Trial monitoring by CSOs and independent media is seen as crucial, in particular as international trial monitoring (conducted by the Organization for Security and Co-operation in Europe [OSCE] until 2012) ended with Croatia's accession to the EU (I-15). Furthermore, international experts from all three countries see a need for domestic war crime institutions to develop more systematic public relations strategies and cooperation with investigative journalists to communicate the legal work to the public. Finally, representatives from international organisations, as well as local CSOs, see a need for the courts to develop gender-sensitive approaches and specific knowledge and procedures in dealing with gender-specific war crimes – an issue that has equally been raised by feminist scholars and practitioners.

The need for gender-sensitivity: feminist contributions to the debate

International researchers and scholars from the Balkans have argued that a holistic understanding of transitional justice needs to apply gender-sensitive approaches. They have helped to shift public attention to the gender dimensions of warfare and war-related crimes. Changing gender roles, it has been argued, were a central feature of social realities in the region. Male constructions of identity were drawn into question that, amongst other factors, contributed to the wars in the 1990s (Blagojevic 2004, 2006). Nationalist discourses were profoundly gendered, as the ethnic "self" and the "other" were both constructed in a gendered way (Zarkov 2007). Furthermore, the wars developed a gender-specific dynamic (Colovic 1994, 2002; Jalusic 2004; Milojevic 2012; Slapsak 2000) – in particular, as sexual violence was systematically applied and rape became a crucial element of warfare aiming at ethnic annihilation in the Bosnian war (Allen 1996; Hromadzic 2004; Skjelsbaek 2012). Against the background of the systematic rape of women in the 1990s wars in the Balkans, researchers and women's rights activists have documented gender-specific violence and advanced the debate on gender-specific war crimes (Kohn 1995; Korac 1994). As a consequence, the debate on transitional justice was further broadened by feminist discourses. Scholars from the Western Balkans, in accordance with human rights and peace activists, have argued that a better understanding of gender, culture and power structures is needed to appropriately analyse the causes, dynamics and consequences of conflict and violence (Djuric-Kuzmanovic et al. 2008; Slapsak 2000).

Feminist research has revealed that as a consequence of campaigns to end impunity for violence against women, legal standards have been modified and advancements have been made in international law; gender-based violence in armed conflict has been recognised as a war crime in international law and prosecutions have been secured. The tribunals for Yugoslavia, Rwanda and Sierra Leone have recognised sexual violence as a grave breach of the Geneva Conventions and as a crime against humanity. The Rome Statute of the ICC, which entered into force on July 1, 2002, recognised rape, sexual slavery, enforced prostitution, pregnancy and sterilisation as crimes against humanity and as war crimes. Courtroom procedures have also been reformed to ensure that victims of sexual violence are not retraumatised by adversarial legal processes.[20] Women's organisations made appeals to respect the rights, needs and inclusion of victims and these were taken into account when the International Tribunal for Lebanon and the ICC were created. It is considered a success that these courts have introduced procedural law for victims[21] and that the representation of women on the staff of the international tribunals has meanwhile increased. Truth commissions have responded to the gender campaigns and tried to find appropriate ways of addressing gender-based violence. In Haiti, Sierra Leone and East Timor, gender aspects and the issue of sexual violence were explicitly incorporated into the mandates; other commissions (in South Africa) have held gender hearings or established special gender units (in Peru) (see Bell and O'Rourke 2007; Ní Aoláin and Turner 2007).

Women's organisations in the Western Balkans have collected testimonies and launched campaigns to break the vicious cycle of silencing sexual abuse as an element of warfare (Vuskovic and Trifunovic 2008). In Bosnia-Herzegovina in particular, the fate of women who suffered rape and torture during the war was largely ignored and silenced by taboos for more than a decade after the war. It was only after the launch of the film *Grbavica*[22] that the Bosnian Parliament formally acknowledged women who had been raped as "war invalids" and decided that they should receive compensation, in a form similar to the payments made to men that fought in the war. This was also a result of campaigns by local and international nongovernmental organisations (NGOs; e.g. the Association of Women of Srebrenica and Medica Mondiale) to raise awareness and generate support for women (Baumann and Müller 2006). Nevertheless, as our field research revealed, the issue of gender justice will remain a particular challenge. As several experts from international organisations mentioned, addressing gender-specific violence related to the war is still hemmed in by a lot of taboos. Although the aforementioned film and NGO campaigns helped to introduce legislation for the payment of compensation for raped women, and although the EU delegation in Bosnia, together with the UN, the Ministry of Justice and the Ministry for Human Rights, developed a strategy to support women, the situation of women affected by sexual violence during the war has not significantly improved in the past decade. Most of these women never received any material compensation and continue to live in very poor conditions (I-16, I-17).

Another problem is that for many women who experienced sexual violence in wartime, there is a continuity and an experience of ongoing suffering also in so-called peace times, not only because of the flashbacks caused by traumatic stress but also in a much more drastic sense, as wartime rape victims often become victims of domestic violence after the war (Simic 2016). Psychological studies of the consequences of the war in Bosnia-Herzegovina have revealed that there is a connection between the unresolved issues and war experiences that war veterans are grappling with and the increase of domestic violence in this postwar society. Many former soldiers continue to suffer from war trauma and post-traumatic stress disorder (PTSD; e.g. Beara and Miljanovic 2007a, 2007b; Sarac-Hadzihalilovic et al. 2008). The experience and the psychological consequences of violence may contribute towards diverse forms of new violence erupting in the domestic context (Beara 2012) or towards a rise in hate crimes occurring in local communities.[23] Social psychologists have emphasised that war veterans face a diversity of challenges when trying to reintegrate and when seeking to adapt their identities to the dynamics of the postwar societies (Moratti and Sabic-El-Rayess 2009). Studies on the impact of demobilisation and reintegration programmes (DDR) in the post-Yugoslav region (Gregson 2000; Heinemann-Grüder and Pietz 2003) outlined that most of the DDR programmes have neglected the need to assist veterans in coping with painful memories.

As changing gender roles have also shaped social relations in the postwar societies, scholars have argued that gender should be considered as an analytical category in the analysis of the roles and identities of former fighters (Becirevic et al. 2011; Jansen 2010; Schroer-Hippel 2011a, 2011b) as well as in studies on transitional justice and reconciliation (Schäuble 2006; Simic et al. 2012). Psychologists argue that efforts geared towards establishing effective legal protection for women are important issues, but that at the same time, programmes focusing on demobilisation and reintegration of former combatants also need to pay attention to the psychological grievances and PTSD symptoms systematically in order to find ways to break this vicious circle. Based on experiences from the Balkans – but also other postwar regions – international peace and human rights organisations have dedicated a great deal of attention towards issues of gender justice in the past decade. These have emphasised that gender justice should be seen as an integral part of social justice and that postwar reconstruction programmes should be geared more towards the specific needs of women (Olsson et al. 2004). It was emphasised in particular that demobilisation and reintegration initiatives for former combatants must be implemented together with local communities – including women – to avoid injustices and to prevent those guilty of war crimes from going unpunished or benefiting from the situation (Farr 2003). In order to serve gender justice, international programmes cannot simply focus on prosecuting crimes committed in war times; they also need to focus on the rule of law and security (Becirevic et al. 2011).

In their analysis of the connection between security and the protection of the rights of women, feminist scholars and practitioners have looked at the activities of international organisations. In this context, they have revealed protection gaps and named the highly problematic side effects of international peace missions.

The need to overcome accountability gaps and protection gaps in international missions

Human rights violations that are committed or supported by international mission staff in postwar realities remain a sensitive topic that is often ignored or silenced. Experiences from the Balkans provide rich material to study this problem. Right after the war, Bosnia-Herzegovina became a central hub for drug trafficking and prostitution (Simic 2012; Stability Pact for South Eastern Europe 2003). The international peacebuilding missions often lacked qualified personnel and know-how needed to effectively counter the structures of organised crime that operated in regional and globalised networks (Buwitt 2001; Stodiek 2006). Unclear mandates of international and local police forces also contributed to a situation in which the rule of law could hardly be established. Reports on forced prostitution (Kartusch and Reiter 2006; Ludwig Boltzmann Institute for Human Rights 2001) have documented the fact that the postwar areas of Bosnia-Herzegovina and Kosovo in particular transformed into hot spots for human trafficking (predominantly of women) from Eastern European countries. This occurred even though several international missions took measures against this; the UN International Police Task Force, for instance, had set up a STOP-Programme in Bosnia. In sum, there was no systematic prosecution of trafficking, forced prostitution and human rights violations.

But how could this sector expand so much and so fast? Both in Kosovo and Bosnia, international staff (NATO, UN and OSCE, including staff from humanitarian organisations) increased the demand for such services and thus indirectly fostered the slavery of women (Böhm 2000; Mappes-Niedek 2003). The number of brothels in Kosovo, for instance, increased substantially with the presence of international actors (Kartusch and Reiter 2006, 220). Furthermore, it was discovered by legal experts that international mission staff were also actively involved in the structures of organised crime, including the trafficking of women and prostitution. A study commissioned by the UN Mission in Bosnia in 2001 revealed that Stabilisation Force (SFOR) soldiers were actively involved in trafficking activities (Ulrich 2001). Those responsible at the UN and NATO did not react and failed to take appropriate means to counteract such criminal structures. Furthermore, political leaders suspected of being involved in these crimes have – apart from only a few exceptions – not been held accountable.

How difficult it is to uncover such practices and bring them to justice becomes clear when one considers the experience of the British lawyer Madeleine Rees, who in 1998 worked for the Office of the High Commissioner for Human Rights (OHCHR) in Bosnia-Herzegovina. She helped to uncover human rights abuses related to the sex trade by testifying together with Kathryn Bolkovac, a UN International Police Task Force (UN-IPTF) monitor. Both women collected evidence on the active involvement of UN mission personnel in sex trafficking and the fate of forced prostitutes. Rees did not hesitate to name the problem of immunity and impunity in peacekeeping that in her opinion has led to a considerable protection gap:

> The explanation lies in how gender plays out in conflict and post-conflict and how institutions that work in those environments, have a nasty habit of replicating the conduct of violence and discrimination which they are there to protect against and to redress.[24]

Both women had to face harsh reactions and negative consequences for their professional career. Rees was dismissed in 2010, although a court subsequently ruled that this dismissal had been unlawful. Bolkovac was also dismissed by her employer – a private firm, which had served as a subcontractor for the UN-IPTF mission.[25] The 2010 film *The Whistleblower* by Laryssa Kondracki brought the problem to public attention and also raised awareness of the topic within the UN system. It was finally explicitly addressed by the UN Secretary-General and an expert report was commissioned. UN agencies reported at a later stage that the number of incidents in which UN military or civilian staff were involved in sexual abuse or related criminal activities had decreased. However, women's organisations doubt these statistics. Pointing to the many more cases of sexual abuse by UN staff that have been reported from other regions (i.e. Haiti, Ivory Coast), they argue that a tendency of silencing such crimes and a culture of impunity for international mission staff in crisis regions is still persisting.[26] Feminist studies have criticised the fact that the measures that have been taken by the UN to regulate sexual conduct in international peacekeeping operations are not satisfying (Simic 2012; Stern 2015). Much more needs to be done in order to establish appropriate standards. The issue of the "accountability of peacekeepers"[27] is still not sufficiently analysed. In fact, international missions often play a factor in the formation of legal grey zones where it is hardly possible to ensure individual responsibility for human rights violations. The accountability gap continues to be a serious problem. Overcoming this gap, and closing the protection gap that comes along with it, represents an important challenge for international organisations engaged in peacebuilding.

Conclusions and challenges for research and practice

In the first part of this chapter, it was illustrated that international tribunals can make important contributions towards establishing accountability in situations where domestic mechanisms are unwilling or unable to do so. However, the shortcomings that have been outlined with respect to the work of the ICTY, and the deficits of legitimacy entailed therein, make it clear that transitional justice mechanisms established by international actors need to be framed in a way that respects the dynamics of war-affected societies. First, international tribunals should be clear and transparent on their principles and mandates. Second, they should connect as much as possible with the war-affected population. The effectiveness of the courts depends on societal acceptance and also on practical support by local communities when it comes to conducting investigations on war events. Furthermore, it is necessary that courts and prosecutors cooperate with civil society actors working to promote human rights and peacebuilding. Both active support by local CSOs and the work of investigative journalists are indispensable for implementing effective initiatives for transitional justice. Finally, international efforts that aim at accountability have to be linked to policies that help to establish well-functioning domestic institutions that address war crimes prosecution and state administrations that guarantee the rule of law. This includes pushing for reforms of the legal system and creating a police apparatus that can actually guarantee an effective protection of victims and witnesses before, during and after the trials.

The second part of this chapter showed that transitional justice approaches need to be gender-sensitive. Court procedures need to pay special attention to gender-based violence. Transitional justice strategies developed and applied in postwar societies need to address gender justice. External interventions in war-torn societies also need to be assessed against the background of gender justice and a gendered understanding of human rights violation and protection. For the sake of assuring their own credibility and legitimacy, international actors that promote transitional justice, democratisation and peacebuilding in war-torn societies need to close the accountability gaps and protection gaps that continue to exist in many peacebuilding missions. More courage is needed by officials to detect human rights abuses committed by the mission staff. Investigation by journalists and researchers is necessary to monitor the gender effects of international missions. As long as accountability and protection gaps persist, they will undermine the credibility and effectiveness of international efforts for transitional justice and peacebuilding. There is definitely an urgent need for ending impunity, not only for those who committed crimes in times of war but also for those responsible for human rights violations, sexual abuse, or who support criminal structures in international peacekeeping missions.

International actors who introduce transitional justice mechanisms in war-torn societies should also be well aware of the limited scope that legal accountability mechanisms can have. They should not promise effects that are beyond the mandates of these instruments. International and domestic courts can establish accountability based on individual responsibility and they can substantially contribute towards setting up databases with undeniable facts. But they cannot provide redress for those affected by violence, enhance processes of healing, or act as drivers for reconciliation. Several structural problems can be said to underlie these limitations: initiatives for establishing truth and justice in a war-torn society will always face a dilemma, as what is perceived as just by some people is seen as unjust by others. What is seen as a fact by one group may be disputed and considered as an inadequate interpretation by another. This is particularly true for societies affected by ethnopolitical conflicts. Different interpretations of history have often fuelled the dynamic of violence, unfolding a particular power in wars of secession. It is therefore typical for societies emerging from such wars that a variety of discourses on the past persist.

While victims and survivors, peace and human rights activists might push for accountability and fact-finding in order to prevent such violence from happening again, political leaders are eager to shape discourses on the past in a way that relativises their own wrongdoings. Frequently, they also seek to make use of distorted versions of history in order to achieve unification and secure positions of political power in a newly established political order. An open question remains: how realistic is the assumption that in such settings a "common memory" (Boraine 2006) can be achieved that will be acknowledged by those who were responsible for an unjust system, those who fought against it, and those who were bystanders? Maybe this aim is too ambitious in societies that have gone through protracted conflict and, in turn, the establishment of different "truths" may be a more appropriate objective. The question of whether and how people deal with painful memories, and when the time has come for entering a process of dialogue on the violent past, is up to the war-affected society, in any case. Outsiders cannot initiate societal debates on the past, but international actors can support such processes by creating spaces where different experiences and interpretations of history can be shared.

As has been outlined in this chapter, the academic discourse has moved on in the sense that transitional justice and reconciliation are increasingly seen as complementary rather than competing concepts. Many more transitional justice experts agree today that societies recovering from oppression or violent conflict need both *legal and restorative approaches* to advance access to truth and justice. Also, most of the scholars who focus on reconciliation would agree that establishing *accountability and facts* is a necessary precondition in society and one that serves to pave the way for such long-term processes.[28] Comprehensive approaches to dealing with the past suggest legal prosecution; reparations and institutional reforms; factual, dialogical and societal approaches to truth recovery; and initiatives for psychosocial healing, trust and relationship-building among individuals and collectives. Reconciliation, however, cannot be achieved by courts or truth commissions alone. This can only be achieved by a set of different tools and a long-term commitment from political leaders and civil society activists. Reconciliation also requires dealing with the root causes of conflict, including power asymmetries and imbalances of suffering (Kriesberg 2004). Transitional justice mechanisms alone have very limited possibilities for bridge-building in divided communities and among individuals and collectives that have been at war with each other.

Initiatives for transitional justice and efforts for reconciliation have two things in common: first, they need engagement from both the top level and the grassroots level of societies (Assefa 2005; Kritz 1995); second, their effects can only be assessed in the long run, after years, decades or even generations. As Pierre Hazan (2007, 11) has outlined, the Nuremberg trials after World War II were regarded as victors' justice by parts of the German population, and did not have an immediate effect in terms of initiating debates in the 1950s. But 25 years later, their archives became an important point of reference for successive generations. Thus, they contributed to informing German society, once initiatives for facing the past had begun to develop on a larger scale and steps for political and cultural reconciliation were actively promoted both by politicians and civil society actors (ibid.).

The literature on transitional justice reveals huge research gaps. Most of the studies that have been published on transitional justice in the past decades have focused on legal mechanisms, their implementation and compliance with international law, and on the underlying policy-making process, regime stability or democratisation. Only very few studies have been devoted to examining the nature of micro-level engagement in transitional justice, or have dealt with societal responses, cultural phenomena, social discourses and narratives.[29] Due to a lack of long-term analysis and systematic empirical research, in fact, there is not much knowledge concerning the effects of tribunals and trials on the respective societies.[30] More research is needed that looks at the scope of different actors and mechanisms and at the dynamics of interaction. It is still unclear how retributive forms of justice and restorative approaches should be sequenced or balanced. Research on the dynamics and transformation of war-related identities, individual and collective memory is still limited. More research is needed on the question of how individual and collective forms of memory constitute and relate to one another, and how war-related identities can be transformed.

Quantitative approaches aiming to measure (short-term) effects of transitional justice mechanisms will in most cases not be appropriate, as these can only be assessed over a longer time frame – decades or generations (Hazan 2006). Qualitative approaches that cover experiences and voices from different levels of society, action research that looks at processes rather than outcomes and results, and interdisciplinary approaches (involving social scientists, legal experts, historians, political psychologists, anthropologists and ethnologists) are much more promising for analysing processes of dealing with the past. Case studies based on qualitative approaches can provide important insights and help to systematise the complex demands and thereby prevent external peacebuilders from rushing into action while upholding unrealistic expectations. Finally, to fill the aforementioned research gaps, the views of those affected need to be included more systematically. In order to achieve more reliable results, research has to involve, as much as possible, experts from the countries under investigation who have to cope with the diverse demands of war-to-peace transition on a daily basis.

Notes

1 For a review of the literature on transitional justice see Backer (2009); Teitel (2014); Thoms et al. (2008); and Van der Merwe et al. (2009).
2 The empirical studies on which this chapter draws were funded by the German Foundation for Peace Research.
3 For an overview see Kerr (2004); Olusanya (2005); Schabas (2006); and Schabas (2013).
4 The Federal Republic of Yugoslavia at that time consisted of Serbia and Montenegro.
5 At the time of writing, proceedings for 141 accused had been concluded. Eighty persons had been sentenced. Proceedings for 14 accused were ongoing (10 before

the Appeals Chamber and four currently on trial). See http://www.icty.org/sid/24 (Accessed: 22 June 2015).

6 Former President of the ICTY, Antonio Cassese, has pointed to this problem. See http://www.icty.org/sid/7420 (Accessed: 22 June 2015).

7 See for instance the statements by former ICTY president Antonio Cassese at http://www.icty.org/sid/7220 (Accessed: 22 June 2015).

8 A Section for War Crimes of the Court of Bosnia-Herzegovina was established in 2005 as a permanent state-level organ. Designed as a hybrid court, international staff were employed and to be phased out after a five-year period. In Croatia, special war crimes chambers were formed in 2003 within the county courts in Zagreb, Osijek, Rijeka and Split. In Serbia a War Crimes Chamber of the Belgrade District Court and a War Crimes Prosecutor's Office were established in the same year (Ivanisevic 2007, 2008).

9 The ICTY was established as a temporary institution at a time where the domestic systems in the region were unable or unwilling to fulfil this task. By 2003 the ICTY's judges developed a *Completion Strategy* to guarantee that the tribunal's mission could successfully be fulfilled in coordination with the legal systems in the region. Initially, it was foreseen that all investigations should be completed by 31 December 2004. Due to the late arrest of prominent fugitives (Ratko Mladic and Goran Hadzic were only arrested in 2011) as well as due to the complexity of some of the cases, the process was delayed. Estimates as of December 2014 suggested that four of the five ongoing appeal cases will be completed in 2015, as well as three of the four cases at trial stage. For the ongoing cases a special *Mechanism for International Criminal Tribunals* (MICT) was established in 2010 (not only for the ICTY but also for the ICTR). The judgement for Ratko Mladic is expected in 2017. All cases that relate to intermediate or lower-level accused have been transferred to national jurisdictions. The domestic prosecutors and courts can initiate cases without involvement of the ICTY. See http://www.icty.org/sid/10016 (Accessed: 27 April 2015).

10 Hoffmann (2016) states that according to the Office of the State Attorney in Croatia, 241 investigations were ongoing in December 2013, and 613 cases pending before first instance courts, while the OSCE Mission to Bosnia counted 1,200 cases involving several thousands suspects, and the OSCE Mission to Serbia counted 20 formal investigations and 1,100 cases in a preinvestigative stage.

11 See http://www.icty.org/sid/10280 (Accessed: 22 June 2015); http://www.icty.org/sid/10850# (Accessed: 22 June 2015).

12 See www.icty.org/sid/10244 (Accessed: 22 June 2015).

13 See http://www.zarekom.org/The-Coalition-for-RECOM.en.html (Accessed: 22 June 2015); for a detailed analysis of the dynamic of the REKOM process, see Petrovic-Ziemer (2013b) and Fischer (2013a).

14 For more details of the purposes, composition and dynamic of the REKOM campaign see Fischer (2013a) and Petrovic-Ziemer (2013b).

15 For an overview on these debates see Thoms et al. (2008).

16 The numbers relate to the interviews conducted in the period 2010–2012 as stored in the Berghof Foundation's database.

17 This assessment is also documented by the Interim Report from the Commission to the Council and the European Parliament on reforms in Croatia in the field of judiciary and fundamental rights, Brussels, 2 March 2011 COM (2011), available online at http://ec.europa.eu/enlargement/pdf/hp/interim_report_hr_ch23_en.pdf (Accessed: 22 June 2015).

18 Some of the county courts were criticised for being biased and poorly prepared for their task. It is reported that earlier practice was "to deal gently with Croatian suspects and preferably to accuse Serbs, based on the argument that Serbs had committed more crimes. For a long time Croatian suspects could rely on a "homeland bonus and more lenient punishments" (I-8).

19 Figures relating to these events are contested. While human rights NGOs refer to 677 persons killed in the aftermath of the military operation, the state attorney argued that there were only 114 victims after 1995, and only recently accepted the number of 677.

20 The ICTY has introduced changes to the procedures of investigation and to the rules regarding evidence, limiting the extent to which consent can be presented as a defence for sexual assault and prohibiting the use of evidence of a victim's past sexual conduct (Bell and O'Rourke 2007, 27).

21 See www.iccwomen.org/publications/resources/docs/Gender_Integration_in_the_Rome_Statute.doc (Accessed: 22 June 2015).

22 The film by Jasmila Zbanic tackles the relationship between a Bosniak woman raped during the war and her teenage daughter, who both try to cope with the past in post-war Sarajevo. It outlines the individual trauma as well as the existing taboos in society. The film was awarded a Golden Bear at the 2006 Berlin Film Festival.

23 An incident in Serbia, when a war veteran who fought in the Croatian war killed 13 relatives and neighbours in a shooting spree in 2013, demonstrated this kind of danger. The government of Serbia declared a day of mourning after this, and Serbian officials said the killings showed that the government must pay more attention to gun control, medical screening for veterans and social problems related to the 1990s wars. The incident occurred on 9 April 2013 in Velika Ivanča near Belgrade. See http://www.guardian.co.uk/world/2013/apr/11/serbian-killer-dies-hospital (Accessed: 22 June 2015).

24 See http://www.opendemocracy.net/print/77442 (Accessed: 22 June 2015).

25 See http://www.theguardian.com/world/2001/jul/29/unitednations/print (Accessed: 22 June 2015).

26 See http://womensenews.org/story/international-policyunited-nations/111023/whistle blower-screening-disturbs-peace-at-un (Accessed: 22 June 2015).

27 The journal *Die Friedenswarte* (2013) dedicated a special issue to the accountability gaps in international law and presented several case studies that outline the deficits of the legal frameworks that regulate the conduct of UN personnel.

28 For an overview of the debate and definitions see Bar-Tal and Bennink (2004); Bloomfield (2006, 2008); Hamber and Kelly (2004); and Kriesberg (2007).

29 See Backer (2009), drawing on a review of 58 comparative studies on transitional justice in Latin America, Europe, Africa and Asia.

30 Thoms et al. (2008), after having reviewed comparative studies conducted in more than 100 countries, found that these studies did not offer a convincing empirical basis for reaching strong conclusions about the systematic effects of TJ mechanisms.

References

Allcock, J. B. (2009). The international criminal tribunal for the former Yugoslavia. In C. Ingrao and T. A. Emmert (Eds.), *Confronting the Yugoslav Controversies. A Scholars' Initiative*. Purdue University Press, West Lafayette, IN, 347–389.

Allen, B. (1996). *Rape Warfare. The Hidden Genocide in Bosnia-Herzegovina and Croatia*. University of Minnesota Press, Minneapolis.

Arzt, D. E. (2006). Views on the ground. The local perception of international criminal tribunals in the former Yugoslavia and Sierra Leone. *Annals of the AAPSS*, 603, 226–239.

Assefa, H. (2005). Reconciliation. Challenges, responses and the role of civil society. In P. Van Tongeren, M. Brenk, M. Hellema, and J. Verhoeven (Eds.), *People Building Peace II: Successful Stories of Civil Society*. Lynne Rienner, London, 637–645.

Backer, D. (2009). Cross-national comparative analysis. In H. Van Der Merwe, V. Baxter, and A. R. Chapman (Eds.), *Assessing the Impact of Transitional Justice. Challenges for Empirical Research*. United States Institute of Peace, Washington, DC, 23–89.

Banjeglav, T. (2016). The micro-legacy of the ICTY in Croatia – A case study on Vukovar. In M. Fischer and O. Simic (Eds.), *Transitional Justice and Reconciliation – Lessons from the Balkans*. Routledge, London, 81–101.

Bar-Tal, D., and Bennink, G. H. (2004). The nature of reconciliation as an outcome and a process. In Y. Bar-Simon-Tov (Ed.), *From Conflict Resolution to Reconciliation*. Oxford University Press, Oxford, 11–38.

Baumann, G., and Müller, N. (2006). Vergangenheitsbewältigung und Erinnerungskultur in den Ländern Mittelost- und Südosteuropas. Working Paper 164/2006. Konrad Adenauer Foundation, Berlin. (http://www.kas.de/wf/de/33.9323) Accessed: 9 February 2015.

Beara, V. (2012). War veterans and family violence. In D. J. Christie, *The Encyclopedia of Peace Psychology*. Blackwell, Oxford, 1–4.

Beara, V., and Miljanovic, P. (2007a). *Gde si to bio, sine moj? [Where Have You Been, My Blue-Eyed Son?]* Centre for War Trauma, Belgrade.

Beara, V., and Miljanovic, P. (2007b). Veterans in peacebuilding. In H. Rill, T. Smidling, and A. Bitoljanu (Eds.), *20 Pieces of Encouragement for Awakening and Change*. Centre for Nonviolent Action, Belgrade, 165–177.

Becirevic, M., Šulc, Z., and Šoštarić, M. (2011). Gender and Security Sector Reform in Bosnia and Herzegovina, Sarajevo. DCAF-Geneva Centre for the Democratic Control of Armed Forces. (http://www.dcaf.ch/Publications/Gender-and-Security-Sector-Reform-in-Bosnia-and-Herzegovina) Accessed: 9 February 2015.

Bell, C. (2000). *Peace Agreements and Human Rights*. Oxford University Press, Oxford.

Bell, C., and O'Rourke, C. (2007). Does feminism need a theory of transitional justice? *International Journal of Transitional Justice*, 1(1), 23–44.

Blagojevic, M. (2004). Conflict, gender and identity. Conflict and continuity in Serbia. In R. Seifert (Ed.), *Gender, Identität und kriegerischer Konflikt. Das Beispiel des ehemaligen Jugoslawien*. Lit-Verlag, Münster, 68–88.

Blagojevic, M. (2006) Serbianhood as manhood: Politics of gender and ethnic identity in Serbia. In M. Grsak, U. Reimann, K. Franke, and T. Bewernitz (Eds.), *Frauen und Frauenorganisationen im Widerstand in Kroatien, Bosnien und Serbien*. Frankfurt: Ed. AV, 69–94. (Online available at http://d-nb.info/982895747/04)

Bloomfield, D. (2006). *On Good Terms. Clarifying Reconciliation*. Berghof Report 14. Berghof Research Center, Berlin.

Bloomfield, D. (2008). Reconciliation. In V. Rittberger and M. Fischer (Eds.), *Strategies for Peace. Contributions of International Organizations, States, and Non-state Actors*. Barbara Budrich, Opladen, 261–270.

Böhm, A. (2000, 13 January). Freier für den Frieden. *Die Zeit*.

Boraine, A. (2006). Transitional justice. A holistic interpretation. *Journal of International Affairs*, 60(1), 17–27.

Brouneus, K. (2008). Truth-telling as talking cure? Insecurity and retraumatization in the Rwandan Gacaca Courts. *Security Dialogue*, 39(1), 55–76.

Buwitt, D. (2001). *Internationale Polizeieinsätze bei UNO-Friedensmissionen. Erfahrungen und Lehren aus Bosnien-Herzegowina und im Kosovo*. Berliner Informationszentrum für Transatlantische Sicherheit, Berlin.

Colovic, I. (1994). *Bordell der Krieger. Folklore, Politik und Krieg*. Fibre, Osnabrück.

Colovic, I. (2002). *The Politics of Symbol in Serbia. Essays in Political Anthropology*. Hurst, London.

Die Friedenswarte. (2013). Accountability of Peacekeepers, Vol. 88(3–4). BWV, Berlin.

Djuric-Kuzmanovic, T., Drezgic, R., and Zarkov, D. (2008). Gendered war, gendered peace. Violent conflicts in the Balkans and their consequences. In D. Pankhurst (Ed.), *Gendered Peace. Women's Struggles for Post-war Justice and Reconciliation*. Routledge, New York, 265–291.

Farr, V. (2003). The importance of a gender perspective to successful disarmament, demobilization and reintegration processes. *Disarmament Forum*, 4, 25–36.

Fischer, M. (2011). Transitional justice and reconciliation – Theory and practice. In B. Austin, M. Fischer, and H. J. Giessmann (Eds.), *Advancing Conflict Transformation. The Berghof Handbook II*. Barbara Budrich Verlag, Opladen, 405–430.

Fischer, M. (2013a). Political context and relevant actors. In M. Fischer and L. Petrovic-Ziemer (Eds.), *Dealing with the Past in the Western Balkans. Initiatives for Peacebuilding and Transitional Justice in Bosnia-Herzegovina, Serbia and Croatia*. Berghof Report 18. Berghof Foundation, Berlin, 5–18.

Fischer, M. (2013b). Analysis of interviews with international actors. In M. Fischer and L. Petrovic-Ziemer (Eds.), *Dealing with the Past in the Western Balkans. Initiatives for Peacebuilding and Transitional Justice in Bosnia-Herzegovina, Serbia and Croatia*. Berghof Report 18. Berghof Foundation, Berlin, 71–87.

Fischer, M. (2013c). Summary analysis. In M. Fischer and L. Petrovic-Ziemer (Eds.), *Dealing with the Past in the Western Balkans. Initiatives for Peacebuilding and Transitional Justice in Bosnia-Herzegovina, Serbia and Croatia*. Berghof Report 18. Berghof Foundation, Berlin, 131–158.

Fischer, M., and Petrovic-Ziemer, L. (Eds.). (2013). *Dealing with the Past in the Western Balkans. Initiatives for Peacebuilding and Transitional Justice in Bosnia-Herzegovina, Serbia and Croatia*. Berghof Report 18. Berghof Foundation, Berlin.

Fletcher, L., and Weinstein, H. (2004). A world unto itself? The application of international justice in former Yugoslavia. In E. Stover and H. Weinstein (Eds.), *My Neighbour, My Enemy. Justice and Community in the Aftermath of Mass Atrocity*. Cambridge University Press, Cambridge, 29–48.

Franke, K. M. (2006). Gendered subjects of transitional justice. *Columbia Journal of Gender and Law*, 15(3), 813–828.

Gregson, K. J. (2000, June). Veterans' Programs in Bosnia-Herzegovina. (http://eww.esiweb.org/pdf/bridges/bosnia/wb-kgregsonveterans.pdf) Accessed: 9 February 2015.

Hamber, B., and Kelly, G. (2004). Reconciliation. A working definition. (http://www.democraticdialogue.org) Accessed: 9 February 2015.

Hayner, P. (1994). Fifteen truth commissions – 1974–1994: A comparative study. *Human Rights Quarterly*, 16(4), 597–655.

Hayner, P. (2009). *Negotiating Justice: Guidance for Mediators*. Humanitarian Dialogue Centre, Geneva.

Hazan, P. (2006). Measuring the impact of punishment and forgiveness. A framework for evaluating transitional justice. *International Review of the Red Cross*, 88(861), 19–47.

Hazan, P. (2007). Das neue Mantra der Gerechtigkeit. Vom beschränkten Erfolg international verordneter Vergangenheitsbewältigung. *Der Überblick*, 43(1–2), 10–22.

Heinemann-Grüder, A., and Pietz, T. (2003). *Turning Soldiers into a Work Force. Demobilization and Reintegration in Post-Dayton Bosnia and Herzegovina*. Brief 27. Bonn International Center for Conversion/DCAF, Bonn.

Hodzic, R. (2007a, 25–27 June). Bosnia and Herzegovina – Legitimacy in transition. Paper presented at the Building a Future on Peace and Justice conference, Nuremberg. (www.peace-justice-conference.info/download/Hodzic_Expert%20Paper.pdf).

Hodzic, R. (2007b). Without dealing with the past, all of it is on some sort of an abstract level. Interview with R. Hodzic. In H. Rill et al. (Eds.), *20 Pieces of Encouragement for Awakening and Change*. Centre for Nonviolent Action, Sarajevo/Belgrade, 137–146.

Hoffmann, K. (2016). The ICTY after 20 years of experience – Assessments from an insider's view. In M. Fischer and O. Simic (Eds.), *Transitional Justice and Reconciliation – Lessons from the Balkans*. Routledge, London, 61–80.

Hromadzic, A. (2004). Kriegsvergewaltigungen in Bosnien. Alte und neue Erklärungsansätze. In R. Seifert (Ed.), *Gender, Identität und kriegerischer Konflikt. Das Beispiel des ehemaligen Jugoslawien*. Lit-Verlag, Münster, 112–130.

International Center for Transitional Justice and Kofi Annan Foundation (2014). *Challenging the Conventional. Can Truth Commissions Strengthen Peace Processes?* New York. (https://www.ictj.org/sites/default/files/ICTJ-Report-KAF-TruthCommPeace-2014.pdf) Accessed: 9 February 2015.

Ivanisevic, B. (2007). *Against the Current – War Crimes Prosecutions in Serbia*. International Center for Transitional Justice, New York.

Ivanisevic, B. (2008). *The War Crimes Chamber in Bosnia and Herzegovina. From Hybrid to Domestic Court*. International Center for Transitional Justice, New York.

Jalusic, V. (2004). Gender and victimization of the nation as pre- and post-war identity discourse. In R. Seifert (Ed.), *Gender, Identität und kriegerischer Konflikt. Das Beispiel des ehemaligen Jugoslawien*. Lit-Verlag, Münster, 40–67.

Jansen, S. (2010). Of wolves and men: Postwar reconciliation and the gender of international encounters. *Focaal – Journal of Global and Historical Anthropology*, 57, 33–49.

Johnstone, G., and Van Ness, D. (Eds.). (2006). *Handbook of Restorative Justice*, Routledge, London.

Kartusch, A., and Reiter, G. (2006). Frauenhandel in Nachkriegsgebieten. Bosnien-Herzegowina und der Kosovo. *Osteuropa*, 56(6), 213–226.

Kerr, R. (2004). *The International Tribunal for the Former Yugoslavia. An Exercise in Law, Diplomacy and Politics*. Oxford University Press, Oxford.

Kerr, R. (2005). The road from Dayton to Brussels? The ICTY and the politics of war crimes in Bosnia. *European Security*, 14(3), 319–337.

Kohn, E. (1995). Rape as a weapon for war. Women's human rights during the dissolution of Yugoslavia. *Golden Gate University Law Review*, 25(1), 199–221.

Korac, M. (1994). Representation of mass rape in ethnic conflicts in what was Yugoslavia. *Sociologija*, 6(4), 495–514.

Kriesberg, L. (2004). Comparing reconciliation actions within and between countries. In Y. Bar-Siman-Tov, Y. (Ed.), *From Conflict Resolution to Reconciliation*. Oxford University Press, Oxford, 81–110.

Kriesberg, L. (2007). External contributions to post-mass-crime rehabilitation. In B. Pouligny, S. Chesterman, and A. Schnabel (Eds.), *After Mass Crime. Rebuilding States and Communities*. United Nations University, New York, 243–271.

Kritz, N. J. (Ed.). (1995). *Transitional Justice. How Emerging Democracies Reckon with Former Regimes* (3 vols.). United States Institute of Peace, Washington, DC.

Kritz, N. J. (2009). Policy implications of empirical research on transitional justice. In H. Van Der Merwe, V. Baxter, and A. R. Chapman (Eds.), *Assessing the Impact of Transitional Justice. Challenges for Empirical Research*. United States Institute of Peace, Washington, DC, 13–22.

Laplante, L. J. (2008). Transitional justice and peace building: Diagnosing and addressing socioeconomic roots of violence through a human rights framework. *International Journal of Transitional Justice*, 2(3), 331–355.

Ludwig Boltzmann Institute for Human Rights (Ed.). (2001). Combat of trafficking in women for the purpose of prostitution. Vienna. (http://www.univie.ac.at/bim) Accessed: 9 February 2015.

Mappes-Niedek, N. (2003). *Die Balkan-Mafia. Staaten in der Hand des Verbrechens – Eine Gefahr für Europa.* Christoph Links-Verlag, Berlin.

McMahon, P. C., and Forsythe, D. P. (2008). The ICTY's impact on Serbia. Judicial romanticism meets network politics. *Human Rights Quarterly,* 30(2), 412–435.

Meernik, J. (2005). Justice and peace? How the international criminal tribunal affects societal peace in Bosnia. *Journal of Peace Research,* 43(3), 271–287.

Mertus, J. (2004). *Women's Participation in the International Criminal Tribunal for the Former Yugoslavia (ICTY). Transitional Justice for Bosnia and Herzegovina.* Women Waging Peace Policy Commission, Cambridge, MA.

Mertus, J. (2007). Findings from focus group research on public perceptions of the ICTY. *Südosteuropa,* 55(1), 107–117.

Milojevic, I. (2012). Transforming violent masculinities in Serbia and beyond. In O. Simic, Z. Volcic, and C. Philpot (Eds.), *Peace Psychology in the Balkans. Dealing with a Violent Past while Building Peace.* Springer Peace Psychology Book Series. Springer Science and Business Media, New York, 57–74.

Minow, M. (1998). *Between Vengeance and Forgiveness. Facing History after Genocide and Mass Violence.* Beacon Press, Boston.

Minow, M. (Ed.). (2002). *Breaking the Cycles of Hatred. Memory, Law and Repair.* Princeton University Press, Princeton, NJ.

Moratti, M., and Sabic-El-Rayess, A. (2009). *Transitional Justice and DDR: The Case of Bosnia and Herzegovina.* International Center for Transitional Justice, New York.

Ni Aolain, F., and Turner, C. (2007). Gender, truth and transition. *UCLA Women's Law Journal,* 16, 229–279.

Olsson, L., Hostens, K., Skjelsbæk, I., and Barth, F. E. (2004). *Gender Aspects of Conflict Interventions: Intended and Unintended Consequences.* Report to the Ministry of Foreign Affairs, Oslo.

Olusanya, O. (2005). *Sentencing War Crimes and Crimes against Humanity under the ICTY.* Europa Law, Groningen.

Orentlicher, D. (2008). *Shrinking the Space for Denial: The Impact of the ICTY in Serbia.* Open Society Institute, New York.

Orentlicher, D. (2010). *That Someone Guilty Be Punished: The Impact of the ICTY in Bosnia.* Open Society Institute, New York.

Petrovic-Ziemer, L. (2013a). Analysis of interviews with TJ institutions. In M. Fischer and L. Petrovic-Ziemer (Eds.), *Dealing with the Past in the Western Balkans. Initiatives for Peacebuilding and Transitional Justice in Bosnia-Herzegovina, Serbia and Croatia.* Berghof Report 18. Berghof Foundation, Berlin, 29–44.

Petrovic-Ziemer, L. (2013b). Analysis of interviews with CSOs. In M. Fischer and L. Petrovic-Ziemer (Eds.), *Dealing with the Past in the Western Balkans. Initiatives for Peacebuilding and Transitional Justice in Bosnia-Herzegovina, Serbia and Croatia.* Berghof Report 18. Berghof Foundation, Berlin, 45–70.

Sajkas, M. (2007). *Transitional Justice and the Role of the Media in the Balkans.* Discussion paper. International Center for Transitional Justice, New York. (http://www.ictj.org/images/content/8/3/833.pdf).

Sarac-Hadzihalilovic, A., Kulenovic, A., and Kucukalic, A. (2008). Stress, memory and Bosnian war veterans. *Bosnian Journal of Basic Medical Sciences,* 8(2), 135–140.

Schabas, W. A. (2006). *The UN International Tribunals: The Former Yugoslavia, Rwanda and Sierra Leone.* Cambridge University Press, Cambridge.

Schabas, W. A. (2013). *Kein Frieden ohne Gerechtigkeit? Die Rolle der internationalen Strafjustiz.* Hamburger Edition, Hamburg.

Schäuble, M. (2006). "Imagined suicide": Self-sacrifice and the making of heroes in post-war Croatia. *Anthropology Matters Journal*, 8(1), 1–14.

Schroer-Hippel, M. (2011a). Männlichkeit und zivilgesellschaftliche Friedensarbeit – Konsequenzen aus der Gender- und Konfliktforschung. *Femina Politika*, 1, 57–67.

Schroer-Hippel, M. (2011b). Kriegsveteranen in der Friedensarbeit – Militarisierte Männlichkeit als Friedenspotenzial? In B. Engels and C. Gayer (Eds.), *Geschlechterverhältnisse, Frieden und Konflikt. Feministische Denkanstöße für die Friedens- und Konfliktforschung.* Nomos, Baden-Baden, 95–112.

Simic, O. (2012). *Regulation of Sexual Conduct in UN Peacekeeping Operations*. Springer, New York.

Simic, O. (2016). Rape, silence and denial. In M. Fischer and O. Simic (Eds.), *Transitional Justice and Reconciliation – Lessons from the Balkans.* Routledge, London, 102–120.

Simic, O., Volcic, Z., and Philpot, C. (Eds.). (2012). *Peace Psychology in the Balkans. Dealing with a Violent Past While Building Peace*. Springer Peace Psychology Book Series. Springer Science and Business Media, New York.

Skjelsbaek, I. (2012). *The Political Psychology of War Rape: Studies from Bosnia and Herzegovina.* Routledge, London.

Slapsak, S. (2000). *Women's Discourse – War Discourse. Essays and Case Studies from Yugoslavia and Russia.* Topas & ISH, Ljubljana.

Spoerri, M., and Freyberg-Inan, A. (2008). From prosecution to persecution. Perceptions of the International Criminal Tribunal for the Former Yugoslavia (ICTY) in Serbian domestic politics. *Journal of International Relations and Development*, 11(4), 350–384.

Stability Pact for South Eastern Europe. (2003). Report on the 5th Meeting of the Stability Pact Task Force on Trafficking in Human Beings. European Union, Stability Pact for SEE, Brussels.

Stern, J. (2015). *Reducing Sexual Exploitation and Abuse in UN Peacekeeping. Ten Years after the Zeid Report.* Civilians in Conflict Policy Brief No. 1. Stimson Center, Washington, DC.

Stodiek, T. (2006). *The OSCE and the Creation of Multi-ethnic Police Forces in the Balkans.* Working Paper 14. Centre for OSCE Research, Hamburg.

Subotic, J. (2009). *Hijacked Justice. Dealing with the Past in the Balkans.* Cornell University Press, Ithaca, NY.

Subotic, J. (2011). Expanding the scope of post-conflict justice: Individual, state and societal responsibility for mass atrocity. *Journal of Peace Research*, 48(2), 157–169.

Sullivan, D., and Tifft, L. (Eds.). (2006). *Handbook of Restorative Justice: A Global Perspective.* Routledge International Handbooks, London.

Teitel, R. (2014). *Globalizing Transitional Justice: Contemporary Essays.* Oxford University Press, Oxford.

Teitel, R. G. (2000). *Transitional Justice.* Oxford University Press, New York.

Thoms, O., Ron, J., and Paris, R. (2008). *The Effects of Transitional Justice Mechanisms. A Summary of Empirical Research Findings and Implications for Analysts and Practitioners,* Working Paper. Centre for International Policy Studies, University of Ottawa, Ottawa.

Ulrich, S. (2001, 11 April). Entfesselte Blauhelme. *Süddeutsche Zeitung*, 8.

Van Der Merwe, H., Baxter, V., and Chapman, A. R. (Eds.). (2009). *Assessing the Impact of Transitional Justice. Challenges for Empirical Research.* United States Institute of Peace, Washington, DC.

Vuskovic, L., and Trifunovic, Z. (Eds.). (2008). *Women's Side of War.* Women in Black, Belgrade.

Zarkov, D. (2007). *The Body of War. Media, Ethnicity, and Gender in the Break-up of Yugoslavia. Durham.* Duke University Press, London.

Zehr, H. (2002). *Little Book of Restorative Justice.* Good Books, New York.

8 Truth commissions, human rights and gender

Normative changes in transitional moments

Susanne Buckley-Zistel[1]

Over the past two decades, dealing with the legacy of violent conflict and repression has become a global norm. The spread of transitional justice has made it a rule rather than an exception, leading Iavor Rangelov and Ruti Teitel to declare that 'we are in what might be called the global phase of transitional justice' (2009, 162). Hardly any peace accord is signed without the inclusion of a truth commission or tribunal, and retributive and restorative measures to deliver justice are being discussed from Afghanistan to Zimbabwe. Importantly, they operate in moments of transition between a violent past and an envisaged peaceful future and thus carry the promise of affecting social relations and rendering them less antagonistic.

This moment of transition might also provide an opportunity for assessing, discussing and unintentionally or intentionally influencing the relationship between women and men in a society and thus for contributing to more gender justice. The latter may require a specific provision in the working of transitional justice mechanisms. As noted by Julissa Mantilla Falcon in a report for the World Bank,

> a gender perspective in TC's [truth commission] report can help bring about changes in existing laws and patterns of behaviour that have contributed to inequality and discrimination. A gender perspective can also promote understanding that women's experiences of conflict, violence, and repression have typically been ignored in favor of males' views. The invisibility of women as victims of, and as active participants in, armed conflict contributes to their overall invisibility in the process of peace negotiation and conflict prevention.
>
> (World Bank 2006, 4)

Against this backdrop, the objective of this chapter is to explore how transitional justice processes incorporate a gender perspective, that is how the categories of women, gender and feminism have been included in its mechanisms and procedures. This shall be done by assessing what kind of crimes are considered to be relevant for transitional justice processes, and if and how redressing them bears the potential of contributing to wider social changes towards gender-just societies in which men and women are treated equally.[2]

In order to limit the scope of the study, this chapter focuses mainly on truth commissions. While there is a large body of literature on the gendered nature of tribunals (Chappell 2012; Ní Aoláin 2012; Studzinsky 2011), mainly due to a vibrant feminist debate in legal studies, truth commissions have so far obtained little albeit rapidly growing attention, both academically and in practice. The objective of this chapter is, however, not to paint a comprehensive picture of one or all truth commissions but to illustrate general historical developments and to underline some tendencies in current practice. To this end, it draws mainly on the mandates and proceedings of the commissions in South Africa, Ghana, Peru and Sierra Leone. These commissions have been selected because they mark milestones in the practice: South Africa was the first to consider women and gender-related aspects; Ghana the first to ensure the strong participation of women in the institutional structures of the commission; Peru brought both these aspects together; and Sierra Leone was the first to expand its enquiry from redressing political and civil rights abuses (against women) to economic, social and cultural rights. The chapter begins with a brief introduction into current thinking about the nexus of women, gender and transitional justice. Next, it explores what measures are being taken to respond to sexual and gender-based crimes before finishing with some reflections as to how their incorporation in transitional justice – here truth commissions – might contribute to affecting wider social change, or what shall be referred to as a feminist, emancipatory concern.

One thread that runs through the analysis is the changing meaning of rights over time and space. The discussion of the notion of justice and its framing in the context of truth commissions reveals the contingent nature of norms more generally which are shaped inter alia through practice, experience and lobbying. Rather than being fixed and permanent, what is considered to be right (or wrong) is constantly debated. Regarding the discussion in this chapter, significant changes have taken place rather rapidly in the course of two decades. Truth commissions thus provide a good example to illustrate how rights are socially and politically constructed.

Gendering transitional justice

While in its initial stages transitional justice was considered to be gender-neutral – rendering it gender-blind – more recent practical and academic contributions challenge this assumption from a gender and/or feminist perspective. A gendered perspective on transitional justice involves identifying and addressing the exclusion, or insufficient inclusion, of the different experiences of women and men in transitional justice processes (Buckley-Zistel and Zolkos 2012). In many incidences, both in literature and practice, this has been understood as synonymous with the social category of women, directing the main focus of research onto the systemic privileging and universalising of male perspectives which renders female perspectives inferior, irrelevant or invisible. This exclusion means that women's potential to contribute to reconstructive processes remains unutilised and that their particular suffering during violent conflict is not recognised. Many efforts to gender transitional justice focus on sexual violence, providing a necessary corrective to the general tendency to ignore or de-emphasise sexual abuses as a form of violence (Cahn 2005). Regarding international jurisprudence and international legal practice, numerous academic contributions discuss the categorisation of different forms of sexual violence, including rape, sexual enslavement and trafficking, impregnation, sterilisation and enforced prostitution, as war crimes (Ní Aoláin 2006). This includes the analysis and discussions of the gendered mandate of ad hoc, hybrid and international tribunals, truth and reconciliation commissions, and gendered violence not only during conflict but also during the transition phase. In addition, issues regarding women's well-being in courtrooms and in the legal enforcement mechanisms, such as the questions of the status of victim-witnesses, interviewing methods, admission of evidence, protection and support of victims of sexual violence to prevent retraumatisation, and their social reintegration are scrutinised (Campbell 2004).

A slightly different direction is taken by approaches of gendering transitional justice which focus on discourses of femininity and masculinity, often criticising 'masculine' conceptions of law and accountability (Ross 2003). They advocated for a deeper attunement to more 'feminine' modes of achieving justice and seeking healing, for example through the production of familial narratives. These approaches have stressed that the nature of gendered exclusions in the transitional justice settings has been conceptual rather than merely situational, rendering female experiences, stories and perspectives largely irrelevant.

In contrast, contributions with a more feminist agenda are not only concerned about the different experiences of men and women during violent conflicts and their transition, but with a wider emancipatory agenda of women's liberation and the establishment of equal power relations between the sexes. In an effort to provide a more systematic analysis of the field, in a seminal article Christine Bell and Catherine O'Rourke ask, 'Where are women, where is gender, and where is feminism in transitional justice?' (Bell and O'Rourke 2007, 23). They criticise that in the first phase of transitional justice, women were more generally absent from institutions and forums for rendering post-violence justice. This was mainly due to the fact that peace negotiations and post-conflict reconstruction remained in the hands of male politicians with women largely missing from the negotiating tables, even though they were often strongly represented in civil society initiatives and peace movements, attempting to assert their presence in transitional justice processes and beyond (Mageza-Barthel 2012).

Responding to this form of criticism may involve the inclusion of more women in transitional processes or what is commonly referred to as an 'add women and stir' approach. Regarding gender, Bell and O'Rourke expand their perspective by arguing that including women in transitional justice processes is not only important in and of itself, but also because of their particular gender-based experiences during violent conflicts and repression, since these frequently differ from those of men (Bell and O'Rourke 2007, 26). This might entail their experience of violence and its repercussions as civilians, for instance in their social roles as mothers and wives, but also as targets of sexual and gender-based violence in the context of human rights abuses. Regarding the latter, it is only since the verdicts of the International Criminal Tribunal for Rwanda and the International Criminal Court for the Former Yugoslavia that rape has been considered a war crime – and, in the particular verdict of Jean-Paul Akayesu in 1996, even a genocide crime – and that it now constitutes a significant aspect of legal prosecution and international criminal law, as part of the Statute of the International Criminal Court.

Enlarging the scope of what constitutes a crime to be addressed in transitional justice processes, including the different experiences of men and women in the proceedings, and recognising that dealing with the past in post-violent societies differs depending on the social category, would form adequate responses to this form of criticism. As a result of debates around these dimensions, an increasing number of provisions in tribunals and truth commissions have been introduced to account for the gendered experience of war and violence. For instance, as we shall see in the following, truth commissions have used various approaches such as gender-mainstreaming (e.g. Ghana) to add women, or including gender-based experiences (e.g. South Africa and Peru) in their proceedings.

Yet Bell and O'Rourke do not stop here. Rather, through their third critique they advocate for a feminist perspective on transitional justice in order to contribute to a more gender just society. As they note, the 'feminist unease with the struggle for inclusion is rooted in more fundamental questions about what exactly transitional justice is transiting "from" and "to"' (Bell and O'Rourke 2007, 35). They argue that transitional justice needs to contribute to the redistribution of power and resources based on a more nuanced understanding of peace and security, which moves beyond the mere absence of physical violence (ibid., 30) and includes political, social and economic equality. At the core of their concern are the wider social changes encouraged for instance by the work of truth commissions and/or their final reports, which incorporate recommendations as to how crimes can be redressed as well as prevented in the future. This moves beyond the mere recognition of the gendered experience of violence and transitional justice processes since it seeks to contribute to reducing the power asymmetries between men and women in societies. Their notion of feminism in transitional justice thus carries a strong emancipatory component.

Using Bell and O'Rourke's categories – women, gender and feminism – as an analytical backdrop, this chapter explores the development of truth commissions regarding the normative frameworks that guide their procedures. Drawing on two questions articulated by Susanne Baer this shall reveal, first, how gender conditions what we understand as (transitional) justice and, second, to what extent (transitional) justice can contribute to facilitating gender relations in the society more broadly (Baer 2008, 556), that is if they carry a feminist potential. This is based on the assumption that a field of social practice – such as transitional justice – is framed by a particular understanding of fundamental norms and conventions, such as what constitutes a crime or human rights abuse in need of redress through transitional justice (Campbell 2007, 420), thus conditioning how we understand it. At the same time, this field shapes the possibilities of how to redress the particular injury, that is how best to respond to crimes by means of transitional justice, as well as how to contribute to changes that challenge the social structures which rendered violence possible in the first place. By drawing on truth commissions, the following analysis shall consider each of these aspects in turn.

Truth commissions

Depending on the definition and description, 20–30 truth commissions have been established worldwide by governments or civil society actors to bring to light human rights abuses in the context of violent conflict or repression (Wiebelhaus-Brahm 2010). Initially conceived as alternatives to state-centred legal proceedings, first in Latin America, they have assumed a complementary role by now. Truth commissions can be understood as temporary establishments that, through a multitude of individual testimonies, uncover the crimes of violent regimes or conflicts and expose patterns of repression and discrimination, such as the persecution of politically, ethnically or racially marginalised groups. The records of truth commissions therefore counteract human rights violations and crimes against humanity by renouncing revisionism as well as by establishing social acceptance of the fact that breaches of the law have taken place, even if their origins and causes remain contentious. This is particularly pertinent if the truth about abuses (i.e. the knowledge about the violence) is unclear or has been suppressed due to social or political forces.

According to Michael Humphrey, truth commissions are composed of two distinct elements: the process and the product (2003, 176). While the process of truth-searching is legitimised by the large-scale involvement of all parties concerned, often through public staging, the product in the form of a final report resembles an attempt at sealing the interpretation of the past. In this sense, the process of speaking the truth serves a performative function, whilst the final report is meant to facilitate a sense of closure. Nevertheless, the final reports of truth commissions are also places where recommendations for wider social, political and economic changes can be articulated and promoted. Regarding the analysis in this chapter, it is important to bear in mind that the process of establishing the truth takes place in the hearings and that it is here where sexual and gender-based violence is articulated – or silenced. These hearings are often disseminated by the media and may thus indirectly affect the attitudes and views of the recipients. In addition, the recommendations of the final report are supposed to contribute to gender justice. This is done through suggesting concrete actions such as the amendment of existing legislation or the establishment of new institutional structures.

As illustrated earlier, gendering transitional justice affects all mechanisms and procedures in the field, not only truth commissions. Yet are truth commissions particularly suitable for addressing women and gender-related human rights abuses and for contributing to a more gender-just society? A number of characteristics would suggest so. First, in contrast to tribunals, truth commissions do not focus on the individual guilt of a perpetrator, but mostly assume a wider social perspective on the crimes committed. As a consequence, they situate atrocities in the prevailing political, social and economic structures of a society and reveal patterns as well as developments over time and space. Second, their uncovering of the truth serves to construct a particular narrative about the events which is open to the inclusion of a gendered perspective, as for instance represented in specific chapters in the final reports of commissions. The dissemination of the final report by the media, in the form of books and public events, moreover bears the potential of bringing these topics to the attention of a wider audience and to stimulate reflection on gender asymmetries in society. Third, most truth commissions release specific recommendations to various interest groups, including the national government, and thus may provide impetus for concrete measures to prevent or redress gendered human rights abuses. This often takes the form of recommending reparations or asking for institutional reforms which, again, can open windows for a more gender-just society.[3] Finally yet importantly, the mandates of truth commissions are drawn up individually for each commission so that insights and lessons learnt from other commissions can be incorporated. As central to this chapter, this allows for a continuously changing normative framework regarding what crimes are to be addressed by truth commissions. Due to a very active and engaged group of norm entrepreneurs in the form of think tank staff, consultants, donor agencies and the like who advise truth commissions, the travelling and expansion of the normative framework – including the introduction of gendered perspectives – is enabled.

Even though it is difficult to identify particular phases regarding the changing normative framework of truth commissions, a cursory look at truth commissions after South Africa's (1996–1998) first inclusion of sexual crimes illustrates the rising awareness of women and gender. In the late 1990s, commissions such as in Guatemala (1997–1999) did not include a gender perspective in their mandate, but in their report and recommendations. As illustrated later, this was also the case in Peru (2001–2003). A turning point in this regard marked the East Timor (2001–2005) and Sierra Leone (2002–2004) truth commissions, which explicitly mentioned rape and other forms of sexual violence in their mandate as crimes to be investigated, as well as dedicating a section of the report to the topic and issuing relevant recommendations. Following this, Liberia (2006–2009) and Kenya (2009–2013) had equally strong provisions, and the most recent commission, the Tunisian Truth and Dignity Commission (2014 to date), has a strong focus on gender and sexual violence in all aspects of its work as well.

Regarding the themes that are of relevance for these commissions, there is a strong focus on sexual violence (not only against women). Moreover, women are often identified as vulnerable groups (next to children and the elderly), suggesting that they are particularly exposed to these forms of crimes. A further tendency is the protection of women (and men) as witnesses when it comes to testifying to acts of sexual violence, and commissions suggest ways of rendering their giving testimony less shameful and harmful. Regarding recommendations, a broad spectrum has been suggested reaching from symbolic gestures such as memorials to material compensation or even land titles.

What crimes?

So what crimes are being addressed by truth commissions? Responding to this query requires first and foremost a perspective that includes what Bell and O'Rourke assume under the category of gender. Earlier commissions such as in Argentina and Chile did not take the gendered experience of conflict and transition into consideration but assumed a supposedly gender-neutral approach to truth (Ní Aoláin and Turner 2007, 257; Theidon 2007, 457). Since the experiences of women were absent, what constituted a crime was mainly based on men's experiences, rendering androcentric what counted as a criminal offence and what did not. In contrast, commissions in Guatemala and South Africa had formally gender-neutral mandates yet decided to pay particular attention to crimes of a sexual or gendered nature, while more recent commissions in Ghana, Haiti, Peru, Sierra Leone, Liberia and East Timor explicitly included them from the beginning (Nesiah 2006, 7). Yet let us look at the developments more closely.

One of the first commissions to realise the omission of women's experiences in its proceedings was the South African Truth and Reconciliation Commission (TRC) which, based on the Promotion of the National Unity Act of 1995, was supposed to investigate gross human rights violations defined as killing, abduction, severe ill treatment and torture during apartheid. In its initial phase, according to Beth Goldblatt and Sheila Meintjes, the TRC excluded crimes against women due to three reasons (Goldblatt and Meintjes 1998, 8): first, the narrow interpretation of the category 'severe ill-treatment' as stipulated in the Act was not wide enough to include the specific plight of women such as forced removals, pass arrests and other systematic forms of violence, and they did not fit the commission's more general definition of gross human rights violations, which focused mainly on physical abuses. Moreover, while certain forms of assault such as rape and genital mutilation were regarded as human rights abuses by the TRC, other methods, such as not providing sanitary towels when needed, body searches performed by men or making women undress in front of male wardens, were not considered as rights violations by the women or in society more generally (ibid., 11).

Second, women's evidence in their social roles as wives and mothers of victims, rather than as direct victims of physical violence, often put them in the group of secondary victims rather than of primary agents in the fight against apartheid, limiting – in their eyes – the relevance of their experiences for the hearings. Due to women's inferior status in South Africa, they tended not to consider their own experiences as important enough for the truth commission (ibid., 10). Their suffering was located in the private realm in their role as supporters of men, rendering it socially inferior, while men were located in the public realm as freedom fighters and resisters of oppression, rendering their agency socially (and politically) more meaningful (Ross 2003, 331). Moreover, early on it was noted that whenever women testified they did so about the abuses of men (mainly male relatives) yet not about their own plight (Graybill 2001, 4). This was despite the fact that the definition of 'victim' in the Act included relatives and dependents of victims – such as wives, mothers, daughters and sisters – even when they were not subjected to direct torture themselves (ibid.). It was however quickly recognised by the commission and lobby organisations that women suffered differently (e.g. that the imprisonment, detention or death of a family member meant the loss of a breadwinner and thus often abject poverty). In addition, it was often impossible for women to find employment if their spouses were known to be politically active, while culturally the loss of a husband was a loss of status and thus detrimental for the women left behind.

Third, Goldblatt and Meintjes argue that the mere setting of the TRC kept women from testifying about sexual and gender-based violence. Due to the fear of stigma and shame, these crimes were often difficult to articulate, particularly in front of a public commission and with hearings broadcast all over the country.

After a petition by advocacy groups, the commission installed three women's hearings in different parts of the country. The first was held in 1996 and provided a platform for females to speak out about gender-specific human rights abuses and degradation related to childbirth and breast-feeding, rape, threats of rape and threats of forced abortion. Women had the option of giving testimony behind screens to conceal their identity and/or to speak before women-only panels and a mainly female audience. Goldblatt and Meintjes hence conclude that 'the hearing gave women an opportunity to speak about themselves and their experiences of detention, harassment and imprisonment which they might not otherwise have had,' they thus provided a space to let both women and gender to come to the fore (1998, 8). Nevertheless, they point out that only a small fraction of sexual assaults and rape were reported to the commission, be it in women's hearings or more generally, since many women still failed to see the political dimension of sexual assaults (ibid., 10). This was confirmed by the TRC's report in 1996 that stated that even though more than half of all deponents were female (54.8 per cent) only 43.9 per cent identified themselves as victims (Graybill 2001, 6).

Regarding Bell and O'Rourke's category of women, the Ghana National Reconciliation Commission (NRC), established in 2002, was one of the first to ensure their participation through its staffing practice, daily operations, hearings and the compilation of the final report. While this form of mainstreaming might have turned the equal participation of women into a relevant organising principle in all aspects of the commission's work, critics hold against it that in the absence of designated staff to address gender issues these concerns were still neglected (Nesiah 2006, 3). In other words, the setup promoted women as persons, yet not their gendered experience of human rights abuses. Helen Scanlon and Kelli Muddell note that in the case of Ghana this led to the subsuming of gender-based violence amongst wider human rights violations and the absence of a special focus on these crimes in the final report. They concluded that 'the lack of focused attention on women – who submitted less than 20 percent of all testimonies – rendered gender-based violence largely invisible within the process' (Scanlon and Muddell 2009, 12).

A different approach was followed by the Peruvian Truth and Reconciliation Commission (PTRC), which sought to incorporate both a women and a gender perspective by establishing a special unit tasked exclusively with gender, by actively seeking out testimonies by women, and by dedicating two chapters of its final report to the matter. The PTRC was created by the Supreme Decree and was tasked with uncovering the truth about murders, kidnappings, forced disappearances, torture and other gross bodily harm, as well as abuses of the collective rights of native communities (Mantilla Falcon 2005, 1–2). Even though the Supreme Decree made no explicit reference to crimes of a sexual or gender-based nature, the commission decided to include them in its mandate due to the importance of the issue and the necessity to provide a space for women to recount the crimes. Yet, similar to the experience in South Africa, women testified mainly about human rights abuses endured by male family members, downplaying their own suffering. At the time, there was only little social awareness about the nature of sexual crimes, even though during the conflict state agents routinely raped females and rebel groups committed sexual assaults on a regular basis (ibid., 2).

In order to develop a definition of sexual violence and refine its normative assumptions, the PTRC drew on sources of international human rights law, humanitarian law and international criminal law, as well as treaties which expressly address violence against women (Mantilla Falcon 2005, 2). Based on this, as well as on previous experiences in other transitional justice processes, the PTRC defined sexual violence as

> the realization of a sexual act against one or more persons or when a person is forced to realize a sexual act by force or threat of force or through coercion caused by fear of violence, intimidation, detention, psychological oppression or abuse of power used against that person or other persons, or taking advantage of a coercive environment or the inability of the person to freely consent.
>
> (Mantilla Falcon 2005, 3)

Against this backdrop, the commission did not only investigate rape but also other forms of gender-based and sexual violence including sexual slavery, sexual blackmail, forced prostitution, pregnancy and nudity – widening the normative remit of what kind of crimes are to be addressed significantly. Regarding its practical translation, in the final report the commission noted that many crimes remained unreported, mirroring the experience of other truth commissions. This was explained by the feeling of guilt and shame of the women, a general social understanding that sexual violence does not constitute a human rights abuse but collateral damage of war, and that it often occurred in the context of other abuses such as massacres, arbitrary detention, summary executions and torture, overshadowing sexual violence (Mantilla Falcon 2005, 3). Nevertheless, two chapters of the final report were dedicated to gender and sexual violence and a gender lens was incorporated in thematic issues such as history, individual human rights abuses and patterns of human rights abuses, as well as in the final recommendations (Nesiah 2006, 4). Vasuki Nesiah thus observes that 'the final report offers an important glimpse of how gendered structures and ideologies shaped the human rights history of Peru' (ibid.).

Despite the significant achievements of the Peruvian commission regarding sexual and gender-based violence against women, Kimberly Theidon adds a word of caution when she notes that by foregrounding this particular form of human rights abuses other nonsexual gender human rights abuses such as structural vulnerability and structural violence remain overshadowed and thus ignored (Theidon 2007, 474). As in other truth commissions, the definition of what constitutes a crime was largely about what can be done to a body, to the neglect of other experiences of pain and suffering (Ross 2001, 252). How conflict impacts differently on men and women might escape truth commissions which focus predominantly on civil and political rights while ignoring social, economic and cultural rights, a criticism that can also easily be extended to the South African Truth and Reconciliation Commission (regarding sexual crimes and beyond) (Schäfer 2011). With some concern it has thus been remarked that

> neglecting other issues has led to the deprioritization of several important dimensions of women's lives and struggles from the human rights radar screen, such as the experience of internally displaced women, women who became sole breadwinners as a result of human rights abuse against spouses, women refugees who fled to other countries, or women prisoners.
>
> (Nesiah 2006, 9)

Amongst the most comprehensive efforts to include women and gender in the work of truth commissions counts the case of the Sierra Leonean Truth and Reconciliation Commission (SLTRC).[4] The SLTRC's (2002–2004) mandate explicitly stated that the commission should 'work to help restore the human dignity of victims and promote reconciliation' and that it should pay 'special attention to the subject of sexual abuses' (Truth and Reconciliation Commission Act 2000, quoted in Nowrojee 2005, 92). Sexual and gender-based violence was thus defined as a crime from the outset. Because staff members had significant experience in the field in addition to comprehensive training, the commission is said to have developed a sound understanding of sexual and gender-based crimes (ibid., 94). Regarding the hearings, the commission discarded its initial idea to have women testify in camera since it was felt that this would undermine the important gesture of raising public awareness for the crimes, perpetuating silence and stigma in society and obstructing wider social change. They thus offered women three options: to testify on camera before the commission, to speak at public hearings where their testimonies would be heard while they were shielded by a screen, or to speak openly and publicly in the course of the hearings.

The final report of the commission included a chapter entitled 'Women in the Armed Conflict', which entailed a detailed analysis of sexual and gender-based violence against women and girls including abduction, dehumanisation, rape, sexual slavery, mutilation, torture and further inhuman acts (Truth and Reconciliation Commission Act 2000, quoted in Nowrojee 2005, 96). Against this backdrop, the report articulates specific recommendations to address the marginalisation of women in politics and society, that is they went beyond merely focusing on the bodily harm of women to include a wider picture of their status in Sierra Leone.

This reveals that significant achievements have been made regarding the treatment of gender and sexual crimes in truth commissions, as well as the inclusion of women in their processes. This ties in with a more general normative change regarding gender aspects in transitional justice as laid out at the beginning of the chapter. To return to Bell and O'Rourke's three critiques, commissions such as in Ghana added women to account for a better gender balance in their daily work; commissions such as in Peru but also in South Africa broadened their scope by adding gender to consider the particular, although still mainly physical human rights abuses during times of violence; and those in Sierra Leone also addressed social issues and structural violence.

Yet where is feminism in all of this? Does the inclusion of women and/or gender in the investigations of truth commissions contribute to creating some form of emancipation and a more equitable society for women? Do they foster a transition to gender justice? This can be considered by looking at how truth commissions suggest adequate ways of responding to the newly defined crimes, as explored in the following.

What response?

When it comes to redressing human rights abuses in transitional justice processes the concern is less *whether* something is done, but *what* (Nagy 2008, 276). Continuing with the earlier examples, the South African TRC was the first commission to become aware of the exclusion of women in truth-finding processes, but its final report did not incorporate concrete recommendations as to how to respond to sexual and gender-based violence or how to prevent it in the future (Sigsworth and Valji 2012). In contrast, the final report of the Peruvian commission included a comprehensive plan of reparations for victims of violence, emphasising that this requires a specific gender perspective (World Bank 2006, 20). This incorporated recommendations regarding symbolic reparations (public gestures, acts of acknowledgement and memorials) with special reference to women. The commission further recommended that women who assumed a leadership role during the civil war should be recognised as well. This was extended by proposing economic reparations for women who had been raped and to children born as the result of rape, as well as health (including mental health) support.

On a more general note, reparations, both monetary and symbolic, may play a vital role as a response to sexual and gender-based violence for a number of reasons (Nesiah 2006): (1) they can assist in drawing attention to the abuses and support the wider social acceptance that harms have been committed while they (2) provide concrete steps to alleviate pain and to undo harm (if ever possible). In addition to reparations, truth commissions may recommend the prosecution of offenders of sexual violence, encourage institutional reforms to improve women's presence in and access to the justice and security sector, create archives as storing places of memory for future generations, or foster public awareness of women as victims but also as agents in violent strife (ibid., 39).[5]

Despite these achievements, Nesiah notes that even though more attention had been paid to gender dimensions in the final report of the PTRC, many Peruvian feminists felt that the whole process of the truth commission was a lost opportunity for a more thorough and systematic engagement with social gender relations (Nesiah 2006, 4). In concrete, the criticism referred to the absence of analysis regarding

> the gendered patterns of human rights abuse, comprehend the diverse ways in which Peruvian women figured in the nation's human rights history, open a national conversation about the enabling conditions of abuse against women, and use such work to mobilize institutional reform and broader political support for enhancing women's access to justice in preventing and redressing human rights abuse.
>
> (Nesiah 2006, 4)

From a feminist perspective, incorporating these aspects is crucial, since truth commissions are rare opportunities where these wider social issues can be articulated and discussed.

Finally, it is important to ask what implication the inclusion of sexual and gender-based crimes in truth commissions has on advancing gender justice, that is on Bell and O'Rourke's category of a feminist emancipation towards more equality. Critically it has been remarked that portraying women as passive and hapless victims – at the mercy of men – perpetuates images of women's inferiority and thus their lesser position in society (Franke 2006, 825). The exclusive focus on sexual crimes is based on a highly selective image of femininity – marked by peacefulness and nonaggressiveness – leading to ignoring women's role as political agents in times of crisis, and consequently also as executors of violence and cruelty, while perpetuating more widespread prejudices that reduce women to sexual beings alone (Nesiah 2006, 10). As Kirstin Campbell notes,

> if women only narrate rape, then they appear as passive victims of sexual violence. Such narrative framing reproduces traditional models of active masculinity and passive femininity. It produces the problem of the legal representation of women's agency, which becomes particularly important in this context of the engendering of naming and witnessing harms of conflict.
>
> (Campbell 2007, 426)

The unawareness of the activity of (some) women is crucial since women, too, might play an active role in a violent conflict – yet this often remains excluded in transitional justice processes. In Liberia, for example the Truth and Reconciliation Commission highlighted the plight of women as 'victims' of violent (sexual) attacks, while it failed to draw attention to the fact that women formed a significantly large part of the warring factions (30 per cent of combatants were female).

Accordingly, their crimes were not considered in the public eye. In doing so, the findings of the TRC undermined the political activities as well as the competences of women to make independent policy decisions; it constructed them as passive objects (Pietsch 2010). Importantly, since much of the gender-based and sexual violence against women is perpetrated as a consequence of their inferior role in society, there is the risk that instead of contributing to more gender justice their social role is reproduced, standing in the way of greater gender justice after transition (Buckley-Zistel 2012). Moreover, it ignores their role as agents in peacebuilding and in other political activities.

Affecting social change and gender justice?

In contrast to other transitional justice mechanisms such as crime tribunals, truth commissions are rather fluid and adaptable to the particular circumstances of a post-violence society. Since they are not enshrined in international criminal law and do not have to adhere to a firm set of standards, they are able to expand their normative framework over the course of time, as apparent in the significant changes that have occurred in the relatively short time span between the South African and the Sierra Leonean truth and reconciliation commissions regarding the inclusion of women and gender aspects. Moreover, their setup provides a space for people affected by violence to tell their story and to have their suffering acknowledged (rather than merely responding to queries such as in courtrooms) (Brants and Klep 2013). In other words, while tribunals are mainly perpetrator-centred, truth commissions have a stronger focus on victims, including women.

In addition, as Vasuki Nesiah points out, truth commissions can move beyond addressing a series of individual cases by investigating conditions in which the abuses occurred and by identifying more general patterns of human rights violations, and they can make recommendations regarding social reforms or reparations, whether with a view to gender or more generally, and thus contribute to what Bell and O'Rourke refer to as feminism (Nesiah 2006, 1). This might lead to more substantive changes in societies, contribute to greater gender justice and prevent sexual and gender-based violence in the future.

While all of this is of major importance, translating thought into action remains a challenge. Many recommendations of truth commissions remain unheard, relevant changes are not introduced and in the absence of political will the situation of women in the society concerned does not improve. It is also important not to overestimate the role of truth commissions in the wider dynamics and struggles of a post-violence society where they might play only a very minor role, and only for a limited period of time. Moreover, even if recommendations are implemented their operationalisation often proves difficult and does not lead to the intended consequences.[6] Thus, even though there is a growing and noticeable recognition of sexual and gender-based crimes and the importance of wider social change in the context of transitional justice mechanisms – a response to all of Bell and O'Rourke's categories – there is still a long way to go for it to have a significant impact on the societies in question.

Normative changes in truth commissions

Assessing the development of women's rights in the context of truth commissions points to a significant change in understanding what constitutes a crime in the transitional justice discourse. By way of conclusions, I thus would like to draw out the normative shifts that have occurred over the past two decades. To start with the category of women, beginning with commissions such as the one in Ghana the inclusion of women in all aspects of their work and their participation in all phases of transition more generally has gained momentum. Next, regarding gender, while the first commissions were blind to the particular gendered crimes committed against women, the South African commission's recognition of sexual and gender-based violence has for the first time led to their prominence. The absence of testimonies regarding women's particular experiences was acknowledged, provision for their inclusion established and the scope of physical abuses widened to incorporate forced abortion, forced nudity and the like. This marks an important turn regarding the nature of the crimes which are being prosecuted by transitional justice and which have, by now, become commonplace in transitional justice discourse and practice. Moreover, in the initial truth commissions, and in transitional justice projects more generally, an androcentric understanding prevailed according to which not only certain forms of violence but also locations (public, not private), certain time spans (during conflict, not after), certain ideas of perpetrators ('foreign enemies', not family members such as in the cause of domestic violence) prevailed so that aspects such as what, when, where and who were strongly influenced by male experiences of violence in times of war or repression. Here, too, a significant normative shift has taken place enabling the inclusion of gendered (male and female) experiences of human rights abuses. Moreover, the notion of rights has been expanded from political to civil rights to incorporate economic, social and cultural rights, which are often more relevant for women who stay behind in abject poverty as a consequence of war and destruction. In other words, rights violations have been extended from mere bodily harm to incorporate other forms of pain and suffering.

Last, regarding feminism the findings of this chapter are inconclusive. From a feminist perspective, this would require transitional justice processes having an impact on power asymmetries between men and women more generally. Yet, if and how social change has occurred towards a more gender-just post-violence society can only be assessed empirically for each individual society and such analyses are still missing, calling for more research in this area.[7] The question where transitional justice societies transition to for women depends on the provisions of truth commissions and their recommendations, yet their impact is also highly conditioned by the existing political climate and the will to change structures to the benefit of women and more a gender-just society.

Importantly, while gender justice is key in its own right, it is also significant regarding the prevention of sexual and gender based violence against women in the future. In many incidences, women become targets of violent assaults due to their inferior position in society. Their social (and biological) role as reproducers of ethnic, religious or national groups through childbirth can turn them into targets of crimes such as rape (inter alia to impregnate them with children from the enemy group), mutilation of their reproductive organs, and forced sterilisation, to name but a few, which all aim to undermine the reproduction of their identity group. This has been referred to as acts of ethnic cleansing (or even genocide, as ruled by the International Criminal Tribunal for Rwanda [ICTR]). Moreover, rape and mutilation can be understood as a symbolic attack on the 'Mother of the Nation', that is the guardian of the respective identity group or on the symbolic representation of the body politic (Elshtain 1987, 67). Cases where husbands, brothers, and sons are forced to witness the rape of female members of their family aim at destroying social and cultural cohesion, insulting them in their socially prescribed role as the protectors of 'their' women. Many of these actions are only meaningful if their objective is to harm men by harming women, reducing women to mere objects of communication between men. In order to prevent this in the future – so is the contention of the present author – women's social role as inferior has to be raised and addressed. Due to their open deliberations of sexual and gender-based violence and their wide outreach, truth commissions might carry the potential to stimulate reflection about women's role in society, to improve their standing and thus, albeit indirectly, contribute to the prevention of violence in the future.

On a more conceptual note, the assessment of truth commissions proves to be a good example to illustrate the social and political construction of human rights. Rather than having some form of metaphysical existence their meaning is contingent and subject to discussion, debate and negotiation between different interest groups. This points to the benefit of feminist investigations or other forms of critical enquiry. More generally, they serve as mechanisms to question what is taken for granted and reveal both the contingency of (normative) concepts as well as the possibility of them being changed.

In conclusion, let us thus return to the two questions posed by Susanne Baer at the outset of this chapter. First, pondering how gender conditions what we understand as (transitional) justice does not point to a fixed notion of justice but rather illustrates how the meaning of this norm changes over time, opening windows of opportunity for the inclusion of both women and gender in discourse and practice. Considering, second, to what extent (transitional) justice can break open gender structures more widely – what we have labelled feminist – the findings of this chapter have not been conclusive and require more empirical research. So far, there is little evidence to suggest that truth commissions contribute substantially to gender justice in post-violence societies. Nevertheless, their influence on changing norms regarding human rights abuses in time of violent conflict or repression is a significant achievement.

Notes

1 This chapter was finalized during a fellowship at the Käte Hamburger Kolleg/Centre for Global Cooperation Research, University of Duisburg-Essen. An earlier draft was presented at the ISA/ECPR Human Rights Joint Conference in Istanbul Kadir Has

University, 16–18 June 2014, and I am grateful to Eric Wiebelhaus-Brahm for his comments as a discussant.
2 The focus of this investigation is on women since it assesses normative changes against what is being considered as an androcentric practice of transitional justices.
3 See also the chapter by Martina Fischer in this volume.
4 A further example could have been East Timor. See Porter (2012).
5 All of this, however, relies on women coming forward to report about their victimization, and hence excludes all persons who chose to remain silent due to shame and fear (Rubio-Marín 2006a, 34).
6 See for instance the case studies on reparations in Rubio-Marín (2006b).
7 To analyse this in three transition countries will be subject to a research project entitled *The Acknowledgement of Sexual Violence in Truth Commissions. Victim Labelling Processes and Their Social Implications in Times of Transition*, funded by the Germany Research Foundation (DFG) at the Centre of Conflict Studies, University of Marburg, 2016–2019.

References

Baer, S. (2008). Recht: Normen zwischen Zwang, Konstruktion und Ermöglichung – Gender-Studien zum Recht. In R. Becker and B. Kortendiek (Eds.), *Handbuch Frauen-und Geschlechterforschung*. VS Verlag, Wiesbaden, 555–563.

Bell, C., and O'Rourke, C. (2007). Does feminism need a theory of transitional justice? An introductory essay. *International Journal of Transitional Justice*, 1(1), 23–44.

Brants, C., and Klep, K. (2013). Transitional justice: History telling, collective memory and the victim-witness. *International Journal of Conflict and Violence*, 7(1), 36–49.

Buckley-Zistel, S. (2012). Redressing sexual violence in transitional justice and the labelling of women as "victims". In T. Bonacker, A. Oettler, and C. Safferling (Eds.), *Victims of International Crimes: An Interdisciplinary Discourse*. T.M.C. Asser Press, The Hague, 91–100.

Buckley-Zistel, S., and Zolkos, M. (2012). Introduction: Gender in transitional justice. In S. Buckley-Zistel and R. Stanley (Eds.), *Gender in Transitional Justice*. Palgrave Macmillan, Basingstoke, 1–33.

Cahn, N. (2005). Beyond retribution and impunity: Responding to war crimes of sexual violence. *Stanford Journal of Civil Rights and Civil Liberties*, 1(1), 217–270.

Campbell, K. (2004). The trauma of justice: Sexual violence, crimes against humanity and the international criminal tribunal for the former Yugoslavia. *Social and Legal Studies*, 13(3), 329–350.

Campbell, K. (2007). The gender of transitional justice: Law, sexual violence and the international criminal tribunal for the former Yugoslavia. *International Journal of Transitional Justice*, 1, 411–432.

Chappell, L. (2011). The role of the ICC in transitional gender justice: Capacity and limitations. In S. Buckley-Zistel and R. Stanley (Eds.), *Gender in Transitional Justice*. Palgrave Macmillan, Basingstoke, 37–58.

Elshtain, J. B. (Ed.). (1987). *Women and War*. Harvester, Brighton.

Franke, K. M. (2006). Gendered subjects of transitional justice. *Columbia Journal of Gender and Law*, 15(3), 813–828.

Goldblatt, B., and Meintjes, S. (1998). Dealing with the aftermath: Sexual violence and the Truth and Reconciliation Commission. *Agenda*, 13(36), 7–18.

Graybill, L. (2001). The contribution of the truth and reconciliation commission toward the promotion of women's rights in South Africa. *Women's Studies International Forum*, 24(1), 1–10.

Humphrey, M. (2003). From victim to victimhood: Truth commissions and trials as rituals of political transition and individual healing. *Australian Journal of Anthropology*, 14(2), 171–187.

Mageza-Barthel, R. (2012). Asserting their presence! Women's quest for transitional justice in post-genocide Rwanda. In S. Buckley-Zistel and R. Stanley (Eds.), *Gender in Transitional Justice*. Palgrave Macmillan, Basingstoke, 136–162.

Mantilla Falcon, J. (2005). The Peruvian Truth and Reconciliation Commission's treatment of sexual violence against women. *Human Rights Brief*, 12(2), 1–5.

Nagy, R. (2008). Transitional justice as global project: Critical reflections. *Third World Quarterly*, 29(2), 275–289.

Nesiah, V. (Ed.). (2006). *Truth Commissions and Gender: Principles, Policies, and Procedures*. International Center for Transitional Justice, New York.

Ní Aoláin, F. (2006). Political violence and gender during times of transition. *Columbian Journal of Gender and Law*, 1(3), 338–354.

Ní Aoláin, F. (2012). Gender under-enforcement in transitional justice contexts. In S. Buckley-Zistel and R. Stanley (Eds.), *Gender in Transitional Justice*. Palgrave Macmillan, Basingstoke, 59–87.

Ní Aoláin, F., and Turner, C. (2007). Gender, truth and transition. *UCLA Women's Law Journal*, 16, 229–279.

Nowrojee, B. (2005). Making the invisible war crime visible: Post-conflict justice for Sierra Leone's rape victims. *Harvard Human Rights Journal*, 18, 85–105.

Pietsch, S. (2010). *Women's participation and benefit of the Liberian Truth and Reconciliation Commission – Voices from the field*. Unpublished MA dissertation, Center for Conflict Studies, Philipps-University Marburg.

Porter, E. (2012). Gender-inclusivity in transitional justice strategies: The women in East Timor. In S. Buckley-Zistel and R. Stanley (Eds.), *Gender in Transitional Justice*. Palgrave Macmillan, Basingstoke, 221–240.

Rangelov, I., and Teitel, R. (2009). Global civil society and transitional justice. In I. Rangelov and R. Teitel (Eds.), *Global Yearbook*. Oxford University Press, Oxford, 162–163.

Ross, F. (2001). Speech and silence: Women's testimonies in the first five weeks of hearings of the South African Truth and Reconciliation Commission. In V. Das, A. Kleinman, M. Lock, M. Ramphele, and P. Reynolds (Eds.), *Remaking a World: Violence, Social Suffering and Recovery*. University of California Press, Berkeley, 250–279.

Ross, F. (2003). On having voices and being heard. Some after-effects of testifying before the South African Truth and Reconciliation Commission. *Anthropological Theory*, 3(3), 325–341.

Rubio-Marín, R. (2006a). Introduction. The gender of reparations: Setting the agenda. In R. Rubio-Marín (Ed.), *What Happened to the Women? Gender and Reparations for Human Rights Violations*. SSRC, New York, 20–48.

Rubio-Marín, R. (Ed.). (2006b). *What Happened to the Women? Gender and Reparations for Human Rights Violations*. SSRC, New York.

Scanlon, H., and Muddell, K. (2009). Gender and transitional justice in Africa: Progress and prospects. *African Journal on Conflict Resolution*, 9(2), 9–28.

Schäfer, R. (2011). Gender in der südafrikanischen Wahrheits- und Versöhnungskommission. In S. Buckley-Zistel and T. Kater (Eds.), *Nach Krieg, Gewalt und Repression. Der schwierige Umgang mit der Vergangenheit*. Nomos, Frankfurt, 151–166.

Sigsworth, R., and Valji, N. (2012). Continuities of violence against women in South Africa: The limitations of transitional justice. In S. Buckley-Zistel and R. Stanley (Eds.), *Gender in Transitional Justice*. Palgrave Macmillan, Basingstoke, 156–183.

Studzinsky, S. (2011). Neglected crimes: The challenge of raising sexual and gender-based crimes before the extraordinary chambers in the Court of Cambodia. In S. Buckley-Zistel and R. Stanley (Eds.), *Gender in Transitional Justice*. Palgrave Macmillan, Basingstoke, 88–114.

Theidon, K. (2007). Gender in transition: Common sense, women, and war. *Journal of Human Rights*, 6, 435–478.

Wiebelhaus-Brahm, E. (Ed.). (2010). *Truth Commissions and Transitional Societies. The Impact on Human Rights and Democracy*. Routledge, Basingstoke.

World Bank. (2006). *Gender, Justice and Truth Commissions*. World Bank, Washington, DC.

Reforming the security sector and rule of law

The hidden transcripts of local resistance

Keith Krause

Introduction

Several years ago, while spending a few days in Liberia as part of a long-term project that examined post-conflict efforts at violence prevention and reduction, I left the capital for a day to see how the state was "producing order and delivering justice" outside of Monrovia. This was not serious or deep field research, but I simply hitched a ride with consultants from an international nongovernmental organisation (NGO) working on peacebuilding. I was in a county capital called Gbarnga and paid a visit to the police, a local human rights NGO with international staff, journalists working at a nearby radio station, the government's gender advisor and other local officials.[1] After one such meeting, the police chief hitched a ride with me back to the station in one of those African taxis that had no real seats in the rear. The new pickup truck – the police vehicle for the county, with the logo of a Western development agency on it – that was parked in front of the police station apparently had no petrol. The cells in the small police station – which were empty at the time – had been refurbished. There were no files or papers of any sort in sight.

One reason the cells were empty became clear when I met with the local human rights NGO, whose staff explained that most of the petty criminals were known to the community, and against these the community practiced a form of rough justice when matters got out of hand. This included occasional beatings or summary executions (three or four per year) of suspected criminals, whose bodies would show up in the town market square in the early hours of the morning. This did not happen frequently, but more frequently than the police would have liked. The NGO, supported also by Western donors, had many files of cases in which people had failed to receive justice for a myriad of different claims. Some of the cases involved people who were trapped in the formal justice system, in jail but not charged, or facing slow-moving procedures. The NGO happened to have an international NGO staff person who worked on rule of law and justice issues. One of her main concerns seemed to be that when bodies turned up, they lay in the streets for several hours before the police did anything about it, which she found shocking, indecent, and – I quote – "terrible for the children to see." Recalling that Gbarnga had been the headquarters of Charles Taylor's National

Patriotic Front of Liberia at one point in the Liberian civil war, I suspected that the occasional display of a dead body was not likely to have been the most "terrible" thing children in that town had witnessed. I also suspected that from the community's perspective the bodies served as a strong message to "wrongdoers," often associated (rightly or wrongly) with the ex-combatants who had converted to moto-taxi drivers (*pehn-pehns*) (*Economist* 2013).

This bit of academic tourism (which did have a more serious context and purpose) encapsulates some of the themes of this volume. The issue of paternalism is reflected in international donor programmes that supply vehicles but not the budgets to run or maintain them, or in international NGO staff that imports unconsciously Western ideas of justice and rule of law. I do not want to focus on this per se, but instead aim to focus on what James Scott (1985, 1990) called "everyday forms of resistance" and the "hidden transcripts" of resistance by local actors, in particular to programmes designed to regulate and restrict the role of and place of violence in post-conflict states and societies.

This is critical since violence and force are both *productive* of particular forms of social order and *purposive* in the sense that they are seldom used or employed as threat randomly. Controlling the use of force and occasionally using it is, as Charles Tilly (1990) and many others have pointed out, at the heart of the state-building process.[2] As international peacebuilding moves away from its emphasis on spreading liberal norms and practices – such as regular elections and the promotion of civil society towards statebuilding and institution building – scholars and analysts need to be conscious of how power is being exercised in these efforts, and what some of the unintended consequences of these programmes and practices may be. Instead of concentrating on the international community and external actors' assessments of the (relative) failure of their projects, I will examine these practices of power and resistance in order to provide a more fine-grained account of the relationship between external and local actors, putting the focus on the way in which local actors take the programmes and policies on offer and bend and fuse them to meet their own purposes and interests.

This chapter will make three propositions. First, there is a tremendous degree of slippage in the transition from the underlying ideas and norms about how peacebuilding works, to the actual policies, programmes and practices that attempt to achieve its goals. This slippage is unidirectional, in the sense that local actors undermine the "liberal peacebuilding" ideal through resistance efforts. Second, the liberal peacebuilding literature – as well as specific arguments about the paternalism of external actors – dramatically overstate the power of external actors, and usually operate with an impoverished notion of power, and how it is exercised, or not. This is what Michael Barnett and Christoph Zürcher (2009) have captured with the notion of the "peacebuilder's contract." Third, peacebuilding is almost always successful – at least from the perspective of some local actors – who use the resources provided by international peacebuilders to achieve their own aims despite the attempts to impose particular models on their practice of politics.

The chapter proceeds first to lay out the normative and institutional underpinnings of the Western (and liberal peacebuilding) notions of the security and justice sector, and offers an account of how these are discursively constructed, rather than being "evidence based" or explicitly validated. It then briefly presents and critiques the way in which power has been conceptualized in the literature on peacebuilding. In the third section, the chapter offers three case studies of forms of resistance to these exercises of power, in the linked domains of security sector reform, post-conflict disarmament, demobilization and reintegration, and promotion of the rule of law. These illustrations are drawn from South Sudan, Burundi and Liberia, and illustrate how resistance operates at the macro, meso and micro levels of interaction.

Peacebuilding and security institutions

At the core of peacebuilding are two ideas about security: the idea that violent conflict, whatever its root causes, must be prevented; and the recognition that providing security to its citizens is one of the core functions/responsibilities of the state. This is to be accomplished through three main ways of designing security institutions:

* First, by creating a relatively sharp institutional divide between internal and external security institutions and functions (police and armed forces, with possible gendarme functions in some cases).
* Second, by establishing democratic or parliamentary oversight of security institutions, which include aspects such as rightsizing, formal budgetary controls, and civil society input into policy-making.
* Third, introducing nonviolent means of resolving conflicts through justice reforms, deeply contentious issues such as land and resource access, entitlements or access to state institutions (jobs, education) are effectively covered up.

This vision is liberal in the simple sense that it reflects the institutional history and development of Western democratic states, but also liberal in the deeper sense that it embodies a vision of the state as a neutral arbiter or honest broker, standing separate from and above competing sociopolitical and socioeconomic claims (and the groups advancing them).

The three elements of this vision were also manifest in particular practices, most notably in security sector reform (SSR), disarmament, demobilization and reintegration (DDR), and rule of law (RoL) programmes. What is most significant about international practices associated with SSR, DDR and RoL is precisely that they were *constructed* as coherent sets of practices. This involved not just the creation of an acronym or label but also the amalgamation of previously disconnected individual domains of action into a unified whole to be "practiced" as a single domain, and causal claims to be made about the impact or importance of the domain. This can be illustrated in all three cases.

In the case of DDR, there is nothing novel about the individual aspects of disarmament, demobilization and reintegration – the D, D and R. We have anecdotal evidence of the demobilization of soldiers and their reintegration into civilian life after the Thirty Years' War, the US Civil War, and World War I, and every major army that included civilian conscripts has, at the end of the fighting, sent its soldiers home (Parker 1997, 162; Holberton 2001; Clarke 1918 cited in Baaré 2006, 20). What *was* new in the 1990s, however, was the fusion of these three into a package that represented "doing DDR." Put schematically, the problem of demobilization of armed actors – which had already been widely recognized as an issue in peace settlements – was coupled to growing concerns over weapons proliferation (and hence the necessity for weapons collection) and then linked to a claim that demobilized former combatants needed assistance to reintegrate successfully in civilian life so as not to pose an ongoing security threat. Each of these claims needed to be advanced individually (x is essential to successful peacebuilding) and then fused (x, y and z are not distinct, but rather one "practice").

The emergence of this practice was neither necessary nor inevitable. Historically D, D and R were *not* linked, and there is little evidence to suggest that all three need to be present, or all three "successful" (however that is understood) in order to make a transition from war to peace. The claim for DDR is discursive and intended to support a particular set of institutional practices, rather than being embedded in any systematic analysis of social realities in conflict and post-conflict zones. While none of the individual elements of DDR was new, the development of a coherent set of practices around DDR represented a conceptual innovation, and an attempt to codify and systematize individual and often disconnected policy responses to a "problem" into a set of practices that shared broadly accepted common standards. This process began in the early 1990s as part of the broader emergence of the peacebuilding paradigm, in places such as Angola, Namibia and Cambodia. The rise of nonstate armed groups and warlordism meant that wars in the Global South were often fought between state and nonstate armed groups who were indistinguishable in terms of training, their commitment to fight and the weaponry employed. The conditions for a (re)establishment of the state monopoly over the instruments and institutions of organized violence after an armed conflict were seldom present.

The idea of security sector reform emerged similarly in recent history and was discursively constructed by the donor community. It was first staked out as an area of importance by the UK in the late 1990s, and focused in particular on Sierra Leone and West Africa, before being generalized throughout peacebuilding practice (OECD 2005). It was instantiated in 2005 and 2007 in two publications from the Organisation for Economic Co-operation and Development's (OECD) *Security System Reform and Governance* and *Handbook on Security System Reform*, which provided a consensus view (from within the international donor community) on why and how to go about reforming and restructuring security sectors. It subsequently found expression in a host of national and international forums, both governmental and nongovernmental (Bryden 2007; Sedra 2010).[3]

Security sector reform thus represented an externally led effort to reshape the security and justice sectors in client states in the name of achieving better (or "good") governance. The security sector was, however, conceived of in extremely broad terms,

> as including: core security actors (e.g. armed forces, police, gendarmerie, border guards, customs and immigration, and intelligence and security services); security management and oversight bodies (e.g. ministries of defense and internal affairs, financial management bodies and public complaints commissions); justice and law enforcement institutions (e.g. the judiciary, prisons, prosecution services, traditional justice systems); and non-statutory security forces (e.g. private security companies, guerrilla armies and private militia).
>
> (OECD 2007, 5)[4]

Although this might be regarded a holistic approach that potentially breaks down policy stovepipes between distinct but interrelated state functions, such a conception effaces the distinction between externally oriented institutions of organized violence (armed forces) and those directed towards providing public order (police forces). The emergence of this division was part of the statebuilding process, and was decisive for achieving public order. Removing the armed forces from the role of domestic security provision (usually repressive), or demilitarizing police forces by changing their organization structure and institutional reporting, were key steps on the road towards creating peaceful states. Treating the security sector holistically in post-colonial states reversed the logic of this process.

Promotion of rule of law by international actors has a somewhat more recent trajectory.[5] The first thing to note is that the concept of rule of law as conceived by the UN system is defined in almost Anglo-Saxon, and probably common law, terms as:

> a principle of governance in which all persons, institutions and entities, public and private, including the State itself, are accountable to laws that are publicly promulgated, equally enforced and independently adjudicated, and which are consistent with international human rights norms and standards. It requires, as well, measures to ensure adherence to the principles of supremacy of law, equality before the law, accountability to the law, fairness in the application of the law, separation of powers, participation in decision-making, legal certainty, avoidance of arbitrariness and procedural and legal transparency.
>
> (United Nations 2004, 4)[6]

This normalization of one tradition of justice (including such concepts as separation of power, transparency and legal certainty) leaves little or no room for informal, community-based, traditional, or local forms of justice, and its promotion is based on the quasi-causal claim that "rule of law is a precondition for sustainable peace and development," and that "in the final analysis, rule of law provides the very foundation for the achievement of the Millennium Development Goals"

(UNDP 2008a, 1, 5).[7] Yet there is little solid empirical evidence to support such claims, and not much of a historical foundation for thinking that this is the role that rule of law – however defined – played in the emergence of Western states and societies (Haggard and Tiede 2011; Browne 2013). Rather RoL represents a claim to knowledge that is used to justify programmes and policies in a competitive resource-scarce environment.

In spite of the unclear causal links and the lack of an empirical record, within a few years, promotion of RoL had become a standard part of UN post-conflict peacebuilding practice. This also gave rise in 2008 – in what could only be described as a fit of institutional madness – to a project to develop "rule of law indicators" for measuring and monitoring programme effectiveness. It came up with 135 distinct indicators to measure the quality of justice, including statistics on the number of assaults on prison officers per 1,000 prisoners per year, whether judges were protected adequately from threats and intimidation, and whether free legal assistance existed (United Nations 2011).[8] Many of these are most likely not easily measurable in advanced industrial states, let alone in the weak institutional contexts of post-conflict societies, and are analytically completely at odds with good practice for measuring and monitoring indicators.

Power, resistance and peacebuilding

How does the international community expect to shape post-conflict peacebuilding and statebuilding through the promotion of DDR, SSR and RoL? Most analyses of the relationship between external and local state builders operate with an undertheorized concept of power, and of the relationship between external and local agents. Monica Toft's (2009, 4) research examining SSR programmes, for example, argues that SSR "offers the potential for both enduring and constructive peace" but does not postulate a mechanism or process by which the programmes that are pushed by external actors actually bring these results, or theorize the nature of the relationship between external and local actors in these efforts.[9]

Barnett and Zürcher's analysis of "the peacebuilder's contract" goes one step further, and conceives of peacebuilding as a strategic bargaining situation between peacebuilders, state elites and subnational elites, all of whom are in a "situation of strategic interaction, where their ability to achieve their goals is dependent on the strategies of others" (2009, 24). Such bargaining leads to four possible outcomes: cooperative, captured, compromised or confrontational peacebuilding. The most likely outcome is compromised peacebuilding, in which local elites and external actors jointly shape how peacebuilding programmes unfold (although they do not exclude "captured" peacebuilding, in which the local elites trump the interests of external actors). Overall, "liberal peacebuilding is more likely to reproduce than to transform existing state-society relations and patrimonial politics" (ibid., 33, 36).

This kind of theorizing remains weak in its ability to describe, explain and understand how local actors can resist the efforts of international peacebuilding programmes, and draw upon the financial, organizational, programmatic and rhetorical resources of the peacebuilding community to advance their own neo-patrimonial statebuilding or rent-seeking agendas. In the bargaining model of Barnett and Zürcher (2009), for example, negotiations are openly (more or less) conducted over the terms for implementation of specific programmes (say, down-sizing an armed force or establishing local and community-based policing), and external parties have a series of carrots and sticks that can be deployed to generate compliance. Yet as most case studies of peacebuilding will acknowledge (and as I will illustrate later), the end result is often not an explicit bargaining game, but rather the deployment of "everyday forms of resistance." Even in situations where local actors are relatively strong, local opposition to external actors' exercises of power will seldom be manifest publicly through, for example, explicit rejec-tion of the idea of democratic elections, power-sharing, or market economics.[10] Rather they will resort to subverting such institutional arrangements, the result being outcomes (such as "democratic one-party rule," "illiberal democracies," the persistence of neo-patrimonial practices or the emergence of hybrid forms) that thwart the stated goals of external actors (free and fair elections) while seeming to follow the hegemonic norms that liberal peacebuilding promotes.

What does such *everyday resistance* look like, and what is the added value of conceptualizing the actions of local actors as an everyday form of resistance? Most fundamentally, resistance differs from the simple opposition of interests manifest in bargaining relationships by its relative invisibility. Following Scott (1985, 1990), one can distinguish between everyday resistance and open defi-ance. Contrasting examples of everyday resistance versus open defiance would include: military desertions versus an open mutiny; pilfering from grain stores versus open attacks on food stocks; and squatting and encroachment on land versus public protests against land policies (Scott 1985, 32). Open defiance is visible, and can be accommodated within a bargaining power understanding of external and local actors' interactions. Everyday resistance, however, is harder to capture. For Scott, it "takes the form of passive non-compliance, subtle sabotage, evasion and deception" (ibid., 31). While Scott (1990) was interested in the relationship between peasants and local power-holders, there is no reason (as he acknowledges) that these everyday forms of resistance cannot be practiced in any relationship between powerful and subordinate groups – as between international and local actors in post-conflict peacebuilding dynamics.[11]

Forms of resistance: DDR, SSR and RoL in South Sudan, Burundi and Liberia

In this empirical section I will offer three case studies – necessarily too brief – to illustrate how everyday resistance is much more important in order to under-stand why external actors fail to achieve their goals, and why local actors – at least powerful ones – often succeed in obtaining theirs. These three examples are drawn from three countries – South Sudan, Burundi and Liberia – all three marked by long engagements of the international community, often of more than a decade, and in which over time the dominance of local actors' interests and concerns have slowly manifested themselves. In addition, each one illustrates local forms of everyday resistance at different levels of local actors: the elite/ macro level, the meso level of nonelite state agents, and the micro level of the local population. While there may be some distinctive features of post-conflict peacebuilding in Africa, similar arguments have been made for cases such as Afghanistan, Bosnia-Herzegovina, Timor-Leste, the Democratic Republic of the Congo or elsewhere.[12]

In essence, the cases illustrate how local actors work *within* the confines (institutional and programmatic) dictated by the liberal peacebuilders, and through different forms of everyday resistance thwart the stated goals of these programmes. While the agendas of local actors may sometimes coincide with those of the international peacebuilding community, more often their actions are designed, through less-visible forms of resistance, to thwart its aims, bending and fusing specific programmes to meet their own local purposes and interests. Peacebuilding is thus often highly successful in achieving the aims of local actors to consolidate and reinforce their economic, political and social power.

South Sudan and macro-resistance by power holders

The comprehensive peace agreement of 2005 between South Sudan and Sudan put an end to a decades-long civil war and paved the way for the independence of South Sudan in 2011. It also marked the opening of an extensive international engagement in South Sudan to deal with the post-conflict legacy and to establish conditions for stable peace – conditions that were dramatically overturned when large-scale factional infighting broke out in December 2013. It illustrates clearly large-scale resistance to internationally promoted initiatives for DDR and SSR, and the hidden logic of elite competition, predation and consolidation of power at the macro level.

One of the first major initiatives was the establishment of a joint (northern and southern Sudan) DDR programme, meant to deal with the vast number of former combatants on both sides. With the institutional establishment of local DDR commissions, the first task was to specify the caseload – the number of ex-combatants to be demobilized (Nichols 2011, 15).[13] The initial figures proposed in 2005 by the Governments of Sudan (1.2 million) and South Sudan (300,000), "were clearly hyper-inflated and unrealistic." After initial discussions, "the two DDR commissions . . . presented a combined initial figure of about 700,000. The total agreed upon, after much negotiation, was 180,000, or 90,000 on both sides."[14]

The arbitrariness of these numbers suggests that local actors viewed potential DDR as a lucrative source of cash, and a means to retain control over the process and destiny of ex-combatants (and many other people!) rather than as a serious exercise in demobilization and reintegration. That this was indeed the case, was be illustrated by the subsequent trajectory of SSR in South Sudan. Analyses of the process of transformation of the Sudan People's Liberation Army (SPLA) and other armed groups into a new national armed forces for South Sudan confirm that, in spite of massive provision of technical and managerial assistance (primarily by the US, UK and UN) for Western-style defence planning and force restructuring, the process was driven by local actors' goals and interests.

To begin, only a tiny percentage of the 90,000 projected southern Sudanese ex-combatants (12,000, or 13 per cent) were processed through DDR between 2006 and 2011 (IRIN News 2011). Until independence in 2011, the South Sudan leadership focused more on maintaining (or even *strengthening*) rather than downsizing their armed forces; to safeguard against a potential future conflict with Sudan; to maintain control over armed elements in society that could pose a future threat to stability; and to distribute resources (jobs, funds) through neo-patrimonial networks. Estimated force strength of the armed forces in October 2010 was 150,000–160,000 (confirming that the 300,000 figure of 2006 was exaggerated), and in early 2011, force strength had actually increased to around 207,000 as former militia combatants were brought in or bought in to the state. As John Snowden (2012, 19) noted: "it is clear that recruitment and subsequent expansion outpaced . . . any other process meant to downsize the SPLA" (see also Munive 2013).[15] This occurred despite the international community having spent more than US$50 million on the process. Between 2009 and 2012, only 12,525 ex-combatants had been processed through DDR, and the (unmet) targets for 2012–2013 were only to process a further 13,500 ex-combatants. This was rather modest given that the stated goal of the SPLA was to reduce its size to 120,000 by 2017. As of 2013, the force size stood at 194,000, and roughly 35 per cent of the national budget was consumed by defence expenditures – hardly an indicator of successful SSR (de Waal 2014, 357; World Bank 2014, 9).

Local elite actors were also successful in understanding, and resisting, the process of SSR in the pre- and post-independence period. The principal fault line within South Sudan – between Nuer and Dinka – was reflected in the SSR process, which attempted to integrate the myriad of former militias into a national army. Yet the central government remained suspicious of the loyalties and identities of the Nuer and whether these were aligned to the South Sudanese Defence Force (SSDF) rather than to the central government. Hence, attempts to maintain peace through buying off militia commanders were central to the government's strategy (Rands 2010, 19). One result was the doubling of SPLA salaries in April 2011 in order to quell unrest. As one analyst wryly observed,

> while one of the aims of defence reform is affordability, the SPLA has no intention of reducing defence spending through salary control . . . . planning . . . took place without any formal in-depth analysis of the current composition and capability of the SPLA, threats (current and future), and financial constraints.
>
> (Snowden 2012, 19–20)[16]

As for other security forces, informal armed militias (such as the so-called White Army) were potent destabilizing factors, and resisted easy reintegration or demobilization. Although ultimately most were brought into the SPLA, they remained factionalized, as evidenced by the rival armed groups that emerged after December 2013 (HSBA 2013). Within the formal sector, the South Sudan Police Service (SSPS) has been largely used as a dumping ground for former SPLA personnel, with the result that "the SSPS leadership finds it difficult to determine the actual size of the force," and that many officers are untrained, illiterate, and may actually be claiming salaries from both the army and the police force! Local ownership in this sense is truly individual (Snowden 2012, 27).[17]

Since the outbreak of civil war hostilities in South Sudan in December 2013, the DDR process has been stalled, with the National DDR commission only manifesting sporadic signs of life. The hostilities in 2014–2015, which displaced up to two million persons, demonstrated the limits of the DDR/SSR peacebuilding strategy. As Jairo Munive concluded,

> the acceptance of the internationally sponsored DDR exercise by the SPLA was balanced with their ability and power to capture and redistribute these entitlements . . . . it [the SPLA] was able to direct the process according to its own priorities.
>
> (Munive 2013, 596)

All of the elements noted above point towards local resistance on the part of ruling elites and parties in South Sudan, who acted in anticipation of further violent conflict, or in order to secure and distribute the spoils of victorious statehood (de Waal 2014). As Alex de Waal puts it, "international partners erroneously assumed that either a nascent institutional, rule-governed system existed, or that South Sudanese leaders were genuinely seeking to establish such a system, and that corruption and rent seeking were deviations from this system" (ibid., 367). This was clearly mistaken, and peacebuilding assistance (including DDR) was just another revenue stream to be tapped for factional and elite interests.

DDR and SSR in Burundi: meso-level resistance by state agents

The post-conflict peacebuilding project in Burundi was subject to the same intense international engagement as in Sudan, albeit with somewhat different dynamics. The experience of genocide in neighbouring Rwanda, as well as the similar sociopolitical context (Tutsi minority, Hutu majority, tight post-independence Tutsi control, civil war), meant that the international community advocated peacebuilding investments after the Arusha peace agreement (2000) across the whole security spectrum as a worthwhile preventive measure. Burundi became a focus country for the UN Peacebuilding Commission; the World Bank made it eligible for the Multi-Country Demobilization and Reintegration Programme (MDRP) for DDR; the European Union and a host of bilateral donors all played significant roles in DDR, SSR, and RoL programming. The international peacebuilding project had a holistic approach, both in the sense that the armed forces and security sector were specifically the object of negotiated reform efforts, and that DDR was part and parcel of efforts to reengineer a new security sector, including the creation a new Burundian National Police (BNP), the resizing of the armed forces to 25,000, and the application of strict 50–50 quotas for Hutus and Tutsis throughout the armed forces.[18]

In this case, I want to focus on meso-level resistance of individual (or small group) state actors, operating not at the elite or regime level. There was, of course, elite resistance at work also, but the DDR programme was particularly subject to meso-level resistance on behalf of countless individuals within the various parts of the security sector. To begin, the World Bank plan for Burundi laid down several conditions for reintegration packages. The total value of the package was to be 600,000 FBU (about US$600) per ex-combatant, but subject to three conditions:

- It could not be given in cash
- It could not be used to build a house
- It could not be used to buy land.

Each of these had a specific macroeconomic rationale: the first two were seen as preventing durable income streams (and hence inconsistent with the goal of the programme), and the last was excluded because of the feared distortive effect that land purchases may have on the displacement of existing residents – in turn, creating new tensions (World Bank 2004).[19] Reintegration included instead several programme streams, including formal education, vocational skills training, entrepreneurial training (e.g. bookkeeping), income-generating activities (market stalls), or the return back to a previous employment (unlikely). In practice, "of the 25,000 ex-combatants who have been reintegrated the vast majority have chosen to engage in AGR [income generating activities]" (Douma and Gasana 2008).

The motivations of ex-combatants did not align themselves with those of the World Bank planners, whose expectations of Burundi as a nation of tradesmen and shopkeepers was at odds with the socioeconomic realities and a context in which more than 75 per cent of the population lives off subsistence agriculture. As a result, a significant number of ex-combatants monetized their reintegration package as quickly as possible, setting up a fictitious small business and stocking it with goods that could then be liquidated for cash. It was easy to determine exactly how many cases of beer or cartons of cigarettes could be acquired for 600,000 FBU, and in the most straightforward monetization, wholesalers simply certified that goods had been delivered, received compensation from the programme, took their cut, and passed the cash onto the ex-combatants.[20]

Local actors also successfully sidestepped or escaped the reach of DDR programmes in other ways. The Burundi DDR process was seen as operating in two phases: in the first, ex-combatants who were not integrated into the national police or armed forces were demobilized into civilian life; in the second, DDR was supposed to reduce the national army to 25,000 soldiers. This raises the question of who selected which ex-combatants went into the different streams – the armed forces, the newly created national police, or "civvy street." The preference of many individual ex-combatants was to join the national police rather than the armed forces – a choice that appears counterintuitive when one recognizes that the army provides for at least the minimum basic needs (food and shelter) of its soldiers, as well as relative stability. Yet joining the police was more attractive, mainly, it appears, because the police enjoyed greater rent-seeking opportunities through their ability to extort funds from the local population with minimal oversight. There was virtually no vetting or oversight of how ex-combatants were selected for the national police, and in the words of one analyst, "essentially, the police have no training in their civilian tasks and have retained their guns and are more-or-less, CNDD-FDD-led" (the ruling party) (Lamb 2008, 20).

Individuals who were demobilized into civilian life were the least well educated of the former combatants and less likely to have the social capital required to be active participants in the patrimonial networks that characterized the armed forces and police. Finally, there was resistance to the process of formally downsizing the national armed forces. Although it eventually approached its target of 25,000, external actors were for a long time unable to verify the actual numbers of soldiers. There were suspicions that the ranks of the army were filled with "phantom soldiers" whose presence allowed officers and high-ranking officials to collect salaries and otherwise pocket allocations (food, materiel, etc.) destined for soldiers ostensibly under their command.

Resistance was also discernible at a macro level, between the international community and the national authorities. The ethnic balance of the security forces proved difficult to achieve. As of 2008, only 30 per cent of senior commanders were Hutu, and almost one-third (31 per cent) of senior commanders hailed from one region (Bururi) – the province from which the first three post-independence presidents came (ruling from 1966–1993). Such concentration testifies indirectly to the persistence of strong neo-patrimonial networks. As the International Crisis Group has noted: "with respect to the police, despite its restructuring, several witnesses from within testify to the existence of a parallel chain of command resting mainly on former elements of the military wing of the CNDD-FDD responsible for repressing the opposition" (ICG 2012, 25). The national intelligence service (*Service nationale de renseignment*, or SNR) remains a potent political tool that has been implicated in repression and extrajudicial executions of political opponents. Overall, and as events in Burundi in 2015 sadly confirmed,

> encounters between international, regional, and local actors have produced governance arrangements that are at odds with their liberal and inclusionary rhetorics. Paradoxically, the activities of international peacebuilders have contributed to an "order" in Burundi where violence, coercion, and militarism remain central.
>
> (Curtis 2012, 1)[21]

Yet there is nothing paradoxical about this result: it is an eminently successful outcome from the perspective of local actors.

Rule of law in Liberia: local, micro resistance

The end of the civil war in Liberia in 2003, and the establishment of democratic rule in 2006 with the election of Ellen Johnson-Sirleaf as president, marked the opening of an intensive international peacebuilding and reconstruction engagement in Liberia.[22] Peacebuilding covered the entire range of activities, but one important element was the promotion of rule of law, generally intended to improve security, justice and respect for human rights, and to "address the weaknesses of the state that have driven poverty, instability and conflict" (UNDP 2008b, 3).[23] Weak rule of law was presented both as a contributing *cause* of conflict and, in turn, was *caused by*

> [correctible] deficiencies includ[ing] recurring absenteeism . . . corrupt practices involving judicial and law enforcement officials; detention facilities that are below minimum human rights standards; large numbers of pretrial detainees awaiting trial for extended periods; and insufficient numbers of qualified corrections officers.
>
> (UNDP 2008b, 6)

It was assumed that correcting these deficiencies through programmes to reconstruct courts and prisons, train judges and lawyers, update the legal code, and put in place new laws and procedures to deal with issues such as violence against women would, in turn, lead to a reduced risk of violence and conflict.

Access to justice for ordinary Liberians, however, operated most often through informal and traditional mechanisms and procedures, or through a parallel legal system that had been originally codified in two formal systems of justice. One system was for the Americo-Liberians (patterned on American legal practice); another, the Hinterland Regulations (from 1905, renewed recently), regulated the indigenous population (mostly rural) through traditional authorities and rules. Although the central government attempted to slowly subsume the rules of the hinterland under the formal Western legal system, these efforts were not always supported or respected by indigenous populations or traditional authorities, who continued to turn to traditional and local authorities (where these still existed) for dispute resolution, including some criminal procedures.[24]

Thus it was easy to anticipate micro-level resistance to post-conflict peace-building efforts for the wholesale reconstruction of the justice sector in Liberia, since the formal sector had never really met Liberians' needs and expectations. A 10-month intensive research project by the US Institute of Peace on Liberian experiences with local justice options found that Liberians saw the formal justice system, almost universally, as falling abysmally short of their expectations. As the report noted: "Liberians report a bewildering array of fees associated with the formal system, including registration fees, gas money for police investigators, requirements that victims pay the cost of food for the detained accused, lawyers' fees, and bribes" (Isser et al. 2009, 3). Perhaps more significantly for our purposes, ordinary people "regard the formal justice system as one of the most effective

mechanisms through which powerful and wealthy social actors are able to per-
petrate injustice in service to their own interests," especially through "deliberate use of opportunistic forum shopping, in which litigants choose the formal
system primarily if they believe it will give them an unfair advantage over their
opponent" (ibid.). Other assessments found endemic corruption, lack of accountability, limited access, and weak capacity throughout the justice system (USAID
2009). Parenthetically, evaluators found that almost no reliable RoL data or indicators had been collected, despite the UN's efforts to do so.

As a result, the customary system has remained the most important way through
which justice is delivered – and sought out – by most Liberians. According to one
analysis, of a total of 3,181 civil cases surveyed, only 3 per cent were taken to a formal court; 38 per cent to an informal forum; and 59 per cent to no forum at all. Of
1,877 criminal cases, only 2 per cent were taken to a formal court; 45 per cent to
an informal forum; and 53 per cent to no forum at all (Isser et al. 2009, 4). If plain-
tiffs are expected to pay the costs of incarceration (including food) for the accused
before court proceedings, it is no wonder that few cases proceeded to the formal
system! Finally, in some cases, policies aimed at regulating the customary justice
system to comply with international human rights and legal standards, had unintended adverse consequences. For example, the association of "human rights" with
issues such as "children's rights not to work" was perceived as operating against
parental oversight (and control) of children and their labour, and the legal framework on sexual violence and rape and its enforcement is perceived as running
against the strong desire for reconciliation and restitution within communities
and between families. I certainly do not want to condone practices such as paying compensation to the family of rape victims as sole punishment, but one must
recognize and understand the social context in which such practices are widely
supported (Isser et al. 2009, 4; Herman and Martin-Otega 2011, 147–148).[25]

One could summarize everyday resistance in Liberia to the imposition of Western ideas of rule of law as having four elements: its high costs, the unfair advantages it appeared to be offering elites, its dissonance with traditional practices, and
the clash between its core principles and local conceptions of justice. One needs
to actively estrange oneself from our deeply ingrained conception of justice (justice is blind, temporally and physically distant from alleged wrongs and offenses,
impersonal in nature, nonrestorative, and so forth) in order to see how bizarre and
inadequate these might seem to local actors. Behind all of this, the core principles
of justice that underlie Liberia's formal system – which is based on individual
rights, adversarialism and punitive sanctions – differ considerably from those valued by most Liberians. As a result, "the imposition of a Western justice system
has been a source of conflict in Liberia and has not strengthened the rule of law.
In fact, imposition has been the enemy of the rule of law" (Compton 2014: 50).[26]

Conclusion

Local actors – whether at the micro, meso or macro level – are almost always able
to bend and shape peacebuilding to their own ends, thus resisting the exercises

of power implicit in externally imposed peacebuilding projects. Although peace-building practices in the security realm have a deep impact upon the relationship between individuals and the state and touch upon existential security concerns, one finds in DDR, SSR and RoL programming little consideration for the poten-tially unanticipated consequences of purposive social engineering in weak and fragile states. Providing resources to some local actors who seek to implement their vision of how (and for whom) security and justice should be delivered also provides them with the opportunity and the means to seize what is often the most instrumentally useful state institution – the security and justice sector – and to use it for their own, often violent and predatory ends. As a result, not only do the projects and programmes promoted by external actors fail to deliver the promised results, but external actors become complicit by default in the power politics of local actors by providing resources that reinforce existing structures, inequalities and forms of overt and covert violence.

If this diagnosis of successful resistance by local actors is correct (and generaliz-able), then what are the normative and practical implications for liberal peace-building? Historically, the process of creating domestic order and security was not completed without a violent struggle against predatory elites, the medieval equivalent of contemporary warlords, repressive and authoritarian rulers, and so forth. The magnitude of the task attempted by the international community in places such as South Sudan, Burundi, Liberia and elsewhere – breaking existing patterns of politics and forcing a reconstruction of social and political relation-ships into a nonviolent or noncoercive mode – is, consequently, enormous. It only makes sense, politically and normatively speaking, if an externally driven social (re)engineering project can accelerate or substitute a more organic histori-cal process of statebuilding that will otherwise be driven by powerful local actors.

This message is cold comfort for those wishing to reform or improve peace-building practices.[27] Local forms of resistance are often deeply embedded in state–society relations, and based on long-standing (and often neo-patrimonial) forms of security and justice. Peacebuilding interventions, while ambitious in their social engineering scope, are often just moments in a much longer process of social and political change. The turn to the local in an attempt to generate sustainable local ownership of peacebuilding is itself fraught, if only because there are multiple locals who do not always have a shared interest in peaceful and inclusive outcomes.[28] *National* ownership – which is what international institu-tions can promote – is not the same as ownership by local communities. Inter-national peacebuilders can themselves be caught between the accountability demands of donors and the legitimacy demands of local actors – and the donors' needs often triumph in the short run.

As a final thought, it is worth asking what kind of subject positioning and commitments are necessary in order to maintain the policies and programmes of security-oriented peacebuilding in the face of the sorts of "successes" detailed earlier. This would require another chapter, but the elements would include the institutional self-preservation incentives within the UN system and the donor community, particular technocratic beliefs ("if only capacities and resources had been greater, or timing better, we would have succeeded"), and likely also a form of peacebuilding orientalism in which local places and spaces are seen as a blank canvas on which the Western imaginary can write its liberal script.[29] What seems to be excluded from much of contemporary peacebuilding practice, however, is the possibility of a genuine dialogue over goals, values and aims of society and forms of governance. In its strong form, this represents a betrayal of core liberal values that not only prescribe particular end points for society, but also make claims about autonomy and individual choice that oppose a narrow vision of the appropriate set of social and political arrangements for any society.

Notes

1 Insights are premised on field notes and interviews, collected in Gbarnga, Liberia, 1 October 2009.
2 For a recent contribution see also Kisangani and Pickering (2014).
3 The Centre for the Democratic Control of Armed Forces has also published a series of volumes on different aspects of security sector reform. See http://www.dcaf.ch/Series-Collections/DCAF-Yearly-Books.
4 The *OECD Handbook* (2007) also claims this as an internationally established definition.
5 For an excellent overview see Sriram et al. (2011).
6 See also United Nations Rule of Law (http://www.unrol.org).
7 Such sentiments were echoed in the UN General Assembly Resolution A/67/L.1, 19 September 2012.
8 The few examples offered here cannot do justice to the nature of the indicators.
9 Much the same could be said about more general works on peacebuilding, such as Paris (2004).
10 As Cooper et al. (2011, 2001) note: "There is little space to (formally) dissent from these policy prescriptions."
11 As Scott (1990, xii) notes: "every subordinate group creates, out of its ordeal, a 'hidden transcript' that represents a critique of power spoken behind the back of the dominant."
12 On Afghanistan, see the special issue of *Central Asian Survey*, 'The Afghan Conundrum: Intervention, Statebuilding and Resistance' (Goodhand and Sedra 2013); on the Democratic Republic of the Congo see Heredia (2012); on Timor-Leste see Richmond and Franks (2008); and on Bosnia see Donais (2009).
13 Analysis in this section is drawn from a series of working papers and issue briefs published by the Sudan Human Security Baseline Assessment (HSBA) Small Arms Survey, Geneva (see Rands 2010; Nichols 2011; Stone 2011; Snowden 2012).
14 In order to maintain parity with the Government of Sudan, the South Sudanese figures were first revised downwards from 300,000 to 60,000, then back *upwards* to 90,000!
15 There were up to 18 other armed groups operating in the south in 2005 before the Comprehensive Peace Agreement.
16 De Waal (2014, 355) reports that after they were doubled to US$150/month, they were increased again to US$220/month – much higher than soldiers in the northern Sudan Armed Forces.
17 Snowden (2012, 27–28) has noted that perhaps half of the SPSS was deployable in 2011–12.
18 For a description of these programmes, see Mora (2008).
19 See World Bank (2004, 26), n.10.

20 Based on interviews with ex-combatants conducted in 2008. For an overview of reintegration as a whole, see Gilligan et al. (2013) as well as Willems and Van Leeuwen (2015).
21 See also Nkundwa and Rosen (2015).
22 Johnson-Sirleaf had previously worked for the World Bank, UNDP, and other financial institutions, as well as having held a high political office in prewar Liberia.
23 See UNDP (2008); the document provides an overview of efforts and rationales in this area.
24 For a brief description of this see Compton (2014, 51–55) and Herman and Martin-Ortega (2011).
25 A poignant example of how restricted access to the formal system in rape cases results in unjust outcomes is offered in Isser et al. (2009, 40). See also Carvalho and Schia (2011). Compton (2014) reports a case in which a tribal governor fined a defendant the equivalent of US$48 for a sexual assault, compared to a potential 10-year prison sentence from the formal system (p. 62). See also Compton (2014, 65–67).
26 Compton (2014, 50) notes that recent, more participatory, initiatives may hold greater promise than the top-down reforms implemented prior to 2008. For a view of how some reforms that worked at improving traditional justice systems could improve RoL outcomes, see Sandefur and Siddiqi (2013).
27 For the debate between reformers and critics, see Paris (2010) and Cooper et al. (2011).
28 For a good overview see Donais (2012) and Richmond (2012).
29 What Cliffe and Manning (2008) call the "fallacy of terra nullius."

References

Baaré, A. (2006). *An analysis of transitional economic reintegration. Stockholm initiative on disarmament, demobilization and reintegration: Background studies.* Ministry for Foreign Affairs, Sweden, Stockholm.

Barnett, M., and Zürcher, C. (2009). The peacebuilder's contract: How external state-building reinforces weak statehood. In R. Paris and T. Sisk (Eds.), *The Dilemmas of Statebuilding.* Routledge, London, 23–52.

Browne, E. (2013). *Evidence on "rule of law" aid initiatives.* GSDRC Helpdesk Research Report 1008. GSDRC, University of Birmingham, 1–12.

Bryden, A. (2007). *From policy to practice: The OECD's evolving role in security system reform.* Policy Paper 22. Centre for the Democratic Control of Armed Forces, Geneva.

Carvalho, B. D., and Schia, N. N. (2011). Sexual and gender-based violence in Liberia and the case for a comprehensive approach to the rule of law. *Journal of International Relations and Development,* 14(1), 134–141.

Cliffe, S., and Manning, N. (2008). Practical approaches to building state institutions. In C. T. Call and V. Wyeth (Eds.). *Building States to Build Peace.* Lynne Rienner, Boulder, CO, 163–184.

Compton, J. (2014). The peril of imposing the rule of law: Lessons from Liberia. *Minnesota Journal of International Law,* 23, 47–78.

Cooper, N., Turner, M., and Pugh, M. (2011). The end of history and the last liberal peacebuilder: A reply to Roland Paris. *Review of International Studies,* 37(4), 1995–2007.

Curtis, D. (2012). The international peacebuilding paradox: Power-sharing and post-conflict governance in Burundi. *African Affairs,* 112(446), 72–91.

de Waal, A. (2014). When kleptocracy becomes insolvent: Brute causes of the civil war in South Sudan. *African Affairs,* 113(452), 347–369.

Donais, T. (2009). Empowerment or imposition? Dilemmas of local ownership in post-conflict peacebuilding processes. *Peace and Change*, 34(1), 3–26.

Donais, T. (2012). *Peacebuilding and Local Ownership: Post-conflict Consensus-Building*. Routledge, London.

Douma, P., and Gasana, J.M. (2008). *Reintegration in Burundi: Between Happy Cows and Lost Investments*. Unpublished manuscript. Conflict Research Unit, Netherlands Institute of International Relations, The Hague.

Economist. (2013, 12 November). *Liberia: The taxis fall silent*. (http://www.economist.com/blogs/baobab/2013/11/liberia) Accessed: 1 December 2013.

Gilligan, M.J., Mvukiyehe, E.N., and Samii, C. (2013). Reintegrating rebels into civilian life: Quasi-experimental evidence from Burundi. *Journal of Conflict Resolution*, 57(4), 598–626.

Goodhand, J., and Sedra, M. (Eds). (2013). The Afghan conundrum: Intervention, state-building and resistance [Special issue]. *Central Asian Survey*, 32(3), 239–422.

Haggard, S., and Tiede, L. (2011). The rule of law and economic growth: Where are we? *World Development*, 39(5), 673–685.

Heredia, D.M.I. (2012). Escaping statebuilding: Resistance and civil society in the Democratic Republic of Congo. *Journal of Intervention and Statebuilding*, 6(1), 75–89.

Herman, J., and Martin-Ortega, O. (2011). Narrowing gaps in justice: Rule of law programming in Liberia. In C.L. Sriram, O. Martin-Ortega, and J. Herman (Eds.), *Peacebuilding and Rule of Law in Africa: Just Peace?* Routledge, London, 142–161.

Holberton, W. (2001). *Homeward Bound: The Demobilization of the Union & Confederate Armies, 1865–66*. Stackpole Books, Mechanicsburg, PA.

HSBA (2013). *Pendulum swings: The rise and fall of insurgent militias in South Sudan. Sudan human security baseline assessment*. Issue Brief No. 22. Small Arms Survey, Geneva. (http://www.smallarmssurveysudan.org/fileadmin/docs/issue-briefs/HSBA-IB22-Pendulum-Swings.pdf) Accessed: 2 March 2015.

ICG (2012, 25 October). *Burundi: Bye-Bye Arusha?* Rapport Afrique No. 192. International Crisis Group. (http://www.crisisgroup.org/~/media/Files/africa/central-africa/burundi/192-burundi-bye-bye-arusha.ashx) Accessed: 1 January 2015.

IRIN News (2011, 8 July). *Analysis: Rethinking DDR in post-independence Sudan*. (http://www.irinnews.org/Report/93180/Analysis-Rethinking-DDR-in-post-independence-Sudan) Accessed: 1 May 2015.

Isser, D.H., Lubkemann, S.C., and N'Tow, S. (Eds.). (2009). *Looking for justice: Liberian experiences with and perceptions of local justice options*. United States Institute for Peace, Washington, DC. (http://www.usip.org/sites/default/files/liberian_justice_pw63.pdf) Accessed: 30 March 2015.

Kisangani, E., and Pickering, J. (2014). Rebels, rivals, and post-colonial state-building: Identifying bellicist influences on state extractive capability. *International Studies Quarterly*, 58(1), 187–198.

Lamb, G. (2008). *Emerging human security issues in the planned implementation of MDRP fund in Burundi*. Centre for International Cooperation and Security, Bradford.

Mora, S. (2008). *La reforme du secteur de la sécurité à Burundi*. Initiative for peacebuilding IFP – Groupe sectorial sur la sécurité, London. (http://www.initiativeforpeacebuilding.eu/pdf/La_reforme_du_secteur_de_la_securite_au_burundi.pdf) Accessed: 1 May 2015.

Munive, J. (2013). Context matters: The conventional DDR template is challenged in South Sudan. *International Peacekeeping*, 20(5), 585–599.

Nichols, R. (2011). *DDR in Sudan: Too little, too late?* Working Paper No. 24. Small Arms Survey, Geneva. (http://www.smallarmssurveysudan.org/fileadmin/docs/working-papers/HSBA-WP-24-DDR-in-Sudan.pdf) Accessed: 2 March 2015.

Nkundwa, J. C., and Rosen, J. W. (2015, 28 April). Burundi on the brink. *New York Times*. (http://www.nytimes.com/2015/04/29/opinion/burundi-on-the-brink.html?_r=3) Accessed: 5 May 2015.

OECD. (2005). *Security System Reform and Governance*. OECD, Paris. (http://www.oecd.org/dac/governance-peace/conflictandfragility/docs/31785288.pdf) Accessed: 1 May 2015.

OECD. (2007). *OECD Handbook on Security System Reform (SSR): Supporting Security and Justice*. OECD, Paris. (http://www.oecd.org/document/32/0,3343,en_2649_33693550_45884768_1_1_1_1,00.html) Accessed: 1 May 2015.

Paris, R. (2004). *At War's End: Building Peace after Civil Conflict*. Cambridge University Press, Cambridge.

Paris, R. (2010). Saving liberal peacebuilding. *Review of International Studies*, 36(2), 337–365.

Parker, G. (Ed.). (1997). *The Thirty Years' War* (2nd ed.). Routledge, London.

Rands, R. (2010). *In need of review: SPLA transformation in 2006–10 and beyond*. Working Paper No. 23. Small Arms Survey, Geneva. (http://www.smallarmssurveysudan.org/fileadmin/docs/working-papers/HSBA-WP-23-SPLA-Transformation-2006-10-and-Beyond.pdf) Accessed: 2 March 2015.

Richmond, O. (2012). Beyond local ownership in the architecture of international peacebuilding. *Ethnopolitics*, 11(4), 354–375.

Richmond, O., and Franks, J. (2008). Liberal peacebuilding in Timor Leste: The emperor's new clothes? *International Peacekeeping*, 15(2), 185–200.

Sandefur, J., and Siddiqi, B. (2013, 20 May). *Delivering justice to the poor: Theory and experimental evidence from Liberia*. World Bank Workshop on African Political Economy, Washington, DC, 1–61. (https://editorialexpress.com/cgi-bin/conference/download.cgi?db_name=CSAE2013&paper_id=1014) Accessed: 2 May 2015.

Scott, J. C. (1985). *Weapons of the Weak: Everyday Forms of Peasant Resistance*. Yale University Press, New Haven, CT.

Scott, J. C. (1990). *Domination and the Arts of Resistance: Hidden Transcripts*. Yale University Press, New Haven, CT.

Sedra, M. (Ed.). (2010). *The Future of Security Sector Reform*. Centre for International Governance Innovation, Waterloo, ON.

Snowden, J. (2012). *Work in progress: Security force development in South Sudan through February 2012*. Working Paper No. 27. Small Arms Survey, Geneva. (http://www.smallarmssurveysudan.org/fileadmin/docs/working-papers/HSBA-WP-27-Security-Force-Development-in-South-Sudan.pdf) Accessed: 2 March 2015.

Sriram, C. L., Martin-Ortega, O., and Herman, J. (Eds.). (2011). *Peacebuilding and Rule of Law in Africa: Just Peace?* Routledge, London.

Stone, L. (2011). *Failures and opportunities: Rethinking DDR in South Sudan. Sudan human security baseline assessment*. Issue Brief No. 17. Small Arms Survey, Geneva. (http://www.smallarmssurveysudan.org/fileadmin/docs/issue-briefs/HSBA-IB-17-Rethinking-DDR-in-South-Sudan.pdf) Accessed: 2 March 2015.

Tilly, C. (1990). *Coercion, Capital and European States, A.D. 990–1990*. Basil Blackwell, Oxford.

Toft, M. D. (2009). *Securing the Peace: The Durable Settlement of Civil Wars*. Princeton University Press, Princeton, NJ.

UNDP. (2008a). *Strengthening the rule of law in conflict- and post-conflict situations: A global UNDP programme for justice and security 2008–2011*. UNDP, New York.

UNDP. (2008b). *Strengthening the rule of law and administration of justice in Liberia: Project Document 2009–2011*. UNDP, New York.

United Nations. (2004). *The rule of law and transitional justice in conflict and post-conflict societies*. Report of the Secretary-General, S/2004/616, 23 August. (http://www.unrol. org/files/2004%20report.pdf) Accessed: 1 May 2015.

United Nations. (2011). *The United Nations rule of law indicators: Implementation guide and project tools*. United Nations, New York. (http://www.un.org/en/peacekeeping/publica tions/un_rule_of_law_indicators.pdf) Accessed: 1 May 2015.

United Nations. (2012). *UN General Assembly resolution declaration of the high-level meeting of the General Assembly on the rule of law at the national and international levels*. A/67/L.1, 19 September. (http://www.un.org/en/ga/search/view_doc.asp?symbol=A/RES/67/1) Accessed: 1 May 2015.

USAID. (2009). *Evaluation of Rule of Law Programs in Liberia*. USAID, Washington, DC.

Willems R., and Van Leeuwen, M. (2015). Reconciling reintegration: The complexity of economic and social reintegration of ex-combatants in Burundi. *Disasters*, 39(2), 316–338.

World Bank. (2004). *Technical annex for a proposed grant of SDR 22.2 million (US$ 33 million equivalent) to Republic of Burundi for an emergence demobilization, reinsertion and reintegration Program*. Report No. T7616-BU, February 24. (http://www.mdrp.org/pdfs/ country_pdfs/burundidoc_techannex.pdf) Accessed: 15 March 2015.

World Bank. (2014). *Republic of South Sudan national DDR programme: 2013–2014 pilot reintegration project*. International Bank for Reconstruction and Development/World Bank, Washington, DC. (http://reliefweb.int/report/south-sudan/republic-south-sudan-national-ddr-programme-2013–2014-pilot-pilot-reintegration) Accessed: 11 June 2015.

10 Corporate peace

Crisis in economic peacebuilding[1]

Michael Pugh

Political economy appears frequently in explanations for the conflicts of the 1990s to which peacekeepers and interventionists were dispatched. Among the inspiring works in the genre are Susan L. Woodward's and Peter Uvin's understandings of Yugoslavia and Rwanda respectively (Woodward 1995; Uvin 1998). The field has also embraced the study of war economies to explain how conflicts were sustained (Reno 1999; Pugh et al. 2008; Berdal and Wennmann 2010). Political economy is also a key to problematising peacebuilding. However, with exceptions (e.g. Paris 2004; Reno 2008), unless corruption and organised crime dramatised economic issues journalists and academics have mainly absconded, leaving economic peacebuilding to the expertise of donor treasuries and international economic institutions.

The argument here is that the general prescription for peacebuilding economies, with modification for local contexts, is derived from a neoliberal vision: 'corporate peace'. It has failed to sabotage the oligarchic legacies of war economies or meet social needs. This thesis does not incubate the kind of vulgar determinism that addles economics-as-science with its emphasis on rational choice materialism. Varied economic systems for material needs are embedded in social relations that shape bureaucratic restraints, mythical beliefs and identity goals. Indeed ideational preferences also create false calculations.[2]

The method adopts Kai Koddenbrock's (2013) linkage of a critical approach to structures and processes of capitalist power with a relational discernment to appraise the practices of post-conflict entrepreneurs. Thus Koddenbrock counterbalances the power of world social structures with a post-colonial turn to the local and the quest for acumen about local sociology, distinctiveness and voice (see Richmond 2011). It reads the experiences of the intervened and the location of peacebuilding 'in the structures of world society with its nation-state form and capitalist logic' (Koddenbrock 2013, 32–33). Cultural differences between peacebuilding hosts and foreign interventionists shape normative justification for interventions because the international tries to improve the local (Chandler 2006). The strategy is applied here with reference mainly to Bosnia and Herzegovina (BiH) but also Kosovo to critique a political economy of international peacebuilding that assumes a linkage between capital and peace, but which adversely affects workers and those with precarious livelihoods. It explores the war inheritances and practices of the plurality of entrepreneurs who accumulate capital and interact with local public authority and global capital. The two post-conflict economies are selected not for comparison but because they represent long-term interventionary peacebuilding. Located beyond the European capitalist core, they are distinguished from other transformations by the costs of war and disruption (to mention only mine clearing and veterans' pensions), by opportunities for primitive accumulation, and by forms of international protectorate. Peacebuilding with international governance attempts to bring peace by integrating domestic and foreign capital accumulation.[3]

Peacebuilding interactions are also mutually constituted to subsidise capital accumulation through corporate welfare and shifting the boundaries of social relations from public to private spaces, such as privatising state assets and services. Yet after 15 (Kosovo) and 20 years (BiH) of administration and institution building, the frustration of international administrators has been plain. Kosovo was described as 'mission impossible' (Spörl 2007); BiH with its exceptional quantities of government is demonised by critical hosts as well as by interventionists as one of Europe's least economically competitive countries (Lagumdžija et al. 2012). Evidently, legacies of conflict enhanced the agency of war entrepreneurs who could determine the implementation of external governance priorities, such as economic liberalisation. Their capital in weapons, followers, network links and wealth from predation and exploitation strengthened new and reinvigorated old bosses. The dominance of business politics articulates both manipulation of and conflict within ethnic politics. In particular, public authority protection of private economic interests and a blurring of formal and unaudited economic activity present notable problems for determining the legitimacy of corporate peace. This reality was imperiously abhorred from an unelected seat in the UK's House of Lords in 2015 by Sir Paddy Ashdown, former High Representative in BiH. He distilled the problem as a lack of international will to overturn the dysfunctional, decentralised constitution deriving the Dayton Framework Agreement (SEESOX 2015, annex). Few would deny that a cumbersome and costly system probably served to end war and suited identity and psychological needs as well as oligarchic interests. Ironically, though, decentralisation is precisely what neoliberals such as Ashdown seek in order to reduce state economic power.

Rather than adopting Ashdown's censure, the analysis here takes a critical approach to the corporate peace project. Following Koddenbrock's design for the structural essence of global capital, the first section is a critique of peace through subsidised capitalism and institutionalism. The second section provides empirical material on BiH war and prewar legacies, with reference to contrasting oligarchic and independent entrepreneurships. Analysis of liberalisation in Balkan cases follow in the third section. A fourth section examines the consequences of the economic intervention in the Balkan cases. The conclusion draws lessons from the cases and conceives peacebuilding in crisis as a problem of political economy.

Peace: a project of subsidised capitalism

The idea of business capital as a pacifying governmentality, encapsulated here as 'corporate peace', has historical anchorage. The nineteenth-century British politician Richard Cobden subscribed to the theory, and the journalist and 1933 Nobel Peace Prize winner Norman Angell developed it in the twentieth. Peace between states through the interdependencies of capital is applied now to domestic conflicts as well. The idea might have been buried by the two world wars, and by the intrastate collapse of free trade in former Yugoslavia. But it continued to find favour in liberal circles when supply-side theories gained ground in the 1970s to address inflation after the oil shocks. This 'neoliberalism' theorised opportunities for finance capital and corporations to drive globalisation and to foster privatisation and wealth creation. Unliberalised parts of the world, such as former socialist-run territories, could be engineered into convergence by financial institutions and Western consultants through processes of globalised competitiveness; outcomes were also dependent on appropriate institutions and cultural dynamics (Holton 2005). For Deepak Lal (1999) and Jeffrey Sachs (2005), the exclusion of societies from capitalism was the global problem to be managed. The market, wrote Lal, is spontaneously adopted worldwide because of its great utility and the failure of dirigism. In the 1990s the International Financial Institutions (IFIs) and UN system countersigned principles to promote open economies, global integration, 'good governance' (commercial law and anti-corruption) and the mobility of capital such as foreign direct investment (FDI).

Note, however, that neoliberalism presents an ontological paradox, for there is no such thing as a self-correcting, free market of the utopian imagination. Even its guru Friedrich August von Hayek acknowledged that the state would need to counter monopoly tendencies. As Antonio Gramsci also noted in the 1920s (1971, 315), the state has to intervene to protect government bonds, to reorganise the economy, and to nationalise private losses by the 'salvaging of large enterprises which are . . . in danger of going bankrupt'.[4] Thus although business and political leaders use free market discourse for ideological simulation, in practice contamination occurs through public protection of profits, rents, dividends and corporate taxes using political patronage, government subsidies and infrastructure support.[5] Ideals of self-help are cultivated while corporate and private debt is converted into sovereign debt (such as the €5 billion used to bail out the private Portuguese *Banco Esperíto Santo* in August 2014; *Guardian* 2014, 14). The power of business–political formations is manifest in such events as the annual World Economic Forum and the Munich Security Policy conference (Rothkopf 2009, 33, 208–209). These formations operate partly through lobbying, corruption, nepotism and revolving door mobility between public and private office (note the example set by the US Ambassador in Pristina who lobbied the Kosovo government to award a road contract to the Bechtel Corporation and was subsequently hired by it; BIRN 2014).

The ideology, clothed in the apparel of scientifically neutral economics, was introduced to societies emerging from conflict. Put coarsely, modern capital peace theory assumed that societies enjoying not only democracy but also fast food retailing would cease fighting one other: a democratic corporate peace (Friedman 2000; critiqued by Mousseau 2010; Schneider and Gleditsch 2013). From that standpoint corporate pacification was no oxymoron. It would democratise consumption, bringing a wide range of products to a wider range of people, cheapening access through open markets without the transaction costs of government intervention. Moreover, redistributing economic control to remove bureaucracy and political interference would lead to greater competitiveness, more transparency and less abuse of public office for personal gain. Low cost areas would also benefit from capital mobility and technological transfer from high cost areas enabling weaker economies to catch up. Thus it was claimed that 'the Kosovo economy, with the assistance of the international community, can eventually converge to the standard of living of its EU neighbours' (Economic Strategy and Project Identification Group 2004, 31).

Indeed, behind the competing narratives on Yugoslavia (the unresolved nationality issues, ethnicity, historical appetites for insurrection and barbarism) lurked discourses of inefficiency and socialist management as causes of conflict. As tested on post-Soviet countries the normative consensus for peacebuilding was that economies had to liberalise as a structural foundation of transition from war to peace. Subsidised private capital accumulation, supported by foreign aid and grant disbursements, would secure a liberal peace. A further consensus assumed that wars were wholly destructive and anti-developmental, exposing a lack of in situ human and physical capital and of the cultural and political will or wherewithal to guide economic reordering (but see Cramer's 2006 critique). Foreign capital had to be mobilised and institutions built. The World Bank orchestrated much of this through donor conferences and the International Monetary Fund (IMF) through standby agreements (Bojičić-Dželilović 2002; Woodward 2013b). Although academic and policy faith in free market hegemony wobbled in the wake of financial convulsions from the mid-1990s, it persisted ideationally in former Yugoslavia with the promise of, and disciplining for, incorporation into the EU.

While the peacebuilding order has the same normative agenda of subsidised capitalism, it also sits with a version of neoliberalism derived from institutional economics. This school emphasised the organisation of economic activity – for establishing and policing commercial law, for instance, and for enabling institutions to mediate between components of an economy (Smelser and Swedberg 1994). Thus, building post-socialist institutions from scratch in BiH and Kosovo ended the clumsy payment clearing in the former Yugoslavia with a private banking structure that subsequently gravitated entirely into the hands of foreign banks. For peacebuilders, institutions are also valuable to instil disciplinary norms and mould behaviour, framed as 'good governance'. Institutionalism has been influential in the UN system where institutionalists such as Jeffrey Sachs (development), Michael Doyle (strategic planning and UN–corporate relations) and Charles Call (peacebuilding) were employed, the first two on secondment from universities as special advisers to UN Secretaries-General. Such influence together with that of the IFIs produced post-conflict anti-corruption institutions to promote development in Timor-Leste, Sierra Leone and Liberia (Paris 2004; Doyle and Sambanis 2011).

From a critical perspective, and mindful of China's rise, a correlation between Western-framed governance and economic development does not prove whether good governance brings development or development brings good governance (Sampson 2010). Peacebuilding to diminish state bureaucracies in the economy (such as abolition of Sierra Leone's Agricultural Marketing Board) can mean a neglect of strategic development for industry and agriculture that could protect producers and employment. Instead, leaving development to private business can stimulate short-term profit-taking and rentier behaviour, as evident in the Balkan cases. Additionally, running a structure for facilitating corporate capital albeit with competition safeguards can replace former bureaucracies with arrangements of managerial complexity and transaction costs. Institutions are socially created. Ambitious projects to systematically generate them for peacebuilding have required elite bargains that can discount broad social needs, but as illustrated next, involve peacebuilders steering through oligarchy (see Richmond 2005, 203).

Oligarchic war legacies

Taking a cue from Koddenbrock's recognition of local autonomy in peacebuilding, this section employs a representative dramatis personae approach to war legacies and the opportunities created by peacebuilding. It details a fragment of a Federation Bosniak oligarchy and complements existing work on Republika Srpska and Western Herzegovina (Bojičić-Dželilović and Kostovicova 2013; Divjak and Pugh 2013). Oligarchy within democracy means elected power in the hands of a few, often with family connections but with wealth acquired by confusing private and general interests, as in the US (Piketty 2014, 514). Such control over social and material capital is a common target of complaint by inhabitants and internationals as being harmful to the liberal peace. But some entrepreneurial career narratives are worth noting.

A former Sarajevo policeman, Alija Delimustafić, exemplifies the war legacy. He had a small prewar trading business and expanded it during the Marković reforms in Yugoslavia in 1989–1990 (for encouraging indigenous small and medium enterprises). He rose to Minister of the Interior in the Party of Democratic Action (SDA)-led government in 1990 under the presidency of Alija Izetbegović. Further business opportunities arose when Croatia and Serbia cut their trade links in 1991; Delimustafić's Bosnian companies could act as intermediaries, shipping goods between adversaries. His interrepublic trade persisted when war broke out; his ministry had its own police and his trucks, some allegedly with weapons, drove through checkpoints. He may have worked to prevent 'Lebanisation' of the country, and maintain a secular state for business reasons (Kumar 1999, 47). But the Izetbegović wing of the SDA sacked him in May 1992, alleging he was plotting with Serbian authorities. Delimustafić then established an anti-corruption magazine, BH Dani, and created the BH Bank to service remittances from the diaspora. As this was the only nonstate bank in operation after the war, USAID and foreign embassies used it to manage aid funds flowing into the country. But without the support of Izetbegović behind him, the bank collapsed in 1998 amid accusations of embezzlement (BBC 2000). Delimustafić was subsequently imprisoned in Serbia for trafficking and in BiH for abuse of power and fraud – though his longest sentence had more to do with an affair of the heart.[6]

From a political economy perspective Delimustafić represents Balkan entrepreneurship at a time of instability and crisis. He took advantage of opportunities presented in peacetime (the Marković period), a time of trade disruption (the Serbia–Croatia boycotts), in wartime (crossing risky borders with scarce goods) and in peacebuilding (servicing aid flows). Essentially a businessman, his operations nevertheless required political protection. His venture into the media was typical in the corporate world of peace dividends: a scramble to control the press and TV to promote political–business interests. For a time he could play the game by his own rules; once his clout evaporated in the politics of 1992 his businesses proved vulnerable to Bosniak infighting.

After the war BH Dani (2004) took stock of the 10 most influential oligarchs in Sarajevo. Two of them – Hilmo Selimović and Fahrudin Radončić – represent corporate war for spoils of peace. Selimović had owned a major shareholding in Sarajevo Brewery since its part privatisation in 1990. The brewery gained 'heroic' status for continuing production during the war and providing a public water supply. The extent to which open tendering occurred in ownership transfers throughout BiH and Kosovo is a matter of controversy – and was hardly above board, for instance, when Mijo Brajković took over Aluminij Mostar (Pugh 2002, 475). During the war Selimović took ownership of the brewery and made other post-conflict acquisitions in food processing and brewing companies without apparently contravening legal norms. He benefitted from IFI nourishment when the World Bank's International Finance Corporation loaned up to US$5.2 million in 1997.

This did not deter a subsequent campaign in the daily newspaper Dnevni Avaz (e.g. 4 June 2012), owned by Radončić. It denounced Selimović as personifying privatisation trickery (also alluding to the construction activities of Bakir Izetbegović, son of Alija, also on the Dani list). Selimović had also acquired Dani and the daily Oslobodjenje. These denied the allegations and counter-alleged that Radončić himself had questionable business links (he admitted to gaining access to a multimillion covertibili kaimark loan from the Federation Development Bank through the Avaz auditor).[7] Radončić certainly had business interests, and two prestige skyscrapers in Sarajevo, that could benefit from political engagement. Splitting from the Izetbegović-dominated SDA he created the Union for a Better Future for Bosnia (SBB), which divided the Bosniak vote in the 2010 and 2014 general elections. He cultivated international opinion as a pro-European and anti-corruption crusader, but was voted out of his ministerial job for failing to respond robustly against Sarajevo rioters in February 2014.

Selimović and Radončić gained from privatisation, corporate welfare and the kind of deregulation or nonregulation of business that the corporate peace environment established. They took advantage of postwar circumstances to operate free market attributes of competitiveness, risk-taking, individual self-help and capital aggrandisement, though the Selimović empire built up debts and could only salvage Sarajevo Brewery and *Oslobodjenje*.

By contrast, other war legatees merely used companies for money laundering, flouting both 'neoliberal rules' and prewar socially constituted morality. Naser Kelmendi, another of *Dani*'s top 10, was a Kosovar trafficker in the wider Balkan region but with BiH citizenship. His property deals included one with the Radončić news corporation. Kelmendi attracted international attention among police agencies and was placed on the US drug baron blacklist in 2012. Arrested in Kosovo in May 2013, the indictment on organised crime charges included evidence from a Sarajevan TV journalist, Šejla Turković (Special Prosecution Office of the Republic of Kosovo 2014). She had also been Radončić's personal assistant and wrote for *Avaz*. She claimed that Radončić attended meetings when, she alleged, it was agreed that Kelmendi would organise the assassination of a wartime racketeer believed to be involved in the murder of Radončić's godfather. As of 2015 Radončić was not charged with any crime. But as if enhancing the potential here for a film noir screenplay, the femme fatale Šejla had married Zijad Turković, who in 2013 was sentenced to 40 years in jail on a range of criminal charges, which was upheld after a subsequent retrial (OCCRP 2014).

Oligarchs thus ran interlocked and sometimes deadly rival corporations. Ethnicity played little part in these feuds. They represented war by other means among Bosniaks for status and defence of corporate welfare – though trespassing across religious and ethnic bounds might be considered a perverted form of peace. Entrepreneurs emerging from war could take advantage of foreign aid whether from Saudi Arabia or Switzerland, and benefit from privatisation programmes to bid for state and public assets. Such patrons usually had little interest in long-term economic growth, agriculture or manufacturing, and more interest in rents for quick returns and difficult for regulatory bodies to police. They could gain additionally from navigating the political distribution of peace with interventionists. Thus the wartime gravitation of Western, particularly US, rhetorical and material support to the politically rigid Izetbegović government partly determined a postwar tolerance of it. This also extended to installing Milorad Dodik as prime minister of Republika Srpska in 1998, though his party had only two seats in the Assembly. Dodik's nationalism was subsequently seen as a threat to peace. In the Bosniak–Croat Federation the Office of the High Representative (OHR) again entered politics by fostering an Alliance for Change among moderate parties for the 2002 elections, but in government the components neglected to relinquish their sources of funds. In turn, Radončić may yet become a suitable candidate for adoption on the basis of his commitments to the EU, NATO and subsidised capitalism.

A Balkan liberalisation: Bosnia and Herzegovina, and Kosovo

Oligarchs aside, rapid economic recovery seemed in the cards for BiH and Kosovo. An influx of foreign aid, diaspora remittances and transfers stimulated booms in the early postwar years (on BiH see Cviić and Sanfey 2010). Growth rates reached double figures with entirely new gross domestic product (GDP) supplements such as rents and services. But growth started from very low levels. The poorest prewar territory, Kosovo, emerged from repression, war and the return of some 800,000 refugees, and incurred about 12,000 civilian deaths. BiH ended war with an estimated 100,000 or more of its population killed, over two million displaced, economic dislocation and massive destruction of housing and capital stock. GDP in BiH was estimated at 20 per cent of prewar levels, industrial production at 5 per cent, energy output at 15 per cent, employment at 10 per cent and per capita income at 25 per cent (Jeffries 2002, 178–183).

As the early boom faded in BiH, a new OHR in 2002 reinforced the mainstream discourse of international peacebuilders in arguing that the BiH elites were failing to conform to a smaller state: 'We need to transform the economy,' argued Ashdown, 'so it becomes capable of creating jobs and generating wealth. This does not mean endless government intervention, but instead, allowing the free market to flourish' (OHR 2002). Potential for more cooperatives and state production let alone the ideological anathema of worker and commune management of yesteryear – even building on prewar market reforms – was rejected as incompatible with subsidised capitalism (Husanović 1997). This conformed to OECD general guidelines for development assistance that specified a balance between, inter alia, debt servicing, noninflationary domestic financing and prioritising the needs of the private sector (DAC 1997). National ownership and local 'capacity building' had also become watchwords for international agencies. The IMF (2001) also fostered this, but made cuts to agricultural subsidies, public sector wages and social benefits as conditions for securing standby funding, pushing responsibility for the consequences onto local authorities. This general consensus does not imply an absence of interagency clashes in the new liberal order – such as a wrangle in the UN Interim Administration Mission in Kosovo which dislocated the privatisation of social and state property (Grasten and Uberti 2015). Moreover, a general critique of the adverse social impacts of corporate peace by the UN Conference on Trade and Development prompted a deliberate suppression of its views by rich countries (Flassbeck 2014). However, fostering corporate-friendly peace in the Balkans, as well as human rights and other standards, fell largely on the EU and the European Bank for Reconstruction and Development.

BiH had early preferential tariff exemptions for its exports to the EU and other markets, but under a 2008 EU stabilisation and association agreement import tariff levels were progressively reduced to zero in 2013. While opening up was less catastrophic than in Iraq subsequently – where the occupying administration suspended all trade restrictions and import charges – it led likewise to a surge of cheap imports that damaged potential local production. At the end of 2012, the value of legal imports exceeded the value of exported goods by 2:1, representing a trade deficit of approximately €3.4 billion, though in 2012 it had separate trade balances with Kosovo, Montenegro and even Austria (BiH Agency for Statistics 2013; Čaušević 2014). Traditional exports of wood products, chemicals, processed metals, leather goods and textiles generally failed to recover.[8]

For the EU and other agents FDI has been an engine to motorise restructuring for a business-friendly environment. In post-conflict settings, economies have to seduce FDI with favourable terms to compensate for security risks, low international credit ratings and sometimes small domestic markets. In some cases FDI has stimulated employment and wealth generation that also meet the needs of the BiH population. German investment in BiH rescued Kakanj Cement (HeidelbergCement Group) with improved environmental safeguards; Bihać Dairy (Megglé Co.) secured the agricultural livelihoods of 4,000 cooperatives in a poor region; and Austrian capital helped to develop cooking oil and bakery products in Brčko (Gudeljević 2011; Hrnjić 2011). But foreign investors negotiate terms that can include repatriation of profits, tax breaks, cheap land, individual rather than general labour contracts, and weak environmental controls. For example, ArcelorMittal's steel plant in Zenica, BiH, has a grim output of pollution (EKOforum–Zenica 2014; see also the company's Liberian deal, Ford and Tienhaara 2010, 365). Investors expect high, often quick returns and exert influence over trading conditions. A foreign supermarket invasion represents classic FDI rent-seeking. Except for tokenistic domestic produce, payment for which locals can wait months, stocks are imported from China or the owner-parent country, Slovenia, Croatia or Serbia (Tomaš 2011).

By contrast, in a context of generally weak export-led growth, locally backed, largely autonomous BiH entrepreneurship achievements are worth revealing. Less perceptibly politicised, they also created nondiscriminatory employment in the audited economy. They exemplify an important lesson: the value of building on prewar development and ingenuity (UNDP 2009). In central BiH the Pharmamed Company is based on a prewar business; it had only six employees in 1997, which increased to over 100 in 2012 for the processing of herbal products such as teas. The wartime besieged 'safe area' of Goražde had become, by 2014, a net exporter with an employment rate at least four times greater than the national average. Goražde's history of precision engineering and returnee entrepreneurs with prewar links to German and Austrian firms facilitated manufacturing for export. For instance, as of 2014 the Prevent Company employed 1,100 to assemble car seat upholstery for VW and Opel. Bekto Precisa employed 450 people to manufacture highly sophisticated industrial machine tools and plastic injection items that include LED lighting for streets and airport runways. They emerged from a prewar knowledge base and experience of production, personal ties to a specific location and prewar contacts with other European companies.

Consequences

Nevertheless, nearly 20 years after the war frustration was palpable in EU reports on lack of BiH progress. In October 2014 the EU Commission reiterated dismay at the dysfunctional institutions and lack of political support for the EU agenda – common enough complaints *within* the EU. The association agreement ratified in

2011, had not entered into force and convergence had stalled, provoking the EU to take disciplinary measures such as reallocating preaccession funds and stalling trade concessions with Croatia (EU Commission 2014).[9] But the EU seemed ambiguous, if not contradictory, about 'endless state intervention'. On the one hand, the commission called for efforts to address the state presence in the economy, condemning stalled privatisation, government spending at 45.6 per cent of GDP and public services employing 27 per cent of the workforce (ibid., 26–27). On the other hand, the EU also required the state to expand the market regulatory and surveillance systems with attendant transaction costs. Understaffed or nonexistent bureaucracies impeded food hygiene standards, labour inspectorates, land registration, refugee housing administration, indirect taxation and, above all, administration for EU integration. Sorting out the labour market also implied bureaucratisation because governments and public employment services lacked both administrative and financial capacity to implement active job creation (ibid., 38–40).

Rather than reinforcing the state's strategic role, the EU clung to the precepts of deregulation for 'free market' welfare. It convened a conference of bankers, employers, employees, nongovernmental organisations (NGOs) and internal and foreign authorities to accept a Compact for Jobs and Growth – imitating the EU's own Jobs and Growth strategy of 2012 (which notably failed to prevent the Greek crisis or quantitative easing by the European Central Bank). The project targeted employment taxes that pay for social security which also benefits those in the untaxed grey economy. Social welfare would be diminished by targeting the most needy (though in theory this would probably include the 35 per cent of the work force that had abandoned the job search). Job protection laws would end, to increase employment turnover and hence provide work for the young. The programme assumed that the formal labour market would expand to absorb the unemployed. Deregulation would lower business transaction costs including fees and licenses that enabled corruption to thrive (though deregulation per se can open up subsidised capital to other levels of corruption and tax avoidance, manifest in global financial centres).

A consequence of economic experience in the Balkan cases has been stubborn unemployment at 30–44 per cent (depending on the methodology used). Youth unemployment was at 50 per cent in 2013, and poverty at 19 per cent in BiH and *extreme* poverty at 10 per cent in Kosovo, where nearly 90 per cent of adult women have no job (World Bank 2013; BiH Agency for Statistics 2014; ESI 2015). Consequently, much of the trade, services and labour markets lurk underground. The unaudited economies of both BiH and Kosovo, not all connected to organised crime and partly a legacy of wartime survival needs, are widely estimated to account for about a third of real GDP (Divjak and Pugh 2013; Hashani 2014; Krasniqi 2014).

Negative GDP growth was recorded for BiH 2009–2010 and 2012. Social unrest followed in 2014, triggered by the collapse of asset-stripped, privatised Tuzla companies with attendant job losses. Protests spread, though mobilising only small minorities. Four canton governments resigned in the Federation, and in the divided city of Mostar disturbances appeared close to reigniting widespread violence. Events briefly cut across ethnic divisions and generated civil society forums, thereby posing a threat to political elites which retaliated with terrorism charges. Torching of government and party headquarters signified the failure of political oligarchs to answer socioeconomic needs. Nor could peacebuilders escape scrutiny. Alarmed by the events, critical friends of the EU took exception to its blanket hostility to state intervention. The public sector, they noted, suffered from a dearth of long-term planning to include development for agriculture, renewal of industry, transport, the environment and regional development (Udovicki and Knaus 2012).Together with extraregional developments, including increasing economic interest in the region from Russia, Turkey and Middle Eastern states, the protests prompted an initiative in November 2014 by Germany and the UK, backed by the US and other EU members. Rhetorically they prioritised socioeconomic issues, but there was no new economic formula other than requiring a written commitment by all BiH parties to institutional and market reform (Hammond 2014). Seemingly devised to recalibrate BiH–EU relations by states whose economic systems had generated economic crisis in the EU, tolerated corporate tax avoidance and provoked Euroscepticism, the tactic's legitimacy is questionable.

Through the political structures of subsidised capitalism, generalised here after Koddenbrock, intervention has attempted to rearrange politics. In BiH and Kosovo it reproduced atomised fiscal social relations and oligarchical governance. On the other hand, the rituals and formalities of 'democratisation' seem perfectly compatible with cosmetic democracy. Elections, assemblies and multiparty systems in the Balkan cases failed to replace cronyism and oligarchy. Reformers who set up citizen forums after the BiH unrest claimed that parties remained authoritarian, run by the same war elites who were only interested in scrambling over assets for personal enrichment (Jansen 2014). They had ridden on a crushing economic transition with the assistance of foreign institutions. For example, the BiH government agreed to an IMF's fiscal budget framework guaranteeing further austerity for 2014–2016, well beyond the reach of any electoral contest (Simić 2014). The approach to subsidised capitalism exhibits common ground with the strategies of war entrepreneurs in crony relationships with ethnopolitical leaders. War entrepreneurs may resist competitive privatisation processes initially. It threatens their war acquisitions and powers (ex-Kosovo Liberation Army leaders were partly curbed). But intervention gave privileged elites, who readily subscribed to the neoliberal goal of facilitating private wealth as the economic generator, a distinct edge in public asset distribution (see Pugh 2002; Čaušević 2013). Liberal peacebuilding did not repoliticise, but arguably exposed a reproduction of neoliberal politics.

Conclusion

Peace has been framed by policies that privilege private capital accumulation as the political economy of choice. In practice the outcomes do not reflect idealised neoliberal purity but are affected by subsidised capitalism and forms of resistance that include unaudited activities. Reflecting the power of global capital, the Balkan cases exhibit elements of convergence with global subsidised capitalism: the corporatisation of peace, the adoption of privatisation and reduction of public space, trade liberalisation, a trend towards services and rents as sources of individual income, and burgeoning income inequalities.

From a problem solving perspective elite enrichment and mass underconsumption seem unlikely to solve the flaws attributed to *dirigiste* political economies. A 2009 review sponsored by the UN Development Programme (UNDP) recognises the need for support to 'local ingenuity', and the evidence presented here from Goražde indicates potential, though success in low wage assembly is dependent on foreign demand. However, without state involvement in education, research and innovation, future competitiveness will founder. Production expertise, long-term strategies, investment in education and local skills add more economic and social value than short-term speculation and rentier behaviour. Paradoxically, whereas champions of global neoliberalism promote self-regulated markets and shrinkage of state activities, indigenous entrepreneurs often have different concerns. The same study for the World Economic Forum that demonstrated BiH's lack of competitiveness (Lagumdžija et al. 2012) shows that enterprises are concerned not only about red tape, but also about access to credit (ultimately controlled by foreign-owned banks), lack of R&D (centred in the capitalist cores), poor communication infrastructure (a low or late priority) and lack of state economic direction (a bête noire of the World Economic Forum).

Obviously this study is limited by the sui generis cases cited. They are proximate to the EU, have socialist histories and particular forms of social capital. But some of the patterns described may have resonance for other peacebuilding economies in relation to global capital. Divergence in other peacebuilding sites may also illuminate the peacebuilding problematique: Rwanda and Ethiopia taking autonomous and statist approaches to political economy with experiences that accord or differ from the Balkans. However, a general malaise is detectable in the peacebuilding industry as a consequence of perceived intervention failures. Confusion is marked by ambiguous or weak Western reactions to crises in Egypt, Syria, Ukraine/Crimea and Israel/Palestine and disturbed by competition from other development sources such as China, India and in the Balkans, Turkey and Russia. Structural cracks in corporate capitalism derive from several sources, including technological change that reduces the labour component in production together with labour casualisation (coded as 'flexibility') that deflates incomes and aggregate demand. A general ferment of critique has perhaps contributed to uncertainty and ambivalence about economic relations with countries undergoing pacification.

From a structural perspective neoliberalism fails, as many economists suggest, because it is overwhelmed by a hyperrational theory of economics. The Cambridge economist Ha-Joon Chang (2014) argues that states and communities have several other theories to pick elements from. But war-affected societies have little choice when, as in the Balkans, they are provided with ready-made solutions and a visionary promise based on global and/or EU integration, the benefits of which have been disputed: richer countries began opening up *after* performing well through trade-protected growth (Chang 2002). Moreover, in peacebuilding a dichotomy (arguably false) between supposed zones of probity and zones of unrest allows the blame for failures to be laid squarely on ethnicity, unruly inhabitants and traffickers, thereby releasing international elites and institutions from responsibility for tension. By the same token domestic elites can blame the internationals. An approach following Koddenbrock that links host interlocutors in peacebuilding strategy to the structures of subsidised capitalism permits a representation of transition as sustaining oligarchs in a democratic system while side-stepping sustenance for the population as a whole. Whether a process of mutual reproduction rather than a dialectic has occurred might stimulate further debate, and whether liberal territories are themselves converging with the Balkan cases through institutional violence that keeps populations economically powerless.

Notes

1 I thank the Leverhulme Trust for research funding under the Leverhulme Emeritus scheme. Responsibility for the text is entirely mine, but I am grateful to Mandy Turner, Professor Oliver Richmond and colleagues at the Centre for International Conflict Analysis & Management (CICAM) for valuable suggestions and to Professor Fikret Čaušević, Merima Zupčević-Buzadžić and Drazen Simić among many in the Balkans for conversations since 1997.
2 As the economist John Kenneth Galbraith quipped, the sole purpose of economic forecasting is to make astrology look respectable. *U.S. News & World Report*, 7 March 1988, 64.
3 Woodward's (2013a) attention to parallels between nineteenth-century imperialism and post–Cold War pacifications of the Balkans by Western powers notes that historical military pacification was accompanied by economic penetrations, partly to secure debt repayments and resources. This dimension has seemingly changed little. In December 1995 an IMF credit of $45m to BiH allowed repayment of a Dutch loan, calculated as its share of an old Yugoslav debt (Boyce 2002).
4 Nor is it social market economics or *Rheinischer Kapitalismus*, a theory in the postwar Federal German Republic which included progressive taxation, distributive justice and indicative economic planning.
5 Collusion between business and political elites has antecedents, for example the British East India Company's control of Indian settlements from the late sixteenth century. On trajectories and cultural meanings of public and private, see e.g. Hibou 2011, 16, 32, 41.
6 A four-year sentence for kidnapping his former lover's husband in Munich in 1996.
7 Radončić was interviewed by police as a potential witness after a rocket attack on the Selimović house in 2003, but no one was arrested.
8 Ironically, the BiH Federation's largest postwar investor was the 90% government-owned BiH Telecom. Albeit prone to political nepotism, it was highly profitable and invested in new equipment. From 2000, when tax was introduced on 25% of the profits, the government used the proceeds to spend on roads and meet a pension fund deficit (Čaušević 2006).
9 A sticking point (ignored by June 2015) was also nonimplementation of the European Court of Human Rights ruling (Sejdić-Finci) for nondiscrimination in political representation of those not belonging to one of the three 'constituent peoples'.

References

BBC World Service. (2000, 5 August). Bosnian police arrest top Muslim banker. (http://news.bbc.co.uk/1/hi/world/europe/816963.stm).

Berdal, M., and Wennmann, A. (Eds.). (2010). *Ending War, Consolidating Peace: Economic Perspectives*. Routledge, London.

BH Dani. (2004). 5 March. (http://www.nato.int/sfor/media/2004/ms040305.htm).

BiH Agency for Statistics. (2013). *International Trade in Goods of BiH*, Thematic Bulletin 06 December 2012. (http://www.bhas.ba/tematskibilteni/robna%20eng.pdf).

BiH Agency for Statistics. (2014). Registered Unemployment January 2014. (http://www.bhas.ba/saopstenja/2014/NEZ_2014M01_01_hr.pdf).

BIRN (Balkan Investigative Reporting Network). (2014, 14 April). US ambassador to Kosovo hired by construction firm he lobbied for. (http://www.balkaninsight.com/en/article/bechtel-hires-us-diplomat-amid-kosovo-contract-controversy).

Bojičić-Dželilović, V. (2002). World Bank, NGOs and the private sector in post-war reconstruction. In E. Newman and A. Schnabel (Eds.), *Recovering from Civil Conflict: Reconciliation, Peace and Development*. Cass, London, 81–98.

Bojičić-Dželilović, V., and Kostovicova, D. (2013). Europeanisation and conflict networks: Private sector development in post-conflict Bosnia-Herzegovina, *East European Politics*, 29(1), 19–35.

Boyce, J.K. (2002). *Investing in Peace; Aid and Conditionality after Civil Wars*. Adelphi Paper 351. Oxford University Press, Oxford.

Čaušević, F. (2006/2014). Discussions with author. Economics faculty, University of Sarajevo, Sarajevo.

Čaušević, F. (2006, 5 September). Discussion with author. Sarajevo.

Čaušević, F. (2013). Bosnia and Herzegovina's economy since the Dayton agreement. In O. Listhaug and S.P. Ramet (Eds.), *Bosnia-Herzegovina Since Dayton: Civic and Uncivic Values*. Longo Editore, Ravenna, 116–117.

Chandler, D. (2006). *Peace without Politics? Ten Years of State-Building in Bosnia*. Routledge, London.

Chang, H.-J. (2002). *Kicking Away the Ladder: Development Strategy in Historical Perspective: Policies and Institutions for Economic Development in Historical Perspective*. Anthem Press, London.

Chang, H.-J. (2014). *Economics: The User's Guide*. Pelican, London.

Cramer, C. (2006). *Civil War Is Not a Stupid Thing, Accounting for Violence in Developing Countries*. Hurst, London.

Cviić, C., and Sanfey, P. (2010). *In Search of the Balkan Recovery: Political and Economic Reemergence in South-Eastern Europe*. Hurst, London.

DAC (Development Assistance Committee). (1997). *Guidelines on Conflict, Peace and Development Co-operation*. OECD, Paris.

Divjak, B., and Pugh, M. (2013). The political economy of corruption in BiH. In O. Listhaug and S.P. Ramet (Eds.), *Bosnia-Herzegovina Since Dayton: Civic and Uncivic Values*. Longo Editore, Ravenna, 81–97.

Doyle, M., and Sambanis, N. (2011). *Making War and Building Peace*. Princeton University Press, Princeton, NJ.

Economic Strategy and Project Identification Group. (2004). *Towards a Kosovo development plan. The state of the Kosovo economy and possible ways forward*. Policy Paper No.1. Pristina.

EKOforum–Zenica. (2014, 21 June). Author's discussion with members. Zenica.

ESI (European Stability Initiative). (2015, 30 April). Why Kosovo needs migration. *ESI Newsletter* 5/2015.

EU Commission. (2014, 8 October). Bosnia and Herzegovina progress report. Enlargement, COM(2014)700.

Flassbeck, H. (2014, 28 July). Interview. *Real News.com*. (http://www.youtube.com/watch?feature=player_embedded&v=GWednAjxWdQ).

Ford, J., and Tienhaara, K. (2010). Too little, too late? International oversight of contract negotiations in post-conflict Liberia. *International Peacekeeping*, 17(3), 361–376.

Friedman, T. L. (2000). *The Lexus and the Olive Tree*. Anchor Books, New York.

Grasten, M., and Uberti, L. J. (2015, 27 February). The politics of law in a post-conflict UN protectorate: Privatisation and property rights in Kosovo (1999–2008). *Journal of International Relations and Development*. (http://www.palgrave-journals.com/jird/journal/vaop/ncurrent/full/jird20154a.html).

Gramsci, A. (1971). *Selections from the Prison Notebooks of Antonio Gramsci* (Ed. Q. Hoare and N. G. Smith). Lawrence and Wishart, London.

Guardian. (2014, 4 August). Portugal to use EU bailout cash to shore up troubled bank.

Gudeljević, P. (2011, 16 June). Discussion with author. Department of Economic Development, Sport & Culture, Brčko.

Hammond, P. (2014, 5 November). UK Foreign Secretary, speech in Berlin. (http://www.gov.uk/government/speeches/bosnia-herzegovina-a-new-strategic-approach).

Hashani, A. (2014, 13 June). Discussion with author, Riinvest Institute, Pristina.

Hibou, B. (Ed.). (2011). *Privatising the State*. Hurst, London.

Holton, R. (2005). *Making Globalisation*. Palgrave Macmillan, Basingstoke.

Hrnjić, K. (2011, 9 June). Discussion with author. Megglé Bihać.

Husanović, S. (1997, 16 July). Discussion with author, office for reconstruction and development, Tuzla.

IMF (2001, 10 February). Conditionality in fund-supported programs – Overview. (http://www.imf.org/external/np/pdr/cond/2001/eng/overview/).

Jansen, S. (2014, 13 February). Can the revolt in Bosnia and Herzegovina send a message to the wider world? *Balkan Insight*. (http://www.balkaninsight.com/en/blog/can-the-revolt-in-bosnia-and-herzegovina-send-a-message-to-the-wider-world).

Jeffries, I. (2002). *The Former Yugoslavia at the Turn of the Twenty-First Century: A Guide to the Economies in Transition*. Routledge, London.

Koddenbrock, K. (2013). Strategic essentialism and the possibilities of critique in peacebuilding. In W. Chadwick, T. Debiel, and F. Gadinger (Eds.), *Relational Sensibility and the "Turn to the Local": Prospects for the Future of Peacebuilding (Global Dialogues 2)*. Käte Hamburger Kolleg/Centre for Global Cooperation Research (KHK/GCR21), Duisburg, 27–35.

Krasniqi, E. (2014, 13 June). Discussion with author. Kosovo Stability Initiative, Pristina.

Kumar, R. (1999). *Divide and Fall: Bosnia in the Annals of Partition*. Verso, London.

Lagumdžija, Z. with MIT Center Group (2012). *Competitiveness of countries and region of Southeastern Europe 2009–2010*. World Economic Forum, Global Competitiveness Report, 2012–13, Geneva.

Lal, D. (1999, 20 September). *Culture, democracy and development: The impact of formal and informal institutions on development*. Paper for IMF conference on Second Generation Reforms.

Mousseau, M. (2010). Coming to terms with the capitalist peace. *International Interactions*, 36(2), 185–192.

OCCRP (Organised Crime and Corruption Reporting Project). (2014, 2 September). Two bosses. (https://reportingproject.net/two-bosses).

OHR (Office of the High Representative). (2002, 31 July). Our reform agenda. (http://www.ohr.int).

Paris, R. (2004). *At War's End*. Cambridge University Press, Cambridge.

Piketty, T. (2014). *Capital in the Twenty-First Century.* Belknap/Harvard University Press, Cambridge, MA.

Pugh, M. (2002). Postwar political economy in Bosnia and Herzegovina: The spoils of peace. *Global Governance,* 8(4), 467–482.

Pugh, M., Cooper, R. N., and Turner, M. (Eds.). (2008). *Whose Peace? Critical Perspectives on the Political Economy of Peacebuilding.* Palgrave Macmillan, Basingstoke.

Reno, W. (1999). *Warlord Politics and African States.* Lynne Rienner, Boulder, CO.

Reno, W. (2008). Anti-corruption efforts in Liberia: Are they aimed at the right targets? *International Peacekeeping,* 15(3), 387–404.

Richmond, O. P. (2005). *The Transformation of Peace.* Palgrave Macmillan, Basingstoke.

Richmond, O. P. (2011). *A Post-liberal Peace.* Routledge, London.

Rothkopf, D. (2009). *Superclass: How the Rich Ruined Our World.* Abacus, London.

Sachs, J. D. (2005). *The End of Poverty.* Penguin, London.

Sampson, S. (2010). The anti-corruption industry: from movement to institution. *Global Crime,* 11(2), 261–278.

Schneider, G., and Gleditsch, N. P. (Eds.). (2013). *Assessing the Capitalist Peace.* Routledge, London.

SEESOX. (2015). *Bosnia and Herzegovina: New International Thinking.* South-East Europe Centre, St Antony's College, Oxford.

Simić, D. (2014, 31 January). Bosnia pays dear for borrowing addiction. *Balkan Insight.* (http://www.balkaninsight.com/en/article/bosnia-pays-dear-for-borrowing-addiction).

Smelser, N., and Richard Swedberg, R. (Eds.). (1994). *A Handbook of Economic Sociology.* Princeton University Press, Princeton, NJ.

Special Prosecution Office of the Republic of Kosovo. (2014, 4 July). Indictment PPS No. 42/13, Pristina. (https://reportingproject.net/two-bosses/Indictment_Kelmendi_OCCRP.pdf).

Spörl, G. (2007, 10 December). The Kosovo failure: Mission impossible in the Balkans. *Der Spiegel.* (http://www.spiegel.de/international/europe/the-kosovo-failure-mission-impossible-in-the-balkans-a-522406-2.html).

Tomaš, R., (2011, 27 June). Discussion with author. Economics faculty, Banja Luka.

Udovicki, K., and Knaus, G. (2012, 7 April). The Balkan employment crisis – An urgent appeal. (http://www.esiweb.org/index.php?lang=en&id=67&newsletter_ID=59).

UNDP (2009). *Post-conflict Economic Recovery: Enabling Local Ingenuity.* UNDP, New York.

Uvin, P. (1998). *Aiding Violence: The Development Enterprise in Rwanda.* Kumarian Press, West Hartford, CT.

Woodward, S. L. (1995). *Balkan Tragedy: Chaos and Dissolution after the Cold War.* Brookings Institution, Washington, DC.

Woodward, S. L. (2013a). The long intervention: Continuity in the Balkan theatre. *Review of International Studies,* 39(5), 1169–1187.

Woodward, S. L. (2013b). The IFIs and post-conflict political economy. In M. Berdal and D. Zaum (Eds.), *Political Economy of Statebuilding: Power after Peace.* Routledge, London, 140–157.

World Bank. (2013). Kosovo overview. (http://www.worldbank.org/en/country/kosovo/overview).

Part III

Rethinking promises and pitfalls of 'the local'

11 What do we mean when we use the term 'local'?

Imagining and framing the local and the international in relation to peace and order

Roger Mac Ginty

Introduction

This chapter begins with an extended personal reflection on the meanings of the term 'local'. The auto-ethnographical approach may be unusual in the context of peace and conflict studies, but it is useful in that it illustrates that many inhabitants of the Global North often have confused attitudes towards the concept and practice of 'the local' in their own lives. This confusion is important because the concept of the local forms a crucial element in peacebuilding, development, stabilisation and counter-insurgency strategies that are developed in the Global North and directed towards the Global South. It will be argued in this chapter that the concept of the local is foundational in the worldviews and policies that shape contemporary liberal peacebuilding. Key documents from international organisations, donor states and INGOs (international nongovernmental organisations) are peppered with the language of localism. Terms such as local ownership, local partnership, local stakeholders, and local wisdom are very common in the documents that form the basis of peacebuilding interventions. But it is worth standing back momentarily and asking: what do we mean when we use the term local?

The chapter argues that we (in the Global North) often hold complex and contradictory views of what constitutes the local in our own lives, yet see the local in overseas peacebuilding and development contexts as somehow simplistic. This contradiction seems like a poor basis for policy. As will be discussed below, the local is one of a number of imaginaries that are constructed and maintained by powerful foreign actors as they engage in building peace and order.

Following an auto-ethnographical section, the chapter then considers how notions of the local are imagined, constructed and hardwired into international peacebuilding efforts. Crucial here is the ability of powerful actors to create an imaginary or series of imaginaries that can construct and shape the local to suit particular narratives and policy aims. The view of the local held by international actors is often partial (in both meanings of the word). As will be discussed in the chapter, a key drawback facing many liberal peace agents is that they have immense difficulty in accessing the local. Security restrictions and their own epistemological limitations mean that many staff from international organisations and donor states who are interested in governance, stabilisation and 'peace' are restricted to their fortified compounds or uninterested in bottom-up processes. In its third section, the chapter then draws on evidence from field research in four sub-Saharan African countries that suggests that the local does indeed matter in how people perceive peace in their own lives. Yet, this version of the local does not necessarily reflect the version of the local that international actors might have. The key purpose of the chapter is to reflect on the construction and framing of the local (and indeed the international) as imaginaries as part of international peacebuilding. As such, much of the chapter is about power – the power to impose narrative frames on others.

Before proceeding, it is worth saying something about terminology and categories. This chapter, and indeed much of the literature on peace and conflict studies and international relations, depends on widely understood but poorly defined terms. The benefits of wide comprehension mean that there can be discourse between many parties. The drawback is that terminological precision may suffer. The danger is that layered and complex definitions lose adherents. Yet, the world that we are discussing – one involving conflict, plural identities and much change – is layered and complex. Nonetheless, this chapter has a job to do: to discuss the meanings of the term local in ways that can, hopefully, be understood by others. This means the use of a range of terms that are political, contingent and conditional. Terms like Global North, Global South, the West, international community and many others are widely understood shorthand terms (Mac Ginty 2011, 1–2). They are used in this chapter with the knowledge that they are approximations. The term Global North, for instance, covers many variations ranging from outright interventionist governments to those that are marginal, peripheral and relatively powerless. Likewise, the term Global South should not be read automatically as equivalent to powerlessness and marginality. The Global South contains individuals and networks that are wealthy and well connected.

This chapter wants to transcend binary notions of the local and the international but it finds itself restricted by the language available to us. So it persists in using the terms local and international but does so in the knowledge that these terms contain enormous variation. When used in this chapter, the term international usually refers to the amalgam of powerful actors: often self-appointed leading states and international institutions that are interventionist to maintain order and 'peace'. While there has been much focus in the academic literature on episodes of belligerent liberal interventionism (with Iraq, Afghanistan and Libya being the most prominent examples), we should be mindful that the international as used in this chapter also refers to a system of power relations, assumptions, compliance and intervention.

An auto-ethnographical reflection

The auto-ethnographical element of the chapter is based on a reflection of a single day when the author attempted to think about what the local means to him and the community he lives in (Dauphinee 2010). The author lives in a rural area of southern Scotland, about 60 miles from the nearest airport, city or university. He travelled to the nearest town, about eight miles away, and walked around the town centre to see evidence of the local. The evidence was not hard to find. Shop windows were adorned with signs saying 'Shop local' or 'Local produce' (Herring 2015). Food retailers in particular used local place names (even the names of particular farms) to assure customers of the authenticity of their produce. The town newspaper offices advertised that they carried reports of 'local news and sport'. A shop selling fishing gear promised potential customers 'local knowledge' of rivers and fishing spots. In short the word local was everywhere and was used with deliberate purpose. It conveyed a sense of advantage: local produce and knowledge was bound to be better, more authentic, more tailored than generic alternatives. Terms like shop local or buy local had a political edge to them – a recognition that many people exercised economic choice and that they could support their own community through their economic habits. There was a communitarian and solidaristic element to the use of the term local.

Yet, a closer look at the town seemed to contradict the very visible emphasis on all things local. While there were advertisements for the local everywhere, it was quite clear that the predominant shopping and commercial practices were actually national and international. The main shops in the town centre were parts of large chains. Indeed, over the past two decades, three out-of-town supermarkets had been built with the result that most trade occurred outside of the town centre. Many locally owned shops had closed down as people transferred their business from the local to the national. In a sign of the online shopping revolution, the town had no book or music shop and there was only one remaining travel agent. And taking a closer look at people, and how they dressed and consumed, it was clear that national and international patterns of behaviour had impacted upon them. Many young males wore football jerseys – not of the local team but of the large English Premiership teams. Among the busiest places in the town centre were two new coffee shops – part of international and UK chains that have been opening everywhere.

The picture that emerged from the brief walk around the town centre was that people talked about the local and clearly attached normative value to it, but they did not necessarily live it in terms of their shopping and cultural behaviours.

The author then travelled to his house – in a small village (less than 100 inhabitants) – and took a walk to the village cemetery. The cemetery was opened about 1900 and its gravestones tell a story about the local area (Rugg 2013). The family names on the gravestones are the names of local families. It is very common for farm names or locality names to be mentioned too. Many of the gravestones are made from stone quarried locally. In many ways, it is difficult to think of something more local than people who were born, lived and died locally being buried in the soil of the locality and their lives being marked by locally hewn stone. Yet, on closer inspection many of the gravestones told stories of migration, empire and war. Although the cemetery is in what might seem like a poorly connected part of Scotland, its gravestones included the names of Polish families who had settled in the locality after World War II. There were references to sons dying in Gallipoli, Flanders and in a German prisoner of war camp. The technology of war is mentioned: Royal Air Force and Machine Gun Corps. Rhodesia, New Zealand and New York are also mentioned on the gravestones, suggesting links with empire and migration.

So again, what initially seemed to be local was, on closer inspection, not particularly local. The gravestones tell stories of transnational political economies and war as well as stories of localism. They suggest that globalisation has a long pedigree and that people are mobile and adaptable. An area that might be described as being rural and poorly connected actually has a history that points to connectivity, migration, the acceptance of incomers and the outward migration of its population. All of this made the author question the term local. Its meaning seems to be elastic in how it is used in our day-to-day lives in the Global North. We talk about local in terms of food, knowledge and people as though localism is a proxy for authenticity, trust and quality. In such usage, the term local has a sociopolitical and cultural meaning that is affective as well as practical. In other words, in its contemporary meaning, the term local can encompass the emotional aspects of life linked with feeling, identity, sense of belonging and place.

The key point of this section has been to point to the fluid and imagined construction, and sometimes contradictory use, of the term local in everyday life in the Global North. It is a term that is used with great frequency and has value attached to it. Yet, the notion of the local has become a key part of the narrative and practice of contemporary peacebuilding strategy as enacted by leading states, international organisations and INGOs. Despite its use and even overuse, the term seems to have been sparsely interrogated in conceptual terms – especially in international relations and peace and conflict studies. It is often accepted without question, and simplistic (even romanticised) views of the local are projected onto peacebuilding and development strategies.

The local as central to international peacebuilding

This chapter is written on the assumption that generalisations (with sensible caveats) can be made in relation to internationally sponsored peacebuilding. In line with arguments on the existence of the 'liberal peace', it believes that leading international organisations, international financial institutions, and leading states collaborate to effect particular types of peace intervention in the aftermath of civil war or transition from authoritarianism (Paris 2004; Mac Ginty 2006; Richmond and Franks 2009). This form of peace intervention is often called the liberal peace because it deploys liberal rhetoric, namely references to freedom, democracy, free markets and rights. As critics point out, the liberal peace often deploys illiberal means and its utilisation of optimistic and emancipatory language often masks a recasting of colonial and stabilisation projects. Even worse, in some analyses, liberal peacebuilding is part of counterinsurgency projects (Turner 2015).

Clearly the term liberal peace is a shorthand that covers a variety of types of intervention. It is not the leviathan that some literature might suggest. Instead, it has weaknesses and limitations, and it is pursued in different places with vary-ing degrees of doggedness (Mac Ginty 2011, 29–32). It should also be noted that China, Russia, India, Iran and a number of other super and mid-range powers with foreign policy ambitions have different views of how peace and order are best achieved. Given the variations in the liberal peace (from the coercive to the incentivising, from democracy at gunpoint to democracy at invitation) it may be tempting to exclude some Western interventions from the liberal peace category. Some of the more violent interventions (for example the invasion of Iraq) might be better defined as realist or neoliberal interventions. Yet, if we examine the justificatory rhetoric that accompanied such adventurism then we see that the language of liberalism was used. Hence it is entirely legitimate to refer to them as liberal peace operations. Indeed, a systematic study of post-1989 comprehen-sive peace accords finds that they do deserve the sobriquet liberal because of the inclusion of so many liberal influenced provisions on rights and democratisation (Joshi et al. 2014).

The liberal peace is able to muster substantial material and symbolic power. Through its capture of international organisations, and by working with national elites and NGOs (nongovernmental organisations) in transition countries, it has considerable reach. This means that peace accords made in international dip-lomatic capitals can have an influence on how life is lived in seemingly remote parts of a transition country. Peace accords, and the conditionality linked to the funding of provisions of those accords, can mean the recalibration of a series of relationships in the post–civil war country: between citizens and the govern-ment, between businesses and the government, and between businesses and citi-zens. It is important not to paint international peacebuilding as being necessarily injurious to the interests of people in the post–civil war state. Instead, the story is likely to be incredibly complex. For some (perhaps national elites or those who will receive new legal protections) an internationally sponsored peace process and peace accord may bring advantages. For others (perhaps members of a former ruling party or soldiers who will lose their jobs) it may bring losses. International peacebuilding agents are usually able to deploy a range of coercive and incentivis-ing powers that encourage compliance if not respect or legitimacy. Local actors can be empowered and can resist, exploit and defer the liberal peace through complex processes of negotiation. As will be discussed later in more depth, lib-eral peace agents often have limited abilities to access the local in substantive and meaningful ways (often they are restricted to the fortified embassy building, capital city meetings or staring at a spreadsheet). Yet their material power means that they can define the local.

It is within the context of the liberal peace (or a dominant form of internation-ally sponsored peacebuilding) that we can turn our attention to the local. The powerful positions of international actors and national elites means that they can often construct and maintain key concepts around which peace, politics and society can be organised (Donais 2009). These concepts are imaginaries. They have no basis in fact or the laws of physics, but the perception is perpetuated that they are real and important. So, for example key actors may be able to construct the idea that they have the legitimacy to engage in peace negotiations. No one mandated to the Kosovo Liberation Army to speak on behalf of Kosovo Albanians, yet they were widely accepted as the legitimate voice of that population in 1999 and 2000 as conflict with Serbia intensified. Or, liberal peace actors may be able to impose their sense of time on peace negotiations, perhaps in the form of a deadline or a sense of urgency. This framing power derives from existing material power, both coercive and incentivising. It takes the form of constructing and maintaining a series of imaginaries. One of these imaginaries is the idea of the local.

The notion of the local, as conceived as part of liberal peacebuilding, is not particularly coherent but it is useful to international actors. While colonial projects traditionally sought to tame the local and bring development, Christianity and 'civilisation' to local populations, contemporary liberal peacebuilding sees the local as being useful to their ends. Four uses are worth considering in this chapter. The first is that by gaining local partners, buy-in and collaboration, international peacebuilding actors may hope to gain legitimacy. A common criticism of international peacebuilding has been that it is a form of remote, top-down intervention that has little connection with the population in war-affected countries (Heathershaw 2008). According to these criticisms, peacebuilding is 'done to' societies rather than in cooperation with them. By emphasising local participation, local partners and local buy-in, international actors can hope to minimise these criticisms and gain legitimacy. Thus, so the logic goes, they can be transformed from being remote colonising powers into participative and enabling partners who are there by invitation. Certainly there is evidence of greater bottom-up peace programming that is reflective of local needs and aspirations. There is also much evidence of local mobilisation for peace, whether at the community level (Hancock and Mitchell 2007) or at the level of national elites of postwar states coming together to lobby for a 'New Deal' in relation to peacebuilding (McCandless 2013).

A second role that the notion of the local, and particularly local participation, can play in international peacebuilding is that it can help lower the costs of intervention. These cost reductions can be material in the sense that local peacebuilders (project officers, NGO workers etc.) are usually often much less expensive to employ than expatriates (Chesterman 2005, 201; Hoffman 2014). Cost reductions can also be symbolic. The notion that local people feel ownership of a peacebuilding process means that the reputational risks of things going wrong can be minimised. Blame can be shifted onto local actors if peacebuilding targets are not met. By using the rhetoric of local empowerment or participation, international actors can portray themselves as neutral outsiders who are merely attempting to facilitate peaceful change (we see this in the rhetoric surrounding international trusteeship [Luckham 2011, 103]). A relatively recent shift in the peacebuilding discourse has been the adoption of the language of local resilience whereby local communities and institutions are to be encouraged to have the resilience to withstand destabilisation (Menkhaus 2012). The implications of resilience have been well critiqued elsewhere (Walker and Cooper

2011), but it depends on a perceptual shift that makes local people (whatever that might mean) responsible for their own circumstances. Thus, if people have been coached to be resilient but war or natural disaster overwhelms them, then that is their own fault for not having adequate coping mechanisms in place. Notions and practices of resilience chime with neo-liberalism and the shifting of blame away from international actors (and structural explanations) and onto local actors (and proximate and localised explanations). It subtly absolves international actors from responsibility and renders any assistance they may give into the realm of facilitation and good-hearted charity. Crucial to the rise and rise of resilience as a buzzword in development and peacebuilding interventions has been the use of terms such as local participation and local buy-in.

A third reason why international actors can be favourable to the notion of local participation in their peacebuilding interventions is that local participation can pave the way for an exit strategy. International peacebuilding actors are often aware of isolationist discourses in their own country that caution against open-ended overseas commitments. These discourses may point to the costs of overseas entanglements, the dangers of blowback, and the opportunity costs of investing in overseas development while neglecting pressing issues at home. Local ownership of a peacebuilding process, evidenced for example through prolonged stability or the staging of a peaceful election, can allow international peacebuilders to withdraw and broadcast a message of 'job done'. The language used by the UK Foreign and Commonwealth Office in relation to its 'mission' in Iraq is revealing:

> Working for stronger, deeper, broader relations between the UK and Iraq. Supporting the people and Iraqi government as they build a stable, prosperous and democratic nation. Increasing UK-Iraq trade and investment, realising Iraq's economic potential, supporting long-term stability and working with Iraq to build partnerships in the region and beyond.
>
> (FCO 2015, n.p.)

The language here includes 'supporting the people' as 'they' engage in post-conflict reconstruction and realise 'their' potential. It is soft language of partnership and mutuality that makes no mention of the power differential between the two states and the UK's central role in the violent toppling of Saddam Hussein and the chaos that followed. 'Shock and awe' (the military codename for the coalition battle plan) seems to have been replaced by a more compassionate and cooperative approach that places an emphasis on relationships. The language gives the impression that the Iraqi people and government are empowered, and can be empowered further. For this to happen, the UK has realised that Iraq is not simply a government in Baghdad but is composed of people.

The fourth way in which the concept of the local has become useful to international peacebuilding interveners is that it provides a justification for their own existence. International peacebuilders and their right to intervene depends on the existence of other actors who 'need' peace, democracy, stability and good governance. The international versus local binary is a gross oversimplification, but it is one of a number of binaries that are used to organise the social world around us. Multiple binaries are at work in relation to peacebuilding intervention: good versus bad, peace versus war, democratic versus nondemocratic, legitimate versus illegitimate and so forth. These binaries give shape to our social reality. The notion and practice of international peacebuilders from the Global North is dependent on the existence of warring, 'incapable' and 'undeveloped' local actors from the Global South. International peacebuilders can portray themselves as necessary and capable in distinction to local actors who may be willing to strive for peace but need the security and technical know-how that only internationals can bring. Aspects of modern peacebuilding can amount to a recasting of the white man's burden whereby international actors convince themselves of their own indispensability. This self-perception can only make sense, though, if local actors exist and can be encouraged or compelled to buy into it. So, the local is co-constitutive of the international.

It should be noted that contemporary policy discourse on peacebuilding is full of references to the local, participation, partnership, national responsibility and positions that seem to be aware of the neo-colonialist connotations of intrusive peacebuilding. The discourse of the democratic engineering of the 1990s, and the neo-conservative and liberal hubris of the early 2000s, have been superseded by a more inclusive language. Yet, there can be no doubting where power (particularly material, symbolic and framing power) lies. The title of a 2014 publication by the Brookings Institution, *Still Ours to Lead*, is revealing of a prevailing worldview that leading states (in this case the United States) are custodians of peace and order and must intervene to maintain them (Jones 2014).

Importantly, liberal peace interveners have come to regard the local as potentially useful: it can be instrumentalised to assist them in their goals of stabilisation, legitimacy, lowering the costs of intervention and exit. In order for the local to become useful and usable they see it as something that is open to persuasion and coercion. This is an important point and is based on a worldview of superiority and liberal optimism that regards the local (like other hierarchy-infused terms such as the third world or undeveloped world) as waiting for technologically superior forms of governance and organisation to arrive (Mac Ginty 2011, 26). It is a worldview that disregards customary ways of doing things (unless they can be harnessed to support the liberal peace). Of course, this depiction is something of a generalisation but, overall, it is accurate to say that liberal peace actors regard the local as something that can be used. In places where the local may object, drag its heels or favour alternative modes of governance, then liberal peace actors may be tempted to use narratives that paint the local as being uncivilised, resistant or given to autocracy (Mac Ginty 2012).

How the local is seen by the international is shaped by multiple factors. As mentioned earlier, the worldview is, in part, influenced by liberal optimism. According to this stance, people and institutions can be reformed for the better through the application of the 'correct' technologies. Indeed, in this logic, not to offer such reforms is a dereliction, and so intervention becomes a necessity.

This worldview is influenced by the long historical trail of colonialism, globalised extraction, ethnocentrism and, it should be said, racism.

An additional element to how the international sees the local is worth mentioning: the extraordinarily limited means with which liberal peace agents have to gauge what the local thinks and feels. Despite technological revolutions and real-time and big data, and despite the multibillion-dollar budgets of governments and intelligence agencies, liberal peace agents have few reliable means at their disposal with which to see the local. There is still a reliance on traditional diplomatic means of gathering data: male, capital city–centric and often restricted to diplomatic compounds for security purposes. Duffield's (2010) characterisation of bunkerised aid in which staff are restricted to a securitised compound is telling of how expatriate staff are often isolated from the societies in which they work. If one considers contemporary conflict-affected societies (Libya, Ukraine, Syria, Iraq, Afghanistan, Gaza, Yemen and northern Nigeria), then we can see that there is a crisis of access for liberal peace agents. For security reasons, and because they failed to cultivate deep-rooted diplomatic linkages, they are unable to gather intelligence on the ground – particularly socioeconomic intelligence. They rely on ersatz means such as satellites and other digital surveillance, or the host government and 'tame' capital city informants. They are also likely to attempt to read the local in terms that are familiar to the organisational culture of the aid agency, intelligence agency or international organisation – even though these terms may be meaningless to the local society.

For example, a liberal peace agent may be interested in economic development in a rural area of a society emerging from violent conflict. His or her first port of call may be national statistics collected and collated by the national government. The veracity of these statistics may be questionable, yet because they come from the national government they may be accepted as fact and find their way into internationally replicated statistics. The liberal peace agent may be particularly attracted to data that can be compared with similar data from other societies emerging from conflict. Yet this data, which is internationally comparable and in a format that economists and statisticians can use, may bear little relation to life as lived in the conflict-affected society. As the case study in the next section shows, the interests of people on the ground, and the idioms they use to express themselves, may differ substantially from the ways in which international actors wish to read data. Moreover, and as James C. Scott (1992) has observed, there is no guarantee that individuals and communities will respond to the questions and data-gathering of international actors with answers that truly reflect their condition. The liberal peace agent may never get a chance to access the 'hidden transcript' because of security fears, translation difficulties, the obduracy of local bureaucracy and the epistemology of the liberal peace itself which is attuned to accept some sources and reject others.

This section has sought to underscore that the notion and practice of the local has become central to contemporary peacebuilding. It is seen by some peacebuilders as the way to address some of the criticisms that have been made of post–Cold War peacebuilding: too expensive, too remote and so forth. Crucially, the term local is used with immense frequency and imprecision. It is often left uninterrogated so that the local can refer to a very broad range of objects that stretch from national government to local communities and neighbourhoods. This definitional imprecision reinforces the necessity to see the local (and indeed the international) as imaginaries that are constructed and reconstructed by those with the power to do so. It seems prudent to think of the local in plural terms – that there are many locals that are fluid and possibly overlapping. Despite their problems of access, liberal peace agents often hold most power in being able to define the local in international, national and policy-related discourses.

Everyday peace

Having discussed the conceptual nature of the local in relation to international peacebuilding, this chapter goes on to draw on an ongoing research project that examines perceptions of peace, security and change at the local level. The project focuses on everyday peace or the tolerance and civility required of people as they navigate their way through socially awkward situations (Mac Ginty 2014). All people engage in these emotionally intelligent activities in the sense of looking the other way, dissembling, avoiding contentious topics or avoiding trouble-makers. These everyday peace skills become more important, however, in deeply divided and conflict-affected societies when minor incidents can escalate into larger ones.

The Everyday Peace Indicators project is based on the premise that individuals and communities often have their own early warning and coping mechanisms that allow them to navigate through potentially awkward or dangerous circumstances. This focus on bottom-up approaches to tolerance and conciliation is different from many orthodox accounts of peacemaking that concentrate on top-down (male and institutionalist) efforts to make peace (for example Mitchell 1999 or Powell 2009) or research projects that use off-the-shelf datasets (for example Hendrix and Haggard 2015 or Rapport 2015). It is influenced by studies in ecology that sought to develop bottom-up and civic epistemologies that would lessen the gulf between the researcher and the researched (Parkins et al. 2001; Miller 2005; Mac Ginty 2013b). Indeed, there has been a relatively recent trend in peace and conflict studies, and in some policy arenas, to solicit bottom-up voices. See, for example the Border Lives project from Northern Ireland (http:// borderlives.eu/project/) or the World Bank's Voices of the Poor programme (http://go.worldbank.org/H1N8746X10).

The project (http://everydaypeaceindicators.org) operates in communities in four sub-Saharan African countries: South Africa, South Sudan, Uganda and Zimbabwe. The communities and localities in the four countries provide a mix of rural and urban, are subject to either much international peacebuilding attention or little, and have experienced violence relatively recently or quite some time ago. Using partner organisations and participatory action research methods, the project seeks to elicit localised understandings of peace and indicators of change. Rather than approaching the communities with ready-made templates, questions or indicators, the project seeks to be ascriptive and encourage community members to identify their own indicators of change (Mac Ginty and Firchow 2014). These indicators may be dismissed as anecdotal or highly localised, yet they are authentic and locally meaningful. For example, a number of communities across a number of countries have pointed to barking dogs as an indicator of insecurity at night (the dogs bark in response to prowlers). Yet those who compile international statistics are likely to regard such an indicator as absurd (Mac Ginty 2013a). Other highly localised indicators included being able to urinate outside at night, being able to possess high-value goods, being able to leave your home unoccupied, and being able to walk to the shops – all signs of safety.

Communities were invited to draw up their own list of indicators via focus groups (separate ones for males, females and youth and then a final verification focus group where community members could agree – consensually – on a combined indicator list). Focus group participants attended on a voluntary basis and we tried to make them as representative of local communities as possible, but there were no guarantees that this came about. The focus group conversations (which were mediated by in-country partner NGOs) provided fascinating considerations in relation to peace security and aspirations. (For a detailed step-by-step account of the project methodology see Mac Ginty 2013b).

The rest of this section reports what these focus group conversations had to say about ideas and practices of the local. There is no pretence from the author that these conversations are representative of the whole of Africa (whatever that may be) or even the communities that they were held in. Focus groups held in neighbouring countries or even neighbouring villages and city neighbourhoods may have yielded very different results. Varshney (2001), for example reflects on the fact that areas relatively small distances apart can experience very different levels of violent conflict. Nevertheless, the focus group conversations are revealing about what the local means, and the relationship between the local and other actors and scales.

Following a review of 35 focus group transcripts from the four sub-Saharan countries, this chapter highlights three points that shed light on the relationship between the international and the local with regard to peacebuilding. The focus group conversations were reasonably open-ended and participants were lightly steered towards the meanings of peace in their own lives and communities. They were then steered towards discussing indicators of peace, security and change. Participation was entirely voluntary and participants were not prevented from discussing what they wanted in the manner of their choosing. The result was wide-ranging discussions. In some of the focus groups there is no doubt that participants felt restrained from talking about sensitive issues (e.g. in Zimbabwe, where there are tensions between regime loyalists and opponents), but the focus group convenors were skilled in sensitively guiding conversations.

The first point that emerges from the focus group discussions is that the international (and it is worth restating the caveat that the international is a broad category) is rarely referred to. In the 35 transcripts that involved several hundred people, only one international organisation, the World Food Programme, was mentioned by name. This is interesting because three of the countries – South Africa, South Sudan and Uganda – have received substantial international peacebuilding and development interventions. Indeed, a pile of rusting signs behind one of the municipality offices in northern Uganda told a fascinating story. These were signs attesting to the assistance of various European government aid agencies in programmes and projects. When each project had come to an end, the sign was taken down and left in a pile at the back of the municipality office. Yet, the focus groups in that locality did not mention the international level, either as a positive or negative factor. There may be a number of reasons for this lack of reference to the international: it occurred a long time ago, the international agencies used local proxies and so local people were unaware of the ultimate patron, or people were simply 'ungrateful'.

Whatever the reason, the lack of reference to the international level is revealing in that it did not show that people saw their own situations as part of a chain that stretched from their village or city neighbourhood to bilateral donors and the international organisations. Their worldview, as can be judged from the focus group discussions, was reasonably local and they did not see a connection with meta-system dynamics of globalisation and geostrategic calculations. This is not to say that people were static and incurious. Many of the focus group participants mentioned migration and upheaval as a result of violent conflict. Visual observation in the areas where the focus groups were conducted revealed plenty of evidence of transnational trade. The lack of mention of the international by focus group participants suggests that the international level was not immediately relevant to people's lives. It was simply not mentioned in terms of everyday livelihood, security and provision of public goods. This is revealing in that it punctures the notion of the 'indispensable international'.

A second point that emerges from the focus group discussions is that people discuss their own safety and security in very localised terms. Consider, for example, the following focus group transcript extracts:

> Safety in the community means that law respecters like myself, I don't come out myself because of insecurity after 8pm. You have to be in. Yesterday the door of my brother was broken for the third time, and the leftover food was collected and everything was collected.
>
> – Male youth, South Sudan

> Criminals used to take advantage of the war situation to break into people's houses, steal crops from the garden and loot people's shops.
>
> – Female, Uganda

> If I take my child to school I have to be careful all the time . . . I have to look wherever she goes. They keep watching. They want your purse or your bag. They want money and they don't believe you if you say you have no money.
>
> – Female, South Africa

The focus group transcripts are full of references to walking to and from the bus stop, the safety of the children in going to school, or the security of homes and crops. Interestingly, all of these references are physically local. While the local must be placed in the context of a transnational world, these focus group insights are a useful reminder that we cannot completely deterritorialise the local. It retains a physical meaning and the transcripts refer repeatedly to physical places that make up the social and economic map of the research participants: homes, vegetable gardens, schools, health centres, bus stops, roads, shebeens, minibus taxis and so forth. This seems important because these spaces (going back to the point on the crisis of access made in the last section) are often very difficult for outsiders to access. They are often zones of informality, yet also the places where important interactions take place that allow individuals and collectives to gauge if a society is becoming more or less peaceful. By and large, international peacebuilders do not queue from dawn outside the health centre, routinely take minibus taxis and tend vegetable gardens in the areas they work. As a result, they can only gain partial, and often generalised, pictures of the areas and communities they work in.

An additional observation is that focus group participants do not link incidences of localised insecurity to broader dynamics such as a transnational political economy and its attendant trading regimes. There is no linkage made between armed criminal gangs and the international arms trade, or between rural poverty and European Union or North American import restrictions. This is not to say that people are necessarily insular and parochial. It is, instead, to highlight the very different top-down and bottom-up worldviews that operate simultaneously in peacebuilding contexts.

A third point is that God and religion (specifically Christianity) is mentioned in a good number of the focus group discussions. This is significant because religion is largely absent from much of the official discourse on international peacebuilding. Programmes and projects by state actors and international organisations often feel distant from religion. In many European countries, religion is regarded as something for the private sphere: it is perfectly acceptable as a private pursuit and outlook, but it rarely enters the workplace. (The United States is somewhat different in that religion can have a more prominent role in politics, especially on the right.) There is a sense in many European public discourses that religiosity is somehow backward or a specialist activity that should have little bearing on public policy issues that should be dealt with via technocracy and best practice. Peacebuilding programmes and projects very rarely mention religion. If they do, it is often part of an attempt to achieve local participation and a recognition that local religious leaders might be useful to have on board. In other words, where religion is recognised by international peacebuilding projects, it is as something to be instrumentalised. This understanding of religion is primarily regarded as a source of social capital and social entrepreneurship and is usually uninterested in the faith aspect of religion. To some extent, religion has even been securitised in some discourses with a focus on (Islamic) extremism.

None of this is to suggest that religion has no role to play in peacebuilding, reconciliation and postwar reconstruction. Indeed, faith actors and communities often play vital roles in such processes, and many explicitly religious organisations have shaped the thinking and practices of conciliation (Appleby 2000; Abu-Nimer 2013). The chief point, however, is that many Western organisations see religion as only a marginal point of reference, or as something to be instrumentalised for its secular (rather than faith) purposes. Even though many Western faith-based organisations are engaged in reconciliation, aid and peacebuilding activities, it tends to be the 'secular international' that dominates (Benthall 2008).

Yet, a cursory reading of the focus group transcripts shows that religion – as a system of faith but also as a source of social capital – plays a significant role in many peoples' lives. Moreover, they were prepared to talk about it. For example, a focus group discussion among South Sudanese males included a number of biblical references. During a discussion on community safety, one participant noted:

> I have to know God because God protects me . . . In Romans, Chapter 18:1–3 a government should take care of their people. If somebody do anything wrong let him face the law but what we are seeing now days these things are not happening. The government is not taking care of that. God has also said in Ephesians 4:11–15, in that chapter it is said that he has given everyone a gift.
> – Male, South Sudan

A fellow focus group member then takes up the theme of scripture-inspired contributions to the discussions:

> It is written in Jeremiah chapter 17:5 that we should be self-reliant. We should not depend on others. We have to work here in our country. Even this soil is money and these stones are money.
> – Male, South Sudan

A little later in the same focus group, yet another participant notes that issues of safety are 'God's will . . . You are under God's hand, he is the one protecting you.'

The reason for highlighting the transcript references to religion is that they are very different from the discourses used by many peacebuilding professionals in their project and programme documents. It is a reminder that the local is likely to contain elements that are not terribly obvious to outsiders and may even make them uncomfortable. These elements, ranging from religious belief systems to practices of patriarchy or the operation of a caste system are likely to be very different from the operating systems and worldviews used by liberal peacebuilding agents. These external agents will have naturalised their own rational justifications for intervention and peacebuilding processes but may be unaware of just how subjective and culturally loaded their own interventions may be. They may see their own work as being based on meritocracy, bureaucratic rationales and value for money, but be unaware that these are cultural constructions.

Concluding discussion

This chapter of *Peacebuilding in Crisis* has concentrated on the relationship between the local and the international. Part of the 'crisis', or at least deficiency, in internationally sponsored peacebuilding is that there is a disjuncture between local and international hopes and practices in relation to building peace. It is recognised that the local and the international are not homogenous entities. Both contain considerable diversity and overlap. Yet, while recognising the imprecision of these terms and the fact that binaries are unsatisfactory, we can move towards three concluding points.

The first of these is that the local and the international are co-constitutive of each other and as such cannot be seen as separate parts of a binary. They are relational concepts and it is difficult to conceive of one without the other. This brings serious problems, especially for the local, in that it is not seen in its own right. Moreover, there is a tendency that such views will be ethnocentric in regarding a Westernised international as the benchmark against which other levels and types of society are to be measured (Sabaratnam 2013). This chapter brings the arguments on ethnocentrism a step further and suggests that the international actually needs the local in order to justify its position of dominance and its interventionism.

The second concluding point is that the international is poorly equipped to see the local. In part this is due to the 'crisis of access', whereby major international powers (guardians of the liberal peace) cannot put their own diplomatic or aid staff in conflict-prone areas to find out what is happening on the ground. Electronic and remote information-gathering systems can go some way to fill in the blanks, but there is clearly a limit to the human intelligence capabilities of technology. The broader problem, however, is that many actors from the Global North – particularly those institutionalised in diplomatic institutions and international organisations – have epistemological biases towards collecting and believing particular types of information. This instititionalised epistemology may privilege official information from other similar institutions, and downgrade the importance awarded to finer-grained and localised information.

The final concluding point is to assert (for here there can be no definitive proof) that many liberal peace agents cannot get beyond attempting to instrumentalise the local and thereby miss the opportunity to have meaningful relationships with it. In this view, the local is something to be used. It is a means to an end: a route to acceptability and legitimacy, a way to lower costs, or the justification for an exit strategy. As such, the connections that many international actors make with the local tend to be transitory and extractive. This is not to say that all local actors are powerless, and all international actors are empowered. Nor is it to say that all international actors are doomed to have shallow relations with the local. It is, instead, to highlight the enormous structural difficulties that liberal peace agents face in seeing the local in its own right. Indeed, in many diplomatic and aid organisations, getting too close to the host society is frowned upon as 'going native'.

208 Roger Mac Ginty

A takeaway point from this chapter is that it is useful to look at the local in our own lives before attempting to imagine or intervene in the local in a peace-building context that may be distant (geographically and figuratively). If we, as scholars and practitioners who often hail from the Global North, maintain a confused picture of what the local might mean in our own lives, then how can we take this as a starting point for constructing policy in other peoples' lives? As has been argued here, the local – in many respects – is an imaginary, made and remade in true constructivist fashion. Some actors, however, have more power than others to make and reshape the local. Often these are liberal peace actors who have material and symbolic power and can wield this to construct discursive geographies and ecologies. Recognising this power is a first step to challenging it.

References

Abu-Nimer, M. (2013). Religion and peacebuilding. In R. Mac Ginty (Ed.), *Routledge Handbook on Peacebuilding*. Routledge, London, 69–80.

Appleby, R. (2000). *The Ambivalence of the Sacred: Religion, Violence and Reconciliation*. Rowman & Littlefield, New York.

Benthall, J. (2008). *Returning to Religion: Why a Secular Age Is Haunted by Faith*. IB Tauris, London.

Chesterman, S. (2005). *You, the People: The United Nations, Transitional Administrations, and Statebuilding*. Oxford University Press, Oxford.

Dauphinee, E. (2010). The ethics of autoethnography. *Review of International Studies*, 36(3), 799–818.

Donais, T. (2009). Empowerment or imposition? Dilemmas of local ownership on post-conflict peacebuilding processes. *Peace and Change*, 34(1), 3–26.

Duffield, M. (2010). Risk-management and the fortified aid compound: Everyday life in post-interventionary society. *Journal of Intervention and Statebuilding*, 4(4), 453–474.

FCO. (2015). UK and Iraq. FCO website (https://www.gov.uk/government/world/iraq) Accessed: 31 May 2015.

Hancock, L., and Mitchell, C. (2007). *Zones of Peace*. Kumarian Press, Bloomfield, CT.

Heathershaw, J. (2008). Seeing like the international community: How peacebuilding failed (and survived) in Tajikistan. *Journal of Intervention and Statebuilding*, 2(3), 329–351.

Hendrix, C., and Haggard, S. (2015). Global food process, regime type and urban unrest in the developing world. *Journal of Peace Research*, 52(2), 143–157.

Herring, R. (2015). *Oxford Handbook of Food, Politics and Society*. Oxford University Press, Oxford.

Hoffman, K. (2014). 4 ways to strengthen global development locally. Devex, 24 November. (https://www.devex.com/news/4-ways-to-strengthen-global-development-locally-84929) Accessed: 8 June 2015.

Jones, B. (2014). *Still Ours to Lead: America, Rising Powers and the Tension between Rivalry and Restraint*. Brookings Institution, Washington, DC.

Joshi, M., Lee, S., and Mac Ginty, R. (2014). Just how liberal is the liberal peace? *International Peacekeeping*, 21(3), 364–398.

Luckham, R. (2011). Democracy and security: A shotgun marriage? In S. Tadjbakhsh (Ed.), *Rethinking the Liberal Peace: External Models and Local Alternatives*. Routledge, London, 89–110.

Mac Ginty, R. (2006). *No War, No Peace: The Rejuvenation of Stalled Peace Processes and Peace Accords*. Palgrave Macmillan, Basingstoke.

Mac Ginty, R. (2011). *International Peacebuilding and Local Resistance: Hybrid Forms of Peace*. Palgrave Macmillan, Basingstoke.

Mac Ginty, R. (2012). Between resistance and compliance: Non-participation and the liberal peace. *Journal of Intervention and Statebuilding*, 6(2), 167–187.

Mac Ginty, R. (2013a). Taking anecdotal evidence seriously: An alternative view of peace indicators. *Shared Space*, 18, 21–35.

Mac Ginty, R. (2013b). Indicators +: Everyday peace indicators – A proposal. *Evaluation and Program Planning*, 36, 56–63.

Mac Ginty, R. (2014). Everyday peace: Bottom-up and local agency in conflict-affected societies. *Security Dialogue*, 45(6), 548–564.

Mac Ginty, R., and Firchow, P. (2014). Capturing local voices through surveys. *Shared Space*, 18, 33–39.

McCandless, E. (2013). Wicked problems in peacebuilding and statebuilding: Making progress in measuring progress through the New Deal. *Global Governance*, 19, 227–248.

Menkhaus, K. (2012). *Making Sense of Resilience in Peacebuilding Contexts: Approaches, Applications, Implications*. Paper No. 6. Geneva Peacebuilding Platform.

Miller, C. A. (2005). New civic epistemologies of quantification: Making sense of indicators of local and global sustainability. *Science, Technology and Human Values*, 30(3), 403–432.

Mitchell, G. (1999). *Making Peace: The Inside Story of the Making of the Good Friday Agreement*. Heinemann, New York.

Paris, R. (2004). *At War's End: Building Peace after Civil Conflict*. Cambridge University Press, Cambridge.

Parkins, J., Stedman, R., and Varghese, J. (2001). Moving towards local-level indicators of sustainability in forest-based communities: A mixed-method approach. *Social Indicators Research*, 56(1), 43–72.

Powell, J. (2009). *Great Hatred, Little Room: Making Peace in Northern Ireland*. Vintage, London.

Rapport, A. (2015). Military power and political objectives in armed conflicts. *Journal of Peace Research*, 52(2), 201–214.

Richmond, O., and Franks, J. (2009). *Liberal Peace Transitions: Between Statebuilding and Peacebuilding*. Edinburgh University Press, Edinburgh.

Rugg, J. (2013). *Churchyard and cemetery: Tradition and modernity in rural North Yorkshire*. Manchester University Press, Manchester.

Sabaratnam, M. (2013). Avatars of Eurocentrism in the critique of the liberal peace. *Security Dialogue*, 44(3), 259–278.

Scott, J. (1992). *Domination and the arts of resistance: Hidden transcripts*. Yale University Press, Yale.

Turner, M. (2015). Peacebuilding as counter insurgency in the Occupied Palestinian Territory. *Review of International Studies*, 41(1), 73–89.

Varshney, A. (2001). Ethnic conflict and civil society: India and beyond. *World Politics*, 53(3), 362–398.

Walker, J., and Cooper M. (2011). Genealogies of resilience: From systems ecology to the political economy of crisis adaptation. *Security Dialogue*, 42(2), 143–160.

12 Peacebuilding goes local and the local goes peacebuilding

Conceptual discourses and empirical realities of the local turn in peacebuilding

Thania Paffenholz

Introduction[1]

The importance of local actors in peacebuilding is undisputed; however, knowledge about who these actors are, what their preferences and values are and how they can be engaged positively in support of peace has proved elusive. The concept of peacebuilding was first developed in the late 1960s by Johan Galtung (Galtung 1969), and underwent substantial revision in the early 1990s after the end of the Cold War. A major component of this reinvention has been the substantial shift in emphasis away from the international and towards local ownership. As a result, the recognition that local actors should be in the driving seat of peacebuilding efforts is firmly established in theory and practice. This has led to a massive rise in peacebuilding projects in support of local organizations.

This so-called local turn in peacebuilding has its conceptual foundation in the work of John Paul Lederach (Lederach 1997), who has inspired an entire generation of peacebuilding practitioners. In recent years, the local turn has been revitalized by scholars from the field of critical peacebuilding research (Mac Ginty and Richmond 2013). This new local turn represents a counter-narrative to the liberal international peacebuilding project.

These two turns, which bring to the fore the "local" in peacebuilding, are marked by commonalities but also fundamental differences. Conceptually, the first Lederach-inspired local turn in peacebuilding, built on frameworks of conflict resolution theory from Azar (1990), Curle (1971), Fisher and Kelman (2003), Freire et al. (2012) and Galtung (1969), in order to advocate for sustainable reconciliation within societies. In contrast, the latest local turn draws from post-structuralist and post-colonial scholarship, including the works of Foucault (1972), Bhabha (1994) and Scott (1985), analyzes power and resistance and aims at more radical changes. Both local turns offer a counter-narrative to outsider driven international peacebuilding, while the latest local turn is more radical and fundamentally challenges the raison d'être of international peacebuilding. Whereas scholars in the first local turn aimed to bridge the gap between academia and policy/practice, the majority of scholars of the second local turn do not engage in this conversation.

What the two discourses on the local turn in peacebuilding have in common, however, is a positive narrative about the role of local actors and their capacity to build sustainable peace. The early local turn in peacebuilding focuses on giving support to local actors through capacity building as a means of enhancing their peacebuilding potential, and has encouraged a generation of civil society support projects around the globe. The newer local turn, on the other hand, constructs the "local" and the "international" as binary opposites – here the "good" local, and there the post-colonial, neo-imperialist, "bad" international. Interestingly, in recent years, more and more empirical research has revised the solely positive narrative about the local, and put forward a more nuanced picture about local actors, their peacebuilding potential and the "peace industry" that has been established in support of the local.

This chapter gives an overview of the development of the local turn(s) in peacebuilding and puts the conceptual discourses into empirical perspective, in order to contribute to a better understanding of local actors' peacebuilding actions, potentials and constraints. This will advance a critical but nuanced assessment of the local turn in peacebuilding. The chapter is structured in two parts. The first part gives a historical and conceptual overview of the local turn(s) in peacebuilding. The second part presents empirical evidence about local actors' peacebuilding action and potential, with an emphasis on local civil societies.

History and theory of the local turn(s) in peacebuilding

The first local turn in peacebuilding emerged in the early 1990s. Peacebuilding by the beginning of the 1990s was mostly focused on mediating and implementing peace agreements in the proxy conflicts characteristic of the Cold War. The end of the Cold War opened up space for the United Nations to act as a proactive peace-builder and raised hopes that – without the stimulus of great power rivalry – conflict would substantially diminish, and peace settlements would be reached more easily. The liberal peace orthodoxy that developed out of this experience expressed the hegemony of the North Atlantic powers, and mandated the establishment of security, democratic political structures and economic liberalization. The UN *Agenda for Peace* (1992) defined peacebuilding as an external intervention in support of national peace processes in conflict countries, with the intention to end conflict and rebuild states. The *Agenda for Peace* became the main reference document for a policy conceptualization of peacebuilding (UN Secretary-General 1992).

Although critiques of the liberal peace project are as old as the liberal peace itself (see, for example, Schmid 1968), liberal peacebuilding orthodoxy was most seriously undermined by the failure of UN missions to achieve sustainable peace in places like Somalia, Rwanda or the Balkans. Responses to this failure can be characterized according to Robert W. Cox's typology of "problem solving" and "critical" (Cox 1981). Conflict management scholars pursued a problem-solving approach and began to research more effective ways to conduct peacebuilding and statebuilding (Barnett and Zuercher 2009; Call and Cousens 2008; de Soto and del Castillo 1994; Hampson 1996; Stedman 1997). Meanwhile, the then newly established conflict transformation school, with John Paul Lederach as its most prominent representative (Lederach 1997), advocated for a critical conception of peacebuilding. This critical approach, the first local turn in peacebuilding, emphasized the necessity of empowering local people as the primary authors of peace instead of advancing externally designed and driven peace interventions.

The first local turn was successful in establishing the importance of local ownership and context sensitivity, at least in the discourse of liberal peacebuilding actors (Mac Ginty and Richmond 2013). However, the continued dismissal of local institutions and perspectives in peacebuilding practice, or the instrumental use of local actors in order to achieve the goals of international actors – as manifested in the failures of the international peacebuilding and statebuilding project in Afghanistan and Iraq – gave impetus to new critical perspectives. The UN, as well as many researchers, reacted to the mixed successes and obvious failures of peacebuilding by analyzing hindering factors and implementation problems within the frame of the liberal peace project.[2] As a result, a new policy consensus emerged which stipulated the importance of context sensitivity in peacebuilding projects (OECD 2007). Nevertheless, the bulk of evaluations commissioned by donors and international actors themselves show that the blueprint/toolbox approach to international interventions in diverse conflict contexts continues relatively unabated. The second local turn thus confronts these universalist ideas of peace, and highlights particularism and resistance (Mac Ginty and Richmond 2013, 772). Within the critical debates of the second local turn we find both moderate critics (Lund 2003; Paris 1997; Paris 2004) and more fundamental ones (Bendana 2003; David 1999; Duffield 2001a; Duffield 2001b; Fetherston 2000; Heathershaw 2008; Jabri 2013; Mac Ginty 2006; Pugh 2004; Richmond 2005).

The current local turn in peacebuilding is now sufficiently consolidated to represent a "school" of peacebuilding theory, and can be numbered alongside other approaches to peacebuilding such as the conflict management, conflict resolution and conflict transformation schools (see Paffenholz 2010 and 2013 for a historical contextualization).

The two generations of local turn scholarship draw from different theoretical traditions, which also lead to quite different conceptions of the local. Lederach and the conflict transformation school built on Galtung's (1969) theory of structural violence and peacebuilding, Curle's (1971) work on transforming relationship, Azar's (1990) work on protracted social conflicts, Fischer and Kelman's (2003) work on relationship-building (also known as the "conflict resolution" school), as well as on Freire et al.'s work – most notably *Pedagogy of the Oppressed* (2012). According to this understanding, international actors should seek to harness local potential in order to achieve sustainable reconciliation within societies. Sustainable reconciliation takes the form of rebuilding destroyed relationships within societies and establishing an infrastructure for peace in the country, and through training of people (human capacity building) within a generation-long time perspective. The role of outsiders here is envisioned as being limited to the support of insiders, mainly those located in the middle level of society.

In contrast, Richmond, Mac Ginty and other representatives of the second local turn in peacebuilding understand peacebuilding as the locus of competing political, economic and social interests (Mac Ginty 2014; Mac Ginty and Richmond 2013; Richmond 2009; Richmond 2011a). Theoretically founded in

Foucauldian, post-structuralist and post-colonial frameworks, including those of Homi Bhaba and James C. Scott (Bhabha 1994; Scott 1985), these authors argue that locally driven peacebuilding is a post-liberal order founded on emancipatory local agency, and a form of resistance against the dominant discourse and practice of the liberal peacebuilding project (Chandler 2013; Richmond 2011b). Emancipation is to be achieved through analyzing structures of power, domination and forms of resistance.

These different theoretical frameworks have led scholars in the first and second local turn in peacebuilding to different understandings of the local and its relationship to the international. The local in Lederach's (1997) theory is identified with the middle level of society (nongovernmental organizations [NGOs], civil society organizations, community leaders etc.), and local actors are thought to have the potential to build peace by working with both the top/national level and the bottom/grassroots level of society (Lederach 1997). Ideally, international actors should support local actors' own agency through training and capacity building, as well as by building peace infrastructures.

Hence, scholars of the first local turn regard international peacebuilders as overconfident about the potential of outside actors to alter local realities rather than as agents of a neo-imperialist agenda. Most representatives of the first local turn are scholar-practitioners who actively work with local groups and communities in order to empower them for peace and reconciliation work. The objective of peacebuilding theory is to conceptualize experiences, which are then transformed into training concepts to support international actors in giving local people agency and power over their peace processes. This capacity building is geared towards two main targets: the international practitioners (NGOs), who need a better understanding of emancipatory conflict transformation, and the local peacebuilders in conflict zones, who need the necessary skills to enhance their role as agents of peace.

This model of the relationship between the local and the international as one of harmonious and unidirectional support has its critics. Some, such as Fetherston (2000) and Miall (2004) argue that the first local turn is overly technical and blind to the domestic and international struggles over influence and access to power that are so often at the heart of conflict. In my work, I have shown that the local in this understanding is still at risk of being dominated by the soft power inherent in the international peacebuilder's interventionist logic of training and peace infrastructures (Paffenholz 2014). Both Mac Ginty (2010a) and I (Paffenholz 2001, 2010, 2014) highlight the risk of the moderate local actor becoming co-opted into the liberal NGO peacebuilding enterprise, and thus being deprived of his or her capacity for resistance.

I have also criticized the lack of internal diversity in conceptualizations of the local in the first generation of local turn scholarship. I argue that the local should encompass not only track II (the middle level of society), but also the top level (track I) and the very local level (track III), and that scholars and practitioners should be aware of the internal division and competition between these actors (Paffenholz 2014). Moreover, none of these levels is internally homogenous; all include constituencies in favour of, and opposed to, peace (Paffenholz 2010). This means that the uncritical valorization of the local as a reliable, peace-supporting constituency is misguided. Despite these criticisms, the model of local agency derived from the first local turn has become thoroughly integrated into almost all organizations working in the field of peacebuilding. The engagement with local actors prescribed by this model thereby risks becoming a form of soft-power domination by other means, especially when it is implemented in a universalist "tool-box" manner (Paffenholz 2014).

In contrast, in the second local turn, the local appears as a site of particularism, autonomy and resistance against the hegemonic international liberal actor. Hence, the local exists in a binary with the international, in which local agency is expressed as resistance to the liberal peacebuilding project. At its inception, the second local turn mainly consisted in conceptual reflections on the continued failure of liberal peacebuilding. This was followed by a new empirical emphasis in critical peacebuilding research that has resulted in a wealth of case studies. The main focus has been on critically analyzing international peace- and statebuilding interventions and their interaction or noninteraction with local communities, as well as hybrid forms of peace and governance structures, characterized by a mixing of local and international norms and procedures, and local infrastructures for peace (Donais 2009; Richmond 2012).[3] Fewer case studies have investigated the local as having agency in its own right (Paffenholz 2010).

The focus on institutional setups, in the form of infrastructures for peace, is a common feature of both local turns. This area represents the opportunity for scholars to go beyond the analysis of domination, power and resistance, and to engage with the practice of peacebuilding. Whereas most post-structuralists do not present any revisions to peacebuilding practice on the basis of their critical analysis (Jabri 2013), other authors such as Boege, Brown and Clements (Boege 2010; Boege et al. 2009) or Belloni (2012) have advocated for hybrid political orders as alternatives to the liberal peacebuilding model. Others, like Mac Ginty (2011), are theoretically agnostic, rejecting counter-narratives as a principle, yet presenting hybrid orders in a solution-oriented manner.[4]

Despite making important contributions to peace and conflict studies, core debates concerning the local turn in the critical peacebuilding literature present contradictions that should be problematized. These mainly concern the construction of the local and the international as binary opposites. I have argued that this construction is at the heart of many problems and contradictions within core debates (Paffenholz 2015), namely the weak conceptualization of the primary actors (the local and the international), including an excessive focus on Western actors within the international; a romanticized interpretation of hybrid peace governance structures; a blindness towards the dominant role of local elites; an overstating of local resistance; and an ambivalent relationship to practice. These issues will be further explained below.

When it comes to the conceptualization of the primary actors, that is the local and the international, both are – especially in most conceptual critical peacebuilding scholarship – not sufficiently analytical, and either uncritical or overly partisan. The international, in these critical studies, is stereotyped as Western and imperialist. This ignores the prominent role of non-Western states such as China or Brazil among international actors. These states have their own interest at stake, and a very different relationship to local organizations of the Global South and their governments. The diversity of local actors is equally vast, and their profiles, behaviours and aspirations vary considerably. There is also an over-emphasis on local civil society actors – mostly portrayed as the "good local" – at the expense of analyzing other local actors, such as local elites (Paffenholz 2010, 2015). Hybrid political orders, the second point mentioned earlier, are too often portrayed as an alternative to the liberal peace model that is free of power rela-tions and that brings the best of both worlds together. However, such an inter-pretation of hybridity ignores elite capture and power relations between local actors on the one hand and between local and internationals on the other hand. Moreover, the mere fact of being a hybrid order does not necessarily contribute constructively to peacebuilding. In fact, research shows that local elites still tend to be in the driving seat of political power and thereby have the capacity to instrumentalize hybrid orders (Debiel et al. 2009). As a consequence, local resis-tance is more often directed against local elites than against international actors.

Local actors in peacebuilding

In the following section I sketch out a response to some of the gaps and weak-nesses identified earlier, by presenting a more complete picture of the actors that make up the local, and their activities. Local actors relevant to peacebuilding include local elites, including national and local governments, parliaments, busi-ness; civil society organizations including professional associations such as unions; special interest groups such as women, minority or human rights groups, but also NGOs and faith-based organizations; traditional institutions; community leaders; research institutions; and mass movements. The following section examines evi-dence drawn from available case study research regarding the role of these local actors in peacebuilding. The main results can be summarized as follows.

First, most studies found that peacebuilding is impossible without at least some degree of local support and consent. Second, studies demonstrate that local actors vary greatly in their degree of support for peace. Third, many case studies found that international donor support to local civil society contributes to the 'NGOization' of peace work. Fourth, only a few studies assessed the relevance and impact of local peacebuilding functions and actors. Lastly, research also identified certain contextual factors seen to enable or constrain the impact of local actors' peacebuilding roles. The following part of the chapter sheds light on these find-ings as they concern different actors.

Civil society

Civil society can play a number of important peacebuilding roles and have an important influence on political change (Kasfir 1998; Ikelegbe 2001a). Most studies analyze local actors' peacebuilding activities in general terms. Only a few studies take a function/role-oriented approach to consider the effectiveness of individual initiatives. Paffenholz and Spurk (2006; 2010, 65–76) take a function-oriented approach to understanding civil society, and group civil society peace-building functions into protection, monitoring, advocacy, socialization, social cohesion, facilitation and service delivery. Other studies focus on end goals, such as giving voice to the unheard (Fetherston 2000; Pearce 1998; Richmond 2005). A number of studies (Barnes 2005; Richmond and Carey 2006; Van Tongeren et al. 2005) illustrate this point with positive examples of NGOs' contribution to peacebuilding. Paris (2004) views the promotion of "good civil society" as an important complement to statebuilding. Until recently, most studies of civil society activities focused exclusively on the social cohesion projects favoured by the conflict resolution school of peacebuilding. These social cohesion work-shops (dialogue projects), which bring together adversarial groups for the pur-pose of reconciliation, have been found in some studies to generate positive results (Cuhadar 2009; Malhotra and Liyanage 2005; Ohanyan and Lewis 2005); however, most of these studies found that the change in individual attitudes is not sustained over the long term, limiting the potential for these workshops to engineer wider social change (Atieh et al. 2004; Cuhadar 2009; Ohanyan and Lewis 2005). Other research suggests that these initiatives are often top-down and pushed by outside actors, rather than being the result of genuine desire or enthusiasm for peace on the part of local actors, whose effectiveness is limited by the fact that civil society organizations in deeply divided societies are often mono-ethnic and radical (Orjuela 2003). Instead, Varshney (2002), Ohanyan and Lewis (2005) and Cuhadar (2009) found that work-related initiatives, focus-ing on a concrete outcome, are more effective.

In my research on civil society (Paffenholz 2010), I have applied a functional approach to 13 case studies of war-to-peace transitions to analyze the wid-est range of civil society actors and initiatives during four phases of conflict/peacebuilding: war, armed conflict, peace negotiations and in the aftermath of large-scale violence (Paffenholz 2010). I found that civil society was not com-prised only of NGOs as implied in many outside-driven discourses. These activi-ties were classified according to seven functions identified earlier (Paffenholz and Spurk 2006; 2010, 65–76), namely protection, monitoring, advocacy, socializa-tion, social cohesion, facilitation and service delivery. In addition to identifying the functions and their relevance in each conflict phase, the study also proposed a set of effectiveness criteria for each function (Paffenholz 2010, 381–404). I found that that civil society actors, and NGOs in particular, generally do not modify their activities to correspond to those most effective for a given phase of peacebuilding. Instead, throughout all phases of the process, they overwhelm-ingly concentrate on activities appropriate to the phase after large-scale violence has come to an end, including training in conflict resolution and transformation as well as dialogue and peace education initiatives (Paffenholz 2010, 381–404). These activities are mandated by the theory and institutional capacities of liberal peacebuilding organizations, and are supported by both funding and discursive pressure. This creates a disconnect between supply and demand in peacebuilding, as affected populations are not provided with the help most appropriate to their situation.

Civil society is not, however, always a reliable peace supporting constituency, contributing towards dialogue and democratization (Orjuela 2004, 210). Civil society can manifest as much division, conflict and hostility as the broader society it is supposed to represent. Research has found that inclusive, civic, bridging and propeace organizations exist alongside exclusivist, sectarian and occasionally even xenophobic and militant groups (Belloni 2001; Ikelegbe 2001a, 2001b; Paffenholz et al. 2010, 414–420). Spurk (2010, 18–19) labels these actors "uncivil society."

An active local civil society is not always indicative of genuine local ownership of peacebuilding. Local civil societies are often products of international donor-driven engagement, manifested most prominently in the preponderance of the NGO as the dominant organizational form in these societies. This had led to the sidelining of local efforts and actors (Kasfir 1998; Pouligny 2005). Additionally, these donor-driven NGO-based civil societies can have the effect of crowding out local capacities and genuinely local ownership of the peace process (Belloni 2001, 2008; Paffenholz 2010, 425–430). This "NGOization" of social protest (Orjuela 2003, 255) leads to the "taming" of social movements (Kaldor 2003, 79) and, hence, shifts the focus away from political peace movements and grassroots civic engagement, which threaten to upset the established order, and towards creating NGOs as service deliverers (Paffenholz 2010, 428; Pearce 1998).

NGOs may have political goals but generally do not aim at radical social change; therefore, the NGO-centric focus of funding by international donors limits the capacity of local civil society to challenge national power hierarchies and other structural factors (Belloni 2001; Orjuela 2003; Paffenholz 2010, 428–430; Pearce 1998). As a consequence, civil society activism has by and large been sapped of its transformative potential (Bendana 2003; Fetherston 2000; Heathershaw 2008; Richmond 2005).

In my research on civil society, I also examined the impact of civil society on peacebuilding (Paffenholz 2010, 425–430). The research identified a large gap between peacebuilding potential on the one hand and the actual track record for a number of civil society actors on the other. Even though mass-based organizations are often the most polarized groups in a conflict – and consequently their peacebuilding performance is rather low and often even counterproductive in many contexts – they also have the potential to promote socialization and social cohesion to a far greater degree than NGOs. Schools have a similarly high capacity. While the research confirmed earlier critique of the NGOization of peace work, it also found that NGOs can be effective in providing protection and in conducting targeted advocacy campaigns, in addition to their more usual roles in conflict resolution training, dialogue and peace education. Additionally, traditional and local actors or institutions, such as elders, or traditional leaders, were found to be effective in the roles of facilitation and protection.

Eminent civil society leaders could be effective in preparing the ground for national facilitation and in helping parties break out of a stalemate in negotiations. Women's groups, as they do not simply reproduce the political fault-lines of the conflict, have the potential to overcome these fault lines to some degree, and can therefore be important in bridging divides between the various parties. In addition, women's groups were almost always responsible for the consideration of gender, women's and minority issues on the agenda. Aid organizations – also generally unaware of their peacebuilding potential – could further support protection, monitoring and social cohesion. Overall, the study found that broader change required that all available change-oriented mass movements unite their efforts.

National elites

Domestic power structures can undermine, block or circumvent well-funded and carefully designed policy reforms. Local or national elites refers to the already politically and economically powerful actors in a given country context. Local elites are not a homogenous group, though by definition they have some vested interest in the current political order. This is especially true if they have risen to power in the context of conflict, as in the case of warlord elites. These elites will resist efforts by peacebuilders to replace them with a more palatable set of usually democratically elected elites. Mac Ginty (2010b) describes the troubled relationship between the warlord elite in Afghanistan and the technocratic and elected political elite post-2001, and international peacebuilders and statebuilders. National elites are often located in urban centres, and more readily accessible and relatable to international peacebuilders. Some studies have shown that peacebuilders engage with elite concerns at the expense of local conflicts (Autesserre 2010). Other studies have shown that national elites are able to absorb and subordinate the "toothless" liberal institutions advocated by peacebuilders to the patrimonial structures on which their power depends (Öjendal and Ou 2015). In my latest research on broader participation in peace negotiations and their implementation (Paffenholz 2015), I could show that local elites that were weakened during political reform processes mostly regained power a few years after the change. Egypt and Nepal are powerful examples of this trend.

Business actors

Local businesses, in the context of peacebuilding, are usually defined as small and medium-sized enterprises (SMEs), as opposed to multinational or transnational corporations (Berdal and Mousavizadeh 2010). Discussion of the role of local business actors in conflict settings has traditionally focused on the negative consequences of "war economies," in particular the importance of extractive industries in providing a source of funding, which leads to the conflict being prolonged, as well as the role of trafficking in humans, weapons and drugs (Gündüz et al. 2006). More recently, scholars have begun to examine the positive potential of business actors in building peace. The peacebuilding potential of the local private sector lies in the provision of employment as a pathway both to self-sufficiency and aspiration for a better future. Certain kinds of businesses have an interest in good infrastructure, stable property rights and an accountable and professional bureaucracy, all of which are abetted by peace and consistent with the program of liberal peacebuilding. According to the typology of Paffenholz and Spurk (2010), business is strongest in the area of intermediation and facilitation. Business groups have built constituencies for peace (as in El Salvador), facilitated the building of personal relationships across conflict lines (as in South Africa) or have held unofficial consultations (as in Colombia) (Tripathi and Gündüz 2008). Factors limiting the potential for local business actors to build peace, include the preponderance of informal and illicit/illegal business in conflict and post-conflict environments (Berdal and Mousavizadeh 2010). Other authors have criticized the narrow neoliberal philosophy underlying international support for the local business sector, as well as the inconsistent investment cycle by the international community, in which funding peaks in the immediate aftermath of conflict – when a society is least prepared to absorb it productively.

Religious or faith-based organizations

Religious organizations are sometimes included under civil society. The activities of religious organizations in peacebuilding are mostly identical to those of civil society. However, religious organizations have special peacebuilding potential in the areas of protection and service provision (Paffenholz and Spurk 2010, 66–75). Religious organizations also share most of the same weaknesses as civil society organizations: in particular, they are not necessarily reliable supporters of peace, and may be as polarized or divided as the society of which they are a part.

Traditional institutions and leadership

Traditional institutions and leaders can represent a parallel leadership structure to the state – being more present and enjoying greater legitimacy in the perception of local actors. Traditional institutions may have peacemaking roles, and these have been engaged effectively by international peacebuilders in Bougainville (Boege 2010). This is particularly important where the conflict itself is structured according to traditional divisions such as clan, tribe or religion. Traditional authorities can also be particularly important in the area of ongoing justice and dispute resolution. In contexts where the state justice system is absent or dysfunctional, this can prevent some conflicts from escalating by providing a mutually satisfactory outcome. Traditional justice may be used by locals because it is already in operation and familiar to the population; because the actors involved are more familiar; because the articulation with local political dynamics creates accountability; due to the weight of social sanction, which is lacking in the formal justice sector; or else, because it is more financially viable – procedures are shorter than in state courts, and there is no need for specialized infrastructure or a full-time, professional staff (Barfield et al. 2006; Dinnen and Peake 2013). However, traditional justice can present a number of problems. It is unlikely to adhere completely to international standards of human rights and procedural fairness (Wimpelmann 2013), it may be biased against certain groups including women (Chopra and Isser 2011) and it may reproduce local inequalities of power and access to resources (Manyena and Gordon 2015).

Enabling and constraining context factors for civil society's peacebuilding impact

In my research, I also found that context factors can seriously open or close the space for local actors in peacebuilding. The main context factors identified in the same study (Paffenholz et al. 2010, 405–424) were:

- *The level of violence:* The overall level of violence had a strong negative correlation with the ability of local actors to perform all of their functions.
- *The behaviour of the state:* Civil society organizations struggle to exercise their functions in the face of outright hostility from the state. Hence, the more repressive the state is towards civil society actors, the more it limits the space for action. Conversely, the more democratic the form of governance, the broader the space for civil society to act. Moreover, the state can alleviate the pressure of civil society by performing the roles of protection and service delivery, for which it is uniquely capable and for which it is conventionally responsible. This allows civil society to concentrate on other functions.
- *The performance of the media:* In general, mass media are among the key opinion leaders in society. Hence, they can tremendously strengthen or limit local actors' peacebuilding roles in different ways. While the media can support peacebuilding, polarized or inflammatory media can close off the space for peace constituencies. In response, donors often choose to support purpose-specific peace media that generally is only capable of reaching a very small audience.
- *The behaviour and composition of major society groups (including diaspora organizations)* influence the peacebuilding impact. This means that the more society is polarized and dominated by radical tendencies, the more difficult it becomes for it to act towards a common cause for peacebuilding. The former also includes diaspora organizations that can often be very influential. Overall, the study also found that men from dominant groups in society (ethnic, religious, caste etc.) hold most of the leading positions in all relevant government but also societal organizations.
- *The influence of external political actors and donors:* External powers – especially those from the region – can have a major impact on the overall level of violence. They can also be important in pressuring the state in certain ways, for example, towards refraining from political repression against civil society

actors. International donors have important influence over the capacities of local actors, through political pressure and dialogue, provision of funding, as well as in setting the direction of the organizations' activities. Donors, especially donor states, may also have a great deal of political leverage over the national government in a conflict context.

Conclusions

The local is a complex object of knowledge for peacebuilders. Even though respect for the local is well established in orthodox peacebuilding theory and practice, there are still gaps and different viewpoints on local actors' peacebuilding actions, potentials, aspirations and limitations.

This chapter has shown that there are a number of reasons for the ambivalent success of local engagement in peacebuilding. The first is that local values are not always consistent with the liberal or neoliberal program of peace and statebuilding. This program posits a set of universal values, such as individualism, free markets, property rights, rule of law and human rights. To the extent that local values contest or resist this program, they are invariably disregarded. The second is that the local is not necessarily always the reliable supporter of peace, as more romantic scholars of the local would have it. Local communities are often as deeply divided as the broader society that they make up.

Looking at the enabling and constraining factors, it is also clear that peacebuilding cannot be achieved in a local vacuum. Conflicts are intertwined. Local, regional and international agendas become interrelated. Hence, local, regional and international peacebuilding go hand in hand. In consequence, supporting local peacebuilding actors alone is not a sufficient guarantee for peace. Other constituencies also need to be addressed, especially those which are against a given peace process. More so, regional and international constellations matter and need to be part of coherent local support strategies. In short, peacebuilding is political and cannot be dealt with in a technical-peacebuilding-NGO-support way. The support to local NGOs also risks creating a peace industry, turning activist movements into project proposal–writing NGOs.

What does this all mean for the future of critical peacebuilding research and the local turn in peacebuilding?

Future research needs to move away from the binary understanding of the local and the international. Much more focus needs to be devoted to the nuanced and critical – but not one-sided – analysis of both players. The local is as good and as bad as society as a whole, and the international is both imperialistic and supportive at times. Hybrid peace governance structures can therefore be an interesting and fruitful system of governance in one place and become a co-opted and manipulated space of power and dominance by local elites in another.

Therefore, much more attention needs to be geared towards understanding local power relations and their meaning for peacebuilding. A critical approach to the analysis of power, dominance and resistance with sensitivity to all power relations and circulations is required. A multidisciplinary approach to address the complex challenge of peacebuilding is needed that also includes joint projects between critical peacebuilding, area studies researchers and other strands of peace research.

Finally, more openness from critical peacebuilding scholars to engage critically with policy practice could enhance the impact of critical debates in real world peacebuilding.

Notes

1 I would like to thank Nick Ross for his excellent assistance as well as Ulrich Schneckener and Tobias Debiel for their helpful comments.
2 Numerous studies and policy papers deal with these issues. See, for example, UN Secretary-General (2009); Call and Cousens (2008); Paris (2004).
3 See, for example, Autesserre (2010); Boege (2010); the special issue of Global Governance – including the introduction by Jarstad and Belloni (2012); Mac Ginty (2011); as well as the special issue of the *Journal of Peacebuilding & Development* – including the introduction by McCandless and Tschirgi (2012).
4 See this point also made in Heathershaw's review of Mac Ginty (2011) in Heathershaw (2013).

References

Atieh, A., Ben-Nun, G., El-Shahed, G., Taha, R., and Tulliu, S. (2004). *Peace in the Middle East: P2P and the Israeli-Palestinian Conflict*. UNIDIR, Geneva.

Autesserre, S. (2010). *The Trouble with the Congo: Local Violence and the Failure of International Peacebuilding*. Cambridge University Press, Cambridge.

Azar, E.E. (1990). *The Management of Protracted Social Conflict*. Aldershot, Dartmouth.

Barfield, T., Nojumi, N., and Thier, J.A. (2006). *The Clash of Two Goods: State and Non-state Dispute Resolution in Afghanistan*. United States Institute of Peace, Washington, DC.

Barnes, C. (2005). Weaving the web: Civil-society roles in working with conflict and building peace. In P. Van Tongeren, M. Brenk, M. Hellema, and J. Verhoeven (Eds.), *People Building Peace II, Successful Stories of Civil Society*. Lynne Rienner, Boulder, CO, 7–24.

Barnett, M., and Zuercher, C. (2009). The peace builders contract. In R. Paris and T. Sisk (Eds.), *Statebuilding after Civil War*. Routledge, New York, 23–53.

Belloni, R. (2001). Civil society and peacebuilding in Bosnia and Herzegovina. *Journal of Peace Research*, 38, 163–180.

Belloni, R. (2008). Civil society in war-to-democracy transitions. In A. Jarstad and T. Sisk (Eds.), *War-to-Democracy Transitions: Dilemmas of Democratization and Peace-building in War-Torn Societies*. Cambridge University Press, Cambridge, 182–210.

Belloni, R. (2012). Hybrid peace governance: Its emergence and significance. *Global Governance: A Review of Multilateralism and International Organizations*, 18, 21–38.

Bendana, A. (2003). *What kind of peace is being built? Stock taking of post-conflict peacebuilding and charting future directions*. Paper prepared for the International Development Research Council (IDRC) on the 10th anniversary of *An Agenda for Peace*. Ottawa, Canada.

Berdal, M., and Mousavizadeh, N. (2010). Investing for peace: The private sector and the challenges of peacebuilding. *Survival*, 52, 37–58.

Bhabha, H. K. (1994). *The Location of Culture*, Routledge, London.

Boege, V. (2010). How to maintain peace and security in a post-conflict hybrid political order – The case of Bougainville. *Journal of International Peacekeeping*, 14, 330–352.

Boege, V., Brown, A., and Clements, K. (2009). Hybrid political orders, not fragile states. *Peace Review*, 21, 13–21.

Call, C. T., and Cousens, E. M. (2008). Ending wars and building peace: International responses to war-torn societies. *International Studies Perspectives*, 9, 1–21.

Chandler, D. (2013). Peacebuilding and the politics of non-linearity: Rethinking "hidden" agency and "resistance". *Peacebuilding*, 1, 17–32.

Chopra, T., and Isser, D. (2011). Women's access to justice, legal pluralism and fragile states. In P. Albrecht, H. M. Kyed, D. Isser, and E. Harper (Eds.), *Perspectives on Involving Non-state and Customary Actors in Justice and Security Reform*. International Development Law Organization (IDLO), Viale Vaticano, 22–38.

Cox, R. W. (1981). Social forces, states and world orders: Beyond international relations theory. *Millennium – Journal of International Studies*, 10, 126–155.

Cuhadar, E. (2009). Assessing transfer from track two diplomacy: The cases of water and Jerusalem. *Journal of Peace Research*, 46, 641–658.

Curle, A. (1971). *Making Peace*. Tavistock Press, London.

David, C.-P. (1999). Does peacebuilding build peace? Liberal (mis)steps in the peace process. *Security Dialogue*, 30, 25–41.

De Soto, A., and del Castillo, G. (1994). Obstacles to peacebuilding. *Foreign Policy*, 94, 69–83.

Dinnen, S., and Peake, G. (2013). More than just policing: Police reform in post-conflict Bougainville. *International Peacekeeping*, 20, 570–584.

Donais, T. (2009). Empowerment or imposition? Dilemmas of local ownership in post-conflict peacebuilding processes. *Peace & Change*, 34, 3–26.

Duffield, M. (2001a). *Global Governance and the New Wars: The Merging of Development and Security*. Zed Books, London.

Duffield, M. (2001b). Governing the borderlands: Decoding the power of aid. *Disasters*, 25, 308–320.

Fetherston, A. B. (2000). Peacekeeping, conflict resolution and peacebuilding: A reconsideration of theoretical frameworks. *International Peacekeeping*, 7, 190–218.

Fisher, R. J., and Kelman, H. C. (2003). Conflict analysis and resolution. In D. O. Sears, L. Huddy, and R. Jervis (Eds.), *Political Psychology*. Oxford University Press, New York.

Foucault, M. (1972). *Two Lectures*. Pantheon, London.

Freire, P., Ramos, M. B., and Macedo, D. P. (2012). *Pedagogy of the Oppressed*. Bloomsbury, New York.

Galtung, J. (1969). Violence, peace, and peace research. *Journal of Peace Research*, 6, 167–191.

Gündüz, C., Vaillant, C., and Banfield, J. (2006). Addressing the economic dimensions of peacebuilding through trade and support to private enterprise. International Alert, London.

Hampson, F. O. (1996). *Nurturing Peace: Why Peace Settlements Succeed or Fail*. United States Institute of Peace Press, Washington, DC.

Heathershaw, J. (2008). Unpacking the liberal peace: The dividing and merging of peacebuilding discourses. *Millennium – Journal of International Studies*, 36, 597–621.

Heathershaw, J. (2013). Towards better theories of peacebuilding: Beyond the liberal peace debate. *Peacebuilding*, 1, 275–282.

Ikelegbe, A. (2001a). Civil society, oil and conflict in the Niger Delta region of Nigeria: Ramifications of civil society for a regional resource struggle. *Journal of Modern African Studies*, 39, 437–469.

Ikelegbe, A. (2001b). The perverse manifestation of civil society: Evidence from Nigeria. *Journal of Modern African Studies*, 39, 1–24.

Jabri, V. (2013). Peacebuilding, the local and the international: A colonial or a postcolonial rationality? *Peacebuilding*, 1, 3–16.

Jarstad, A., and Belloni, R. (2012). Introducing hybrid peace governance: Impact and prospects of lberal peacebuilding. *Global Governance: A Review of Multilateralism and International Organizations*, 18, 1–6.

Kaldor, M. (2003). *Global Civil Society: An Answer to War*. Polity Press, Cambridge.

Kasfir, N. (1998). Civil society, the state and democracy in Africa. *Commonwealth & Comparative Politics*, 36, 123–149.

Lederach, J. P. (1997). *Building Peace: Sustainable Reconciliation in Divided Societies*. United States Institute of Peace Press, Washington, DC.

Lund, M. S. (2003). What kind of peace is being built? Assessing post-conflict peacebuilding, charting future directions. International Development Research Centre, Ottawa.

Mac Ginty, R. (2006). *No War, No Peace*. Palgrave Macmillan, Basingstoke.

Mac Ginty, R. (2010a). Hybrid peace: The interaction between top-down and bottom-up peace. *Security Dialogue*, 41(4), 391–412.

Mac Ginty, R. (2010b). Warlords and the liberal peace: state-building in Afghanistan. *Conflict, Security & Development*, 10, 577–598.

Mac Ginty, R. (2011). *International Peacebuilding and Local Resistance: Hybrid Forms of Peace*. Palgrave Macmillan, Basingstoke.

Mac Ginty, R. (2014). Why do we think in the ways that we do? *International Peacekeeping*, 21, 107–112.

Mac Ginty, R., and Richmond, O. (2013). The local turn in peace building: A critical agenda for peace. *Third World Quarterly*, 34, 763–783.

Malhotra, D., and Liyanage, S. (2005). Long-term effects of peace workshops in protracted conflicts. *Journal of Conflict Resolution*, 49, 908–924.

Manyena, B., and Gordon, S. (2015). Resilience, panarchy and customary structures in Afghanistan. *Resilience*, 3, 72–86.

Miall, H. (2004). *Conflict Transformation: A Multi-Dimensional Task*. Berghof Research Center for Constructive Conflict Management.

OECD. (2007). *DAC Principles for Good International Engagement in Fragile States & Situations*. Paris: Organization for Economic Cooperation and Development.

Ohanyan, A., and Lewis, J. (2005). Politics of peacebuilding: Critical evaluation of inter-ethnic contact and peace education in Georgia-Abkhaz Peace Camp, 1998–2002. *Peace and Change*, 30, 57–84.

Öjendal, J., and Ou, S. (2015). The "local turn" saving liberal peacebuilding? Unpacking virtual peace in Cambodia. *Third World Quarterly*, 36, 929–949.

Orjuela, C. (2003). Building peace in Sri Lanka: A role for civil society? *Journal of Peace Research*, 40, 195–212.

Orjuela, C. (2004). *Civil society in civil war, peace work and identity politics in Sri Lanka*. PhD dissertation, Department of Peace and Development Research, University Göteborg.

Paffenholz, T. (2001). Western approaches to negotiation and mediation: An overview. In L. Reychler and T. Paffenholz (Eds.), *Peacebuilding: A Field Guide*. Lynne Rienner, Boulder, CO, 75–81.

Paffenholz, T. (2010). Civil society and peacebuilding. In T. Paffenholz (Ed.), *Civil Society and Peacebuilding: A Critical Assessment*. Lynne Rienner, Boulder, CO, 43–64.

Paffenholz, T. (2013). *Critical peacebuilding research, power and politics*. HCRI Conference "Power and Peacebuilding". Manchester.

Paffenholz, T. (2014). International peacebuilding goes local: Analysing Lederach's conflict transformation theory and its ambivalent encounter with 20 years of practice. *Peacebuilding*, 2, 11.

Paffenholz, T. (2015). Unpacking the local turn in peacebuilding: A critical assessment towards an agenda for future research. *Third World Quarterly*, 36, 857–874.

Paffenholz, T., and Spurk, C. (2006). Civil society, civic engagement and peacebuilding. *Social Development Papers, Conflict Prevention and Reconstruction*. World Bank, Washington, DC.

Paffenholz, T., and Spurk, C. (2010). A comprehensive analytical framework. In T. Paffenholz (Ed.), *Civil Society and Peacebuilding. A Critical Assessment*. Lynne Rienner, Boulder, CO, 65–78.

Paffenholz, T., Spurk, C., Belloni, R., Kurtenbach, S., and Orjuela, C. (2010). Enabling and disenabling factors for civil society peacebuilding. In T. Paffenholz (Ed.), *Civil Society and Peacebuilding*. Lynne Rienner, Boulder, CO, 405–424.

Paris, R. (1997). Peacebuilding and the limits of liberal internationalism. *International Security*, 22, 54–89.

Paris, R. (2004). *At War's End: Building Peace after Civil Conflict*. Cambridge University Press, Cambridge.

Pearce, J. (1998). From civil war to "civil society": Has the end of the Cold War brought peace to Central America? *International Affairs*, 74, 587–615.

Pouligny, B. (2005). Civil society and post-conflict peacebuilding: Ambiguities of international programmes aimed at building "new" societies. *Security Dialogue*, 36, 495–510.

Pugh, M. (2004). Peacekeeping and critical theory. *International Peacekeeping*, 11, 39–58.

Richmond, O. P. (2005). *Understanding the liberal peace*. Experts' Seminar on "Transformation of War Economies". University of Plymouth, Plymouth, UK.

Richmond, O. P. (2009). Becoming liberal, unbecoming liberalism: Liberal-local hybridity via the everyday as a response to the paradoxes of liberal peacebuilding. *Journal of Intervention and Statebuilding*, 3, 324–344.

Richmond, O. P. (2011a). De-romanticising the local, de-mystifying the international: Hybridity in Timor Leste and the Solomon Islands. *Pacific Review*, 24, 115–136.

Richmond, O. P. (2011b). *A Post-liberal Peace*. Routledge, Abingdon.

Richmond, O. P. (2012). A pedagogy of peacebuilding: Infrapolitics, resistance, and liberation. *International Political Sociology*, 6, 115–131.

Richmond, O. P., and Carey, H. (2006). *Subcontracting Peace. NGOs and Peacebuilding in a Dangerous World*. Ashgate, Aldershot.

Schmid, H. (1968). Peace research and politics. *Journal of Peace Research*, 5, 217–232.

Scott, J. C. (1985). *Weapons of the Weak: Everyday Forms of Peasant Resistance*. Yale University Press, New Haven, CT.

Spurk, C. (2010). Understanding civil society. In T. Paffenholz (Ed.), *Civil Society and Peacebuilding. A Critical Assessment*. Lynne Rienner, Boulder, CO, 3–27.

Stedman, S. J. (1997). *Spoiler Problems in Peace Processes*. MIT Press, Cambridge, MA, 5.

Tripathi, S., and Gündüz, C. (2008). *A role for the private sector in peace processes? Examples, and implications for third-party mediation*. Background paper. The Oslo Forum Network of Mediators.

UN Secretary-General. (1992). *An agenda for peace: Preventive diplomacy, peacemaking and peace-keeping*.

UN Secretary-General. (2009). *Report of the secretary-general on peacebuilding in the imme-diate aftermath of conflict*. UN document no. A/63/881-S/2009/304 (New York: United Nations, 2009).

Van Tongeren, P., Verhoeven, J., and Wake, J. (2005). People building peace. Key mes-sages and essential findings. In P. Van Tongeren, M. Brenk, M. Hellema, and J. Verho-even (Eds.), *People Building Peace II. Successful Stories of Civil Society*. Lynne Rienner, Boulder, CO, 83–93.

Varshney, A. (2002). *Ethnic Conflict and Civic Life: Hindus and Muslims in India*. Yale Uni-versity Press, New Haven, CT.

Wimpelmann, T. (2013). Nexuses of knowledge and power in Afghanistan: The rise and fall of the informal justice assemblage. *Central Asian Survey*, 32, 406–422.

13 False promise

'Local ownership' and the denial of self-government

Pol Bargués-Pedreny

Introduction[1]

This chapter unpacks how the concept of local ownership has been employed within policy frameworks in the context of peacebuilding since the late 1990s (OECD 1996; UNDP 2001; World Bank 2000). The term has been widely understood in the literature as 'the extent to which domestic actors control both the design and implementation of political processes', which is essential because, as the wisdom goes, 'any peace process not embraced by those who have to live with it is likely to fail' (Donais 2009, 3). The concept is portrayed positively first for its practical benefits, in terms of improving the results of the mission if local authorities are able to take the initiative; second, it is endorsed because of its ethical connotation of transforming externally dominated and overly invasive practices and correcting 'a paternalistic attitude of donor countries towards local actors' (Reich 2006, 7; see also OECD 2011, 45). While the practical and ethical importance of ownership is seldom disputed, there is also a wide consensus that ownership is rarely realised in practice. Indeed, one of the biggest concerns in the literature is how to operationalise this concept more successfully in post-conflict scenarios. As Ganson and Wennmann (2012, 6) write: 'the challenge is that the international rhetoric of "local ownership" must be made substantially more real.'

What is intriguing is that even if there are policy reports (and academic critiques of these reports), which continuously highlight the need to enable genuine local control of peace processes, these processes exclude de facto self-determination and self-government. This is intriguing because, as Chesterman (2007, 20) notes, in its broadest sense, ownership means self-determination, a basic principle of international law (e.g. UN Charter, ICCPR, ICESCR), which nowadays seems to have lost its punch.[2] Rather than understanding ownership as akin to self-determination, studies increasingly define it as 'a shorthand way of describing the relationship between different local and international actors' (Martin and Moser 2012, 3). Within this narrower definition, in which self-determination itself is not contemplated, the big question is how to improve the nature of the exchange between partners. Reich (2006, 4), for example who calls literal or 'full' ownership an 'unfulfillable goal', wishes to make the relationship between donors and recipients more emphatic by introducing the notion of 'learning sites'. For Donais

(2009, 21), similarly, local ownership is 'a delicate, complex, and often shifting balancing act, in which the division of responsibilities between outsider and insider is constantly calibrated and adjusted as a means to advancing the peace process'. Krogstad (2014) criticises the fact that the debates on ownership have mainly focused on the difficulties faced by donors. However, instead of uncompromisingly defending recipients and their right to self-determination, he focuses on the cases in which local authorities ask for an international supervision of their country. For Krogstad (2014, 1), there is no longer a conflictive relation between international and local, 'coloniser' and 'colonised' because sometimes receivers are the ones 'inviting the coloniser back'. To this I wish to add: what if receivers do not invite the coloniser back? Or what if they do not even have the prerogative to make the invitation?

This chapter thus explores the apparent paradox that lies in the increasing willingness to transfer ownership to the local population and the explicit assumption that self-determination and self-government have to be avoided in democratisation and post-conflict situations. Local ownership – increasingly understood by most policy reports and the academic literature as a learning relationship, cultural exchange or reflexive cooperation between donors and recipients, in which self-government is no longer an issue demanding a response – has sought to overcome the wrongs of both top-down and bottom-up processes of peacebuilding. However, the conclusion of this chapter is that the concept of ownership, as it has been interpreted by the approaches to peacebuilding analysed here, has been of little value to post-conflict societies and has even denied their moral and political autonomy. This denial, disguised as a discourse that promises to embrace difference, is particularly flawed because it seems to permanently defer the equality between internationally supervised populations and the rest of the sovereign nations.

Local ownership: facing a governance dilemma

In 1996 the Organisation for Economic Co-operation and Development (OECD), reflecting on the experience of the last five decades of international development, published a report that sought to set a new strategy for the twenty-first century. 'Success will depend', it argued, 'upon an approach that recognises diversity among countries and societies and that respects local ownership of the development process' (OECD 1996, 9). The concept of local ownership soon became a mantra for international organisations. From the UN to the World Bank, international institutions believed that development could not be imposed from an external perspective. For this reason, it was argued, developing people – rather than international administrators importing successful institutions from elsewhere – ought to be in the driver's seat of economic and political reforms, and the specific sociocultural context of every society would need to be taken into account (CIDA 2002; Stiglitz 1998a, 1998b; UNDP 2001, 20–30; World Bank 2000, 8–9; 2001, 191–192).[3] As one of the World Bank (2001, vi) reports stressed, 'action must also take place with local leadership and ownership reflecting local realities. There is no simple, universal blueprint.'

In postwar scenarios, the policy strategy of transferring local ownership was considered more burdensome than in developing contexts, as it posed a delicate dilemma. On the one hand, local ownership was introduced to correct the highly invasive international administrations that have been in place since the end of the 1990s. These administrations have proved inefficient, economically and politically costly and lacking in legitimacy among the local population (Chesterman 2002). On the other hand, local ownership seemed difficult to promote in postwar societies in which there were periodic relapses of violence after the peace agreement. By the end of the 1990s, it was assumed that free and fair democratic processes, which respected the priorities of the local population and devolved responsibility to the nationals, would disturb the efficiency of peacebuilding missions (Carothers 2002; Mansfield and Snyder 1995; Paris 2004, 151–178; Snyder 2000).

It is against this dilemma that I seek to unravel the dominant understanding of local ownership. For instance, had ownership been taken literally – for example as a synonym for self-government – international administrators would have disregarded the widespread assumption shared by academics and policy-makers that democracy was a destabilising factor in postwar societies. Nevertheless, as I shall demonstrate, international administrators were to understand local ownership as being detached from its meaning of self-government precisely to resolve this governance dilemma: being able to avert the dangers of democratisation, which could lead to conflict, and of top-down interventions, which could be reminiscent of colonialism.

The case of Bosnia is useful to illustrate how international agencies introduced local ownership as a way to manage this dilemma. In 1999, the UN High Representative, Wolfgang Petritsch (1999), stated that the UN was undertaking a new approach, which he referred to as ownership. For him, this new approach meant that the responsibility for the peace process and implementation of the Dayton Peace Agreement lay with the Bosnian electorate and its elected leaders. However, while Petritsch was defending ownership, he was, at the same time, discriminating in favour of the leaders he preferred and was convinced that Bosnians were not yet ready to make the 'appropriate' (read here nonnationalistic) democratic choices (Chandler 2000, 201–202; Hughes and Pupavac 2005, 882). In an apparent incongruity, the UN affirmed its commitment to local ownership *after* its ruling administration had been prolonged indefinitely and the High Representative had adopted further substantial powers in a meeting in Bonn only two years earlier. The point here is not that Petritsch was hypocritical or fallacious, but to understand that for the High Representative the approach of ownership did not imply self-government and that it was certainly not contrary to further international assistance. With the benefit of hindsight, it seems obvious to say that even if international policy-makers have increasingly transferred responsibilities to the local population, the process of ownership initiated by Petritsch has continuously limited self-government on the premise that Bosnians are not capable of taking autonomous actions.[4]

Throughout most of the decade 2000–2009, the concept of local ownership was meant to rectify the limits of highly invasive missions led almost exclusively by international administrators. Rather than transferring full responsibility to the locals and falling into the trap of democratising post-conflict environments, though, international administrators focused on developing the structural socio-economic conditions that would make national ownership 'efficient' (UNDP 2010, 23).[5] In 2005, in a manual for conflict resolution and peacebuilding, the OECD (2005, 4, 7) wrote: 'In all peace-building interventions particular emphasis should be given to national ownership of the process. Work may need to be done to ensure that it is truly representative and not perpetuating existing divisions in society.' This statement needs careful attention. While the OECD does not specify why the 'existing divisions in society' are not representative, it nevertheless assumes that there is the need to work on building favourable country conditions and institutional capacity to achieve ownership that is 'truly representative'. For the OECD, therefore, ownership does not imply the right to autonomously own or choose, but it is tied into prerequisites or amendments that internationals allocate and that indicate how ownership ought to be.

The assumption that postwar societies are not yet ready, and therefore in need of international interference, is indicative of the dominant conceptualisation of ownership since its initial formulations (Chesterman 2007; Narten 2009; Pouligny 2009; Reich 2006; Scheye and Peake 2005). Rather than understanding ownership as a democratic right to self-determination that populations have or do not have (Philpott 1995), it is formulated as a process that can be enhanced or built from a co-ownership perspective. As Chesterman (2007, 7) argued: 'Ownership is certainly the intended end of such operations, but almost by definition it is not the means.' In the next section, I focus on contemporary policy approaches, which have pushed this conceptualisation of ownership further in order to resolve the governance dilemma 'forever'.

Local ownership as a process: the denial of self-government?

By the end of the decade 2000–2009, international organisations progressively placed greater emphasis on the requirement that the local population take command of postwar situations. A quick glance at contemporary reports is enough to identify systematic efforts to transfer responsibilities to the locals, while respecting the specificity of every context (Ganson and Wennman 2012; OECD 2008, 2011; UNDP 2010). As the UN (2010, 6) argues, 'peacebuilding strategies must be coherent and tailored to the specific needs of the country concerned, based on national ownership.' The OECD has a similar position: 'It is absolutely necessary to give the state space to establish itself and to ensure that local ownership leads to locally grown institutions' (OECD 2008, 101; see also OECD 2011, 23–25).

In contrast to the previous approach in which ownership was the end of the process that justified other externally driven means, now ownership is increasingly understood to be the means of the peacebuilding process.[6] In this vein, international agencies have limited their role to mere assistance, support or facilitation of the locally owned process of cultivating resilience to violence and other crises. Now, achieving local ownership requires international partners to become more self-reflexive throughout the process, aware of their limits and culturally biased assumptions, and more open to the sociocultural backgrounds of other societies. At the same time, however, their role as facilitators is still considered to be important to ensure that ownership actually results in a plural and all-encompassing execution of domestic politics (OECD 2011; UNDP 2012).

The result is that efforts to enhance more substantial local ownership within contemporary governance frameworks are rarely translated into de facto self-government. Rather than providing full autonomy or ownership to the local, local ownership has turned into a long-term emancipatory process in which autonomy is, at the same time, enhanced and supervised – without these positions being seen as contradictory. Schmidt (2016, 131) goes a step further to argue that, within current internationally administered democratisation practices, populations come to 'fully acknowledge and realise their lack of autonomy'. However as counter-intuitive as this claim may sound, the EU Mission (2008 to present) in the statebuilding project in Kosovo seems to be translating this idea into practice.

From its inaugural report, the European Union Rule of Law Mission in Kosovo (EULEX 2009, 9) has stressed that 'there would be total ownership of the reform process by the relevant Kosovo institutions.' Its commitment towards effectively operationalising local ownership seems clear in this statement:

> The EULEX Programmatic Approach is based on a rigorous adherence to the principle of 'local ownership'. In practice this has meant that the final responsibility for translating each recommendation into a[n] MMA Action has rested with the relevant institutions of Kosovo's rule of law. In this way, the EULEX programmatic approach is designed to help Kosovo's rule of law bodies to make the changes themselves, rather than rely upon an international presence to do it for them.
>
> (EULEX 2010, 6)

The willingness to transfer responsibility and leadership to the Kosovars is purposely different from the intrusive strategy led by the UN administration during the immediate postwar period. However, EULEX's predisposition to promote ownership is belied by the important fact that it entered into force just before the Kosovo Assembly declared the country's independence in February 2008. This implies that EULEX, which operates under UN Resolution 1244, and which does not recognise Kosovo's independence,[7] is enhancing ownership to a population that is not sovereign. But the approach by EULEX does not appear to entail an inherent inconsistency: it understands ownership as if there were no longer a conflictive binary or opposition between international supervision and local leadership. That is, ownership has turned into a process that removes any tension between international supervision (potentially neo-colonialist) and local sovereignty (potentially problematic). Within this framing, in which full sovereignty is a priori eclipsed as an immediate possibility, ever more genuine local ownership can indeed become the means of a cooperative process of peacebuilding that has an unclear end.[8] Although the dilemma of transferring ownership may be 'solved', the discourse of promoting ownership seems to constrain the political agency of the Kosovars who, to paraphrase Schmidt, acknowledge and fulfil their lack of autonomy.

At least in the case of Kosovo, the process of granting ownership to some degree and discarding self-determination and full self-government from the equation is problematic because this process goes against the preferences of the immense majority of the Kosovars. The cause of self-determination has been a priority for the Kosovars at least since the summer of 1990, when the majority in the Assembly voted to declare Kosovo a republic within the Yugoslav Federation (IICK 2000, 43–44). It is therefore very likely that – particularly since the possibility of self-government is left out of EULEX's schema – international policy-makers are doing little to resolve the concerns of the majority of Kosovars. The efforts to respect and support the preferences and priorities of the local population, which are explicit in contemporary policy texts, remain vacuous if these do not include or respond to their principal plea.[9] To be clear, the conclusion drawn here is not that Kosovo (and other post-conflict societies) ought to be independent or freed from international interference. What I seek to understand, however, is the logic of a strategy that promotes ownership and seeks to offer deep respect for local sensitivities, but still places firm restrictions regarding self-government. It is important to interrogate this particular conceptualisation of ownership because, at least in the cases of Bosnia and Kosovo, its logic seems to go against one of the central items on the citizens' agenda.

Rethinking ownership at the cost of equality

The critics of liberal peacebuilding highlight two main problems when concerned with the question of how ownership is operationalised and when explaining the unsatisfactory outcomes of peacebuilding missions.[10] First, these authors point out that recent policy concerns about local ownership represent only a rhetorical shift that is not realised in practice, where international and national agents still maintain asymmetrical power relations. For Mac Ginty and Richmond (2013, 775), for example local ownership – like partnership or participation – are merely 'buzz phrases' used by practitioners to gain local legitimacy and support.[11]

Second, critical scholars are wary of how ownership is being promoted. They suggest that international administrators that seek to transfer authority to the local population rely on a narrow and 'self-referential vision of civil society' – working, for example with liberal NGOs – and thus underestimate the plurality of views and possibilities that can be found in the everyday life of conflict-affected zones (Belloni 2001, 175–178). A direct consequence is that war-prone entrepreneurs, nationalist groups or other local spoilers, which do not represent the majority of the population, have co-opted ownership and dominated postwar political transitions. Donais argues that, besides capacity building, work should be done to promote 'capacity disabling' of some groups or some practices. This means that there ought to be 'efforts to disable, marginalize, or co-opt those

domestic political power structures that stand in the way of the effective establishment of new institutions' (Donais 2009, 16). For the critics, liberal peacebuilding operations should pursue a deeper engagement with diverse civil society
groups in order to develop a bottom-up version of peace and thereby overturn the
risk that unrepresentative groups pose in terms of co-opting the conflict resolution process (Orjuela 2003; Pouligny 2005).

Against the two flaws identified earlier, critical frameworks seek to reno-
vate the actual promotion of local ownership. The way forward depends on the
involvement of a great variety of actors, with specific attention to be paid to the
powerless, in a truly inclusive peace endeavour. Richmond writes:

> Reform[ing] the liberal peace model . . . requires an engagement with not
> just the currently fashionable and controversial issues of local ownership or
> local participation, but the far deeper 'local-local' (i.e. what lies beneath
> the veneer of internationally sponsored local actors and NGOs constitut-
> ing a 'civil' as opposed to 'uncivil' society), which allows for genuine self-
> government, self-determination, democracy and human rights.
>
> (Richmond, 2011, 10)

While Richmond states that the aim of 'a post-liberal peace' is to allow for
'genuine self-government', this is not automatically conceived. Granting self-
government depends on the possibility of engaging with the 'local-local'.[12] This
deeper level is 'hermeneutic, diverse, fluid, transnational and transversal' and
cannot be represented, analysed or governed from an external perspective. Based
on this assumption, peacebuilding requires a plural, flexible and open understanding of difference, which does not essentialise or reduce difference to existing
(Western-informed) forms of representation (see also Mac Ginty and Richmond
2013, 764).

This emancipatory form of peacebuilding – post-liberal or 'hybrid peace' –
is committed to transferring responsibilities to 'the local', beyond 'ethnocentric
ways of knowing culture', as Brigg (2010, 336–341) puts it. As a critical reap-
praisal of liberal peace, proposals for hybrid peace demand the need to foster a
context-sensitive peacebuilding process, which prevents this process from being
either controlled by domineering policy advisors or co-opted by unrepresentative local leaders. Hybridity in this context is seen as a framework that corrects
international peace practitioners and nationalist entrepreneurs, who both tend
to conceptualise identity as static, homogenous and essentialist, and thus undermine multiple forms of being and doing (Mac Ginty 2010, 397). There is confidence that a reflexive and agonistic conversation between multiple actors opens
up new possibilities for cultivating a peace project that embraces difference and
enables the local-local (Donais 2009, 19; Richmond 2012, 125).

These critical perspectives are thus very similar to contemporary policy
approaches of peacebuilding, which have already sought to abandon the top-
down and intrusive projects of the late 1990s in order to facilitate and enhance a
real process of ownership that is inclusive of diverse views. To be sure, although

proposals for hybrid peace promise an even greater appreciation of the dynamics and resources of everyday life and a more sensitive engagement with the local (or the local-local), the process of transferring local ownership has not been translated into local self-government either.

Critical perspectives, in wanting to respect and negotiate with the local-local of postwar societies, eschew or belittle the autonomous demands openly voiced by different local actors. The willingness to build peace *beyond* current forms of political representation and identification gives little meaning to the *present* struggles faced by these societies. For example, Richmond (2011, 130) argues that the promise of a post-liberal peace goes 'beyond mere rationalism and sovereignty', beyond 'state institutions' or 'territorial' constraints in order to aspire to true 'democracy and self-determination'. But this promise is of little value for the people in post-conflict societies who want sovereignty, territory and state institutions (e.g. Bosnia and Kosovo). Wishing to build peace beyond 'established constellations of identity and difference', as William Connolly (1995, 192) would say, these frameworks disregard the preferences and political positions that make sense for the local population.

My suspicion is therefore that, according to contemporary policy frameworks and their academic critics, the Other is not taken as the sovereign *equal*, but as the *different*, whose peace ought to be approached through a careful conversational and reflexive process of cooperation among multiple actors. In conclusion, the cost of a discursive shift, which has sought to move away from universal approaches (considered intrusive and disrespectful of diversity) and towards emphasising difference, may be summed up as the difficulty of considering post-conflict populations as equals. Based on the assumption that these people are momentarily 'inferior',[13] incapable of being autonomous, the approaches analysed here (international peacebuilders from the beginning of the first decade of the twenty-first century until the present and authors critical of the liberal peace) have promoted ownership while adjourning self-government.

Conclusion

This chapter has explored the apparent paradox in contemporary democratisation and post-conflict settings of a growing commitment to promote local ownership and the reluctance to grant self-government to war-affected populations. I have argued that far from being understood as a strategy containing a paradox, the concept of local ownership is increasingly seen as a learning relationship or a process of reflexive cooperation between international and national actors that is able to resolve a fundamental dilemma affecting governance missions: either having overly invasive international actors or devolving power to unrepresentative or potentially violent local agents. Liberal peacebuilding frameworks introduced ownership at the end of the 1990s, both as a mechanism for bettering the results of previous missions and as a politically correct concept to improve the practices and relations between interveners and those intervened upon. However, the notion of ownership appeared at a time in which there was great scepticism towards democratic processes and thus it had to be postponed until certain social and political conditions were met.

In the last few years, local ownership has become the means of a process in which the outcome is constantly adjourned. The role of peacebuilders has become secondary in order to facilitate a cooperative process of peace. However, even if ownership has become a sine qua non principle for any peacebuilding process, this has not been translated into de facto self-determination or self-government. In this sense, the promotion of ownership has undermined the moral and political autonomy of postwar societies. At the very least, processes of local ownership are in constant tension with the pleas and interests of the (majority of the) people.

Hybrid peace frameworks seek to rectify international domineering attitudes without transferring ownership to unrepresentative local agents, predominantly by cultivating a process of agonistic relation between multiple self-reflexive actors. Yet it has been argued that the attempt to transfer ownership to the local-local seems to offer solutions of little value to conflict-affected people. In short, critical frameworks project an inclusive peace process in which statehood, territory or security are no longer relevant and hence are not exclusive of nonmajority groups.[14] Meanwhile, before this promise of peace can be fulfilled, sovereignty, territory and security are the desires of the majority of postwar populations. The question remains whether, within frameworks of peacebuilding that have increasingly sought to embrace difference and promoted a more inclusive local ownership process, the *equality* of postwar societies has been degraded.

Notes

1 I would like to thank Blai Bargués, David Chandler, Tobias Debiel, Frank Gadinger, Aidan Hehir, Volker Heins, Thomas Mills, Elisabet Portavella, Mathieu Rousselin and Jessica Schmidt for comments on previous drafts. The chapter is based on a more comprehensive paper published in the Research Paper Series of the Centre for Global Cooperation Research, Duisburg (Bargués-Pedreny 2015).

2 To clarify, this chapter is not a defence of self-determination. Indeed, it is not even about self-determination as such. It is about how local ownership has been understood in peacebuilding settings so that it means something different than self-determination and self-government. For a defence of the principle of self-determination see, for example, Philpott (1995).

3 Along the lines of the OECD, most of the reports have considered ownership as one of the principles of effective development. The Canada International Development Agency, for example, has written: 'development strategies, if they are to be sustainable, must be developed by recipient countries – their governments and people – and they must reflect their priorities, rather than the priorities of donors' (CIDA 2002, 4).

4 For critiques along these lines, see Chandler (2000, 194); Pupavac (2004, 391–394). Both authors argue that the apparent contradiction between denying self-government and promoting ownership is not a contradiction according to the lens of international policy-makers. This is because there has been a redefinition of the traditional meaning of democracy and citizens' political rights: now these come to be understood as processes that can be enhanced or empowered to meet international standards (Chandler 2000, 162–163; 2010; Pupavac 2004, 393).

5 For example, the *Utstein* group advises that a 'simple commitment to local ownership' without preconditions can be 'fatal to hopes of successful peacebuilding'. Instead,
'there needs to be very careful research about the identity and background of project
partners, and recognition that it will be best to attempt to increase the degree of local
ownership slowly and carefully as experience offers a growing basis of trust. Otherwise, local ownership risks being a code for working with the most powerful and most
opportunistic sectors of society' (Smith 2004, 26–27).

6 See Chesterman's quote earlier. Recently, the OECD (2011, 20) specified that 'statebuilding is primarily a domestic process that involves local actors, which means that
the role of international actors is necessarily limited.'

7 It is important to add here that most scholars emphasise that there are many domestic
and international constraints that make it difficult for EULEX to recognise Kosovo as
an independent state (Greiçevci 2012; Papadimitriou and Petrov 2012; Weller 2008).
However, the point here is to highlight that EULEX intends to promote ownership
without transferring self-government to the Kosovars.

8 See Krogstad (2014) for an interpretation that undoes this binary.

9 For instance, it is unsurprising that citizen satisfaction with the work of EULEX has
been very low (below 30% most of the periods) and with EULEX police even lower,
regardless of ethnicity (IPOL 2012, 15–17).

10 By critics of liberal peace, I refer here to authors who emphasise that practitioners
have ignored or undermined the social and cultural dynamics of postwar societies and
therefore critique the way local ownership is practised (e.g. Brigg 2010; Donais 2009;
Mac Ginty and Richmond 2013; Pouligny 2005; Richmond 2011).

11 Note that international administrators and more policy-oriented academics also share
the belief that ownership has not been translated into practice when they assess some
negative results of earlier international interventions (Chesterman 2007, 17; Nathan
2007, 1; Reich 2006, 14–15).

12 Mac Ginty and Richmond (2013, 774–775) define it as 'the local that cannot be
described as subscribing to liberal and neoliberal rationalities'.

13 See Friedman for a critique of the hierarchical assumptions underpinning hybrid
approaches (2002).

14 See, for instance, Richmond's promise of peace: 'A deterritorialised, non-sovereign
polity would be the outcome of incorporating the everyday as a key priority of peacebuilding in desecuritised form, maximising critical agency rather than the national
interest of the state or interests of donors' (2011, 138–139).

References

Bargués-Pedreny, P. (2015). *Conceptualising Local Ownership as "Reflexive Cooperation":
The Deferral of Self-government to Protect "Unequal" Humans?* Global Cooperation
Research Papers 11. Duisburg: Käte Hamburger Kolleg/Centre for Global Cooperation
Research. doi:10.14282/2198-0411-GCRP-11

Belloni, R. (2001). Civil society and peacebuilding in Bosnia and Herzegovina, *Journal of
Peace Research*, 38(2), 163–180.

Brigg, M. (2010). Culture: Challenges and possibilities. In O. P. Richmond (Ed.), *Palgrave
Advances in Peacebuilding: Critical Developments and Approaches*. Palgrave Macmillan, London, 329–346.

Carothers, T. (2002). The end of the transition paradigm. *Journal of Democracy*, 13(1), 5–21.

Chandler, D. (2000). *Bosnia: Faking Democracy after Dayton*. Pluto Press, London.

Chesterman, S. (2002). *Tiptoeing through Afghanistan: The Future of UN State-Building*.
International Peace Academy, New York.

Chesterman, S. (2007). Ownership in theory and in practice: Transfer of authority in UN statebuilding operations. *Journal of Intervention and Statebuilding*, 1(1), 3–26.

CIDA (Canadian International Development Agency) (2002). *Canada Making a Difference in the World: A Policy Statement on Strengthening Aid Effectiveness*. Canadian International Development Agency, Quebec.

Connolly, W. E. (1995). *The Ethos of Pluralization*. University of Minnesota Press, Minneapolis.

Donais, T. (2009). Empowerment or imposition? Dilemmas of local ownership in post-conflict peacebuilding processes. *Peace & Change*, 34(1), 3–26.

EULEX (European Union Rule of Law Mission in Kosovo). (2009). *The EULEX Programme Report*, Programme Office. (http://www.eulex-kosovo.eu/docs/Accountability/EULEX-PROGRAMME-REPORT-July-2009-new.pdf) Accessed: 21 September 2014.

EULEX (European Union Rule of Law Mission in Kosovo). (2010). *The EULEX Programme Report*, Programme Office. (http://www.eulex-kosovo.eu/docs/tracking/EULEX%20Pro gramme%20Report%202010%20.pdf) Accessed: 15 September 2014.

Friedman, J. (2002). From roots to routes: Tropes for trippers. *Anthropological Theory*, 2(1), 21–36.

Ganson, B., and Wennmann, A. (2012). *Operationalising conflict prevention as strong resilient systems: Approaches, evidence, action points*, Geneva Peacebuilding Platform, Paper No. 3. (http://www.gpplatform.ch/sites/default/files/PP%2003%20-%20Operationalising %20Conflict%20Prevention%20as%20Strong%20Resilient%20Systems%20-%20January%202012_0.pdf) Accessed: 21 September 2014.

Greiçevci, L. (2012). EU actorness in international affairs: The case of EULEX mission in Kosovo. *Perspectives on European Politics and Society*, 12(3), 283–303.

Hughes, C., and Pupavac, V. (2005). Framing post-conflict societies: International pathologisation of Cambodia and the post-Yugoslav states. *Third World Quarterly*, 26(6), 873–889.

IICK (The Independent International Commission on Kosovo). (2000). *The Kosovo Report: Conflict, International Response, Lessons Learned*. Oxford University Press, Oxford.

IPOL (Balkan Policy Institute). (2012). *EULEX and the Rule of Law*. (http://policyinsti tute.eu/images/uploads/EULEX_and_Rule_of_law_May_2011_English.pdf) Accessed: 15 September 2014.

Krogstad, E. G. (2014). Local ownership as dependence management: Inviting the coloniser back. *Journal of Intervention and Statebuilding*, 8, 1–21. (http://dx.doi.org/10.1080/1 7502977.2014.901030) Accessed: 10 September 2014.

Mac Ginty, R. (2010). Hybrid peace: The interaction between top-down and bottom-up peace. *Security Dialogue*, 41(4), 391–412.

Mac Ginty, R., and Richmond, O. P. (2013). The local turn in peace building: A critical agenda for peace. *Third World Quarterly*, 34(5), 763–783.

Mansfield, E. D., and Snyder, J. (1995). Democratization and the danger of war. *International Security*, 20(1), 5–38.

Martin, M., and Moser, S. (Eds.). (2012). *Exiting Conflict, Owning the Peace: Local Ownership and Peacebuilding Relationships in the Cases of Bosnia and Kosovo*. Friedrich-Ebert-Stiftung. (http://library.fes.de/pdf-files/id-moe/09181.pdf) Accessed: 22 September 2014.

Narten, J. (2009). Dilemmas of promoting "local ownership": The case of postwar Kosovo. In R. Paris and T. D. Sisk (Eds.), *The Dilemmas of Statebuilding: Confronting the Contradictions of Postwar Peace Operations*. Routledge, London, 252–284.

Nathan, L. (2007). *No Ownership No Commitment: A Guide to Local Ownership of Security Sector Reform*. Technical Report, University of Birmingham. (http://epapers.bham. ac.uk/1530/1/Nathan_-2007-_No_Ownership.pdf) Accessed: 12 September 2014.

OECD (Organisation for Economic Co-operation and Development). (1996). *Shaping the 21st Century: The Contribution of Development Co-operation*. OECD Paris. (http://www. oecd.org/dac/2508761.pdf) Accessed: 11 August 2014.

OECD (Organisation for Economic Co-operation and Development). (2005). *Preventing Conflict and Building Peace: A Manual of Issues and Entry Points*. Development Assistance Committee, DAC Network on Conflict, Peace and Development Co-operation. (http://www.oecd.org/development/incaf/35785584.pdf) Accessed: 5 September 2014.

OECD (Organisation for Economic Co-operation and Development). (2008). Concepts and dilemmas of state building in fragile situations: From fragility to resilience. *Journal on Development*, 9(3), 1–79.

OECD (Organisation for Economic Co-operation and Development). (2011). *International Engagement in Fragile States: Can't We Do Better?* OECD, Paris. (http://www.oecd. org/development/incaf/48697077.pdf) Accessed: 14 September 2014.

Orjuela, C. (2003). Building peace in Sri Lanka: A role for civil society? *Journal of Peace Research*, 40(2), 195–212.

Papadimitriou, D., and Petrov, P. (2012). Whose rule, whose law? Contested statehood, external leverage and the European Union's rule of law mission in Kosovo. *Journal of Common Market Studies*, 50(5), 746–763.

Paris, R. (2004). *At War's End: Building Peace after Civil Conflict*. Cambridge University Press, Cambridge.

Petritsch, W. (1999, 17 September). The future of Bosnia lies with its people. *Wall Street Journal*. (http://www.ohr.int/ohr-dept/presso/pressa/default.asp?content_id=3188) Accessed: 15 September 2014.

Philpott, D. (1995). In defense of self-determination. *Ethics*, 105(2), 352–385.

Pouligny, B. (2005). Civil society and post-conflict peacebuilding: Ambiguities of international programmes aimed at building "new" societies. *Security Dialogue*, 36(4), 495–510.

Pouligny, B. (2009). *Supporting local ownership in humanitarian action*. Policy Paper No. 4. Global Public Policy Institute, Berlin. (http://www.gppi.net/fileadmin/user_upload/ media/pub/2009/Pouligny_2009_Supporting_Local.pdf) Accessed: 15 June 2014.

Pupavac, V. (2004). International therapeutic peace and justice in Bosnia. *Social & Legal Studies*, 13(3), 377–401.

Reich, H. (2006). "Local ownership" in conflict transformation projects: Partnership, participation or patronage? Berghof Occasional Paper No. 27. Berghof Research Center for Constructive Conflict Management, Berlin. (http://www.berghof-conflictresearch.org/ documents/publications/boc27e.pdf) Accessed: 22 September 2014.

Richmond, O. P. (2011). *A Post-liberal Peace*. Routledge, London.

Richmond, O. P. (2012). A pedagogy of peacebuilding: Infrapolitics, resistance, and liberation. *International Political Sociology*, 6(2), 115–131.

Scheye, E., and Peake, G. (2005). Unknotting local ownership. In A. H. Ebnöther and P. H. Fluri (Eds.), *After Intervention: Public Security Management in Post-conflict Societies. From Intervention to Sustainable Local Ownership*. Bureau for Security Policy at the Austrian Ministry of Defence and National Defence Academy, Vienna and Geneva; Geneva Centre for Democratic Control of Armed Forces, 235–260.

Schmidt, J. (2016). *Rethinking Democracy Promotion in International Relations: The Rise of the Social*. Routledge, London.

Smith, D. (2004). *Towards a Strategic Framework for Peacebuilding: Getting Their Act Together*. Overview report of the joint Utstein study of peace-building, International Peace Research Institute. Royal Norwegian Ministry of Foreign Affairs, Oslo.

Snyder, J. (2000). *From Voting to Violence: Democratization and Nationalist Conflict*. W. W. Norton, New York.

Stiglitz, J. (1998a, 7 January). *More Instruments and Broader Goals: Moving toward the Post-Washington Consensus*. The World Bank Group, Speech presented at Helsinki. (http://web.worldbank.org/WBSITE/EXTERNAL/NEWS/0,,contentMDK:20025088~menuPK:34474~pagePK:34370~piPK:34424~theSitePK:4607,00.html) Accessed: 6 June 2014.

Stiglitz, J. (1998b, 19 October). *Towards a New Paradigm for Development: Strategies, Policies and Processes*. The 1998 Prebisch Lecture presented at Geneva. (http://web.worldbank.org/WBSITE/EXTERNAL/TOPICS/TRADE/0,,contentMDK:20025537~menuPK:167371~pagePK:64020865~piPK:149114~theSitePK:239071,00.html) Accessed: 24 April 2014.

UN (United Nations). (2010). *UN Peacebuilding: An Orientation*. United Nations Peacebuilding Support Office. (http://www.un.org/en/peacebuilding/pbso/pdf/peacebuilding_orientation.pdf) Accessed: 15 September 2014.

UNDP (United Nations Development Programme). (2001). *Development Effectiveness: Review of Evaluative Evidence*. Evaluation Office, New York.

UNDP (United Nations Development Programme). (2010). *Beyond the Midpoint: Achieving the Millennium Development Goals*. (http://uncdf.org/gfld/docs/midpoint-mdg.pdf) Accessed: 19 September 2014.

UNDP (United Nations Development Programme). (2012). *Governance for Peace: Securing the Social Contract*. (http://www.undp.org/content/undp/en/home/librarypage/crisis-prevention-and-recovery/governance_for_peacesecuringthesocialcontract/) Accessed: 21 September 2014.

Weller, M. (2008). *Negotiating the Final Status of Kosovo*. Chaillot Paper No. 114. Institute for Security Studies, Paris. (http://www.iss.europa.eu/publications/detail/article/negotiating-the-final-status-of-kosovo/) Accessed: 7 May 2014.

World Bank. (2000). *Comprehensive Development Framework Country Experience: March 1999–July 2000*. Report on Country Experience. (http://web.worldbank.org/archive/website01013/WEB/IMAGES/CEXP_WEB.PDF) Accessed: 8 June 2014.

World Bank. (2001). *World Development Report 2000/2001: Attacking Poverty*. Oxford University Press, New York. (http://www.ssc.wisc.edu/~walker/wp/wp-content/uploads/2012/10/wdr2001.pdf) Accessed: 8 June 2014.

14 Rethinking the local in peacebuilding

Moving away from the liberal/ post-liberal divide

Tobias Debiel and Patricia Rinck

Introduction[1]

After the end of the Cold War, peacebuilding became a 'blooming business', frequently accompanied by large-scale intervention from outside. The UN expanded its traditional peacemaking and peacekeeping activities and created a multidimensional, second-generation approach in order to cope with the many civil wars of the post–Cold War era. Peacebuilding, in this context, can be defined as a deliberate strategy of external and/or domestic actors, aimed at moving a country away from the mere absence of armed conflict and towards preventing the outbreak of renewed collective violence. Peacebuilding includes ideational and value-oriented shifts, socioeconomic policies, governance-related reforms and new arrangements for the distribution and control of power.

The number and size of new operations since the 1990s has been breathtaking – in particular, when compared to the past decades. Over the last five years, personnel contributions to UN peace operations alone ranged between 90,000 and 100,000 (Debiel and Rinck 2015). Peacebuilding became a "collective commitment" (Tschirgi 2004, i) by the UN and other international actors, who had – against the background of the changed global security situation – developed a clear normative understanding of how these countries could be helped. The academic debate about peacebuilding has over the last 15 years focused on what has been called 'liberal peace' and its critiques (Newman et al. 2009; Paris and Sisk 2009; Paris 2010; Campbell et al. 2011; Richmond 2011a; Tadjbakhsh 2011; Mac Ginty 2013). After the end of the Cold War, liberal approaches remained rather unchallenged and provided a seemingly sound and rather elaborated theoretical and conceptual basis for international engagement in war-torn societies, as these put forward an explicit normative and conceptual framework as well as detailed policy-oriented prescriptions.

Liberal blueprints promised to provide institutional stability, welfare, democracy and peace – though possible trade-offs featured prominently from early on. Large-scale peace operations based on these assumptions and recipes, however, were not able to fulfil these promises. In some cases, at least short-term stability could be provided, such as in Cambodia, Namibia, Mozambique or Central America. In other cases, more or less obvious failure had to be acknowledged.

The mission in the Democratic Republic of the Congo (DRC) is one outstanding example in the UN context. It is controversial whether the US-led military interventions in Iraq and Afghanistan can be properly subsumed under the liberal peacebuilding framework or whether these were mainly shaped by other motivational factors and ingredients. However, most proponents of liberal peacebuilding would concede today that the original top-down approaches were problematic and included a rather superficial understanding of local realities.

This crisis of liberal peacebuilding has brought critical approaches in the ascendant. They are rooted in post-colonial thinking and Critical Security Studies and conceptualise peacebuilding not as a technocratic exercise in social engineering that can be planned and administered by all-powerful (and benign) dominant external actors, but rather as an interface, as relational and interactive – hence as a field of contestation and politics. Linear models of transforming states and societies are replaced by a new ontological understanding of nonlinearity and complexity. The preoccupation with external strategies is countered by the discovery of the 'local', its interaction with the 'external liberal' and its ability to build resilient structures. Still, the local remains a rather vague, underconceptualised phenomenon therein and is mainly framed as representing the 'other side' of the liberal international.

The chapter starts off with a brief reflection on different conceptualisations of the term local as used in the social sciences over the past 25 years and highlights that definitions of the local as marked-off systems with clearly defined actors have become highly problematic. It continues with a critical review of liberal approaches, their standard, frequently sequenced models of peacebuilding (Doyle and Sambanis 2000, 2006; Collier et al. 2003; Paris 2004, 2010) as well as post-liberal approaches in the context of Critical Security Studies (Richmond 2009, 2010, 2011a; Mac Ginty 2010, 2011; in a different way: Chandler 2012, 2013). We argue that the liberal template of the Weberian state has contributed towards understanding the local in war-torn societies as a misfit and, in turn, restrained perspectives of the local that go beyond formal institutions and their challengers. Post-liberal approaches have rightly pinpointed these deficiencies but tend to romanticise or culturalise the local as the 'locus' of resilience or even resistance and overemphasise its potential for emancipatory peace.

While liberal approaches are entrapped by 'methodological nationalism' (Wimmer and Glick Schiller 2002), the post-liberal 'local turn' risks falling into the trap of another variant of 'methodological reductionism', namely one which neglects power structures and domestic politics, upholding the dualism between the naturalised liberal international and the local-local and failing to overcome existing blind spots regarding the role of formal institutions and the state. Although we appreciate the validity of the post-liberal critique and its potential to explore ground, we advocate that future peacebuilding research should move beyond the liberal/post-liberal divide. The contest of the two competing paradigms has sidelined crucial issues in peacebuilding such as the distribution of authority and power that is negotiated in the context of political orders and which transcends the reach of the 'formal state'. Without integrating such structural analysis in peacebuilding research, the turn to the local runs the risk of collecting anecdotal evidence for everyday peace instead of identifying its underlying causes.

What and who is 'the local'?

Before we turn to the role of the local in liberal and post-liberal thinking, we want to provide a brief conceptual overview which shows that the local and locality have been contested concepts in social sciences, anthropology and geography (and here in urban studies in particular) for quite some time. The current turn to the local in peacebuilding has partly acknowledged this debate, but still fails to take account of the quite elaborate debates that have been carried forth in other fields. For the purpose of this chapter, we would like to highlight five notions that the term local can relate to: (1) territorial space in which specific social practices emerge; (2) politically or administratively bounded territories; (3) spatial patterns or arenas; (4) actors and their origins and/or senses of belonging; and (5) social or political representations as present in everyday practices or as constructed in discourses. These manifold meanings imply different ontologies and have profound consequences for how we can conceptually grasp empirical realities and engage in specific practices.

Originally, the term local was taken to refer to a *space or sphere* of manageable size, in which the world can be directly experienced in its material as well as its symbolic forms. In this space, social practices emerge which follow specific and often implicit logics and stocks of knowledge, have a material dimension and become well established without being completely predictable (Reckwitz 2003). Owing to globalisation and transnationalisation studies, however, an understanding of the local as a marked-off system has been drawn into question. Instead, in times of the transnational flux and migration of ideas, values, people and objects, attention is increasingly directed towards how the local develops in relation to other locations as well as their mutual interactions.

A second understanding of the local (or here: locality) refers to "*bounded territories*, such as local authority areas, which are recognized politically and administratively for the discharge and conduct of public services" (Jones and Woods 2013, 33, emphasis added). This conceptualisation defines local politics as primarily embedded in formally institutionalised arrangements. With regard to vertical power-sharing and governance reforms, the local herein can also become a policy field, for example, in the context of decentralisation measures (Hartmann and Crawford 2008; Leonardsson and Rudd 2015).

Third, the local can be regarded as a *spatial arena* in which a variety of agents and institutions interact and produce social meaning (Duncan and Savage 1989, 181). Such arenas can be regarded as analytical constructs that help to understand, among others, how norms, rights, institutions or access to resources are being negotiated in particular spheres. This understanding of the local is particularly well suited for analysing patterns of cooperation, conflict, adaptation and resistance in circumstances where multiple actors interact in a specific setting.

Fourth, the local can be understood as an *actor-related term*. The recent debate on local ownership in development cooperation and peacebuilding very much relies on such actor-related understandings and has addressed the difficulties of identifying the actors who represent the local (von Billerbeck 2015, 312). Coming from ethnology, the local was conventionally defined with reference to a specific territorial origin. This rather primordial definition now gives way to more differentiated understandings of local actors, which, among others, stress their sense of belonging. This sense relates, according to Yuval-Davis (2011, 5), to social locations as well as to emotional ties and value systems. Thus, it overcomes the idea that actors can be 'naturally' identified as being linked to a certain territory.

Finally, the local can be conceptualised within the theoretical framework of social representations. The latter means "organizational mental constructs which guide us towards what is 'visible' and must be responded to, relate appearance and reality, and even define reality itself" (Halfacree 1993, 29). Such an understanding departs from an emphasis on the materiality of space as well as from the idea that the local or localities have to be shaped by a dense network of structures or causal interrelations. Instead, this approach focuses on how a specific term is used in everyday talk or is reflected in specific social practices. Referring to K. H. Halfacree, who relied on theories of social representations in order to make sense of 'the rural', one could argue that this fifth approach conceptualises the local "in terms of the disembodied cognitive structures which we use as rules and resources in order to make sense of our everyday world, through both discursive and non-discursive actions" (Halfacree 1993, 23).

Liberal peacebuilding: the local as misfit

Liberal peacebuilding is oriented towards the core concepts of liberal thinking – such as the right to property, liberty and individual freedoms (in particular: freedom of opinion), rule of law and balance of power (Paris 2004). It understands the local in the sense of politically and/or administratively bounded territories and focuses on their institutionalised representations (formal authorities etc.) and the respective designs for exercising, restricting and controlling power. The approach puts national institutions at the forefront, but also includes measures for the devolution of power to the subnational level. It also draws on actor-related notions of the local, determined by formal legitimation and official mandates. Still, it sees the local as an object of external intervention rather than as a subject in peacebuilding.[2]

With the end of the Cold War, this form of liberal thinking was reflected and conceptualised in key concepts such as the UN *Agenda for Peace* (1992) and the *Agenda for Democratization* (1996). At its core are, as Jan Selby puts it,

> liberal democratic political structures and processes (multi-party elections, good governance, human rights provisions, the development of a limited but functional state and the empowerment of civil society) and liberal or

neo-liberal economic practices (the privatisation of public enterprises, reduced state subsidies, the deregulation of capital markets and the lowering of barriers to international trade).

(Selby 2013, 61)

The rather naïve design, following a top-down rationale of social engineering, clashed with empirical realities. Though fully fledged, market-based democracies offer the best insurance for preventing collective violence at the domestic level, processes of transformation are risky, in particular in fragile states and war-torn societies. As empirical research has shown, democratisation in these contexts contributes to polarisation, destabilisation and often even the (re)emergence of collective violence (Collier et al. 2003; Mansfield and Snyder 1995a, 1995b; State Failure Task Force 2003). Transition periods are not seldom shaped in a vacuum in which the old rules of the game have eroded, while new rules have not yet been institutionalised. This offers excellent opportunities for political entrepreneurs who can capitalise on ethnic, religious or regional cleavages and use the emerging 'liberal space' in politics to pursue rather sectarian or authoritarian agendas. Economic liberalisation, on the other hand, contributes to social tensions and leads to an increased vulnerability of poor strata of society. In many cases, it thus turned out that the local has reacted to the liberal peacebuilding package in rather unforeseen and unexpected ways (Debiel and Lambach 2009).

Proponents of the liberal peacebuilding discourse, such as Roland Paris, were among the first to acknowledge and criticise the shortcomings of dominant peacebuilding strategies. Interestingly enough, though, they abstained from an in-depth analysis of local structures, readily attributing the 'pathologies' of liberal peacebuilding (proneness to violence, social fragmentation etc.) to the 'deficiencies' of the local as measured against the liberal model – in particular the lack of a functioning state (Paris 2004, 46, 159–168). In this reading, the establishment of formal institutions is the prerequisite for successful liberalisation. From an ideational perspective, one could argue that this is in the tradition of John Locke or Adam Smith, whose writings cannot be properly understood without Hobbes's thinking and his construct of the Leviathan, which was not to be abolished but to be relied upon and tamed by liberal strategies.

A more elaborated version of liberal peacebuilding thus replaced the *Liberalisation First* approach through a strategy of "Institutionalisation Before Liberalisation" (IBL). According to this strategy, elections should be delayed until moderate forces have had a chance to establish themselves, and electoral designs should make sure that politicians have to seek support beyond ethno-regional cleavages. Assistance for civil society groups should be rather selective at this stage and directed towards those associations that bridge societal divides. In some countries, international actors in the first phases strongly focused on the reform and strengthening of the security sector without pursuing a broader institutional perspective – a strategy thus labelled *Security First*. More bottom-up oriented versions of liberal peacebuilding advocated a kind of *Civil Society First* approach (Schneckener 2011).

Within IBL, as well as the *Security First* approach, the local level comes into the picture merely if the attempted transfer of institutions goes wrong, which is then attributed to the incapability of elites or to the resistance of illegitimate elites trying to maintain their control of power, patronage and resources. *Civil Society First* approaches, on the other hand, put forward a different narrative of liberal thinking and stress that institutional reform has to be embedded in societal transformation. At the same time, this narrative tends to project the achievements and strategies of social movements and civil society in liberal democracies (in particular in the 1970s and 1980s) onto non-Western contexts. This projection of 'sameness' has its pitfalls as it might also reflect some idleness. They often portray particular nonstate actors in an exclusively positive way (Chandler 2013, 17–19) and tend to romanticise them as potential agents of change (Belloni 2012, 34). Though these varieties of liberal peacebuilding differ substantially in their concrete recommendations, they all share a linear understanding of peacebuilding and a particular sense of governmentality according to which the transformation of a war-torn country can be planned and administered (Donais 2009; Jabri 2013; Mac Ginty 2012). As war-torn countries are seen as being unable to help themselves, the responsibility for creating peace is transferred to interveners.

Post-liberal peacebuilding: engaging with the local

In contrast to liberal (and neo-liberal) thought, the peacebuilding discourse has in recent years been strongly influenced by post-liberal approaches. Several core assumptions of liberal thinking have, in turn, been drawn into question – including linearity, the belief in the autonomous individual and the universal applicability of normative concepts. A case for peacebuilding 'post' or beyond the liberal peace is made, which follows notions of nonlinearity, hybridity, the local and the everyday (Boege et al. 2009a, 2009b; Mac Ginty 2011; Richmond 2009, 2010, 2011a, 2011b; Richmond and Mitchell 2011).

Countering linear and reductionist understandings of peacebuilding, the notion of complexity offers a new lens for peacebuilding, postulating that societies and communities that peacebuilders intervene in cannot be understood and manipulated if these are reduced to their individual components. Instead, social actions within and across complex systems have to be analysed in terms of their interconnections (Loode 2011, 70–71). As Cedric de Coning points out,

> complex social systems, like a post-conflict society, develop the ability to organise and maintain themselves not because of a centrally controlled hierarchy, such as a strategic framework or a strategic plan, but as a result of emergence – the ability of non-linear interactions to spontaneously result in self-regulating behaviour through complex feedback systems.
>
> (de Coning 2013, 3–4)

This implies a profound critique of peacebuilding and external interventions in general and requires peacebuilders to fundamentally change their approach.

With the shift from linear to nonlinear understandings, the focus of post-liberal approaches moved from the formal sphere of government and elite processes to the local and societal level. Roger Mac Ginty and Oliver Richmond understand the local as

> a range of locally based agencies present within conflict and post-conflict environments, some of which are aimed at identifying and creating the necessary processes for peace – with or without international help, framed in a way in which legitimacy in local and international terms converges.
>
> (Mac Ginty and Richmond 2013, 769)

They are thus close to an understanding of the local as a spatial arena in which agents produce meaning with regard to how and what kind of peace could be achieved.

A local peace may be influenced by a formal peace accord or national political dynamics, but it is designed locally and may resist national or international trends. Since the political, social and economic factors that influence people's everyday lives are different from place to place, peace cannot be the result of measures taken as part of the international community's peacebuilding template (Belloni 2012, 34). Peace, accordingly, is a complex process and of an "everyday and emancipatory type, in which authority, rights, redistribution and legitimacy are slowly rethought" (Mac Ginty and Richmond 2013, 769, 771).

In post-liberal thinking, the local is a rather broad category, which subsumes actors at the national, regional, city, village and community level without explaining how these levels differ. Post-liberal thinking constructs the local in its interaction with the international. Through various forms of agency – obstruction, resistance, subversion, capture, reappropriation, co-optation, adoption, adaptation, mimicry, redirection etc. – local actors are able to appropriate international agendas and resources for their own purposes. For instance, Richmond associates the local with either a civil society (but not in a Western understanding) or an everyday context (Richmond 2010, 667, 670). A special emphasis is placed on the so-called local-local – a term which, in particular, captures actors who do not fit into the Western liberal format of either state, civil society or business/economy (Richmond 2011a, 133). Instead, it refers to the sphere of local societies and their institutions and actors – such as chiefs, healers, traditional authorities, religious leaders, customary laws, vigilantes, and clan and lineage affiliations.

Answering to charges of romanticising the local, Mac Ginty and Richmond point out that local actors and contexts can be partisan, discriminatory, exclusive and violent, and contain power relations and hierarchies. Furthermore, they admit that the local is often less local than imagined; it can be transnational, transversal and be comprised of a geographically dispersed network (Mac Ginty and Richmond 2013, 770). Still, as Claudia Simons and Franzisca Zanker (2014, 5) observe, "the impression remains that the 'local' in critical peacebuilding is a panacea of legitimacy, and is everything and anything, as long as it fits the image of being in opposition to liberal peacebuilding."

The notion of resilience has become key for post-liberal peacebuilding. The concept has travelled from the field of engineering to medicine, psychology, humanitarian assistance to peacebuilding. It focuses on peoples' and communities' existing capacities and abilities to maintain or build peace rather than the external provision of policies or programmes (Chandler 2012, 217; 2015, 2). A community's resilience depends on its internal social capital, that is "dense patterns of trust networks, hybrid coalitions forged across a wide range of actors, shared narratives, common interests, multiple lines of communication, good leadership, and a commitment by local leaders to take risks for peace" (Menkhaus 2013, 6, 2–3). The resilience approach thus focuses on existing local capacities for conflict transformation as opposed to imported institutions, policies and strategies. Resilience, as conceptualised by post-liberals, differs from related neo-liberal understandings, as it does not primarily focus on the individual, its vulnerability and its market-oriented coping mechanisms, but rather on communities.

'Methodological reductionism': blind spots of the local turn

Liberal approaches mostly ignore the local and, in a rather technocratic enterprise, offer a certain peacebuilding template, with which all-knowing, interest-free and benign international actors can fix local problems – obviously overestimating their own capacities, and without really engaging with the local or even analysing the contexts in which they intervene. By advocating state- and institution-building, this school of thought has remained entrapped in methodological nationalism that can be defined as "an ideological orientation that approaches the study of social and historical processes as if they were contained within the borders of individual nation-states" (Glick Schiller 2009, 4). This "coherent epistemic structure" (Wimmer and Glick Schiller 2002, 308) conceptualises modernity only in national frameworks. It takes shared norms, values and institutions for granted and ignores how the 'project of modernity' is prone to undermine alternative frameworks that exist beyond, or cut across, the nation state. Furthermore, methodological nationalism 'naturalises' empirical realities by reifying the nation state and its characteristics, in turn, limiting the scope of analysis to the territorial boundaries of the nation state (Wimmer and Glick Schiller 2002).

Through the local turn, research on peacebuilding has in recent years been marked by a newfound theoretical emphasis on realities on the ground and has also become more empirical in nature (Mac Ginty 2015). It can thus be seen to reopen a debate on social justice and emancipation and on the relation between interveners and those intervened upon (Mac Ginty and Richmond 2013, 780). Indeed, the discourse on the international and the local shows a "new level of self-reflexivity on the part of the interveners, an attempt to reconfigure power relationships with the 'local' and a questioning of previous assumptions about the ability to achieve predetermined outcomes" (Chadwick et al. 2013, 9).

The post-liberal turn to the local can be interpreted as a counter-movement to the implicit methodological nationalism of liberal thought. Still, it risks replacing one variant of methodological reductionism with another. In particular, the epistemic structure of 'localism' tends to conceptualise peace mainly in the framework of the everyday at the local level and neglects how it is embedded in wider power structures and domestic politics. Second, it naturalises the international as being almost inevitably 'liberal' and tends to assume that the local – and in particular the local-local – is somehow imbued with authority or legitimacy defined by local norms and practices rather than by liberal values. Not least by primarily studying the local and its interactions with the international, it reveals epistemic boundaries regarding the role of formal institutions and the state.

Neglecting power and domestic politics

Post-liberal approaches take everyday peace at the local level as a starting point for exploring alternatives to liberal peace. Accordingly, there is an implicit assumption that *local peace* is primarily based on actors and institutions that derive their authority and legitimacy from the local level. As empirical research shows, however, local problems do not necessarily warrant strictly local solutions. In a study on the DRC and Burundi, for example, Simons and Zanker found out in focus group discussions that those actors considered most important for peace-building were those who are influential at the national level – because these had, according to their findings, much more power to influence the local situation (Simons and Zanker 2014, 10–11).

Post-liberal perspectives are at odds with findings that stress the relevance of the national level as the local is herein primarily conceptualised in relation to international and not domestic politics. Thus, they potentially mask political, economic and military power relations at the local level, and also tend to romanticise trust in local self-regulating forces. Richmond touches on this topic, acknowledging that the everyday is a "terrain of conflicts over needs, rights, custom, culture, identity, citizens and imported state frameworks" (2009, 335), and suggests that local actors can have a positive or negative impact on peace (2012, 120). Mac Ginty analyses where the power (moral, cultural, material etc.) lies in different hybridised versions of peace (2010, 408). These answers to the respective critiques however remain rather abstract and do not give any analytical grip on the exact nature of power and conflict. An alternative perspective would assume that agency is not primarily constructed in the context of local–international interactions, but rather determined by conflicts of interest and identity that, in turn, result in competing claims for authority and control at the local/national interface (Debiel et al. 2009).

Naturalising the liberal international and the autochthonous local-local

As methodological nationalism naturalises the modern state, methodological localism tends to naturalise crucial concepts such as the liberal international versus the not-so-liberal local or even the rather autochthonous local-local. Within this framework, the international is indispensably conflated with liberal, top-down approaches and a lack of knowledge, while local authorities stand for embedded legitimacy and appropriate understandings. This makes it difficult to take situations into account in which the international actually neglects liberal standards or in which local resistance is motivated by liberal ideas. The juxtaposition reminds us of critiques of locality research, which had already by the end of the 1980s problematised inherent dualisms

> that relate the necessary and the contingent, the social and the spatial, and the global and the local. Thus the abstract, the necessary, the social and the global melt into one another; likewise the concrete, the contingent, the spatial and the local.
>
> (Cox and Mair 1989, 121–122)

Post-liberal dualisms tend to subsume any kind of international engagement under the rubric of liberal peace and regularly turn a blind eye to the heterogeneity of actors and missions. This leads to strange generalisations. For example, the failure of military interventions and stabilisation missions in Iraq or Afghanistan are taken as evidence for the inadequacy of liberal peace without considering how much these interventions differ from UN-led multidimensional peace operations as they were implemented, for example, in Namibia, Mozambique or Central America in the 1990s. While the international is always liberal and entrapped in its 'blueprints', the local is conceived "as actually or potentially politically progressive" (Hughes et al. 2015, 820–821).

As Simons and Zanker rightly noted, the legitimacy of local authorities is often hastily taken for granted. For instance, traditional authorities and institutions are often automatically assumed to be the authentic representatives of local people – although they may in fact be highly contested, depending on the historical context, their entanglement with political and military power and their role during the civil war. Even if a traditional institution itself still carries legitimacy, this does obviously not mean that the person holding the position is also legitimate in the eyes of the population. Furthermore, as in any other society, perceptions on this issue vary, and generational differences play a role. Therefore, the most visible local actor – which may well be a traditional authority – is not necessarily the most legitimate one (Simons and Zanker 2014, 9–14).

Post-liberal notions of the local-local, in particular, tend to repeat mistakes of former locality research by conceptualising marked-off systems and neglecting the relationality of such categories. Indeed, nothing and nobody can be regarded as purely local. Local actors are connected to actors at the national and international level, are influenced by them and try to influence them in turn: As Simons and Zanker put it:

> A "local-local" sphere entirely decoupled from national, regional or international agency simply does not exist. Most civil contexts today are characterised by regionalisation or even internationalisation processes, which strongly relativize the scope and impact of local agency.
>
> (Simons and Zanker 2014, 14)

Formal institutions and the state as analytical lacunae

The post-liberal focus on local agency, as well as on everyday practices, tends to underestimate the relevance of institutional rules and structures. Accordingly, post-liberal theory lacks a distinct analysis of how formal institutions – like the state security apparatus, justice system, parliament, parties and authorities – impact the causes of violence, and how they can help to overcome these. While claiming to create space for negotiating local solutions, they do not pay close attention to the question which rules are to apply in this space and whether the political constitution of regimes is significant or not. In a similar vein, Caroline Hughes et al. highlight that research in the wake of the local turn partly "has proceeded on the assumption that international interveners and local communities either do or could interact in a manner that is unmediated by state intervention" (Hughes et al. 2015, 821).

Such an approach might reveal new insights in settings where the state is either very distant or has collapsed entirely. Peace processes in Bougainville or in Somaliland come to mind. At the same time, the focus on the local seems to be inappropriate in cases where a national government is at least partly functional and claims legitimate rule over a territory. Approaches that turn a blind eye to the state in such settings might even be instrumentalised for the modernisation of counterinsurgency strategies – as was the case in Afghanistan, where traditional authorities were used as allies in the fight against the Taliban. It might, in addition, unwillingly also pave the way for 'neo-liberal' strategies that welcome anti-state sentiments in order to free private actors from alleged fetters and seek to advance an integration of war-torn states into the global market.

Towards more pluralist research: bringing power, authority and order back in

Post-liberal thinking has discovered new ground, and it is evident that future research on peacebuilding will be strongly influenced by the insights resulting from the local turn. Still, the controversy with the liberal school has veiled the fact that this approach is still rather reductionist and that it has not been able to develop a comprehensive epistemic system that on the one hand avoids the naturalisation of the local, and on the other hand effectively links the analysis of local agency with a distinct analysis of political structures and power relations. As a result, current peacebuilding research, trapped in the liberal/post-liberal divide, has partially been closed off from related and relevant research fields that focus, among others, on the transformation of war-torn societies, the role of political order and state institutions, the relevance of transnational networks for peace and conflict and the political economy of development cooperation.

Future peacebuilding research might thus have to move away from the liberal/post-liberal divide and integrate a more comprehensive set of theories, methodologies and fields of knowledge in order to grasp the multidimensionality, multicausality and complexity of peacebuilding processes. Such a pluralist approach would seek to free itself from the confirmation bias in current research and would rather put those inconsistencies and frictions that have been attached to the contested and power-related character of peacebuilding processes into the limelight. Selby accordingly highlights how peacebuilding is significantly shaped by the mode by which a war ended and the resulting power bargains. As a matter of fact, and despite their liberal framing, "the detailed content of peace agreements is often distinctly illiberal and non-democratic" (Selby 2013, 74), as they redistribute power and are influenced by the respective interests of domestic actors and geopolitical considerations (Selby 2013, 76). As a consequence, "to explain failed war-to-peace transitions solely in terms of shortcomings in post-conflict peace-building, or the liberal peace paradigm, would be reductionist in the extreme" (Selby 2013, 80).

If success and failure of peacebuilding depend on more than the underlying paradigms, political order in postwar societies and the underlying bargains become crucial – a field that is not adequately covered by recent research. A closer analysis of such political settlements reveals that the local is all but homogeneous, and instead shaped by

> intra-elite contention and bargaining (political versus economic elites, landed and non-landed elites, regional elites, rural and urban elites, religious and secular elites, etc.); contention and bargaining between elites and non-elites (the rich and the poor, employers and employees, land-owners and tenants or farmworkers); inter-group contention and bargaining (between genders, regional groups, ethnic or linguistic communities, or religious communities); and contention and bargaining between those who control the state and the wider society.
>
> (Putzel and di John 2012, 1)

Though comparative politics and area studies offer a great variety of theoretical concepts (neopatrimonialism, rentier state etc.), these approaches fall short of capturing the complexities and specifics of war-torn societies. The mainstream fragile states discourse, firmly rooted in liberal thinking, is equally limited, as it suffers from the heavy footprint of the ideal-type Weberian state (Kraushaar and Lambach 2009; Migdal and Schlichte 2005). Finally, post-liberal thinkers remain tellingly agnostic how they position themselves in this context. Richmond acknowledges that engaging with local understandings might imply "a polity that does not conform with the modern liberal state" (Richmond 2010, 687). Still, it remains unclear how such a polity can be conceptualised and how internationals can cope with the implicit and explicit normative dilemmas they face when dealing with these polities.

A promising starting point for analysing political order in war-torn societies might be an analytical framework that Volker Boege et al. developed. They interpret such societies as

> places in which diverse and competing institutions and logics of order and behaviour coexist, overlap and intertwine: the logic of the "formal" state,

the logic of traditional "informal" societal order, the logic of globalisation and international civil society with its abundance of highly diverse actors, such as non-governmental organisations (NGOs), multinational enterprises (MNEs), international organisations, development aid agencies, private military companies (PMCs) and so on.

(Boege 2011, 433)

The resulting structures which decide about the distribution of power and authority are described as hybrid political orders (HPO) in which the state has to share its sovereignty with a peculiar mix of local, private, transnational and international actors and institutions (Boege et al. 2009c; Carbonnier and Wennmann 2013). This notion of hybridity partly integrates the post-liberal idea of a hybrid peace (Belloni 2012; Mac Ginty 2010), combining and reconciling liberal peace-building concepts with local perceptions. At the same time, it is more differentiated with regard to the variety of domestic and transnational/international actors and refrains from attributing any kind of normative value to hybridity. As the concept of HPOs avoids the local-international dichotomy, it also has the potential to take account of the relationality of such categories. In the age of globalisation and transnationalisation, many agents – such as diaspora networks, civil society cooperation, religious associations, but also intelligence agencies and PMCs cross the lines – form competing, collaborating and conflicting coalitions of interest. Power geometries determine which actors gain agency and whose agency is restrained. Since power is located in diverse spheres and since actors from different levels are deeply entangled, "generalizations about the powerlessness of 'the local' in a globalizing world" can be regarded as "unwise" (Jones and Woods 2013, 33).

To give but one example: The recent turn to the local within the peacebuilding business has already had an impact on the distribution of authority in HPOs. As Stefanie Kappler argues, "being 'local' becomes a political resource as actors who are 'most local' act as gatekeepers to communities and to the political legitimisation of intervention projects" (Kappler 2015, 882). As this example shows, power and authority are permanently negotiated and renegotiated in war-torn societies – and this process meanwhile includes actors from all levels. Donor discourses substantially impact on this dynamic since related policies are closely linked to the acknowledgement of specific actors as legitimate and the respective distribution of resources. Under certain circumstances, this might contribute to a donor-driven "politics of belonging" (Yuval-Davis 2011), which offers a premium on identifying oneself as local in order to strengthen one's position in these negotiation processes.

Conclusion

As we have argued, liberal peacebuilding approaches have so far mainly looked for ways of improving the manner in which the local fits into democratisation or marketisation strategies. Interactive engagement with the local remained marginal, as Western actors are mainly framed as being interest-free and enlightened by liberal approaches – making the negotiation about principles and practices of peacebuilding inherently difficult. Post-liberal approaches, on the contrary, state that decisions about peace should be taken at the local level, and have indirectly been confirmed by the failure of many top-down attempts. At the same time, it is striking to which degree the post-liberal debate is shaped by "naïve assumptions about locals knowing best, since such assumptions are surely as dangerous as the currently dominant assumption that internationals know best" (Donais 2009, 22). Furthermore, the rather bounded conceptualisation of the local leads to a methodological reductionism which results in a neglect of the role of power and domestic politics, the naturalisation of the liberal international and the local(-local) as well as blind spots regarding formal institutions and the state.

At the same time, post-liberal approaches have gone beyond the critique of the liberal paradigm and its implementation. These have raised hope: with their focus on the prerequisites of local peace and their emphasis on everyday practices, they formulated validity claims that can be conceptually scrutinised and empirically tested. This chapter addressed some of the current shortcomings inherent to post-liberal peacebuilding research and indicated that empirical realities might not always coincide with its core assumptions. Post-liberal thinkers have partly taken up such sceptical perspectives and responded to the respective objections and suggestions. Still, the narrow focus on the local might turn out to be an epistemological corset or even a trap. Its 'opponent', the liberal school of thought, on the other hand, is a bit 'cornered' and does not currently provide an attractive option – not least due to the fact that it has not been able to convincingly contribute to problem-solving.

Future peacebuilding research should therefore move beyond the liberal/post-liberal debate. A more pluralist approach would pay more attention to those crucial issues that have been neglected so far – this includes how authority and power are distributed in the context of particular political orders as well as their underlying bargains. By integrating such structural analysis, research would benefit from focusing more on frictions, contestations and negotiations and would be able to better grasp the multidimensionality and complexity of peacebuilding processes.

Notes

1 Among many other colleagues, we would like to thank Volker Boege, Stephen Brown and David Carment for their helpful comments on this chapter.
2 We abstain in this chapter from reconstructing the neo-liberal discourse in peacebuilding research since our starting point is the controversy between the liberal and post-liberal school. Suffice it to say that neo-liberal thought stresses individual freedoms. Compared to liberal thinking, it emphasises to a lesser degree the state's role in the establishment of a institutions and instead favours the unrestricted unfolding of the logic of the (global) market. The local, accordingly, is not primarily conceptualised in terms of institutions or political agency, but rather in terms of individuals who exercise agency within the limits of the existing system. In fragile environments, neo-liberal governance strategies stress the resilience of individuals rather than institutional or political reform (Aradau 2014, 1–2).

References

Aradau, C. (2014). The promise of security: Resilience, surprise and epistemic politics. *Resilience: International Policies, Practices and Discourses*. (http://dx.doi.org/10.1080/216 93293.2014.914765) Accessed: 18 January 2015.

Belloni, R. (2012). Hybrid peace governance: Its emergence and significance. *Global Governance*, 18, 21–38.

Boege, V. (2011). Potential and limits of traditional approaches in peacebuilding. In B. Austin, M. Fischer, and H. Giessmann (Eds.), *Advancing Conflict Transformation. The Berghof Handbook II*. Barbara Budrich, Opladen, 431–457.

Boege, V., Brown, A., and Nolan, A. (2009a). Building peace and political community in hybrid political orders. *International Peacekeeping*, 16(5), 599–615.

Boege, V., Brown, A., Clements, K., and Nolan, A. (2009b). On hybrid political orders and emerging states: What is failing – States in the global South or research and politics in the West? In M. Fischer and B. Schmelzle (Eds.), *Building Peace in the Absence of States: Challenging the Discourse on State Failure*. Berghof Handbook Dialogue Series 8. Berghof Research Center, Berlin, 15–35.

Boege, V., Brown, A., Clements, K., and Nolan, A. (2009c). Undressing the emperor: A reply to our discussants. Building peace in the absence of states: Challenging the discourse on state failure. In M. Fischer and B. Schmelzle (Eds.), *Building Peace in the Absence of States: Challenging the Discourse on State Failure*. Berghof Handbook Dialogue Series 8. Berghof Research Center, Berlin, 87–93.

Campbell, S., Chandler, D., and Sabaratnam, M. (Eds.). (2011). *A Liberal Peace? The Problems and Practices of Peacebuilding*. Zed Books, London.

Carbonnier, G., and Wennmann, A. (2013). Natural resource governance and hybrid political orders. In D. Chandler and T. Sisk (Eds.), *Routledge Handbook of International Statebuilding*. Routledge, London, 208–218.

Chadwick, W., Debiel, T., and Gadinger, F. (Eds.). (2013). *Relational Sensibility and the "Turn to the Local": Prospects for the Future of Peacebuilding (Global Dialogues 2)*. Käte Hamburger Kolleg/Centre for Global Cooperation Research (KHK/GCR21), Duisburg.

Chandler, D. (2012). Resilience and human security: The post-interventionist paradigm. *Security Dialogue*, 43(3), 213–229.

Chandler, D. (2013). International statebuilding and agency: The rise of society-based approaches to intervention spectrum. *Journal of Global Studies*, 5(1), 1–20.

Collier, P., Elliott, L., Hegre, H., Hoeffler, A., Reynal-Querol, M., and Sambanis, N. (2003). *Breaking the Conflict Trap: Civil War and Development Policy*. A World Bank Policy Research Report. World Bank, Washington, DC.

Cox, K., and Mair, A. (1989). Levels of abstraction in locality studies. *Antipode*, 21(2), 121–132.

Debiel, T., Glassner, R., Schetter, C., and Terlinden, U. (2009). Local state-building in Afghanistan and Somaliland. *Peace Review*, 21(1), 38–44.

Debiel, T., and Lambach, D. (2009). Global governace as self-deception. How the western state-building project neglects local politics. In M. Brzoska and A. Krohn (Eds.), *Overcoming Armed Violence in a Complex World. Essays in Honour of Herbert Wulf*. UniPress, Budrich, 163–184.

Debiel, T., and Rinck, P. (2015). Liberal peace in crisis: Armed conflict in a contested world order. In M. Roth, C. Ulbert, and T. Debiel (Eds.), *Global Trends 2015. Prospects for World Society*, 33–57. (www.global-trends.info/fileadmin/Globale-Trends/beitraege_ kapitel/debiel_rinck.pdf) Accessed: 20 July 2015.

De Coning, C. (2013). Understanding peacebuilding as essentially local. *Stability: International Journal of Security and Development*, 2(1), 1–6. (http://dx.doi.org/10.5334/sta.as) Accessed: 19 January 2015.

Donais, T. (2009). Empowerment or imposition? Dilemmas of local ownership in post-conflict peacebuilding processes. *Peace & Change*, 34(1), 3–26.

Doyle, M., and Sambanis, N. (2000). International peacebuilding: A theoretical and quantitative analysis. *American Political Science Review*, 94(4), 779–801.

Doyle, M., and Sambanis, N. (2006). *Making War and Building Peace: United Nations Peace Operations*. Princeton University Press, Princeton, NJ.

Duncan, S., and Savage, M. (1989). Space, scale and locality. *Antipode*, 21(3), 179–206.

Glick Schiller, N. (2009). *A Global Perspective on Transnational Migration: Theorizing Migration without Methodological Nationalism*. Working Paper No. 67. University of Oxford: Centre on Migration, Policy and Society.

Halfacree, K. (1993). Locality and social representation: Space, discourse and alternative definitions of the rural. *Journal of Rural Studies*, 9(1), 23–37.

Hartmann, C., and Crawford, G. (Eds.). (2008). *Decentralisation in Africa: A Pathway Out of Poverty and Conflict?* Amsterdam University, Amsterdam.

Hughes, C., Öjendal, J., and Schierenbeck, I. (2015). The struggle versus the song – The local turn in peacebuilding: An introduction. *Third World Quarterly*, 36(5), 817–824.

Jabri, V. (2013). Peacebuilding, the local and the international: A colonial or a postcolonial rationality? *Peacebuilding*, 1(1), 3–16.

Jones, M., and Woods, M. (2013). New localities. *Regional Studies*, 47(1), 29–42.

Kappler, S. (2015). The dynamic local: Delocalisation and (re-)localisation in the search for peacebuilding identity. *Third World Quarterly*, 36(5), 875–889.

Kraushaar, M., and Lambach, D. (2009). *Hybrid Political Orders: The Added Value of a New Concept*. Occasional Papers Series 14/2009. The Australian Centre for Peace and Conflict Studies (ACPACS).

Leonardsson, H., and Rudd, G. (2015). The "local turn" in peacebuilding: A literature review of effective and emancipatory local peacebuilding. *Third World Quarterly*, 36(5), 825–839.

Loode, S. (2011). Peacebuilding in complex social systems. *Journal of Peace, Conflict & Development*, 18, 68–82.

Mac Ginty, R. (2010). Hybrid peace: The interaction between top-down and bottom-up peace. *Security Dialogue*, 41(4), 391–412.

Mac Ginty, R. (2011). *International Peacebuilding and Local Resistance: Hybrid Forms of Peace*. Palgrave Macmillan, New York.

Mac Ginty, R. (2012). Routine peace: Technocracy and peacebuilding. *Cooperation and Conflict*, 47(3), 287–308.

Mac Ginty, R. (2013). Indicators+: A proposal for everyday peace indicators. *Evaluation and Program Planning*, 36(1), 56–63.

Mac Ginty, R. (2015). Where is the local? Critical localism and peacebuilding. *Third World Quarterly*, 36(5), 840–856.

Mac Ginty, R., and Richmond, O. (2013). The local turn in peace building: A critical agenda for peace. *Third World Quarterly*, 34(5), 763–783.

Mansfield, E., and Snyder, J. (1995a). Democratization and the danger of war. *International Security*, 20(1), 5–38.

Mansfield, E., and Snyder, J. (1995b). Democratization and war. *Foreign Affairs*, 74(3), 79–97.

Menkhaus, K. (2013). *Making Sense of Resilience in Peacebuilding Contexts: Approaches, Applications, Implications*. Paper No. 6. Geneva Peacebuilding Platform.

Migdal, J., and Schlichte, K. (2005). Rethinking the state. In K. Schlichte (Ed.), *The Dynamics of States: The Formation and Crises of State Domination*. Ashgate, Aldershot, 1–40.

Newman, E., Paris, R., and Richmond, O. (Eds.). (2009). *New Perspectives on Liberal Peacebuilding*. United Nations University Press, New York.

Paris, R. (2004). *At War's End: Building Peace after Civil Conflict*. Cambridge University Press, New York.

Paris, R. (2010). Saving liberal peacebuilding. *Review of International Studies*, 36(2), 337–365.

Paris, R., and Sisk, T. (Eds.). (2009). *The Dilemmas of Statebuilding: Confronting the Contradictions of Postwar Peace Operations*. Routledge, London.

Putzel, J., and Di John, J. (2012). *Meeting the Challenges of Crisis States*. LSE Crisis States Research Centre Centre Report.

Reckwitz, A. (2003). Grundelemente einer Theorie sozialer Praktiken. Eine sozialtheoretische Perspektive. *Zeitschrift für Soziologie (ZfS)*, 32(4), 282–301.

Richmond, O. (2009). Becoming liberal, unbecoming liberalism: Liberal-local hybridity via the everyday as a response to the paradoxes of liberal peacebuilding. *Journal of Intervention and Statebuilding*, 3(3), 324–344.

Richmond, O. (2010). Resistance and the post-liberal peace. *Millennium: Journal of International Studies*, 38(3), 665–692.

Richmond, O. (2011a). *A Post-liberal Peace*. Routledge, London.

Richmond, O. (2011b). De-romanticising the local, de-mystifying the international: Hybridity in Timor Leste and the Solomon Islands. *Pacific Review*, 24(1), 115–136.

Richmond, O. (2012). A pedagogy of peacebuilding: Infrapolitics, resistance, and liberation. *International Political Sociology*, 6(2), 115–131.

Richmond, O., and Mitchell, A. (Eds.). (2011). *Hybrid Forms of Peace: From Everyday Agency to Post-liberalism*. Palgrave Macmillan, Houndmills.

Schneckener, U. (2011). State-building or new modes of governance? The effects of international involvement in areas of limited statehood. In T. Risse (Ed.), *Governance without a State? Policies and Politics in Areas of Limited Statehood*. Columbia University Press, New York, 223–261.

Selby, J. (2013). The myth of liberal peace-building. *Conflict, Security & Development*, 13(1), 57–86.

Simons, C., and Zanker, F. (2014). *Questioning the Local in Peacebuilding*. Working Papers of the Priority Programme 1448 of the German Research Foundation, Nr. 10.

State Failure Task Force (2003). *State Failure Task Force Report. Phase III Findings*. Prepared by Jack A. Goldstone et al. (www.cidcm.umd.edu/inscr/stfail/SFTF%20Phase%20III%20Report%20Final.pdf) Accessed: 10 October 2004.

Tadjbakhsh, S. (Ed.). (2011). *Rethinking the Liberal Peace: External Models and Local Alternatives*. Routledge Cass Series on Peacekeeping. Routledge, Abingdon.

Tschirgi, N. (2004). *Post-conflict Peacebuilding Revisited: Achievements, Limitations, Challenges*. Prepared for the WSP International/IPA Peacebuilding Forum Conference. International Peace Academy, New York.

Von Billerbeck, S. (2015). Local ownership and UN peacebuilding: Discourse versus operationalization. *Global Governance*, 21, 299–315.

Wimmer, A., and Glick Schiller, N. (2002). Methodological nationalism and beyond. Nation-state building, migration and the social sciences. *Global Networks*, 2(4), 301–303.

Yuval-Davis, N. (2011). *Power, Intersectionality and the Politics of Belonging*. Institut for Kultur og Globale Studier, Aalborg Universitet, Aalborg. (FREIA's tekstserie; No. 75).

Index

Note: Page numbers with *t* indicate tables.